T5-CQC-530

The Human Way

Introducing Anthropology, Psychology, and Sociology

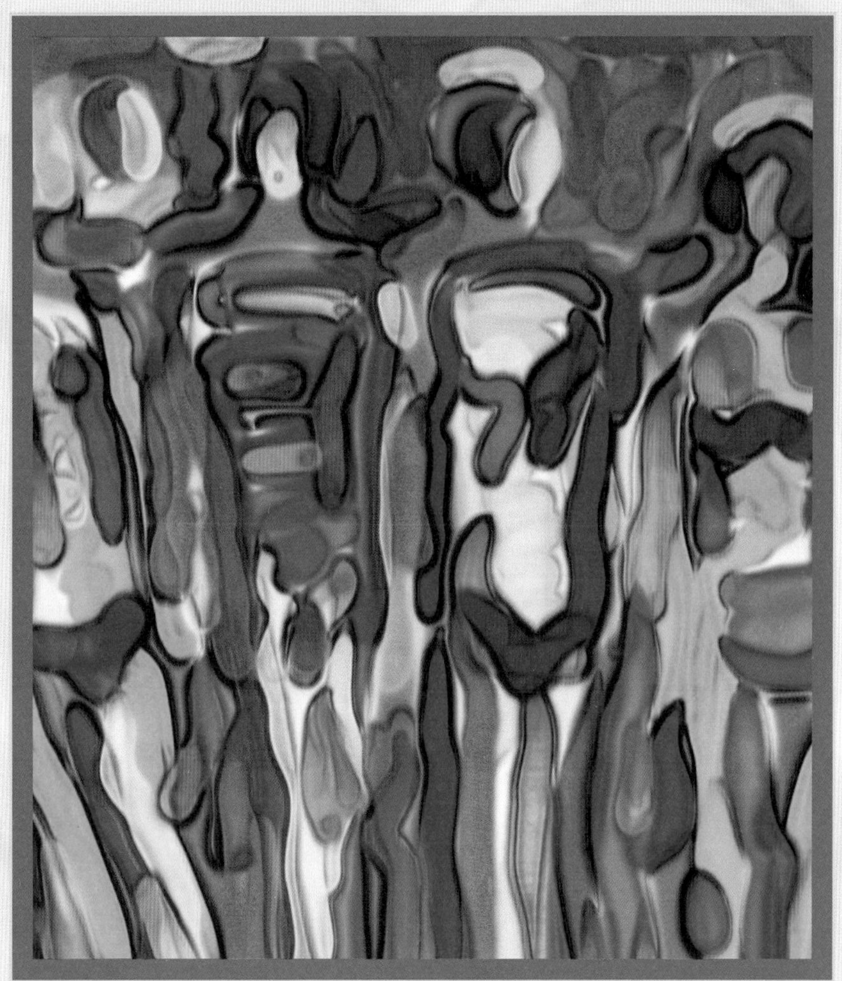

Colin M. Bain / Jill S. Colyer

70 Wynford Drive, Don Mills, Ontario M3C 1J9
oup.com/ca

Oxford University Press is a department of the University of Oxford.

It furthers the University's objective of excellence in research, scholarship, and education by publishing worldwide in

Oxford New York
Athens Auckland Bangkok Bogotá Buenos Aires Cape Town Chennai Dar es Salaam Delhi Florence Hong Kong Istanbul Karachi Kolkata Kuala Lumpur Madrid Melbourne Mexico City Mumbai Nairobi Paris São Paulo Shanghai Singapore Taipei Tokyo Toronto Warsaw

with associated companies in Berlin Ibadan

Oxford is a registered trade mark of Oxford University Press in the UK and in certain other countries

Published in Canada
By Oxford University Press

First published 2001

National Library of Canada Cataloguing in Publication Data

Bain, Colin M.
The human way: introducing anthropology, psychology, and sociology

For use in grade 11.
Includes bibliographical references and index.
ISBN 0-19-541557-4

1. Sociology. 2. Anthropology. 3. Psychology. I. Colyer, Jill. II. Title.

HM586.B34 2001 301 C2001-930532-X

Printed and bound in Canada
This book is printed on permanent (acid-free) paper

1 2 3 4—04 03 02 01

Cover and text design: Brett Miller
Illustrations: Dave McKay
Cover image: "Family Ties," Diana Ong/SuperStock

Acknowledgements

This book is the result of many people's efforts.

At Oxford University Press Canada, we have worked closely with and valued the varied contributions of MaryLynne Meschino (Director, Education Division), Loralee Case (Editorial Manager), Patti Henderson (Acquisitions Editor), and Tiina Randoja (Developmental Editor). To Tiina, a special thank you for being a supremely competent editor, who provided us with many excellent suggestions and the research material with which to develop them. We have had less contact with others who have nonetheless made valuable contributions. We thank Vince Morgan (Production Manager) and Brett Miller (Design Manager). Freelance workers Elaine Aboud (Copy/Production Editor) and Maria DeCambra (Photo Researcher) have added value to this product while working against tight deadlines. To the many others whom we have not named, our thanks go out to you.

We must thank our spouses, Scott Grondin and Vi Bain, for their assistance with technical matters, research materials, and editorial suggestions. Without your constant love and support, we could not have completed this project in the available time.

Jill S. Colyer
Colin M. Bain

This book is dedicated
to the memory of
Catherine M. Bain
(1911-1997)

Contents

Contents

Contents

Contents

Features Contents

Open For Debate Contents

Point and Counterpoint Contents

Film Link Contents

Case Study Contents

Classic Study Contents

Voices of Youth Contents

Skill Development Contents

Remarkable People Contents

Welcome to The Human Way

The Human Way is about how we as human beings behave in the many situations and stages of our lives. In this text you will find questions, issues, and theories relating to our development as human beings. The tools used to bring you this information are those of anthropology, psychology, and sociology. After reading and working through this text, you will have a greater understanding of yourself, your society, and the people and institutions of many other cultures.

Features of *The Human Way*

Use the design features of *The Human Way* to focus and streamline your learning:

- The Unit Study Guide identifies learning expectations and organizes chapter topics by the three disciplines of anthropology, psychology, and sociology
- Each chapter begins with an overview, a list of learning expectations, and an Open for Debate article to get you thinking about the chapter.
- Each section begins with focus questions and a list of Key Concepts
- Icons are used to indicate the focus of each major subsection as anthropological, psychological, and/or sociological.

- Frequent Recap questions help you review and summarize information in your own words.

Information in each section is delivered through a variety of features to spark your interest and challenge you intellectually.

- Ask the Expert presents the perspective of professional social scientists on various issues.
- Voices of Youth gives you the perspectives of your peers on various issues.
- Case Studies extend the information in the text with real-life examples.
- Point and Counterpoint offers arguments on two sides of an issue and invites you to form your own opinions.
- Internet Resources directs you to relevant Web sites and useful activities to try at that site.

- Film Link describes how a recent film relates to a topic.
- Photographs, flow charts, diagrams, tables, graphs, and cartoons provide information and invite you to reflect on situations and patterns of behaviour.

Skill Development in *The Human Way*

The Human Way includes a wide variety of activities to help you develop the skills of a social scientist.

- The activities at the end of each chapter develop a variety of inquiry skills.
- *Show your knowledge* activities enable you to demonstrate your understanding of facts, terms, concepts, principles, and theories.
- *Practise your thinking skills* activities provide opportunities for you to think analytically and creatively.
- *Communicate your ideas* activities provide opportunities for you to communicate orally, in writing, and through the use of visual displays in ways that are accurate and effective.
- *Apply your knowledge* activities enable you to transfer what you have learned to new situations.
- Specific social science skills are developed in the Skill Development feature found in Chapters 4 through 10. These skills include: locating and selecting information for research; evaluating and citing sources; creating a survey; interpreting and presenting survey results; designing a field observation; and interpreting and reporting field observation results. Each feature includes Follow-Up activities.
- *The Human Way* also invites you to develop skills related to doing a long-term project. The Summative Project Outline at the end of Unit 1 provides guidance on the development of these skills.

The Experts Gallery

Shirley Fedorak (Chapter 4)

Shirley Fedorak is a sessional lecturer in archaeology and anthropology at the University of Saskatchewan, where she has taught since 1991. She holds a master's degree in anthropology from the University of Saskatchewan, with a research emphasis on public anthropology. Between 1991 and 2000, she worked on several curriculum committees to develop anthropological materials relevant to today's students and the general public. She has traveled extensively and worked on several archaeological projects in Canada and the Near East. She has authored several novels with an anthropological theme and is hard at work on a collection of children's short stories and a fictionalized biography of her paternal grandmother's life as a Canadian pioneer.

Dr. Jennifer Connolly (Chapter 5)

Dr. Jennifer Connolly is a professor in the department of psychology at York University in North York, Ontario. She received her Ph.D. in 1981 from Concordia University and is a registered psychologist in the province of Ontario. Dr. Connolly conducts research on adolescents' peer relationships, particularly in school contexts. She studies the influences of friends and peer groups on teenagers' attitudes and behaviours. She also studies adolescents' romantic relationships. A particular interest is the romantic relationships of aggressive and troubled youth. She has written extensively on adolescent development, teaches university courses on adolescence, and often speaks in the community on adolescent issues and violence in adolescents' peer and romantic relationships.

Dr. Vincent Sacco (Chapter 6)

Dr. Vincent Sacco is a professor of sociology and former head of department at Queen's University in Kingston, Ontario. A native of Niagara Falls, Ontario, Dr. Sacco received a bachelor's degree in sociology from McMaster University in 1972 and a master's degree in the same area from the University of Western Ontario in 1973. In 1980, he was awarded a Ph.D. in sociology from the University of Alberta. During his career, Dr. Sacco has taught at the School of Criminology at Simon Fraser University, the University of Calgary, and the University of Toronto.

Dr. Ann D. Duffy (Chapter 7)

Dr. Ann D. Duffy is a professor of sociology at Brock University in St. Catharines, Ontario. She obtained her Ph.D. from McMaster University in 1979. In 1995, she was awarded the OCUFA Award for Excellence in Teaching. Long active in the women's studies and labour studies programs at Brock, she has written extensively in both areas. Among her books are *The Part-Time Paradox* (co-authored with Professor Norene Pupo), *Few Choices: Women, Work and Family* (co-authored with Professors Nancy Mandell and Norene Pupo), and *Family Violence: A Canadian Introduction* (co-authored with Professor Julianne Momirov).

Dr. George J. Sefa Dei (Chapter 8)

Dr. George J. Sefa Dei is professor in and associate chair of the department of sociology and equity studies at the Ontario Institute for Studies in Education of the University of Toronto (OISE/UT). Between 1996 and 2000, he served as the first director of the Centre for Integrative Anti-Racism Studies at OISE/UT. His teaching and research interests are in the areas of anti-racism education, development education, international development, indigenous knowledges, and anti-colonial thought. He recently completed a three-year study on "Making Excellence Accessible and Equitable: The Examination of Best/Exemplary Practices of Inclusive Schooling in Ontario Public Schools."

Dr. Robert J. Brym (Chapter 9)

Dr. Robert J. Brym received his Ph.D. from the University of Toronto. His main areas of research are political sociology, race and ethnic relations, and sociology of culture. Most of his research has focused on Canada and Russia. His publications include *From Culture to Power: The Sociology of English Canada*, *The Jews of Moscow, Kiev, and Minsk*, and *New Society*, one of Canada's best-selling introductory sociology textbooks. From 1986 to 1989, Dr. Brym served as editor of the *Canadian Review of Sociology and Anthropology* (the journal of the Canadian Sociology and Anthropology Association) and from 1992 to 1997 as editor of *Current Sociology* (the journal of the International Sociological Association).

Paul F. McKenna (Chapter 10)

Paul F. McKenna began his career as a researcher/librarian at the Centre of Criminology, University of Toronto, followed by a term as associate law librarian at Osgoode Hall Law School, York University. In 1983, he joined the staff of the Ontario Provincial Police Academy, where he eventually became Deputy Director (Administration). Mr. McKenna has been a Police Services Advisor within the Ontario Ministry of the Solicitor General and a member of the working group amending the *Police Services Act*. Mr. McKenna is currently the president of Public Safety Innovation, Inc., a consulting business formed to provide a broad range of services and assistance to police organizations. He has written extensively on public safety in Canada.

Unit 1

An Introduction to the Social Sciences

Among all the academic disciplines, the social sciences are the most closely related to our lives as individuals and as members of society. Three of the social sciences—anthropology, psychology, and sociology—focus particularly on human behaviour. Each of these sciences has undergone its own historical development and has formulated its own set of questions to answer. Different methodologies are used to find the answers to these questions.

This unit will introduce you to these three social sciences and provide you with an overview of their evolution, their major practitioners, and their methodologies.

UNIT STU

Unit Contents

Overall Expectations

In this unit, you will

- describe some differences and similarities in the approaches taken by anthropology, psychology, and sociology
- begin to use appropriate social science research methods effectively and ethically
- begin to conduct research to determine the critical differences and similarities among the approaches and concepts of anthropology, psychology, and sociology, and summarize your findings

Topics by Discipline

Anthropology

Chapter 1

- How social science research can improve the quality of life
- How social science research can resolve issues
- An anthropological explanation of the OC Transpo shooting rampage

Chapter 2

- Fields of study in anthropology
- An anthropology hall of fame: Margaret Mead, Ruth Benedict, Bronislaw Malinowski, Raymond Dart, the Leakey family, Jane Goodall, Biruté Galdikas, Dian Fossey
- Anthropology in Canada today: Asen Balikci, Robin Ridlington, Jean Michaud, Patricia Spitta

Chapter 3

- Reliability in research
- Participant observation and the challenges of fieldwork
- Reflexive observing and note-taking
- Ethical dilemmas in research

Psychology

Chapter 1

- How social science research can improve the quality of life
- How social science research can resolve issues
- A psychological explanation of the OC Transpo shooting rampage

Chapter 2

- Fields of study in psychology
- A psychology hall of fame: Sigmund Freud, Alfred Adler, Carl Jung, Ivan Pavlov

Psychology in Canada today: Gerald Wilde, David Dozois

hapter 3

Reliability in research
Studying human intelligence: IQ testing, reaction-time experiments
Studying personality: experiments, case studies
Studying privacy and intimacy: cross-cultural observations, experiments
Ethical and privacy issues

Sociology

hapter 1

How social science research can improve the quality of life
How social science research can resolve issues
A sociological explanation of the OC Transpo shooting rampage

hapter 2

Fields of study in sociology
A sociology hall of fame: Auguste Comte, Émile Durkheim, Karl Marx, Max Weber, Talcott Parsons, George Murdock
Sociology in Canada today: Wallace Clement, John Porter, Jay Goldstein, Rita Bienvenue, David Lyon, Edna Einsiedel, Marc Raboy, Reginald Bibby, Marlene Mackie

hapter 3

Reliability in research
Statistical analysis
Developing theories from statistics
Questionnaires
Case studies
Ethical issues

Skill and Project Guide

In Chapter 3 of this unit, the skills and methods of anthropologists, psychologists, and sociologists are introduced.

At the end of the unit, an opportunity is given to work on a "summative project" in which you can apply the skills. This project, described on pages 68 to 70, is to be worked on throughout the rest of the year.

Other opportunities to practise skills are found in Units 2, 3, and 4. See the Unit Study Guides of these units for more information.

Research and Inquiry Skills Learning Expectations

The skill development in this unit will enable you to

- correctly use the terminology of anthropology, psychology, and sociology
- define the concepts that are central to anthropology, psychology, and sociology
- demonstrate an understanding of the factors that explain human behaviour from the perspective of anthropology, psychology, and sociology
- describe the steps involved in social science research and inquiry, including developing and testing a hypothesis
- demonstrate an understanding of various research methodologies for conducting primary research
- demonstrate an understanding of the ethical guidelines of social science research

Chapter 1

The Social Sciences

Overview of Chapter

1.1 The Importance of the Social Sciences
1.2 Social Scientific Analysis

Learning Expectations

By the end of this chapter, you will be able to

- identify the major questions posed by anthropologists (for example, What are the cultural patterns that help to define societies?), by psychologists (for example, What is going on inside the mind?), and sociologists (for example, What are the roles of the various groups inside a particular society?)
- describe the differences in approach and understandings that are characteristic of each of the disciplines

Open for Debate

Workplace Stress Hurts, Bosses Learning

Most bosses now agree that helping employees cope with workplace stress boosts the bottom line, the Conference Board of Canada says.

Just over half of employers in a recent survey by the economic think-tank said they had a program to help employees reduce stress, up from only one third a half decade ago.

The conference board's survey last spring found that 40 per cent of the employees who felt little stress in balancing work and their personal lives reported being "very satisfied" with their jobs. In contrast, only one quarter of those who complained of being under a great deal of stress reported the same level of job satisfaction.

Employer programs for workers, which provide counselling or stress management courses, can help, the board said.

"But if working conditions are causing the stress, problems will resurface unless conditions are changed," it warned.

Some of the conditions that generate worker stress, according to a recent study by the National Institute for Occupational Safety and Health, include:

- Long hours and a heavy workload.
- Conflicting responsibilities.
- Overbearing management, which leaves the employee out of the decision-making process, and poor communication.
- An unhealthy work environment, including the lack of family-friendly policies which, for example, will allow for flexible hours.
- Career concerns and job insecurity.

Estimates of the cost to employers of absenteeism due solely to stress have run as high as $2.7 billion a year.

Kevin O'Connor, vice-president of CHC-Working Well, the country's leading provider of employee assistance programs, said worker stress will become a more important issue to employers "the more that the very senior levels of management begin to realize the cost of having people absent from work, or on disability, or so on."

Abridged from: Beauchesne, Eric. 1999. "Workplace Stress Hurts, Bosses Learning." *Calgary Herald*. 10 September 1999.

Think About It

1. Do you think it is sensible to pour money and effort into researching people's job satisfaction, stress levels, and workplace conditions? Why or why not?
2. How do you think the National Institute for Occupational Safety and Health went about conducting its study on worker stress?
3. What recommendations would you make to Canadian companies on how to achieve a higher level of workplace health? Classify your recommendations into those addressing personal, social, and environmental factors.

Section 1.1

The Importance of the Social Sciences

Focus Questions

- What are the social sciences?
- What techniques do the social sciences use?
- Why are the social sciences important?

Key Concepts

social sciences
statistics
humanities
retribution
deterrent

The Social Science Disciplines

You may be sitting in this class wondering what the **social sciences** are. (Just to add confusion, they are sometimes called social studies.) You probably have a good idea what mathematics and science are, and you are probably familiar with English and technological studies. But what are the social sciences?

The social sciences are those disciplines that use research and analysis to examine human behaviour. They use such techniques as collecting and analyzing **statistics**, conducting experiments, and examining what people have written and created, in an attempt to understand why people act as they do. The social sciences include such subjects as anthropology, economics, geography, history, politics, psychology, and sociology. In some ways, the social sciences are related to the **humanities**, or the subjects that focus more on the creative side of the human experience. These include art, literature, and philosophy. But where the humanities are concerned more with human expression, the social sciences focus more on human behaviour.

The social sciences are valuable disciplines. For example, history allows us to understand why the relationship between Aboriginal and non-Aboriginal peoples is sometimes difficult. Economics shows us whether there really is a link between lower taxes and job creation, as some politicians claim. Geography illustrates how it is necessary to balance economic production and protection of the environment.

The focus of this textbook is a set of three social science disciplines. In alphabetical order, they are anthropology, psychology, and sociology. You will learn the perspective each of these disciplines takes on human behaviour. You will examine some of the important social issues related to these sciences. You will discover the techniques and methods used in each discipline to reach conclusions about people and their behaviour. The remainder of this chapter presents some examples that show the importance of these social sciences to our everyday concerns.

Improving Quality of Life

To illustrate the importance of the social sciences, let us think of human stress.

Scientists and doctors can show us the medical consequences of stress, such as high blood pressure, heart attacks, and death. But social scientists can analyze the factors that lead to stress. In the workplace, for example, studies have shown that employees become stressed when they feel they have little control over the pattern of their daily work lives. At one time, this feeling was widespread among assembly-line workers in car plants. As a result, these workers experienced abnormally high rates of absenteeism, substance abuse, and marriage breakup. Workers and unions became concerned with the stressful conditions at the car plant workplace. At the same time, management became concerned that production costs were rising as a result of declining worker productivity. Teams of social scientists were called in to examine the problem.

The first step they took was to observe the existing production lines in operation. They also gave questionnaires to the workers and conducted experiments in the assembly lines.

Their examination showed that workers felt rushed to keep up with the cars coming down the line. At the same time, they got bored doing the same task all day long. These two problems resulted in mistakes in the assembly process that were expensive to fix later on.

The social scientists eventually recommended that manufacturers create teams of workers to carry out a number of steps in the assembly process. Teams of six to ten people, depending on the complexity of the steps, could decide for themselves how to complete the steps and also how to divide the steps among the team members. They could agree to rotate steps every

Figure 1.1 Social scientists have an important role to play in showing how stress can be reduced in the workplace as well as in other areas of life.

hour, day, week, or any other unit of time they chose. As long as all the steps were accomplished in the amount of time budgeted for them, and met quality-control standards, the team could decide virtually anything else for itself.

The Honda Canada assembly plant in Alliston, Ontario, was a pioneer in the team concept. Right from the opening of the plant in the mid-1980s, it was found that worker satisfaction was higher, quality control better, and absenteeism lower than in older plants. The Alliston plant was more profitable as a result, so a new production shift was added, creating more jobs. The economy in the Alliston area expanded as houses, schools, and stores were built to accommodate the workers' families. Customer satisfaction with vehicles assembled in the plant was higher than elsewhere. Customers were also more likely to buy a similar vehicle later on. Everyone seemed to benefit. The social scientists had had a significant impact.

Resolving Issues

Social scientists can also help people make informed decisions about issues. For example, let us consider the issue of the death penalty for convicted murderers. Canadians are divided on this issue, with some in favour of the death penalty and others opposed. Those in favour may argue that anyone who deliberately kills another person has lost the right to life. This is known as the **retribution** argument. It claims that murderers deserve the death penalty for the evil act they have committed. This argument focuses on murder as a violation of society's moral order. Punishment is justified as a means of re-establishing this moral order. A social scientist can help people evaluate this argument by clarifying the values and assumptions about a moral order they hold. In other words, a social scientist can help people understand that the meaning of crime is dependent on one's perspective. How people respond to factual data depends on the perspective they bring to crime. The other key contribution a social scientist makes is to actually provide the factual data—the statistics—that bear on the issue.

Some supporters of the death penalty say that it is a **deterrent**. This means that the execution of murderers serves as an example to society and will encourage others not to commit the same act—they know what could happen to them if they do. The deterrence argument, like the retribution argument, assumes that individuals have free will. It also assumes that people are rational or calculating in their thinking. Someone who commits a criminal act, such as murder, at some level feels the benefits of the act outweigh its cost. For most people, the pain of being caught and punished by death is enough to make them think twice about committing murder. A social scientist can help people evaluate this argument by clarifying its assumptions and collecting statistical data. Social scientists also work to gain a better understanding of the characteristics of people who kill. How rational and calculating are they? Can they be deterred? How? The "Point and Counterpoint" on the following page presents two points of view on deterrence.

POINT and COUNTERPOINT

Is the Death Penalty a Deterrent?

In September 1995, George E. Pataki, governor of the State of New York, reinstated the death penalty for first-degree murder. Opinion was divided on whether or not such a move served any real purpose. Whose opinion and statistics below do you find the most convincing?

Yes:

The death penalty is a necessary tool to fight and deter crime. Capital punishment deters crime by causing would-be murderers to fear arrest and conviction and by preventing convicted murderers from killing again. In recent years, violent crime in New York has dropped dramatically, due in part to the restitution of the death penalty.

Since I took office in 1995, violent crime has dropped 23 per cent, assaults are down 22 per cent, and murders have dropped by nearly one-third. ... I believe this has occurred in part because of the strong signal that the death penalty and our other tough new laws have sent to violent criminals and murderers. You will be punished with the full force of the law.

Abridged from: Pataki, George E. 1998. "The Death Penalty Is a Deterrent." In Steve Schonebaum, ed. *Does Capital Punishment Deter Crime?* San Diego. Greenhaven Press.

No:

Capital punishment actually makes the fight against crime more difficult. Executions waste valuable resources that could be applied to more promising efforts to protect the public. Additionally, innocent people are sometimes executed and the brutalizing effect executions have on society may result in more murders.

In 1994, 6100 criminals were sentenced to the state prison in Manhattan [New York], and 9000 more were sent to city jail. In 1975, when I became District Attorney, there were 648 homicides in Manhattan; in 1994, there were 330. The number has been cut virtually in half without executions—proof to me that they are not needed to continue that trend.

Abridged from: Morgenthau, Robert M. 1998. "The Death Penalty Hinders the Fight Against Crime." In Steve Schonebaum, ed. *Does Capital Punishment Deter Crime?* San Diego. Greenhaven Press.

1. Summarize the arguments for and against the death penalty.
2. Explain how you think both sides are able to use statistics to support their viewpoints.
3. Which point of view do you most agree with? Why?

The Social Scientific Verdict

The last capital punishment hanging in Canada took place in 1962. Social scientists have studied homicide rates in the country from the nineteenth century until that year. They have compared them with the period from 1962 until 1976, when the death penalty for murder was officially abolished. They have also added to the comparison the homicide rates from 1976 until the present. If the death penalty were in fact a deterrent, you would expect homicide rates as a percentage of total population to rise during each period after

Figure 1.2 In 1976, Prime Minister Pierre Trudeau held a free vote on Bill C-84, abolishing capital punishment. The bill passed by a narrow margin of 6 votes: 130 to 124. In 1987, in another free vote, the Canadian Parliament voted against reinstating the death penalty. In a 1994 Fraser Forum survey, 59 per cent of Canadians were in favour of reinstating the death penalty. Where do you think Canadians today stand on the issue?

1962. In fact, they remained fairly stable until 1967. They rose somewhat in the 1970s, hitting an all-time high in 1985. But the rates from 1997 to 1999 were the lowest since 1969.

Social scientists have also looked at homicide rates in American states that use the death penalty (such as Texas) and ones that do not (such as Michigan). Criminologist Steven Messner has concluded that homicide rates are actually between 48 and 101 per cent higher in death penalty states than in non-death penalty states (Bonner and Fessenden, 2000, A23).

Such studies suggest that homicide rates are related more to social and economic conditions in individual states than to how murderers are punished. So when a politician or a citizen says, "I believe that the death penalty for murder is a deterrent," we know that most social scientists who have examined the issue do not agree.

RECAP

1. On what areas of the human experience do the social sciences concentrate? On what areas of the human experience do the humanities concentrate? How are these areas different?
2. What changes to assembly line production did Honda Canada make when it built its Alliston plant? Which groups benefited and why?
3. What conclusions have most social scientists arrived at about murder and the death penalty? How have they reached their conclusions?

Section 1.2

Social Scientific Analysis

Focus Questions

- What assumptions do psychologists make when analyzing people's behaviour?
- What assumptions do sociologists make?
- What assumptions do anthropologists make?

Key Concepts

psychology
personality
sociology
anthropology

The Incident

On 6 April 1999, at around 2:40 p.m., city bus maintenance workers for OC Transpo in Ottawa saw a former employee drive his car into the parking lot. He got out carrying a loaded Remington hunting rifle. Pierre Lebrun walked deliberately into the bus garage. In less than six minutes, he killed four co-workers and seriously injured two others. He entered a bus where eight workers were finishing their afternoon coffee break, swore at them but did not fire a shot, and finally killed himself.

An inquest was held to investigate the incident. Joseph Casagrande, one of the workers at the bus garage that day, was asked how Lebrun seemed when he entered the garage. Casagrande replied: "He was blank, just blank. He didn't sway. He didn't even blink an eye."

The Killer

Pierre Lebrun was a quiet and reserved man who appeared to live an isolated life. He did not really have close friends, and there is no evidence that he had any romantic relationships. His parents lived in Ottawa, and they were virtually his only social contacts. Many of his problems at work related to his stutter, which became worse when he was agitated or frustrated. Some of his co-workers mocked him by mimicking his speech, which naturally made the problem worse.

Lebrun had no criminal record and had given no indication that he was capable of such violence. He had been in trouble only once. In August 1997, he punched a co-worker at the bus garage. He was moved to another garage and forced to take a twelve-week anger management course. In a self-evaluation at the end of the course, he wrote that he did not feel he had met the goals he had set for himself. He offered no further explanation for what this meant. After completing the course, he returned to his usual location, but quit a few months later. Almost exactly a year after completing the course, he returned to the garage and went on his shooting rampage

A Psychological Explanation

The question: **Psychology** is the systematic study of people's thoughts, feelings, and behaviour. Thoughts, feelings, and behaviour are largely determined by **personality**—someone's relatively unchanging personal characteristics. Thus, psychologists attempting to explain the reasons for Pierre Lebrun's behaviour would examine his life in detail in order to answer the question: *What factors in his personality led Lebrun to commit this crime?*

The assumption: Psychologists assume that an individual's personality is moulded by a combination of biological factors (that is, hereditary traits determined by genetics) and prior experiences. Finding out about Lebrun's significant personal experiences is therefore one way to gain an understanding of his personality.

The explanation: At the coroner's inquest, Dr. John Joanisse provided information about over fifty visits Lebrun made to his office over eight and a half years. Lebrun complained of stomach cramps, insomnia, depression, diarrhea, and a host of other conditions. He would sit quietly in the doctor's waiting room, for hours if necessary, until his turn came.

On many occasions, Lebrun complained that people from OC Transpo were following him all over town. By July 1994, Dr. Joanisse was writing "paranoid" in Lebrun's medical history, meaning that the patient was suffering from delusions. This diagnosis indicated that Lebrun had

Figure 1.3 Paramedics carry in stretchers for shooting victims at the OC Transpo bus garage.

a mental illness characterized by irrational feelings of persecution from others. People with such an illness are likely to feel that family or co-workers are out to get them, even when there is no evidence to support such a feeling.

Lebrun made genuine efforts to deal with his problems. He did not miss a single class at his anger management course. Nor did he miss a class when he was being treated for his speech impediment in 1997.

But Lebrun was never fully able to solve the problems that overwhelmed him. His sense of reality began to fail. He tried unsuccessfully to deal with the demons that haunted him. On a trip to British Columbia and Las Vegas in March 1999, he wrote in his diary that union officials from OC Transpo were following him. Evidence given at the inquest showed that he cut short his trip, drove the 5000 km from Las Vegas to Ottawa in three days, and went on his rampage the following day.

A Sociological Explanation

The question: **Sociology** is the scientific study of the development, structure, and functioning of human society. It includes the study of how groups of people who share some common characteristic(s) function. A sociologist trying to explain the reasons for Pierre Lebrun's behaviour would attempt to answer the question: *What common factors are there in the lives of people who have gone on shooting sprees at their former place of work?*

The assumption: Sociologists assume that an individual's acts can only be understood when they are compared with the acts of similar individuals.

The explanation: In recent years, there have been a number of recorded cases of men returning to their former places of work and shooting former colleagues. Most of these cases have occurred in the United States. Many of the men who did such things shared some common characteristics.

In many ways, Pierre Lebrun fit the image of such a person. He was unpopular. He was a loner. He had felt the pain of being mocked by others. He appeared to have a low tolerance for frustration and had problems controlling anger.

During the inquest, there was a lot of testimony that showed Lebrun's behaviour was unusual. At OC Transpo, he spent his breaks alone, eating quickly then sleeping until it was time to go back to work. There were a number of "red flags" (warning signs) whose significance was not understood until after the rampage. These included the assault, being harassed at work, low self-esteem, and access to a rifle. Such experiences and factors are common among people who have shot their workplace colleagues.

Mass murderers have difficulty dealing with their emotions. Frustration and anger frequently take control of their lives. Inside they are deeply tormented. Pierre Lebrun was typical of this group. After years of frustration from injuries real or imagined, he finally cracked, killing four former co-workers and seriously injuring two others.

An Anthropological Explanation

The question: One of the branches of **anthropology**—cultural anthropology—is the study of the culture and customs of human beings. A cultural anthropologist seeking to explain Pierre Lebrun's actions would ask: *What were the values of the cultures in which he grew up and later worked?*

The assumption: An anthropologist would assume that there are factors in Canadian culture in general, and in the "subculture" of OC Transpo in particular, that encouraged Lebrun's violent behaviour.

The explanation: Powerful images of violence are widespread in today's Canadian culture. People witness violence in sports, media, and video games. They hear and see violent lyrics and images in music and music videos. "Mighty Morphin Power Rangers" may be plastic toys, but the message they implant in the minds of their young owners is that violent methods are a good way to deal with opponents. Many TV shows and movies feature characters, including the heroes, who solve their problems by behaving aggressively toward others, rather than by learning to reflect on and deal with their feelings of frustration and anger. The message in this culture is clear. When things get out of hand, acting violently will gain the attention and even the respect of others.

Many employees at the bus garage spoke at the inquest. The OC Transpo bus garage had nurtured a poisonous environment, characterized by hostility and aggression. Employees felt that managers did not respect them and treated them, in the words of one witness at the inquiry, "like children." Morale was low, he continued. People had expected that one day an employee would come into the office and "shoot a manager."

Figure 1.4
The movie Natural Born Killers *(1994) released a storm of controversy when it was accused of inspiring copycat killings. Should our culture be labelled "violent" because such movies exist?*

This workplace culture may have contributed to a sense of worthlessness, causing employees to act in antisocial ways. Virtually all of the mechanics and support workers were male, and there was much macho behaviour. Many had nicknames such as "Moose" or "Gonzo." They talked about fishing trips, hockey, and women. There was great pressure to accept the values of this culture in order to fit in and be accepted.

INTERNET RESOURCES

Do you want to find out how a sample of Canadians account for violence in schools? Visit the CBC News Online letters site on the killings in Taber, Alberta, at

http://cbc.ca/news/indepth/taber/yourletters.html

Summarize the perspectives by tallying how many offer psychological, sociological, or anthropological explanations for school violence. Which submission most closely reflects your own viewpoint?

There was a lot of teasing, much of it harmless. Supporters of the Ottawa Senators hockey team were ribbed when the team lost, a common occurrence at the time. But such teasing could cross the line of acceptability when someone did not fit in, and clearly Lebrun did not. Co-workers imitated his stutter, openly laughing at him. On one occasion, a co-worker pretended to be laughing so hard that he fell to the ground holding his stomach. The values and culture of his workplace increasingly frustrated Lebrun.

Social scientists have shown that workplace culture is a major factor in workplace violence. The level of personal harassment that was apparently accepted in the OC Transpo culture seemed only to increase over time. Lebrun finally rejected this culture, and the values that went with it, in the only way he knew how. Four deaths were the result.

RECAP

1. Make a timeline of events involving Pierre Lebrun as told in this section. Do you think anyone at any stage could have done anything to prevent this tragedy? Give reasons for your answer.
2. Do you think that anyone at the OC Transpo bus garage on the day of the shootings could have prevented the tragedy? Give reasons for your answer.
3. Complete a copy of the following organizer in your own words to summarize different social scientists' analyses of the Pierre Lebrun incident.

	Psychological	Sociological	Anthropological
Question			
Assumption			
Explanation			

Activities

Show your knowledge

1. Create a New Vocabulary glossary of the terms and phrases you learned in this chapter.
    a) Record the definition of each term.
    b) Use these terms to create four questions to ask a classmate. Make each question more difficult than the last. Follow the model used for these activities ("Show your knowledge," "Practise your thinking skills," "Communicate your ideas," "Apply your knowledge").
2. What are the social sciences? What one word identifies the chief focus of social scientific investigation?
3. What are some key questions asked by each of the following disciplines?
    a) anthropology
    b) psychology
    c) sociology

Practise your thinking skills

4. Imagine your school asks you to conduct a study on stress experienced by students over school workload and part-time jobs.
    a) Which different groups would you consult?
    b) What questions would you ask them?
    c) What other evidence would you want to gather?
    d) What process would you go through to come up with a recommendation?
5. Do some research into the arguments for and against capital punishment.
    a) Identify the three strongest arguments from both sides of the debate.
    b) Rank each set of arguments from most to least persuasive.
    c) How would an opponent respond to the supporters' strongest argument?
    d) How would a supporter respond to the opponents' strongest argument?

Activities

6. Present your opinion on the plausibility of each of the three explanations for Pierre Lebrun's crime (anthropological, psychological, and sociological). Give reasons for your opinion.

Communicate your ideas

7. Write a letter to the editor in praise of how social science research can help improve the quality of life and/or resolve issues.
8. Make a wall poster that illustrates factors that can cause workplace stress, and remedies that social scientists have recommended. Use the poster as a basis for a discussion on class members' personal experiences with the factors and/or remedies.
9. Imagine a Canadian news show is devoting a program to the Lebrun incident. A team of experts (one anthropologist, one sociologist, one psychologist) is gathered for a freewheeling discussion of violence in the workplace. In groups, role-play the participants in the discussion (moderator plus the three-member team of experts).

Apply your knowledge

10. How might an anthropologist, psychologist, and sociologist explain the following incidents?
    a) A group of thugs attack and injure two men they see coming out of a gay bar.
    b) A church group sponsors a refugee family from a wartorn country.
    c) Canadian peacekeeping troops put their lives at risk in a foreign country, where a civil war has just ended but may break out again.
    d) Soccer fans overseas riot and get into fist fights with opposing fans after a World Cup qualifying game.
11. Which social science disciplines have the most potential to help someone wanting to be one of the following?
    a) a good teacher
    b) a good boss
    c) a good parent
    d) a good spouse or partner

    Give reasons for each answer. Then look over all four answers. Do you see any pattern? Explain why you think the pattern exists.

Chapter 2

The Development of the Social Sciences

Overview of Chapter

Learning Expectations

By the end of this chapter, you will be able to

- evaluate the major contributions to our understanding of the idea of self in relation to others made by at least one of the leading practitioners in each of the social sciences
- correctly use the terminology of the social sciences
- define the concepts that are central to the social sciences
- demonstrate an understanding of the factors that explain human behaviour from the perspective of the social sciences
- formulate appropriate questions for research and inquiry relating to one or more of the main areas of concern in the social sciences

Open for Debate

What a Difference a Gene Makes

The Great Ape Legal Project has a plan for extending rights typically considered to be the solely human to all of the members of the great ape clade (or group of related species): humans, chimpanzees, gorillas, orangutans, and bonobos.

The Great Ape Legal Project has a uniquely genetic twist: the remarkable similarity between human and chimpanzee DNA. We now know that humans and chimpanzees share 98.4 per cent of their genetic material. A number of people have taken a look at the data and have come to a conclusion called the Identity Thesis—humans are not like chimpanzees, humans *are* chimpanzees.

The Identity Thesis is an imaginative mix of genetics with ethics, philosophy, and law.

A little *too* imaginative, actually, since the holders of the Identity Thesis have bent the science involved past the breaking point.

The 1.6 per cent difference between humans and chimp DNA accounts for roughly 500 000 points of difference between the average human genome and the average chimp genome—in other words, 500 000 places in which our DNA has drifted apart. You could make an analogy with a skydiver: In the first second after a jump, a skydiver will have fallen only sixteen feet [4.9 m] from the plane. But no matter how small the distance separating them, skydivers do not fall up into planes. Likewise, no matter how close species are, they will never reclose the gap between them.

The extension of legal rights to primates may make moral sense, but basing this idea on a supposedly small and permeable border between humans and chimpanzees bases good morals on bad science.

Abridged from: Shirky, Clay. "What a Difference a Gene Makes." *FEED Magazine*. [Online]. Available http://www.feedmag.com/feature/fr335lofi.html 15 May 2000.

Think About It

1. Why is the 1.6 per cent difference in the genetic material of humans and chimpanzees causing a controversy?
2. Do you think we should extend the same moral and legal rights to apes as to humans? On what do you base your opinion?
3. Using what you learned in Chapter 1, briefly analyze the validity of the Great Ape Legal Project from the point of view of a sociologist, a psychologist, and an anthropologist.

Section 2.1

The Development of Sociology

Focus Questions

- What different schools of thought exist in sociology?
- Who were the leading sociologists?
- What do Canadian sociologists today study?

Key Concepts

functionalist school
conflict school
neo-Marxist
symbolic interactionist school
social statics
social dynamics
equilibrium
positivism
egoistic suicide
altruistic suicide
anomic suicide
class conflict
bourgeoisie
proletariat
bureaucracies
universals
gender socialization

Fields of Study in Sociology

Sociologists take on a wide range of topics in their research. These topics include relationships between ethnic groups; relationships between social classes; gender roles and expectations; the family; criminology and deviance; and the structure of the workplace.

Different schools of thought exist within the discipline of sociology. The first two sociologists you will read about, Comte and Durkheim, as well as Parsons (see pages 20 to 21 and 22), were of the **functionalist school**. The third sociologist, Marx (see page 21), was of the **conflict school** (also known after Marx's time as the **neo-Marxist** school). The fourth sociologist, Weber (see pages 21 to 22), was of the **symbolic interactionist school**.

Functionalism

Functionalists believe that society is best studied as an organic system, very much like the human body. Just as each organ in the human body performs a function, so each institution in society has a specific job to do. When all the parts of society work together as they should, the interests of each individual member are protected. Large-scale patterns can be discovered as the functioning of each institution, and the relationships among institutions, are analyzed.

The Conflict School

Neo-Marxists, or conflict theorists, believe that the most significant characteristic of human beings is their ability to produce goods to meet their needs and wants. Neo-Marxists are therefore interested in how the forces of production operate, and in the social structures and relationships that are created from these forces. Not everyone can be in control of these forces (also known as the economy)—in other words, different groups struggle or compete for resources and power. Conflicts arise as a result, and different social classes form, with some classes having power over others. Conflict theorists study the social patterns and structures that develop as classes struggle against each other.

Symbolic Interactionism

Unlike both functionalists and conflict theorists, symbolic interactionists focus on small-scale patterns in the everyday interactions between individuals. They believe that the most significant characteristic of human beings is their ability to reason abstractly and think symbolically. This ability enables us to have a sense of "self" and a sense of who others are. By using it in our face-to-face interactions, we jointly create the patterns of connecting and relating to one another that form the basis of "society." Together with others, we create the rules for how to behave in our daily lives. We learn what roles to play depending on who our audience is.

FILM LINK

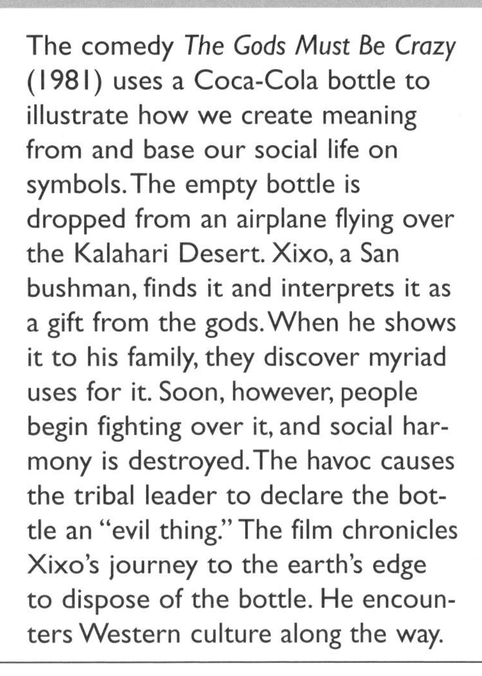

The comedy *The Gods Must Be Crazy* (1981) uses a Coca-Cola bottle to illustrate how we create meaning from and base our social life on symbols. The empty bottle is dropped from an airplane flying over the Kalahari Desert. Xixo, a San bushman, finds it and interprets it as a gift from the gods. When he shows it to his family, they discover myriad uses for it. Soon, however, people begin fighting over it, and social harmony is destroyed. The havoc causes the tribal leader to declare the bottle an "evil thing." The film chronicles Xixo's journey to the earth's edge to dispose of the bottle. He encounters Western culture along the way.

The Goals of Sociology

Sociologists can also be divided into pure, applied, and clinical camps. "Pure" sociology is focused on research; its goal is the understanding of life in human groups. "Applied" sociology uses research findings to solve social problems. "Clinical" sociologists try to go beyond solving specific problems to bringing about social change.

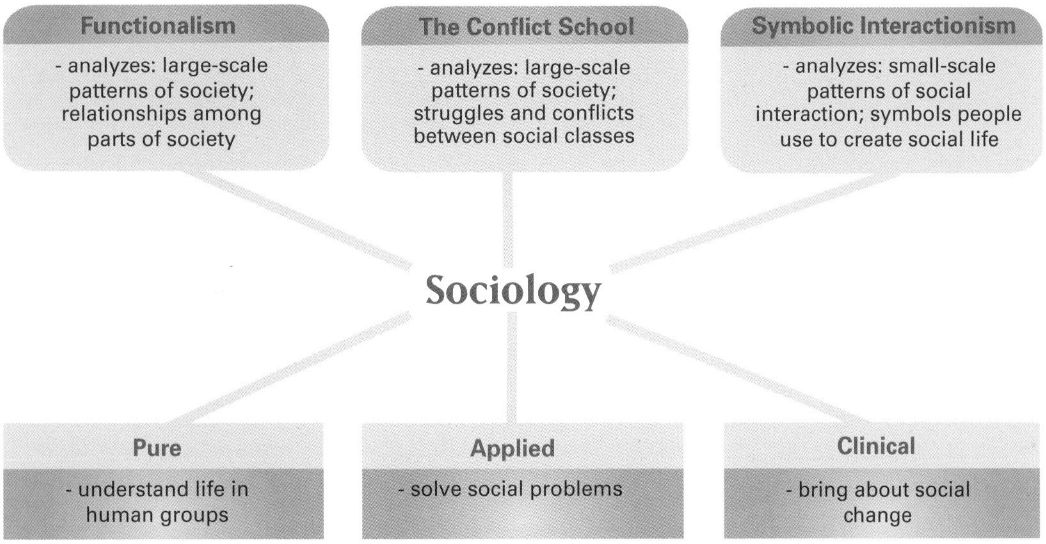

Figure 2.1 Schools of thought and goals of sociology

A Sociology Hall of Fame

Of the three social sciences that form the basis of this book, sociology is the oldest. It had its origins in France in the early nineteenth century. Later in the century, it became important in Germany. During the twentieth century, it became increasingly important in the United States. It is now truly a worldwide discipline.

Figure 2.2 Auguste Comte (1798–1857)

Auguste Comte

The first person to study sociology, and the inventor of the term, was Auguste Comte (1798–1857). Comte originated the use of scientific methods such as observation and analysis to study society. His methods are now regarded as crude, but his contribution to sociology and the social sciences in general cannot be denied.

Comte observed that societies change over time. Such changes cause difficulties for people as they try to adapt. He tried to identify the factors that cause society to change and to measure the effect of these changes. He formulated two major categories for analyzing society. The first category he called **social statics**—the study of society's customs, institutions, and laws, and their interaction. He called the second category **social dynamics**—the stages through which societies must go as they experience change.

Figure 2.3 Harriet Martineau (1802–1876) translated Comte's ideas into English, and wrote Society in America *(1837).*

Comte believed that societies have a natural tendency to reach a state of **equilibrium**, or balance. If one institution declines in importance, another will emerge to fill the void, so balance is maintained. While change causes discomfort, Comte observed, in the long run society adapts and survives.

Perhaps Comte's most important contribution to sociology was **positivism**—his insistence on the rigid application of the scientific method in order to arrive at the truth. He believed that scientists and sociologists, working together, could reach a better understanding of society than could church authorities or politicians. He even went so far as to suggest that sociologists should make *all* decisions about the future of society! This idea was largely rejected by his successors.

Émile Durkheim

Another French philosopher, Émile Durkheim (1859–1917), is generally regarded as the founder of modern sociology. Like Comte, Durkheim believed in applying the scientific method to the study of society. He believed this could result in a more perfect society. Durkheim concentrated on the *changing* nature of society, largely because he lived in an era of great social upheaval in Europe (the Industrial Revolution).

Durkheim established a lasting relationship between sociology and the criminal justice system. Ancient societies had punished lawbreakers by inflicting severe and barbaric punishments. In Durkheim's time, many European societies abandoned this approach. Restitution, or paying for the crime, became the norm. Durkheim was the first to argue that reform of criminals was more effective than vicious punishment.

Durkheim is perhaps best remembered for his *Studies on Suicide* (1897). Why do people kill themselves? he asked. He identified three major types of suicide. The first was the **egoistic suicide**, which resulted when an individual shared none of the values or goals of society. The second type was the **altruistic suicide**, in which a person deliberately entered into an impossible situation, sacrificing himself or herself to protect others. Third was the **anomic suicide**, which occurred when the person was overwhelmed with sudden change in society and could not cope with social breakdown. Durkheim predicted that the anomic suicide would become more common as the rate of social change increased. Durkheim is considered the founder of functionalism—the belief that society works in a logical manner and protects the interests of most of its members. With this belief, Durkheim was confident that society would survive, dealing effectively with the forces of change.

Karl Marx

Karl Marx (1818–1883) was a German scholar. Like Durkheim in France, Marx lived though the Industrial Revolution, when factories were replacing small workshops. Why, he asked, had the few become fabulously wealthy while the majority had nothing?

Marx, looking to history for the answer, concluded that uneven distribution of wealth was a normal condition in society. It led to a struggle between rich and poor for wealth and power. He coined the term **class conflict** to describe this struggle. He called the wealthy, who owned the factories and machinery, the **bourgeoisie**. The poor, who survived by selling their labour, he called the **proletariat**.

Marx was the founder of the conflict school of sociology. This school claims that the struggle for power and wealth is the driving force behind society. Marx argued that capitalist society left most people with no control over their own destiny. Society's problems would not be solved until power was redistributed among the people. Many of Marx's ideas were later incorporated particularly into the study of alienation and conformity.

Max Weber

German sociologist Max Weber (1864–1920) modified Marx's conflict approach. Weber believed that Marx had placed too much emphasis on economic factors in explaining power differences among social groups. Religion, education, politics, and family structure, he argued, are as important as economics in moulding people's values.

Weber believed that power came in many forms. People could obtain it by belonging to a political party or an elite status group. Wealth alone, he believed, was not enough to give a person power. He felt that Marx's division of society into capitalists and proletariat was too simple. It ignored the growing professional middle class, which owned property and survived by selling valuable skills to society.

Weber also disputed Marx's belief that armed revolution was the only way of bringing about change. He favoured the creation of government **bureaucracies** to provide essential social services, such as safe drinking water, sewage disposal, and schooling. These bureaucracies, he believed, would improve many of society's problems and make revolution unnecessary.

Weber was one of the most influential

Figure 2.4 Émile Durkheim (1858–1917)

Figure 2.5 Karl Marx (1818–1883)

Figure 2.6 Max Weber (1864–1920)

Figure 2.7 Talcott Parsons (1902–1979)

of the early sociologists. He popularized the belief that society could be reformed and improved. He began focusing sociology on the study and solution of society's problems and inequities. This focus remained central as sociology developed throughout the twentieth century.

Talcott Parsons

The twentieth century saw leadership in the field of sociology turning to the United States. Talcott Parsons (1902–1979) was one of the people who spearheaded this change. His approach to sociology began with the recognition of people's freedom to make choices. For example, we are free to decide how to dress, what to study in school, and what career to pursue. In making these choices, however, we are motivated to fit into society. We adopt the dress, language, and behaviour of the group with which we most strongly identify. Business leaders, sports figures, and punk rockers, for example, all have their preferred styles of dressing, speaking, and behaving. These draw group members closer together.

Parsons's works included *Sociological Theory and Modern Society* (1967) and *Politics and Social Structure* (1969). He demonstrated an optimistic view of a society in which most members' needs could be met. His critics contend, however, that he focused too much on the forces of law and order. He was unable to explain the disorder, upheaval, and change that exist in all societies.

Figure 2.8 Parson's view of society

Cultural System

Social System

Society

Personality System

Behavioural System

George Murdock

George Murdock (1897–1985), an American sociologist and anthropologist, studied societies around the world. He believed that these societies shared many similar characteristics. His approach contrasted with that of many other researchers, who focused on what made societies unique. Murdock's most important work, *Social Organizations* (1949), focused on human **universals**. Years of research produced a list of over 100 characteristics that Murdock believed could be observed in every human culture and society. They included bodily adornment (such as tattoos and makeup), ethics, gestures, superstitions, and sexual restrictions.

Murdock's findings demonstrated that sociologists must not concentrate solely on the forces of division in society. He highlighted the need to explain why religion, social status, and concepts of good and bad are recurring themes in human societies.

Sociology in Canada Today

From the 1960s onward, Canadian sociology expanded significantly. The gap between rich and poor ("social stratification") featured prominently in the works of Wallace Clement (Carleton University) and John Porter (University of Toronto). In the 1970s, ethnicity and multiculturalism were a focus for investigation. Jay Goldstein and Rita Bienvenue's *Ethnicity and Ethnic Relations in Canada* (1980) was the result of years of work. Another continuing theme has been gender relations, of which you will read more below.

Many present-day Canadian sociologists have established an international reputation. They study a wide range of topics. A brief mention of a few of these scholars indicates the range of their work.

David Lyon, of Queen's University, Kingston, Ontario, has written about the impact of electronic media on our consciousness. He has shown how all Canadians, whether they realize it or not, are affected by this phenomenon. University of Calgary's Edna Einsiedel has studied communication patterns in the modern world. University of Montreal's Marc Raboy is a professor of communication who investigates "the journalism of alternative media."

Communication is only one of the fields that Canadian sociologists study. Reginald Bibby, of the University of Lethbridge, has written about young people—their values, hopes, and fears. He is particularly interested in how young people's values affect the way they lead their lives and view the future. He has found that religious principles are part of the moral beliefs of more young people than had previously been imagined. Marlene Mackie, from the University of Calgary, does research into the effect of early life experiences on development. She has written widely about **gender socialization**—the distinct ways in which girls and boys are commonly socialized.

Virtually every aspect of human group behaviour is being examined by a famous sociologist somewhere in Canada. Much research has been done into such topics as schools, prisons, job cuts, teenage gangs, and differences in communication patterns between males and females. If you choose to study sociology after you have graduated from high school, you have an almost unlimited set of topics from which to choose.

RECAP

1. List five different topics or issues that have been important to sociologists.
2. How are the topics of study of today's sociologists different from the topics studied in the past?
3. Which of the sociologists described here do you find the most interesting? What are your reasons for picking this person?
4. Which of the sociologists do you think has focused on ideas that are most important or helpful in trying to solve problems in society today? Explain your answer.

Section 2.2

The Development of Psychology

Focus Questions

- Where and how did psychology originate as a field of study?
- How has the understanding of personality developed over time?
- What are some current topics of psychological study in Canada?

Key Concepts

psychoanalysis
behavioural psychology
cognitive psychology
conscious mind
unconscious mind
free association
id
ego
superego
defence mechanisms
psychiatry
individual psychology
inferiority complex
analytical psychology
introvert
extrovert
unconditioned stimulus
unconditioned response
conditioned stimulus
conditioned response

Fields of Study in Psychology

As a discipline, psychology has gone through periods when different schools of thought have dominated.

Psychoanalysis

Following the pioneering work of Sigmund Freud (see pages 26 to 27), the main emphasis of psychological research was directed toward **psychoanalysis**. Followers of this school tried to probe the innermost experiences (thoughts, feelings, emotions, fantasies, and dreams) of their subjects, with a view to treating patients who suffered from severe anxieties and tensions.

Behavioural Psychology

In the early part of the twentieth century, growing numbers of psychologists became dissatisfied with psychoanalysis. They turned away from the study of the mind, believing that such study was unreliable because it depended on the patient's ability to describe her or his innermost experiences. Instead, they moved toward studying behaviour, which is observable and therefore can be studied more

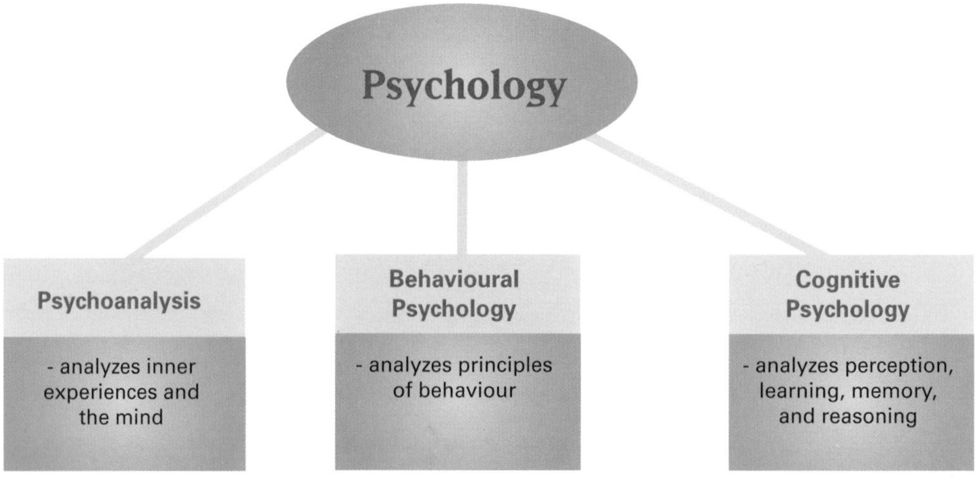

Figure 2.9 Schools of thought in psychology

objectively than the invisible mind. The American behaviourist John Watson described the goal of **behavioural psychology** in 1913 as "the prediction and control of behavior." This school of psychology encouraged the use of animals in psychological experiments, believing that principles of behaviour would remain consistent among all species. Behavioural psychology dominated the discipline until the 1950s.

Experiments in Behaviourism

Edward Lee Thorndike (1874–1949) was an American behavioural psychologist. In 1898, he began a series of experiments on animal learning. In one of the more famous experiments, he put cats in a cage, left food outside it, and timed how long it took the cats to learn how to open a small door that would let them out of the cage. He returned individual cats to the same cage a number of times, discovering that the cats could escape more quickly each time. They did so by avoiding the techniques that they knew from prior experience did not work and concentrating on those they knew would lead to success.

From such experiments, Thorndike developed his law of effect. This states that behaviours that result in a positive outcome will be repeated, and those that result in negative consequences will be avoided. It also goes on to state that the more satisfying the result of a particular action, the better it is learned.

Thorndike went on to apply the law of effect to school classrooms. He believed that school curriculum should be designed to include some subjects that were more practical and less intellectual than subjects like mathematics or languages. Thorndike claimed that students would see the immediate benefits of such practical subjects and would therefore apply themselves to these subjects, so increasing the likelihood of success.

Studies like those of Thorndike convinced behavioural psychologists that it was a short step from the animal experiment cage to the classroom as well as the workplace.

Classic Study

RESEARCHER:
Edward Lee Thorndike, Psychologist

TIME:
1898

SUBJECT:
The Law of Effect

Cognitive Psychology

In the second half of the twentieth century, **cognitive psychology** became prominent. This school studies how people perceive and deal with their environment, how people learn and remember, where in the human brain memories are stored, how humans acquire and use language, and how they reason and make decisions. Because much of formal education involves learning and remembering, cognitive psychologists have spent considerable time investigating how schools operate and suggesting improvements. They have also investigated abstract phenomena like values and beliefs, examining how humans acquire them and what role they play in their lives.

A Psychology Hall of Fame

Psychology first emerged as an area of study in Europe during the last half of the nineteenth century. Austrian, Swiss, and Russian researchers led the field for three generations. In the early twentieth century, American researchers became increasingly important. Although psychology has practitioners in many countries, a significant amount of study is still carried out in the United States.

Figure 2.10 Sigmund Freud (1856–1939)

Figure 2.11 Anna Freud (1895–1982) extended and transformed Freud's work. Other female scholars who extended or radically revised Freud's work include Karen Horney (1885–1952) and Melanie Klein (1882–1960).

Sigmund Freud

Sigmund Freud (1856–1939) is generally regarded as the founder of psychology. In his practice in Vienna, Austria, he developed the theory and method of psychoanalysis. This development came about from Freud's assumption that the human mind is divided into two parts. The **conscious mind** contains the memories that we can recall. The **unconscious mind** harbours the memories we cannot recall. Of the two, he believed that the unconscious mind was the more powerful influence on human behaviour. In order to treat patients for mental disorders, he believed, it was necessary to "unlock" the unconscious mind and explore the memories stored there.

Freud initially believed that hypnosis was the key to unlocking the unconscious. He later came to doubt its reliability and developed the technique of **free association**. Patients were placed in a state of complete relaxation, and the therapist would read from a list of words. The patient would respond with the first idea that came to mind. Freud believed that by analyzing the patient's responses, it was possible to see what secrets lay hidden in the unconscious mind. He believed that our unconscious mind speaks to us in dreams. *The Interpretation of Dreams* (1900) outlined his techniques of dream analysis and the importance of dreams in understanding personality.

Further investigations led Freud to conclude that there are three elements to the human mind. The **id** is the pleasure-seeking element. It contains all the primitive parts of our personality, including aggression and sexual drive. In encouraging us to satisfy our desire for pleasure, the id can lead us to be self-destructive. The **ego** is the element that urges us to do good things to obtain positive results. It also is the driving force that spurs us to work for personal success. While the id might tempt us to sleep late and skip classes, the ego tells us to get up and study for a test. But which will win? The **superego**, the third element, referees between the id and the ego. The superego acts as our conscience, helping us judge right from wrong. More than that, it urges us to strive for perfection.

Some of Freud's most interesting work related to what he called **defence mechanisms**. These are techniques that the human mind uses to deal with anxiety and to maintain self-esteem (see page 77 in Chapter 4 for a detailed look at four defence mechanisms). A brief list includes denial (refusing to acknowledge your own problem behaviour), displacement (shifting your anger and frustration over a situation or person to a less threatening object), and repression (removing damaging experiences from your conscious memory). A person who uses such mechanisms persistently runs the risk of losing touch with reality. In such a case, Freud believed, the person would need psychoanalysis. It is in the area of defence mechanisms that Freud's pioneering work has perhaps had its most lasting impact.

Sigmund Freud was undoubtedly one of the most important thinkers of the twentieth century. Although certain followers later rejected some of his theories, his work was enormously significant in the development of **psychiatry**. This is the study and medical treatment of mental disorders.

Alfred Adler

Alfred Adler (1870–1937), an Austrian psychoanalyst, worked with Freud from 1902 to 1911. Initially a follower of Freud, he b appro Adler that s ing p ple w conq taine powe peop

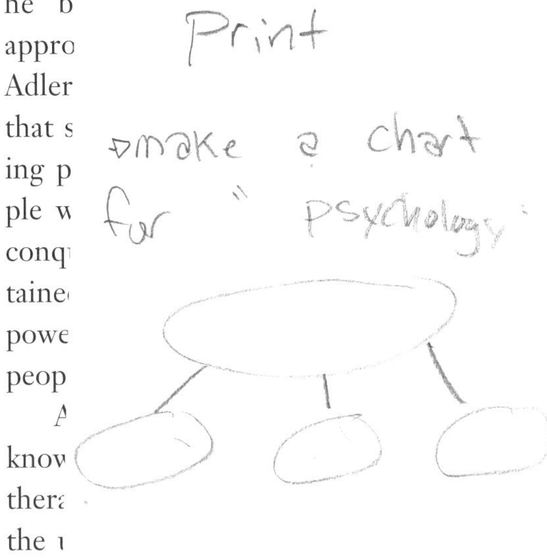

A know thera the u Instead, it assumed that people were nor-mally aware of the goals and values that guided them.

Adler also introduced the concept of the **inferiority complex**. All people, he stated, feel inferior at certain times in their lives, especially as children. They try to compensate by seeking experiences that give them a feeling of power. For some people, this might involve having an important job with many junior employees reporting to them. For others, having a large house and an expensive car satisfies their need for power. For still others, exerting extreme control over their spouse helps them overcome inferior feelings.

In *Understanding Human Nature* (1927), Adler laid out his basic theories. Like Freud, he believed that dreams were extremely important in understanding human personality. But he rejected the idea that our dreams reveal more about our sexuality than anything else. Nor did he accept Freud's theory that people who have difficulty relating to others probably had damaging sexual experiences as chil- People are maladjusted, he argued, they pursue goals that are useless and society. They choose to pur- ch goals because they lack self- Becoming well-adjusted requires self-esteem and, as a result, the of worthwhile goals.

ler is one of the most important sychologists. He broadened psych- focus beyond Freud's concentra- n sexuality. His approach was an ant influence on other theoreti- nd practitioners.

Figure 2.12 Alfred Adler (1870–1937)

Jung

Swiss psychoanalyst Carl Jung (1875–1961) founded **analytical psychology**. Having read many of Freud's works, Jung carried out his own experiments in word association. After having some success with the technique, he went to Vienna in 1907 to work with its inventor. Like Adler, he found Freud a difficult colleague, eventually splitting with him over the issue of sexuality and its role in the human personality.

Jung believed that Freud's idea of the unconscious mind was too simplistic. He theorized that the unconscious mind has both a personal and a collective aspect. The personal unconscious is unique to the individual. In contrast, the collective unconscious is shared by all, containing

Figure 2.13 Carl Jung (1875–1961)

the memories of our ancestors. It is the more important of the two.

Jung originated the concept of four psychological functions: sensation, intuition, thinking, and feeling. He believed that human personality types could be defined by which function is dominant. Jung also made a distinction between two ways people use their psychological power. Some individuals use their psychological power to look inward into themselves. They are often emotionally self-sufficient and do not need many close personal relationships to give them reassurance and confidence. Jung called these people **introverts**. Other people use the same power to draw closer to others. They are outgoing and more comfortable in a large group of friends. These people are the **extroverts**.

Figure 2.14 Ivan Pavlov (1849–1936)

Like Adler, Jung expanded the base of research into the human mind. His ideas continue to have a strong following today.

Ivan Pavlov

Russian Ivan Pavlov (1849–1936) trained as a medical doctor before becoming a behavioural psychologist. In 1904, he was awarded a Nobel Prize in Medicine. He is best remembered, however, for his studies of conditioned behaviour.

Pavlov was interested in the relationship between stimulus and response. If, for example, you lightly touch a baby's nose (stimulus), she or he will smile (response). Pavlov wondered if the stimulus-response pattern could be used to teach animals new behaviours.

He decided to test his theory on dogs. He discovered that squirting small quantities of food into a dog's mouth (**unconditioned stimulus**, or UCS) caused the dog to drool or salivate (**unconditioned response**, or UCR). This response was "unconditioned" in that it was a natural reaction that required no learning. Pavlov also discovered that if the experimenter rang a bell just before squirting the food, the dog would associate the bell with the food. Pavlov called the ringing of the bell the **conditioned stimulus** (CS). If the experimenter rang the bell without squirting the food, the dog still salivated. This was the **conditioned response** (CR).

Figure 2.15 Pavlov's stages of conditioning

This experiment showed that responses can be conditioned—in other words, behaviour can be manipulated—with the right kind of stimulus.

Pavlov extended his research with dogs to generalize about human behaviour. He believed that humans are also conditioned to act in particular ways. We have a tendency to engage in behaviours that we know from prior experience will reward us, perhaps with money, admiration, or a feeling of self-worth. Like the dogs who salivated when they heard the bell, humans can respond positively or negatively to a piece of music or a particular smell, because we have already experienced it in another setting. In developing these generalizations about human behaviour based on animal research, Pavlov was demonstrating the important behaviouralist principle that aspects of behaviour can be consistent across species.

Pavlov changed the direction of psychology. Whereas earlier psychologists were concerned with the mind's internal structure, Pavlov placed more value on observable behaviour. His experiments were to form the basis for much modern research into conditioning.

Psychology in Canada Today

There are a large number of Canadians currently active in the field of psychology. Gerald Wilde, of Queen's University in Kingston, Ontario, studies accidents. He specializes in analyzing how mechanical breakdowns, system failures, and human error cause accidents.

Researchers are trying to find out to what extent certain medical conditions, such as anorexia or depression, are caused by physiological or emotional factors. The University of Western Ontario's David Dozois is devoting research time to depression.

The Native Physicians Association has set up a branch called Native Psychologists in Canada, which investigates psychological health among Aboriginal peoples.

Corrections Canada, which runs the federal penitentiary service, employs psychologists to research and treat many of its violent offenders.

RECAP

1. Make a list of five different topics or issues that have been important to psychologists.
2. How are the topics of study of today's psychologists different from the topics studied in the past?
3. Which of the psychologists described here do you find the most interesting? What are your reasons for picking this person?
4. Which of the psychologists do you think has focused on ideas that are most important or helpful in trying to solve problems in society today? Explain your answer.

Section 2.3

The Development of Anthropology

Focus Questions

- How did the development of anthropology differ from the development of sociology and psychology?
- What different types of anthropologists are there?
- Why is anthropology important to the study of human behaviour?

Key Concepts

cultural anthropology
social anthropology
physical anthropology
culture
ethnographic studies
myth
kinship
participant observation
functional theory
cultural evolutionism
ethnocentric
cultural diffusion
primate

Fields of Study in Anthropology

Three types of anthropology have developed over the course of the twentieth century and continue to be practised. **Cultural anthropology** examines and compares the cultures of living peoples. In a similar manner, **social anthropology** focuses on the social organization of living peoples. **Physical anthropology** has links with natural sciences such as biology and genetics. It examines the evolution of humankind over the last few million years, and compares the genetic characteristics of humans with other biologically similar animals, such as apes, gorillas, and chimpanzees.

In examining distinct peoples, anthropologists concentrate on a number of key concepts. Perhaps the most important of these is the concept of **culture**. To an anthropologist, culture means any information about behaviour that is transmitted from one person to another and that enables people to live together

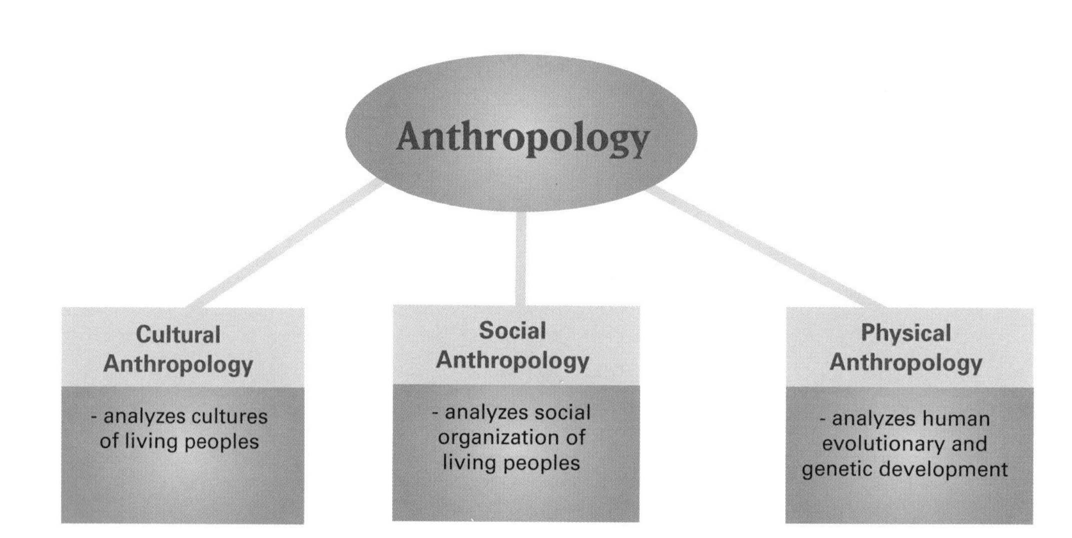

Figure 2.16 Fields of study in anthropology

successfully. Culture is intended to provide a framework to make everyone a better person. It consists of three major elements. The first element is material objects that we might possess or desire (for example, a car or a cow). Second, culture includes attitudes that are considered acceptable (for example, "people of all races are equal," "knowledge about your ancestors makes you a better person"). Third, culture consists of behaviours that are considered proper (for example, not eating with your fingers, or only eating with your fingers, depending on the culture).

Early **ethnographic studies**—that is, studies of the culture and traditions of distinct peoples—implied that culture is static and clearly defined. In fact, culture changes over time, and there are usually grey areas about human attitudes or behaviour. Good examples of changing cultural attitudes in modern Canadian society relate to drinking and driving and unmarried couples living together. Where a generation ago, teenagers might have thought of drinking and driving as a person's right and a demonstration of independence, there is less tolerance for this behaviour today. Schools have successful anti-drinking-and-driving programs, and designated driver schemes are relatively common. As for unmarried couples living together, tolerance for this behaviour has increased over the past generation. Not everyone accepts these changes, but there has been a general shift in Canadians' attitudes.

A second concept that is important to anthropologists is **myth**. Myths include stories that explain the origins of the world and of human beings. Myths also recount the lives of cultural heroes and beings with supernatural powers. Myths are intended to reassure people about where they have come from and where they are going. In addition, they provide reasons why people should practise the most important attitudes and behaviours of their culture. To an anthropologist, the story of Adam and Eve would be regarded as an origin myth. It is a story that communicates certain truths about the nature of humanity and its relationship to God. When anthropologists consider a story to be a "myth," they do not mean that the story is false. Indeed, myths are the most powerful stories in a culture. They are the means by which cultural values are transmitted from one generation to the next.

Another important anthropological concept is **kinship**. This involves the idea that members of a social group define themselves as descended from common ancestors. The most obvious kinship system is the family. We identify with other family members because of common

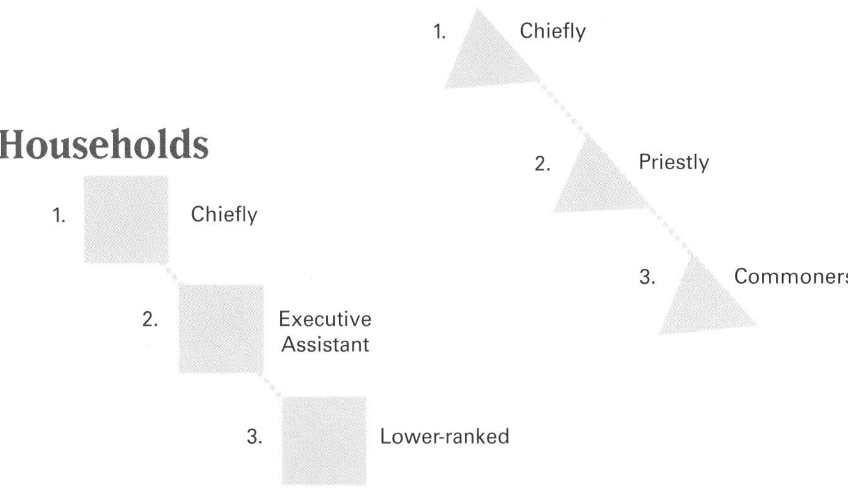

Figure 2.17 In the Tikopian kinship system, each ranked clan was divided into ranked lineage groups, and each ranked lineage group was divided into ranked households.

descent, and we assign special importance to family relationships because of this. As anthropologists have found, kinship structures vary enormously.

For example, in nineteenth-century China, the ideal family structure was headed by two married sons, often called a joint family. Girls were often adopted into families as child brides so that they would marry the sons. Such girls were completely dominated by their future mothers-in-law, even after they had married. Since kinship was recognized down the male side of the family, women played a subordinate role. They were virtually obliged to marry. If a woman died unmarried, it was possible for her spirit to be married after death, so that she would then belong to a kinship group (Bodley, 2000, 24).

On the island of Tikopia, in the South Pacific, all kinship groups were ranked by order of importance and ruled over by a single chief. The chief's kinship group, or clan, was given precedence at religious and social ceremonies, and each other group took part based on its rank. Higher-ranked groups played the more important roles. There was also a ranking of household membership within each clan. The importance of any household was based on its seniority within the clan. Consequently, there was a complete ranking of all groups, families, and individuals that permitted or prevented specific behaviours according to position in the hierarchy. The rules of proper behaviour were clearly outlined, and it was the duty of all members to obey them (Bodley, 2000, 172–173).

Anthropology originally tended to concentrate on non-industrialized peoples, while sociology focused on industrialized, Western nations. This distinction is no longer as great as it once was because anthropologists are now equally involved in studying modern, industrial societies. Sociologists have likewise expanded their study beyond Western, industrialized nations. Perhaps the most important difference between anthropology and sociology today lies not so much in the area of study but in the methods used. Sociologists prefer to rely on analysis of statistics to explain trends in society. Anthropologists more commonly rely on **participant observation**. This means living with the people being studied, sometimes for years, in order to understand how they believe their culture and society work.

An Anthropology Hall of Fame

Of the three social sciences that form the basis of this book, the youngest is anthropology, which originated as a discipline in the twentieth century. Its development differed from sociology and psychology in two significant ways: many of its founders were American, and many were female. This latter difference may well account for the different focus that it initially took.

Margaret Mead

Margaret Mead (1901–1978) was the most famous of the early anthropologists. A cultural anthropologist, she began her career studying the cultures of the Pacific islands. Her earliest investigations took place in the islands of Samoa, where she compared Samoan and American cultures. She specifically compared the adolescent experience in Samoa and America. She

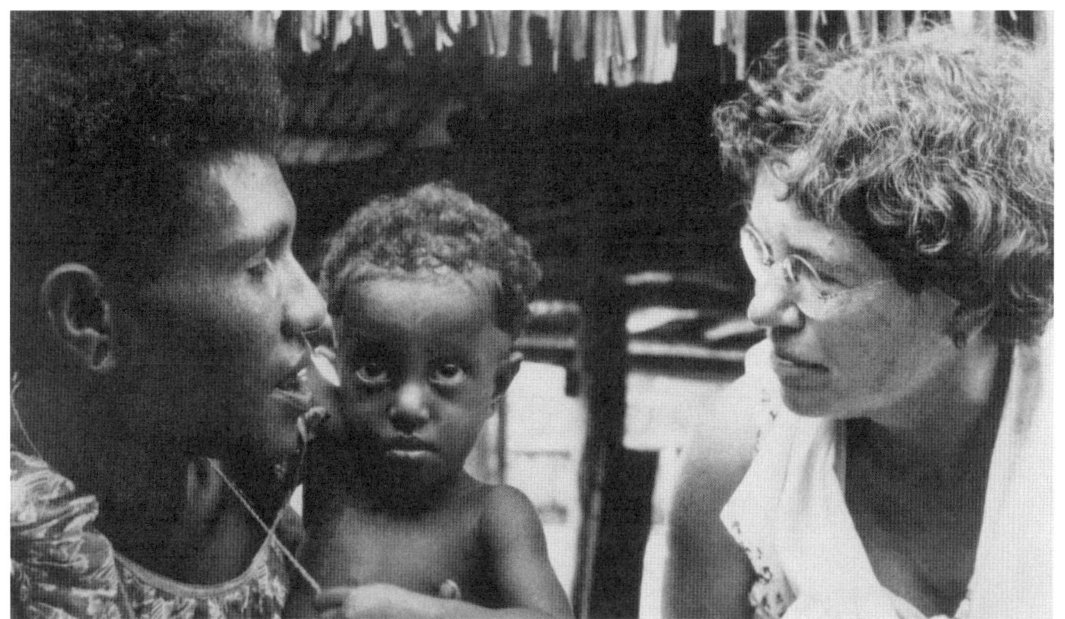

Figure 2.18 Margaret Mead made several expeditions to the Admiralty Islands of Papua New Guinea to study the culture of the Manus.

observed that adolescence was not a particularly troubling time for Samoans, who were considered adults when they reached physical maturity. Samoan youth did not experience teenage conflicts, unlike North American youth, who had to wait until their early twenties to be regarded as adults.

Mead concluded that our personalities are largely influenced by the society in which we live. Americans were raised to compete against each other, while Samoans were taught to co-operate. This made Americans generally more aggressive than Samoans. Her book *Coming of Age in Samoa* (1928) documented her findings.

Mead subsequently focused her attention on gender roles. This topic was particularly relevant to Mead, who broke gender roles herself by becoming a world-famous scholar. In *Sex and Temperament in Three Primitive Societies* (1935), she examined the roles of women and men in different cultures.

Although many consider Mead to have been the most important cultural anthropologist who ever lived, later researchers have accused her of sloppy methods. She relied too heavily, they argue, on personal stories, and too little on the gathering of objective statistics. Derek Freeman's *The Making and Unmaking of an Anthropological Myth* (1983) lays out these charges in great detail. In the late 1990s, other researchers charged that her claims of sexual liberation among young Samoans were greatly exaggerated. But Mead did popularize the study of anthropology through her research and is therefore regarded as one of its most important pioneers.

Ruth Benedict

Ruth Benedict (1887–1948) was another pioneering American cultural anthropologist. Her work included studies on the role of religion in developing and shaping human personality. Much of her work was with the Aboriginal peoples of

Figure 2.19 Ruth Benedict (1887–1948)

the American Plains. Her investigations heightened interest in, and increased our knowledge of, Aboriginal societies in North America.

In 1934, Benedict published her famous *Patterns of Culture*. In it she concluded that culture was "personality writ large"—in other words, a sum of all the personality types of its people. Benedict shared with Mead this belief in a strong link between the characteristics of a culture and its people's personality types.

During the Second World War, the US government hired Benedict to study Japanese culture. The government hoped her findings would help in planning for Japan's redevelopment after the war. Her work was eventually published in *The Chrysanthemum and the Sword* (1946). This book detailed the nature of Japanese society and its national personality. With this very practical contribution, Benedict brought respect to the field of anthropology. The concerns of anthropology were becoming part of the mainstream of American life.

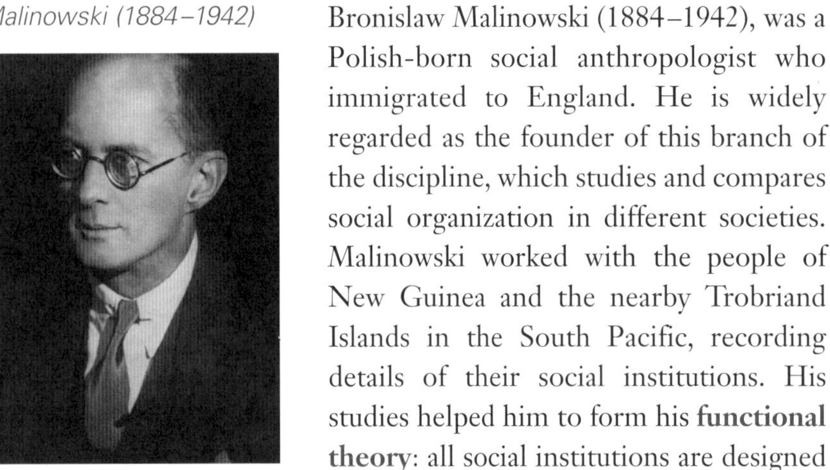

Figure 2.20 Bronislaw Malinowski (1884–1942)

Bronislaw Malinowski

Bronislaw Malinowski (1884–1942), was a Polish-born social anthropologist who immigrated to England. He is widely regarded as the founder of this branch of the discipline, which studies and compares social organization in different societies. Malinowski worked with the people of New Guinea and the nearby Trobriand Islands in the South Pacific, recording details of their social institutions. His studies helped him to form his **functional theory**: all social institutions are designed and modified to serve the needs of most of the population.

Malinowski rejected **cultural evolutionism**, the theory common among anthropologists at the time. This theory hypothesizes that all societies and cultures develop in a regular series of predictable stages. Cultural evolutionism was built on the work of Charles Darwin (1809–1892), a British scientist, who claimed that each civilization built on the foundation left by its predecessor. The three stages of development asserted in the theory were "savage," which evolved into "primitive" and finally into "sophisticated." One of the theory's greatest supporters was Sir James Frazer (1854–1941), first professor of anthropology at the University of Liverpool, in England, in 1908. His thirteen-volume *The Golden Bough* suggested that the development of religion followed a common path among all cultures.

Cultural evolutionism had first been attacked by Franz Boas (1858–1941), who was born in Germany but immigrated to the United States in 1881. His studies of Aboriginal peoples in North America, such as the Kwagiulth of the Pacific Northwest, led him to reject the idea that cultures should be labelled as "savage" or "primitive" and therefore be considered less evolved.

Malinowski supported Boas. He found cultural evolutionism to be racist, with its implication that the newer civilizations of northern Europe were more advanced than the older civilizations of Africa or the Pacific. He stated that the theory was **ethnocentric**, in that it judged Western

Cultural Evolutionism Today

Discussions among anthropologists about whether or not cultures evolve through predictable stages have continued since Malinowski's time. In 1949, Leslie White wrote *The Science of Culture*, in which he proposes that cultural development was directly related to the amount of energy consumed by a society. Foraging cultures were underdeveloped, he states, because they only had human energy available to them. Early farming cultures had water, wind, and animal power available to them, and so developed into more advanced societies. Commercial-industrial cultures have all sorts of energy available (for example, human, natural, fossil, and nuclear) and have therefore developed into advanced technological societies.

Richard N. Adams takes a slightly different approach. In his 1988 book *The Eighth Day: Social Evolution as the Self-Organization of Energy*, he argues that the key factor in the development of cultures is whether or not they permit the differentiation of members into different classes. He believes that if a small ruling class and a much larger working class develop, cultures can become far more complex and meet the needs of a much wider range of people. If everyone is to belong to the same class, the range of needs that can be met is smaller. The more complex cultures today, he says, are those in which a relatively small group of people plan and regulate society, and a much larger group carry their plans into action.

A more extreme version of cultural evolutionism, called **cultural diffusion**, was popular for a brief time in the twentieth century. This theory held that "civilization" began in one specific place and from there spread throughout the world, though sometimes in a deteriorated form. Many diffusionists regarded Egypt as the cradle of all civilizations. A number of British anthropologists, notably Sir Grafton Elliot Smith and W.J. Perry, were ardent diffusionists, but the theory fell out of fashion in the 1920s.

civilizations to be most advanced and judged other cultures on how close they were to the Western model. For example, the law in Western Christian nations permitted people to have only one spouse, and sexual infidelity was regarded as grounds for divorce. But in many cultures that the early anthropologists studied, having more than one spouse was acceptable. In a number of these cultures, spouses were encouraged to take lovers and have children with them, with their partners being fully aware of the situation. The marriages remained intact and healthy. Christian missionaries who encountered these cultures tried to change such behaviour, believing that it was immoral and contrary to the Christian God's rules for all humanity. Like the missionaries, early anthropologists who were cultural evolutionists cited such practices as evidence of cultural backwardness. They believed that these cultures would eventually adopt Western concepts of marriage.

In contrast, Malinowski believed that the role of the anthropologist was not to judge but to explain. Anthropologists should not, he concluded, try to rate cultures, but merely point out their similarities and differences. This could only be done by exhaustive observation and detailed record-keeping. Only then would conclusions be valid.

Raymond Dart

Raymond Dart (1893–1988) was an Australian physical anthropologist. In this branch of anthropology, researchers locate and examine fossils and other remains to learn about the evolutionary development of humans.

Dart's most famous discovery was a skull he found in South Africa in 1924. He believed that the skull represented a transitional stage between apes and humans. He named it *Australopithecus*, meaning "Southern Ape." Contemporary critics were skeptical of Dart's claim, however—

Figure 2.21 Raymond Dart (1893–1988)

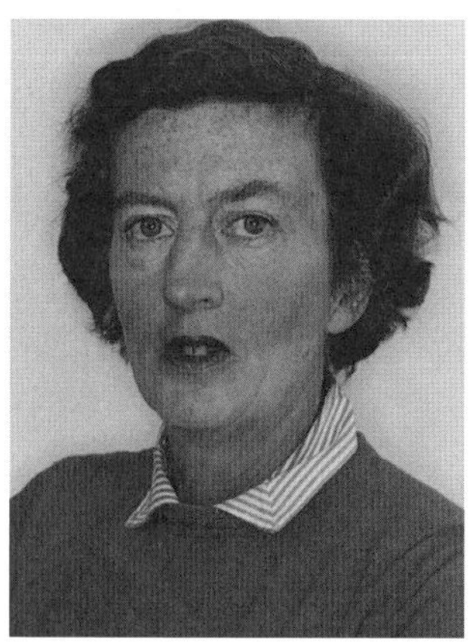

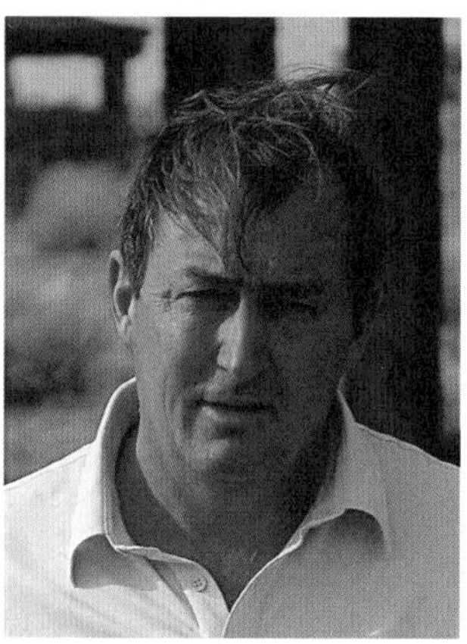

Figure 2.22 Louis Leakey (1903–1972) (top), Mary Leakey (1913–1996), (middle), and Richard Leakey (b. 1944) (bottom)

his findings were disputed for over twenty years. But in 1947 he discovered other fossil remains that supported his original claim. *Australopithecus* was accepted by most physical anthropologists as a valuable discovery. Today, Dart's research is continued at the University of Witwatersrand, in Johannesburg, South Africa. The Institute for the Study of Man in Africa has been established there for this purpose.

The Leakey Family

Louis Leakey (1903–1972), his wife Mary (1913–1996), and their son Richard (b. 1944) are probably the most famous family of physical anthropologists in the world. Born in Kenya of British ancestry, they have all been major contributors to physical anthropology.

When Louis studied at Cambridge University in the 1930s, physical anthropologists believed that humans had their origins in Asia. Rejecting this theory, Louis went to Africa, where he and Mary made numerous discoveries of fossilized human forms. In Kenya and Tanzania, they reconstructed a series of human civilizations dating from 100 000 years BP (before the present) to over 2 million years BP. In the process, they uncovered samples of two of anthropology's greatest finds: *Australopithecus* (1.5 to 2.5 million years BP) and *Homo habilis* (2.2 million years BP).

The Leakeys experimented with Stone Age tools, such as axes and scrapers, to discover how our ancestors hunted for food. Louis also felt that greater understanding of our ancestors' lives lay in the study of other **primates** (for example, apes, monkeys, and gorillas). Believing that women tend to have more accurate powers of observation than men, he deliberately recruited three females to conduct these studies. They were Jane Goodall from Britain, Dian Fossey from the United States, and Biruté Galdikas from Canada.

Since the death of his parents, Richard has continued their work. He was seriously injured in a small plane crash, however, which has considerably reduced his ability for fieldwork.

Jane Goodall

Jane Goodall (b. 1934) has become internationally celebrated for her work with the Leakeys in Tanzania. Through funding from *National Geographic*, Goodall spent twenty years, beginning in the mid-1960s, observing and recording the lives of chimpanzees.

Initially, Goodall was forced to observe the chimpanzees from a distance. Eventually winning the trust of the community, she was able to observe them from close-up. There she observed things that were previously unknown to Western anthropologists. She discovered that the chimps used tools for some of their daily activities. They would push sticks into holes bored in trees by colonies of ants; the ants would cling to the sticks, which the chimps would then withdraw from the holes and place in their mouths. They could feed on the ants at will! Goodall also discovered that chimpanzees were not strictly vegetarian as previously believed. Sometimes they killed another chimp and ate the meat from the carcass.

Figure 2.23 Jane Goodall observes chimpanzees at the Sweetwaters Chimpanzee Sanctuary in Kenya in 1997.

Perhaps the most significant of Goodall's discoveries was the highly developed social structure of the chimpanzee community. An alpha male wins supremacy over other males by sheer aggression and strength. He alone has the right to mate with all the females. The remaining males are not allowed to mate with the females as long as the alpha remains in charge. Eventually, a younger male will defeat an aging alpha and take his place as the supreme male. The old alpha remains in the community, but his privileged position is gone, and he lives like a respected grandparent.

Goodall's research has given social scientists valuable insights into what the human kingdom might have been like a million years ago. Anthropologists have been able to conclude that our early ancestors had a highly developed social structure, based largely on aggression and intimidation. Originally vegetarian, they probably became meat-eaters as they learned to co-operate in the hunting of wild animals. Goodall's observations have provided a fascinating window into our own ancient past.

Biruté Galdikas

Biruté Galdikas (b. 1945) first became interested in the work of the Leakey family while she was studying anthropology at the University of British Columbia. She eventually met Louis Leakey when she was a graduate student at the University of California at Los Angeles (UCLA). He subsequently offered her the opportunity to study orangutans—a type of ape that shares 98 per cent of its genetic material with humans. In 1968, she set up camp in Borneo, Indonesia, to study the wild orangutans that live there.

Figure 2.24 Biruté Galdikas (b. 1945)

In *Reflections of Eden: My Years with the Orangutans of Borneo*, Galdikas wrote of the terrible conditions she and her husband, Rod Brindamour, encountered in the rainforest. They had to put up with ticks, fleas, and leeches that got under their clothes and into their skin. They were always wet and lived on a diet of fried sardines and rice. It was months before they could get close enough to the orangutans to make any reliable observations.

Galdikas became foster parent to Surgito, a one-year-old male orangutan that was being kept in a cage as a pet. He became intensely jealous of Rod and acted with hostility toward him. Surgito slept with his foster parents, and often bit Rod in a show of dominance and hatred. Rod equally disliked Surgito, and after eight years he secretly released Surgito when Galdikas was in the United States completing her Ph.D. She never saw Surgito again, and her marriage with Rod broke up soon afterwards. She later married an Indonesian man named Pak Bohap, and together they continued the observations.

In many ways, Galdikas's findings were similar to those of Jane Goodall about chimpanzees. Orangutans live in highly structured social communities. Violence is ever-present, lurking just beneath the surface. Although largely vegetarian, orangutans, too, occasionally kill one of their community for meat.

Galdikas agreed with Louis Leakey that humans can learn much about their early ancestors from the study of primates. In *Reflections*, she wrote: "Looking into the calm, unblinking eyes of an orangutan, we see … the image of our own creation. … [W]e recognize that there is no separation between ourselves and nature. We are allowed to see the eyes of God."

Dian Fossey

Dian Fossey (1938–1985) was an American anthropologist famous for her studies of Rwanda's mountain gorilla community. Beginning in 1966, Fossey spent most of the rest of her life living with gorillas, which are normally gentle animals, despite their size and fierce reputation.

At first, Fossey found it difficult to get

Figure 2.25 Dian Fossey's studies of gorillas inspired the movie Gorillas in the Mist *(1988).*

close enough to the gorillas to observe them accurately. She eventually learned to imitate their habits and sounds, and thus gained acceptance into their society. She documented the gorillas' highly structured social system. She observed them demonstrating affection toward family members and aggression toward outsiders. Like Goodall and Galdikas, she believed that gorillas shared much in common with our earliest ancestors.

The mountain gorillas were constantly threatened by poachers, who frequently tried to frighten Fossey into abandoning her work so that the gorillas would be unprotected. But she could not be intimidated. Her fearlessness eventually cost her her life—in 1985, she was murdered by persons unknown. Much of her work remained unfinished.

Anthropology in Canada Today

Canadians studying anthropology today have retained the link that the discipline first established with values and culture. Ethnographic studies are an important part of modern research. The University of Montreal's Asen Balikci is famous for his studies of the Netsilik people of the Arctic. Robin Ridlington, retired from the University of British Columbia, has examined the Dunne-za people of the Subarctic. The University of Montreal's Jean Michaud is an expert on the mountain peoples of Thailand, Laos, and Vietnam.

Not all anthropologists are cultural anthropologists doing ethnographic studies. Social anthropologists examine modern culture to find the roots of social problems. The University of Victoria's Patricia Spittal, for example, has done groundbreaking work into the causes of domestic violence. Much of the work in modern anthropology is along such lines, and there is considerable common ground between social anthropologists and sociologists.

Anthropology offers students the opportunity to examine cultures in distant parts of the world. It also encourages students to investigate the cultural features of everyday life in their own society. Its bounds are almost unlimited, and it enjoys close links with a number of other social science disciplines.

RECAP

1. Make a list of five different topics or issues that have been important to anthropologists.
2. How are the topics of study of today's anthropologists different from the topics studied in the past?
3. Which of the anthropologists described here do you find the most interesting? What are your reasons for picking this person?
4. Which of the anthropologists do you think has focused on ideas that are most important or helpful in trying to solve problems in society today? Explain your answer.

Activities

Show your knowledge

1. Make a list of five significant topics that anthropologists have studied, along with the names of the individuals who studied them. Write down, with definitions, three significant terms that are used by anthropologists.
2. Make a list of five significant topics that psychologists have studied, along with the names of the individuals who have studied them. Write down, with definitions, three significant terms that are used by psychologists.
3. Make a list of five significant topics that sociologists have studied, along with the names of the individuals who have studied them. Write down, with definitions, three significant terms that are used by sociologists.
4. Review the information about the three disciplines on pages 18 to 19, 24 to 25, and 30 to 32. Using this information, make a list of the types of questions each discipline tries to answer. For each discipline, try to include one question that is
   a) factual (What is…?)
   b) defining (What is the meaning of...?)
   c) causal (What is the cause of…?)
   d) decision-making (What is the most important/dangerous, etc.…?)

   For example, a factual question anthropology tries to answer is: *What genetic characteristics do humans share with chimpanzees?* A defining question would be: *What is the meaning of culture?* A causal question psychology tries to answer is: *What are the causes of severe anxieties and tensions?* A decision-making question sociology tries to answer is: *What should be the most important focus or goal of sociology?*

Practise your thinking skills

5. Identify a social issue in Canada today that would be of interest to sociologists. How would you go about finding information about this topic? What methods would you use in order to provide a solution for the issue?
6. Identify a social issue in Canada today that would be of interest to psychologists. How would you go about finding information about this

Activities

topic? What methods would you use in order provide a solution for the issue?

7. Identify a social issue in Canada today that would be of interest to anthropologists. How would you go about finding information about this topic? What methods would you use in order to provide a solution for the issue?
8. Sigmund Freud identified the following defence mechanisms used by humans:
   - denial (refusing to recognize threatening behaviours or thoughts)
   - displacement (replacing a threatening object with a less threatening one)
   - projection (attributing to others behaviours that we know apply to ourselves)
   - rationalization (deliberately finding excuses for our own personal failures)
   - reaction formation (finding reasons why others should not do the things that we have done)
   - regression (returning to less mature behaviour as a cover for disappointment or frustration)
   - repression (removing traumatic experiences from our conscious memory)
   - sublimation (channelling our impulses into outlets that are likely to be socially acceptable)

   Do some research into these mechanisms. Two good places to start are
   http://www.members.tripod.co.uk/chrispab/freud.htm
   http://www.prenticehall.ca/wood/home/tryit/defence.html
   Describe
   a) how defence mechanisms work
   b) why humans use them
   c) examples of defence mechanisms from your own experiences
9. Many social scientists accept Comte's principle of positivism—that solutions to social problems are to be arrived at by the rigid application of scientific principles. This point of view is disputed by many religious leaders.
   a) Identify a social issue or problem, such as homelessness or the high rate of marriage breakdown.

Activities

b) Present a social scientific and a religious explanation for the issue or problem.
c) Present your opinion on the validity of both explanations. Give reasons for your opinion.

Communicate your ideas

10. Make a wall poster illustrating one of the disciplines in this chapter (anthropology, psychology, or sociology). Using both pictures and words, present
    a) the contributions made to the discipline by one of the discipline's founders and/or some modern researchers
    b) the topics examined by researchers in the discipline
    c) which colleges or universities in your area offer courses in the discipline

    Give your poster a catchy heading or slogan.
11. Choose one of the social scientists mentioned in this unit.
    a) Do some further research to find out more about the person's work.
    b) Role-play the person telling a conference about her or his latest findings.
    c) Invite pointed but fair questions from the class about your work.
12. Read an excerpt from the writings of the Leakeys, Jane Goodall, Dian Fossey, or Biruté Galdikas. List the aspects of their work that would interest you and those that would bore you. Ask a classmate to look at your list and assess your suitability for this type of work. Do you agree with your classmate's assessment? Why or why not?
13. There is considerable evidence to suggest that women's role as food gatherers in early human societies was more important than the hunting role of males. Do some research into this topic. You might consider such sources as Riane Eisler, *The Chalice and the Blade: Our History, Our Future*, and Rosalind Miles, *The Women's History of the World*. What conclusions have they reached? Present your findings to the class.
14. Physical anthropologists who believe in the theory of evolution—that humans developed from less complex forms over millions of years—are called evolutionists. Fundamentalist Christians who believe that the world exists now in the form that it was originally created by God are

called creationists. The University of Toronto's Web site maintains an excellent resource on the discussions between the two groups. Visit http://bioinfo.med.utoronto.ca/~lamoran/Evolution_religions.html Click on The Handy Dandy Evolution Refuter and on Statement on Teaching Evolution—the statement of the National Association of Biology Teachers (USA)—for the two sides of the argument.

   a) Present your opinion on the validity of the arguments on both sides. Give reasons for your viewpoint.
   b) Do you think that a compromise between the two views is possible—that is, that one can believe in elements of both? Present your viewpoint to the class.

15. The 1925 John T. Scopes "Monkey Trial" in Dayton, Tennessee, was a challenge to physical anthropologists. Scopes was prosecuted for teaching the theory of evolution and using fossil evidence as unearthed by anthropologists (the movie *Inherit the Wind* is based on this true story). As a class, research the trial. Role-play the characters of Scopes, William Jennings Bryan (prosecution), and Clarence Darrow (defence) during the trial. Does the class think the jury reached the right decision? Why or why not?

Apply your knowledge

16. Imagine Auguste Comte, Sigmund Freud, and Margaret Mead were still alive today.
    a) How would each researcher explain teenager behaviour today (good and bad)?
    b) Which one do you think would be closest to the truth? Why?
17. Review the Canadian social scientists mentioned in this chapter.
    a) Use the Internet and other sources to find out more about each of their lives.
    b) What social issue(s) does each person research?
    c) What conclusions has each person arrived at?
18. Social scientists frequently make predictions about the future.
    a) Make three predictions about the future of Canadian people and society from the viewpoint of each discipline.
    b) Which discipline do you think can make the most helpful predictions? Explain your answer.

Chapter 3

Social Science Skills and Methods

Overview of Chapter

Learning Expectations

By the end of this chapter, you will be able to

- describe the steps involved in social science research and inquiry, including developing and testing a hypothesis
- demonstrate an understanding of various research methodologies for conducting primary research
- demonstrate an understanding of the ethical guidelines of social science research
- evaluate the relevance and validity of information gathered through research

Open for Debate

Racial Intelligence at Issue

It arrived at *The Hamilton Spectator* in a plain brown envelope, which in itself might be fitting given the subject matter.

Inside was a 108-page paperback booklet entitled *Race, Evolution and Behavior: Special Abridged Edition*, by J. Philippe Rushton.

Yes, that Philippe Rushton.

Who doesn't remember the controversy he created in 1989 with his highly criticized theory that Asians are smarter than whites, who in turn are smarter than blacks?

More than 35 000 copies of the booklet were mailed out to psychologists, sociologists, and anthropologists across North America.

"The goal of this book is to be scientific," Rushton writes in the preface.

"It's lousy science," said [Dr. Fred] Weizmann [a psychology professor at York University]. "We found that there was not much of a scientific basis for what he was claiming at all."

Most of Rushton's conclusions have been drawn by re-analyzing data that has already been collected. Some of that data is decades old. Some of it even dates back to the 19th century.

"[Another problem is] the selective aspect of the data," said [Dr. Michael] Peters [a psychology professor at the University of Guelph], "picking those bits that look good to him and then not commenting on those bits that don't look so good."

What may be most dangerous about works such as *Race, Evolution and Behavior* is that, in some pseudoscientific way, it can sound believable.

"It's so tempting," Peters said. "It sort of fits in with people's prejudices."

Abridged from: Buist, Steve. 2000. "Racial Intelligence at Issue." *The Hamilton Spectator*. 15 April 2000

Think About It

1. Elsewhere in the article a psychology professor says many psychologists "were shocked to find an academic work with no list of references identifying the source of [Rushton's] assertions." Why would these scholars expect to find references?
2. In 1989, Rushton was barred from using students for his research after conducting a survey without the approval of an ethics committee. Why should ethics committees approve research?
3. Rushton cites 1934 data of the head measurements of black Kenyans to support a conclusion about "race." He does not mention that the subjects were severely malnourished. How could such selective citing of information affect the reliability of Rushton's conclusions?

Section 3.1

Scientific Research

Focus Questions

- What factors make an experiment reliable?
- What are the differences in research conditions between the natural sciences and the social sciences?
- What external forces can influence social science research?

Reliable Research

Scientists can be divided into two groups: "natural" scientists and social scientists. These two groups differ not only in *what* they study, but also in *how* they study—that is, how they conduct experiments and other types of research.

Natural scientists work in a variety of fields, including chemistry, biology, and physics. When conducting research, natural scientists have one key advantage over social scientists: they usually work in strictly regulated conditions, such as temperature- and humidity-controlled environments. In these conditions, they can take extremely precise measurements (for example, they can control exactly how much of a chemical goes into a test tube, or how much resistance is built into an electronic circuit). The controlled environment also eliminates contact with all foreign material, preventing contamination of their research materials. These features of a controlled environment ensure that the research results of natural scientists are reliable. An experiment is **reliable** if it produces exactly the same results whenever it is repeated.

If we compare the research conditions of natural scientists with those of various social scientists, we see important differences. Let's begin with the case of anthropologists doing fieldwork. Their research consists of observing and receiving information from the members of the culture being studied, who are called **informants**. Note that the anthropologist cannot treat informants as if they were chemicals in an experiment, manipulating them to see what reactions result. The anthropologist also cannot ensure that external forces do not contaminate the research material. In fact, the anthropologist's presence among the informants is itself an external force that "contaminates," or affects, the culture's members. By speaking to, eating with, or giving small presents to them, the researcher affects their behaviour. If a second researcher were subsequently to observe the same informants, different results might emerge. The differences could stem from factors in the researchers' backgrounds that have influenced their varied interpretations of what they see (for example, their gender, personality, age, and ethnic or cultural background).

Key Concepts

reliable
informants

Sociological or psychological experiments are beset with the same challenges as anthropological research. As in fieldwork, the experimental proceedings and the results obtained are highly sensitive to the researcher's presence and participation. For example, if an experiment involves giving verbal instructions to subjects, the researcher must give those instructions in exactly the same manner to each participant. She or he must ensure that the instructions given just after breakfast are as clear as the instructions given four hours after lunch. Problems can arise if one researcher has a gentle manner while another is abrupt. Such factors, if uncontrolled, affect the reliability of experiments.

The existence of such challenges does not mean that social science findings are inaccurate. It does mean that social scientists must try to identify all factors that could affect their findings. They should eliminate as many of the contaminating factors as possible. They should ensure that their research is extensive—that is, they must repeat their experiments and find a consistency in results before their experiment can be deemed reliable. They must identify and deal with their own biases and those of their associates, as well as those of their subjects. Although natural scientists are also required to take precautions in their experiments, social scientists must contend with a greater number and range of biases and contamination issues.

Figure 3.1 How can a natural scientist control the research environment? Why is such control important?

RECAP

1. What research advantages do natural scientists have over social scientists?
2. What must social scientists do to ensure that their research is as reliable as possible?
3. Do the challenges faced by social scientists make their findings less reliable than those of natural scientists? Explain your answer.

Section 3.2

Anthropology Skills and Methods

Focus Questions

- Why must researchers live entirely like their subjects during participant observation?
- What must participant observers do in order to make sure that they do not "contaminate" their subjects?
- What advantages do teams of female and male participant observers have in obtaining a complete picture of their subjects?

Participant Observation

Chapter 2 introduced the work of famous cultural anthropologists such as Margaret Mead and Ruth Benedict (see pages 32 to 39). Such researchers pioneered what is still the basic tool of the cultural anthropologist, namely **participant observation**. This technique involves living with a subject group for an extended period and engaging in their daily activities. The researcher makes detailed notes about what goes on and draws conclusions about what has been observed. In addition, the researcher may carry out interviews with members of the subject group, administer questionnaires, or even carry out psychological tests. These additional methods are purely supplemental, however—no anthropologist would rely exclusively on these procedures because they are not sensitive to the context of the subject group. The anthropologist's most important method of gathering information, by far, is meticulous observation and note-keeping.

Fieldwork Challenges

Whether anthropological research, or "fieldwork," is conducted in the researcher's own country or in another region, the task is laborious and challenging. Many early cultural anthropologists went to tropical climates where they had to cope with unfamiliar conditions. The climate was draining, and both dietary practices and hygiene standards were different from what they were accustomed to. The same challenges are faced by anthopologists researching inner cities or isolated areas in their own country.

Consider the work of Bettylou Valentine and her husband Charles. In the late 1970s, they participant-observed a poor neighbourhood in one of North America's large cities (the city was never identified, and the neighbourhood was given the fictitious name of Blackston). They lived on one-quarter of their normal income, and for the final six months lived on the same budget as neighbouring families on

Key Concepts

participant observation
vague notes
concrete notes
reflexivity
polygyny
informed consent

welfare. Here is how Charles Valentine described their conditions.

> For five years we inhabited the same decrepit rat- and roach-infested buildings as everyone else, lived on the same poor quality food at inflated prices, trusted our health and our son's education to the same inferior institutions, suffered the same brutality and intimidation from the police, and like others made the best of it by some combination of endurance, escapism, and fighting back.... For several cold months we lived and worked in one room without heat other than what a cooking stove could provide, without hot water or windows, and with only one lightbulb (Valentine, 1978, 5).

Figure 3.2 The Valentines lived in conditions similar to those shown here. A stove provides the only heat, so residents dress as warmly inside as outside.

Such conditions would test the most experienced cultural anthropologist. But the Valentines knew that if they were to be accepted by their informants, they had to live with and adopt their standard of living. This was the only way to gain their subjects' trust, which was necessary for them to obtain reliable information.

Observing and Note-Taking

Effective fieldwork requires learning the skill of detailed observation. Hand-in-hand with this skill goes the habit of meticulous note-taking. A cultural anthropologist's field notes will be referred to over a research period of many months or years, so no aspect of a described event should go unrecorded. Consider the following examples, describing an incident in a high-school class.

Example 1

Student C spoke angrily to Teacher G.

Example 2

After Teacher G asked Student C to get her feet off the desk, Student C became loud and angry. She said: "You're always picking on me. Why don't you give the other kids a rough time when they do something you don't like?" She slammed her textbook shut and walked out of the room.

Anthropologists would describe the notes in Example 1 as **vague notes** because they merely describe something that happened and who was involved. Example 2 illustrates **concrete notes** because they describe all the necessary elements: the tone of the incident, who was involved, where it took place, an example of what was said, a physical action, and how the incident ended. The anthropologist will be able to return to such concrete notes years later and draw useful information from them.

Participant observers must not only observe carefully and in detail—they must also try to understand the world as their informants see it. This means that they do not try to judge what they see, using standards from outside the informants' own culture. To achieve such an understanding, they practise **reflexivity**. In other words, they examine their own thought processes and reflect on how their life experiences affect their thinking patterns.

The following example shows the importance of reflexivity. Suppose you were a researcher who had been beaten as a child. You are studying a community in which parents commonly beat children who behave badly. If you fail to be reflexive, you might want to write about how brutal the community appears to be. You might even go a step further and tell the parents, from personal experience, how bad the effects of family violence can be. However, anthropologists practising reflexivity would take neither of these steps. They would try to understand the context of the culture in which the behaviour takes place. They would then explain the behaviour in terms of that context, rather than judging the behaviour in terms of their own culture.

The Blackston study perfectly illustrates reflexivity. Bettylou Valentine believed that there should be a partnership between herself and her informants. When her manuscript was complete, she showed it to her informants and welcomed their comments. In her final chapter, she allowed her informants to state what they agreed with and what they thought was wrong. This is reflexive writing, allowing a complete partnership between the researcher and the informants. It recognizes that every interpretation of human culture and behaviour may be challenged. It values above all a full understanding of the context in which behaviour occurs.

Gender Issues

It is important that anthropologists respect and fully understand the culture that they study. This can be made more difficult when the culture has defined gender roles. Such roles often identify certain situations as open to females only (for example, a bridal shower) or males only (for example, an initiation ritual). An anthropologist of the opposite gender who observes such situations will likely affect the behaviour of the participants, making the data unreliable. Alternatively, the anthopologist may be refused admission altogether.

The issue of gender makes it more appropriate for certain types of participant observation to be done by male-female teams of anthropologists. Charles and Bettylou Valentine's study of Blackston, for example, was made stronger by having a female and a male observer.

Ethical Dilemmas in Research

In trying to understand another culture rather than judge it, anthropologists usually avoid intervening in community affairs. Sometimes, however, this stance can lead to ethical dilemmas.

Intervening in Crises

Colin Turnbull participant-observed the Ik people of Uganda, in southeast Africa. Facing great hardship because of drought and famine, the Ik did not have enough food and water to ensure their survival. As a last resort, they decided to leave old or fatally ill members of the community to die without food. This would make more scarce resources available for the remaining members. Those few who wanted to help the dying were mocked by the larger group. If Turnbull had intervened to help the dying himself, the Ik would probably have stopped co-operating with him. Not wanting to ruin his study, Turnbull did not intervene, but his manuscript shows the mental torture caused by his dilemma.

Case Study: The Chagnon Contoversy

Napoleon Chagnon is an American cultural anthropologist. He has devoted his life to the study of the Yanomami people, who live in the Amazon region of Venezuela. In 1968, he published *Yanomamö: The Fierce People*, in which he described a culture containing much male violence. Wife beating was common, and men tried to provoke each other into violent confrontations. In the 1988 edition of his book, Chagnon wrote that up to 30 per cent of adult men die violently.

Chagnon observed that much of the fighting among men was over women. There is a shortage of women in Yanomami society. **Polygyny**—a man having a number of wives—is practised, and Chagnon uncovered evidence of selective female infanticide. Given the shortage of women, female abduction is prevalent among the Yanomami.

A reputation for fierceness and swift retaliation made it easier for men to attract wives. Violent men would obviously increase the level of family violence, but they would also protect the women against abduction. Those men who were regarded as killers had more wives than those who were not.

Chagnon's book became one of the most widely read cultural anthropology books of all time, and a standard text in anthropology classes. But, Chagnon wondered, were such killers genetically selected, or was it a cultural adaptation to the conditions in which the Yanomami live?

In 2000, Patrick Tierney, an American writer, published *Darkness in El Dorado*. After ten years of research, he concluded that journalists, scientists, and anthropologists who studied the Yanomami had not merely *observed* the violence—they had *triggered* it By interfering in a culture they did not understand, they created conflict and division.

Tierney notes that a major disaster stemming from scientific studies of the Yanomami was that measles were carried into the area. With no natural resistance, the Yanomami suffered horribly in measles outbreaks.

Tierney singles out Chagnon for particular criticism over what happened next. Observing the devastation caused by measles, Chagnon arranged to inoculate the Yanomami. But it is known that genetically isolated people such as the Yanomami are prone to dangerously high post-vaccination fevers that can kill. Over the three months following the vaccinations, the worst epidemic in Yanomami history broke out, killing hundreds. It is not clear whether the killing fevers were from the vaccine or what effect the vaccine had on the many who died from measles, even after they were inoculated. Tierney charges that Chagnon knew of the dangers the vaccine posed. He claims that what Chagnon was really trying to do was to see if the dominant males—the fiercest of the "killers"—would survive the inoculation at a greater rate than the general Yanomami population. Finding this out would answer one of Chagnon's most pressing research questions: Is extreme violence among the the Yanomami a cultural adapatation, or is it a result of a genetic difference in the killer males? It would be this same genetic difference that would enable them to survive the inoculation while others died.

Tierney's charge is unproven, and debate over Chagnon's intentions will probably rage for a number of years. If the charge is true, the measles inoculations clearly violated ethical standards in that the researcher did harm to the group being studied.

To ensure that researchers do not inflict suffering on their subjects, anthropologists today are expected to get **informed consent** to proceed with research. This expectation is included in documents such as the American Anthropological Association's "Principles of Professional Responsibility." In this statement, anthropologists are charged to "clearly communicate the aims of all their professional activities," "assess both the positive and negative consequences of their activities," and "inform individuals and groups likely to be affected of any consequences relevant to them that they anticipate" (American Anthropological Association, 1997).

Figure 3.3 In 1968, Chagnon put on tribal feathers as part of his participant observation of the Yanomami.

1. Explain the charge that Patrick Tierney has laid against Napoleon Chagnon's work.
2. If the charge is true, how did Chagnon's work violate ethical principles of research?
3. Patrick Tierney spent fifteen months in the field, over a ten-year period, studying the Yanomami. His findings differ sharply from Chagnon's descriptions of the "fierce" Yanomami culture. What reliability issues arise from these different findings? Explain.

Violating Personal Beliefs

Ken Pryce experienced an ethical dilemma while participant-observing the West Indian community of a British city. Religion was very important to the community, and many activities revolved around the local charismatic Christian church. Although Pryce attended church regularly with the community, he knew that he was not completely accepted. One Sunday morning, the minister invited members of the congregation to step forward for baptism.

There were good reasons for him not to respond to the invitation—and there were good reasons for him to be baptized.

Reasons against baptism included the following:

- It would be dishonest—Pryce did not believe in baptism.
- It would be culturally insensitive. Pryce was an agnostic white man studying a strongly religious black community. He could never be a completely integrated member of this community. Being baptized in an effort to erase the differences between himself and his informants would be unrealistic and insulting.

Reasons for baptism included the following:

- It would allow Pryce to get closer to his informants. They would accept him more fully if he were a baptized church member.
- It would give him the insights of a participant observer. Just as anthropologists such as the Valentines needed to lower their standard of living to participate in Blackston community life (see pages 47–48), Pryce needed to experience church membership to gain an insider's perspective into his informants' culture.

In the end, Pryce did step forward and became baptized. His relationship with the community changed immediately—his informants opened up to him and began honestly sharing their experiences. There is no question that his research benefited from his decision.

Where should anthropologists draw the line on what they do to win acceptance? Surely, anthropologists studying criminal groups should not take part in illegal activities in an effort to "fit in." Was Pryce's decision more like an "illegal act"? Or was it more like the Valentines' commitment to make their public lives as similar as possible to the lives of their informants?

RECAP

1. How do vague notes differ from concrete notes? Why is it important to keep concrete notes?
2. What is reflexive writing? How did Bettylou Valentine's Blackston study illustrate this?
3. What ethical principles should anthropologists follow in participant observation?

Section 3.3

Psychology Skills and Methods

Focus Questions

- How is human intelligence generally measured?
- How do psychologists study human personality?
- What methods are used to study humans' sense of privacy and intimacy?

Three Areas of Study

Psychology, like anthropology and sociology, is a broad discipline. You have read in Chapter 2 about some of the major divisions of psychology—psychoanalytical, behavioural, and cognitive (see pages 24 to 25). Each of these is further divided into a number of other subcategories. In order to get some understanding of how psychologists work, we will look at three of these subcategories and what psychologists have discovered about them. In the first subcategory, human intelligence, IQ testing, and reaction-time experiments are described. In the second subcategory, personality, the experimental method, and case studies are introduced. In the third subcategory—privacy and intimacy—further experiments and their ethics are discussed.

Human Intelligence

Alfred Binet produced the first standardized intelligence test in 1904. In 1916, the Standford-Binet test introduced what has become one of the most common ways of measuring human intelligence—the **intelligence quotient (IQ)** method. In this method, a candidate answers a series of multiple-choice questions that do not rely on previously acquired knowledge. The number of right and wrong answers is calculated, and a raw score is given in relation to an average score of 100. A person who scores 110 is theoretically more intelligent than average, while a person scoring 90 is theoretically less intelligent.

IQ is a somewhat crude measurement tool. People with high IQs do not necessarily lead happier or more successful lives than people with low ones. Nevertheless, it is still used as an intelligence measure, since the testing procedure is relatively simple, and we have scoring records going back for almost a century.

Several issues have arisen with respect to measuring intelligence. One issue is whether certain groups of people are inherently more or less intelligent than others. This question has been answered with massive amounts of test result data from a wide range of population samples. The data show that the distribution of IQ scores throughout population samples is

Key Concepts

intelligence quotient (IQ)
regression to the mean
double-blind principle
heritable

Figure 3.4 Percentage distribution of IQ among total population

IQ	60–69	70–79	80–89	90–99	100–109	110–119	120–129	130–139
% of population	2	7	17	25	25	17	7	2

Note: Percentage total does not add up to 100 because of rounding.
Source: Eysenck and Eysenck, 1989, 106.

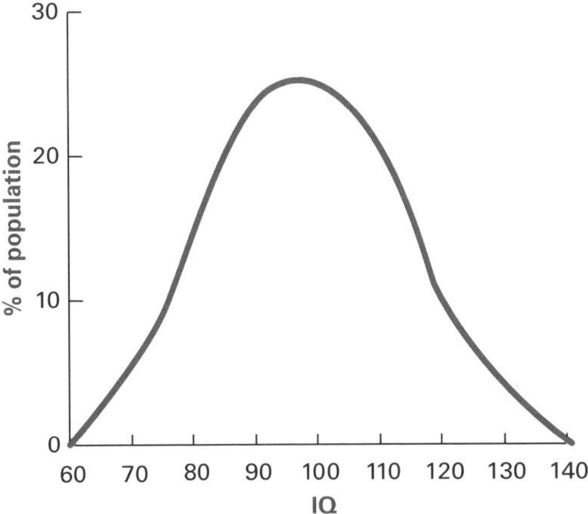

Figure 3.5 The bell curve

consistent, as shown above in Figure 3.4. When the data is shown on a line graph, a classic "bell curve" results, as shown in Figure 3.5.

Figures 3.4 and 3.5 show that 50 per cent of the population has an IQ of between 90 and 110, with decreasing percentages toward each end of the scale. The same bell-curve distribution has been found throughout different age groups, ethnic or cultural groups, and social or economic groups. These findings disprove the nineteenth-century notion that some races are more intelligent than others.

A second issue related to intelligence testing is whether intelligence is inherited. Since the distribution of IQ scores shown in Figure 3.4 remains the same from one generation to the next, does this mean that parents with higher IQs have passed on their intelligence to their children, as have parents with lower IQs? Many studies have found that the answer is no. Although the distribution of intelligence in one generation is the same as that of the previous generation, there is no direct intelligence link between individual sets of parents and their children. Psychologists use the term **regression to the mean** to describe the persistence through time of the overall intelligence distribution pattern.

A third issue in intelligence studies is whether intelligence can be linked to physiological factors. Measurements of head and brain size have been found not to be reliable predictors of intelligence. But there is evidence of some correlation between reaction time and IQ. In a typical reaction-time experiment, the subject is placed before a console on which there are a number of coloured buttons that correspond to different lights on a board. When one of the lights on the board is lit, the subject must press the corresponding button on the console. When a number of lights are lit, the subject must press all matching buttons. People with high IQs tend to have quicker reaction times, especially as the task becomes more complex. How can we account for this finding?

Studies of brain waves have shown that there is a link between the speed at which the brain can interpret information and IQ score. Despite such study results,

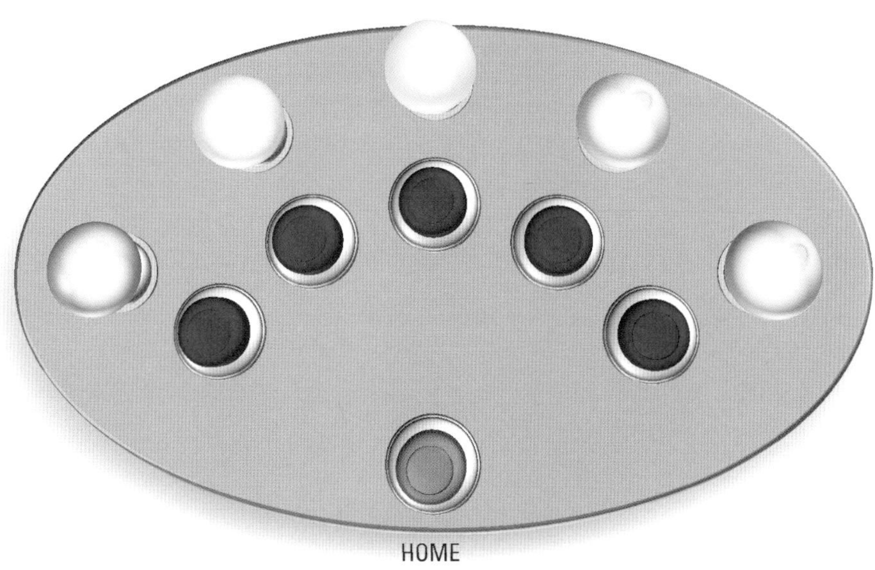

Figure 3.6 Reaction-time experiments are conducted using consoles such as this one. When one or more bulbs light up, the subject must press any matching buttons. How have the results of reaction-time experiments been linked to intelligence?

however, there is still no clear understanding of how intelligence affects brain physiology and vice versa.

Personality

The human personality is one of the most heavily researched areas in psychology. Social scientists consider personality to be the consistent practice of specific behaviours. Optimistic people, for example, may smile more in their personal contacts with others than pessimists do. Because such behaviours as smiling are observable, personality can be measured.

The main means of obtaining research results on personality is through experiments. Here is an example of an experiment based on the distinction between introverts and extroverts introduced in Chapter 2 (see page 28).

Hypothesis: Introverts are more stimulated by external factors than extroverts.

Method: Proceed through the following stages.

1. Obtain two groups of subjects. One group consists of people who have been measured as introverts, while the members of the second group have been independently classified as extroverts. Neither the subjects nor the testers should know to which group each subject belongs. (This experimental technique, called the **double-blind principle**, is used to ensure that the participants do not influence the experimental results through their own expectations.) In addition, the subjects should not know the purpose of the experiment.
2. In a random order, each subject is asked to hold a cotton ball in her or

his mouth for twenty seconds. Tester #1 weighs the ball before and afterwards. The difference in weight is used as a measure of how much saliva has been absorbed. Tester #2 tabulates the results (dividing up these tasks among two testers ensures that the experiment is bias-free).

3. Each subject is given a rest, and then the test is performed a second time. In the second trial, tester #1 puts four drops of lemon juice on the subjects' tongues (lemon juice is known to increase the salivation rate of most people). The cotton balls are again weighed to determine the amount of salivary flow. Tester #2 again tabulates the results.
4. The results of all the introverts are put together, as are the results of the extroverts. The increase in salivary flow between trial #1 and trial #2 is calculated for each group.

Results: The introverts have a greater increase in salivary flow than the extroverts do. This outline shows the methodical way in which psychological experiments must be conducted. Every effort should be taken to ensure that the participants (subjects and testers) do not influence the results of the experiment. When the experiment is completed, the hypothesis, method, scores for each subject, group results, and conclusion should be clearly recorded and communicated to colleagues.

Case Study: Twin Research

A great deal of psychological research has been done on identical twins who have been separated at birth. Will their personalities be different, depending on their different upbringings? Or will their personalities be the same because of their genetic similarities? Thomas Bouchard founded the University of Minnesota's Center for Twin and Adoption Research to find out the answers to such questions. The center currently tracks over 100 pairs of identical twins separated at birth. One well-documented case is that of Barbara Herbert and Daphne Goodship.

Herbert and Goodship are identical twins born in London, England, in 1939 and separated immediately afterwards. They did not meet until they were forty years old. The similarities shared between them are breathtaking.

- Both left school at fourteen.
- Both fell down stairs at fifteen, weakening their ankles.
- Both worked in local government and met their husbands at sixteen.
- Both had miscarriages in the same month.
- Both eventually had two boys and a girl.
- Both tinted their hair auburn as teenagers.
- Both drank coffee cold.
- When they met, they were both wearing cream-coloured dresses and brown velvet jackets. Their style of clothing was virtually identical.
- Both had the habit of pushing up their noses with the palm of their hands.
- Both had a distinctive way of laughing that caused the Twin Center to nickname them the "Giggle Twins" (Angle and Niemark, 1997, 36–52).

Figure 3.7 Reunited identical twins Daphne Goodship and Barbara Herbert—the "giggle twins"

One of the goals of collecting such case study data is to determine what percentage of a given characteristic is **heritable** (coming from the genes). Intelligence has been found to be between 69 and 78 per cent heritable, with between 22 and 31 per cent coming from life experiences. In various studies, sexual orientation has been found to be anywhere from 20 to 50 per cent heritable ("The Mirror," 1998, 74–77).

Other studies have concluded that personality type is more similar among identical twins separated at birth than among those who have lived together. One study reported in the *Economist* (1998) confirmed this finding using a database of over 12 000 pairs of identical twins. The explanation is that twins who live together may emphasize what little natural difference exists between them in order to express their individuality. Separated twins have no need to do this, and so their "natural" personality emerges unaltered. Studies such as these have underlined the importance of nature or genes in determining personality. This issue is explored further in Chapter 4 (see pages 82 to 87).

1. What is the purpose of the University of Minnesota's Center for Twin and Adoption Research?
2. What is the meaning of "heritable"? According to identical twin studies, to what extent is intelligence heritable?
3. Why do identical twins separated at birth have personalities more similar than those of identical twins raised together?

Privacy and Intimacy

How and why we encourage or avoid closeness with others is another greatly researched topic in psychology. To a large extent, our culture determines out tendencies toward privacy or intimacy. For example, men's kissing each other as a form of greeting is more common in southern European and Middle Eastern cultures than in North America. Likewise, how close we stand while speaking to our parents, our teachers, or our boss varies from culture to culture.

Classic Study

RESEARCHER:

Michael Argyle, Sociologist, Janet Dean, Sociologist

TIME:

1965

SUBJECT:

Techniques for Controlling Intimacy

Regulating Intimacy

Michael Argyle and Janet Dean's classic study (1965) analyzed the techniques humans use to regulate interpersonal intimacy. These techniques involve controlling factors such as physical distance between oneself and others, eye contact, smiling, and leaning. The more we make eye contact or lean toward another person, the more intimate we consider our relationship to be. But if we make too much eye contact, the other person can become uncomfortable and look away, rejecting our intimacy.

There is a wide variation among cultures in the amount of touching that goes on in a conversation. In one study, observations of pairs of people conversing in cafés and coffee shops yielded the results shown in Figure 3.8.

In another experiment reported by Argyle and Dean, individual subjects engaged in conversations with another "subject" (actually an experimenter) at distances of 30 cm, 90 cm, and 3 m. In some conversations, they sat facing each other, while in others they sat at 90 degrees to each other. The results, one set of which is given in Figure 3.9, showed that eye contact is greater between same-sex pairs than between opposite-sex pairs. Also, the amount of eye contact increases with distance. What reasons can you think of to explain these patterns?

San Juan, Puerto Rico	180
Paris, France	110
London, England	0

Figure 3.8 Number of times one person touched another in one hour

Distance between subjects	Subjects of same sex	Subjects of different sexes
30 cm	55	30
60 cm	61	55
3 m	72	58

Figure 3.9 Percentage of available time in which eye contact was maintained

Figure 3.10 What observations can you make about physical distance, eye contact, and smiling and leaning behaviours in this café scene in France?

Ethical Issues

Conducting experiments such as those in the Classic Study can raise important ethical questions for psychologists. Consider the following experiment conducted by Oklahoma State University researchers. The site of the experiment was a three-urinal men's washroom. The hypothesis of the experiment was that anxiety delays the onset of urination and reduces the duration of urine flow. The experimenters found that men standing alone began urination on average after 5 seconds and continued for 25 seconds. When an experimenter stood at an adjacent urinal, onset took place at 8.5 seconds, while flow lasted only 17.5 seconds. After collecting their data, the experimenters informed all the subjects about what had transpired. The experimenter claimed that none of the subjects raised any objections to their unwilling participation in the experiment.

Was this experiment an invasion of personal privacy? Is it ethical to monitor what unsuspecting people do at their most private moments? These are important ethical questions. Psychologists conducting experiments must consider whether they are legitimately observing human behaviour, or simply spying on others.

RECAP

1. Is intelligence passed directly from one generation to the next? Explain your answer.
2. How is it possible for psychologists to measure human personality?
3. According to Argyle and Dean, what are some of the techniques that humans use to regulate intimacy during conversations?

Section 3.4

Sociology Skills and Methods

Focus Questions

- What are the main features of statistical analysis?
- What are the main features of questionnaires?
- For what type of sociological research are case studies normally used?

Key Concepts

causal theories
consequential theories
hypothesis
independent variable
dependent variable
intervening variables

Statistical Analysis

Sociologists examine and analyze the characteristics of present-day societies. They try to identify a society's key elements, as well as its power structure and value system. After they organize their observations and analyses, they develop theories to explain their findings.

A favoured method of inquiry among sociologists is statistical analysis. Sociologists gather numerical data that reflect what is happening in society regarding matters such as income distribution, educational levels, changing family structures, and crime rates. In this section, we will examine how statistical analysis is used to understand homicide rates in Canada.

Homicide Statistics

Statistics Canada defines criminal homicide as "first degree murder, second degree murder, manslaughter, or infanticide. Deaths caused by criminal negligence, suicide, accidental or justifiable homicides are not included in this definition" (Statistics Canada, 2000). A number of striking conclusions can be formed when examining homicide statistics. The 1999 figures are fairly typical. In that year, almost 90 per cent of convicted murderers and almost 66 per cent of victims were male. These are striking proportions in light of the fact that slightly less than 50 per cent of the population was male.

Spousal murders made up one of the largest categories of homicides. Just over 28 per cent of total homicides were female victims murdered by their husband or former husband. In contrast, only 6.4 per cent of total homicides were male victims murdered by their wife or former wife.

Another striking figure is that about 86 per cent of 1999's murder victims knew their assailant—that is, the assailant was a family member, friend, business associate, or acquaintance. Sociologists conclude that the chances of being murdered as a result of a random act of crime are fairly small.

The sociological use of statistics goes beyond just creating a statistical snapshot of society at a given time. Sociologists make these statistics meaningful by comparing them with equivalent figures in other countries. They then seek to explain why homicide is more or less prevalent in Canada than elsewhere.

Sociologists also examine Canadian rates over a period of time to see what, if any, changes are taking place. In the following section, we look more closely at how sociologists use statistical data to perceive trends.

Determining Trends

The first step in perceiving a possible trend is to get raw data. Every year, Statistics Canada, the federal government's statistical agency, publishes homicide statistics. Its 2000 report contains homicide data from the previous thirty years. The findings are shown in Figure 3.11.

Sociologists make sense of these figures by calculating what proportion of the total population each year's homicide numbers represent. In other words, they calculate the rate of homicide relative to the population in a given year. This calculation will indicate what kind of a chance a typical citizen stands of being murdered from year to year. The standard measure for homicide rate is the number of homicides for every 100 000 members of the population. Converting the totals from Figure 3.11 into figures per 100 000 gives the rates shown in Figure 3.12.

Now the figures are more meaningful. Figure 3.12 shows that murder rates

INTERNET RESOURCES

Statistics Canada maintains an up-to-date site with statistics relating to sociological topics. Go to

http://www.statcan.ca/english/Pgdb/

Under the major heading "The People," you can access statistics on

- population
- education
- labour
- health
- families
- culture

Year	Number of homicides	Total population (000)
1970	467	21 324
1975	701	22 813
1980	592	24 564
1985	704	25 882
1990	660	27 731
1995	588	29 400
1999	536	30 454

Figure 3.11 Total homicides and population in Canada, selected years, 1970–1999

Year	Homicide rate per 100 000 population
1970	2.19
1975	3.03
1980	2.41
1985	2.72
1990	2.38
1995	2.00
1999	1.76

Figure 3.12 Homicide rate in Canada, selected years, 1970–1999

peaked in 1975 and, other than a slight rise between 1980 and 1985, have declined since then.

Such findings are extremely useful in correcting inaccurate public perceptions. For example, there is a perception, fuelled by politicians during election campaigns, that violence is on the increase among criminal gangs and young people. The statistics show that the rate of *gang-related* homicide, frequently related to drug trafficking or revenge, did in fact rise through the 1990s. But the *overall* homicide rate among young offenders fell during the period from 1990 to 1998. Fifty-two homicides were committed by young offenders in 1989, while in 1999 the figure was forty-eight. Thus, a politician who bases an election platform of being "tough" on crime *solely* on the claim that youth homicide has been rising is misinforming the public.

Developing Theories from Statistics

Once sociologists have identified a trend or change, they try to explain it. Sociological theories tend to fall into two categories: **causal theories** and **consequential theories**. Causal theories try to relate two variables and to determine whether one causes the other. Consequential theories try to predict what will happen to society if a particular variable is changed.

You have already read about a causal theory in Chapter 1 (see pages 7 to 9). Claiming that the variable of capital punishment is related to the variable of homicide rates—that, in fact, capital punishment causes a decrease in homicide rates—is a causal theory. Let us look more closely at the sociological method of analyzing this issue.

Sociologists examining the effect of capital punishment on murder rates in Canada first create a **hypothesis**. In ancient Greek, this word meant "a proposition," or something that someone tries to prove. A hypothesis is presented as a statement as opposed to a question. In this case, the hypothesis might be, "The death penalty is an effective deterrent to murder."

There are two variables in this hypothesis: the death penalty and homicide rates. The two variables have a specific relationship to each other. The hypothesis puts forth that the death penalty affects homicide rates; it does not assert the reverse—that homicide rates affect the death penalty. Thus, the death penalty, as the factor that is "doing the affecting," is called the **independent variable**. The second variable, homicide rates, is called the **dependent variable**. It is the variable that "is affected by" the independent variable.

To prove the hypothesis, the sociologist compares homicide rates in countries having the death penalty with those of countries with no death penalty. In making this comparison, the sociologist must be sensitive to **intervening variables**. These are variables that cause difficulty in making a simple link between the independent and dependent variables. Sociologists usually encounter numerous intervening variables when they analyze data because the issues they study tend to be extremely complex. The intervening variables in comparing homicide rates from country to country include the following:

- In the countries being compared, the percentage of the population that is male and between the ages of twenty-five and forty-nine may differ. This is an intervening variable because we know that this population sector is the most likely to commit murder.
- The standard of living may differ in the countries being compared. This is an intervening variable because poverty and economic hardship may have an effect on crime rates.
- The definition of homicide may differ in the countries being compared. For example, Canada does not consider death caused by criminal negligence as homicide, while other countries do.

All the intervening variables need to be identified, and their effects need to be understood, in order for research conclusions to be valid.

Suppose you, as the sociologist, have gathered your evidence and have come up with the data in Figure 3.13 (the statistics are fairly typical for the years cited). What would your conclusion be?

Looking only at the 1958, 1967, and 1980 data, you might conclude that the non-use of the death penalty after 1962 caused homicide rates in Canada to increase. But, as Figure 3.12 shows, an increase in the rate from 1980 to 1985 has been followed by a steady decline since then. Thus, the data fail to prove the hypothesis. In Canada at least, homicide rates are falling even though the death penalty has long been abolished.

Questionnaires

Questionnaires are another tool favoured by sociologists. One kind of questionnaire is the administered questionnaire. In this questionnaire, the researcher asks subjects questions and fills in their responses on a sheet. In contrast, in the self-administered questionnaire, the subjects themselves answer the questions and return the questionnaire.

Figure 3.13 Status of death penalty, homicide rate, and number of executions, Canada, selected years, 1958–1999

Year	Status of death penalty	Homicide rate per 1000 000 population	Number of executions
1958	Could be imposed as punishment for first-degree murder.	1.15	2
1967	Could be imposed for first-degree murder, but all death sentences after 1962 were automatically commuted to life imprisonment.	1.66	0
1980	Death penalty for first-degree murder abolished in 1976. Replaced by minimum of 25 years' imprisonment.	2.41	0
1999	As above.	1.76	0

Sources: Urquhart and Buckley, 1971, 14, 649. Statistics Canada, 2000, http://www.statcan.ca/Daily/English/001018/d001018b.htm

The self-administered questionnaire has some advantages over the administered method. First, it is more effective in getting data about private aspects of people's attitudes or behaviours. People might be reluctant to reveal themselves to a flesh-and-blood researcher, but may provide data in an anonymous setting. The self-administered method is also cheaper, eliminating the need to pay for a researcher to ask questions.

There are difficulties associated with the questionnaire method as a whole. One difficulty is not having any guarantees that subjects have answered questions honestly. A second is having to limit the subject pool to people with reasonable reading and writing skills. A third is finding willing subjects—urban societies are saturated with questionnaires about all sorts of topics, and many people have neither the time nor the interest to participate.

Case Studies

Another method that sociologists use is the case study. This method is favoured when researching deviant behaviour. To see why, imagine you were trying to find out about the type of people who sexually abuse young children. Since the vast majority of people do not engage in this behaviour, questionnaires on people's sexual lives would not be a fruitful information source. Furthermore, a sexual abuser would be unlikely to admit to the behaviour in a questionnaire for fear of being identified.

When people do admit to a deviant behaviour, they become the focus of avid research. Sociologists and psychologists conduct extensive interviews with them, often in a prison setting. Information from these interviews is collated, compared, and written up as case studies. Such

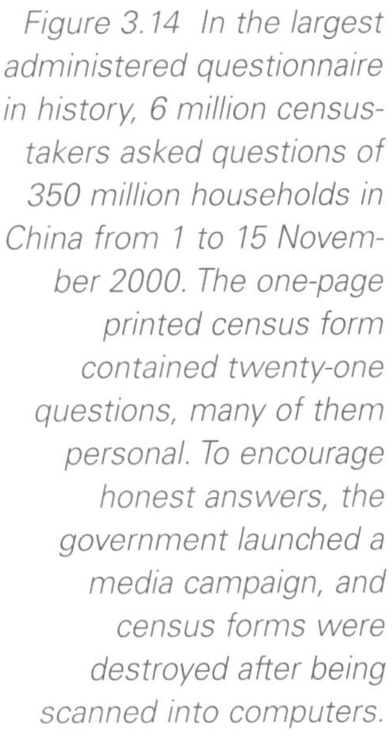

Figure 3.14 In the largest administered questionnaire in history, 6 million census-takers asked questions of 350 million households in China from 1 to 15 November 2000. The one-page printed census form contained twenty-one questions, many of them personal. To encourage honest answers, the government launched a media campaign, and census forms were destroyed after being scanned into computers.

methods of investigation have produced valuable findings—for example, we now know that most child abusers were themselves abused as children.

Ethical Issues

As in all social science inquiry, it is important to consider ethical matters.

When asking subjects questions in questionnaires, it is important to respect their anonymity. Questionnaires must not contain numbers or codes that could be traced back to a particular respondent.

When conducting interviews for case studies, questions should be confined to only those topics that are really necessary. The researcher must also be careful to maintain an emotional distance from the respondent. This stance ensures that the researcher does not express disgust or revulsion at any of the behaviours and activities the respondent may describe. Equally important, the sociological researcher must avoid trying to change a deviant respondent's behaviour. That is the role of the psychological team. Case study research in sociology requires that the researcher does not become involved in the respondent's treatment.

When working with statistics, the researcher must practise intellectual honesty. It is fairly easy to manipulate statistics. Manipulation can involve only selecting the statistics that support your hypothesis and ignoring the ones that contradict it. Manipulation also includes the deliberate falsification of numbers. Any kind of tampering with data is unethical and must be avoided.

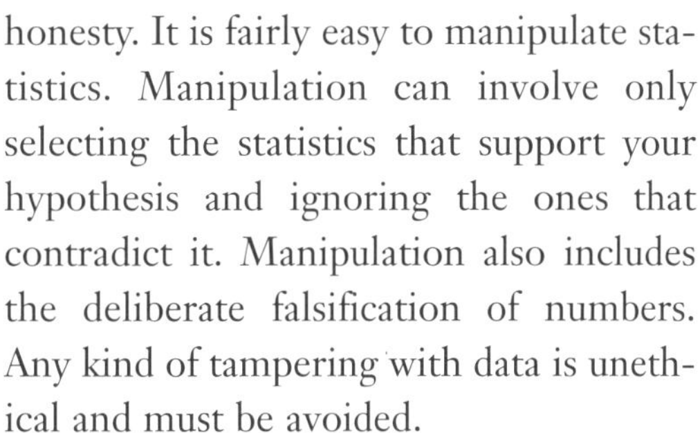

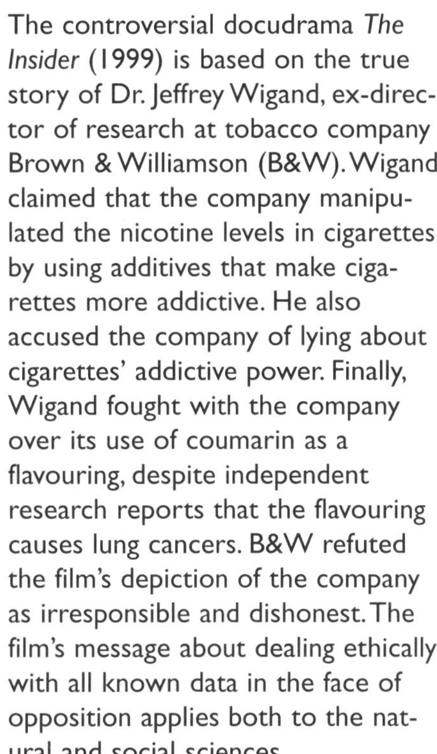

The controversial docudrama *The Insider* (1999) is based on the true story of Dr. Jeffrey Wigand, ex-director of research at tobacco company Brown & Williamson (B&W). Wigand claimed that the company manipulated the nicotine levels in cigarettes by using additives that make cigarettes more addictive. He also accused the company of lying about cigarettes' addictive power. Finally, Wigand fought with the company over its use of coumarin as a flavouring, despite independent research reports that the flavouring causes lung cancers. B&W refuted the film's depiction of the company as irresponsible and dishonest. The film's message about dealing ethically with all known data in the face of opposition applies both to the natural and social sciences.

RECAP

1. How are homicide rates calculated?
2. How did homicide rates in Canada change between 1970 and 1999? Include specific figures in your answer.
3. What ethical considerations must sociologists bear in mind when conducting research?

Activities

Show your knowledge

1. How can a cultural anthropologist ensure that participant observation fieldwork is reliable?
2. Describe three areas of human behaviour that psychologists study. For each area, summarize the conclusions reached.
3. Describe how a sociologist does statistical analysis.

Practise your thinking skills

4. Imagine that you are a cultural anthropologist doing a participant observation. In each of the following situations, choose the ethical response. In each case, explain your answer.
   a) An informant tells a racist joke. The rest of the group laughs. Do you?
   b) You are a vegetarian for moral reasons. The informants are all meat-eaters. Do you eat meat with your informants while you do your participant observation?
   c) Every Friday night your informants get drunk to the point where they throw up. What do you do?
   d) Your informants believe that most police officers are corrupt. You don't. They ask what you think. What do you say?
   e) Your informants use a lot of slang and swearing in their talk. You are not familiar with this slang and don't swear much. Do you change the way you speak?
5. From among all the experiments and studies described in this chapter, choose one that you think makes a significant contribution to our understanding of human behaviour. Explain your choice.
6. Imagine you are conducting a sociological inquiry into the dating habits of the students in your school.
   a) What would be the advantages and disadvantages of obtaining information with a self-administered questionnaire?
   b) What do you think would be the best method of gathering data? Explain your choice.

Communicate your ideas

7. Outside your classroom, observe a short interaction among people. Write both a vague and a concrete note about the interaction. Then,

Activities

compare your work with that of a classmate. What characteristics of the concrete notes make them more useful than the vague notes?

8. Choose one of the following psychology research areas: human intelligence, personality, or privacy and intimacy. Find out what experiments and studies have been done in the area. Report your findings to the class.
9. Go to the Statistics Canada Web site at http://www.statcan.ca/english/Pgdb/. Describe the statistical information provided about one of the following topics:
   a) population
   b) education
   c) labour
   d) health
   e) families
   f) culture

   Report to the class on current trends in the topic.

Apply your knowledge

10. Imagine you are conducting an experiment to measure people's reactions to violent images. The experiment involves showing a selection of pictures to subjects. Some pictures contain violence and are upsetting. To keep your results reliable, you do not want to reveal the purpose of the experiment to your subjects. On the other hand, to be ethical, you feel the subjects' informed consent is necessary. How might you obtain informed consent without giving too much away beforehand?
11. Create a set of rules for psychologists to follow to ensure that they do not violate their subjects' sense of privacy when conducting experiments. Explain how you arrived at the rules.
12. You are a sociologist investigating whether or not there is a link between involvement in extracurricular activities and academic success in school. You plan to use a self-administered questionnaire to obtain information. Identify
    a) your hypothesis
    b) your independent variable
    c) your dependent variable
    d) possible intervening variables
    e) the method you would use to prove your hypothesis

SUMMATIVE PROJECT OUTLINE

You may be asked to work on a summative project over the course of the term or year. This text suggests three choices for such a project. The following outline breaks each project down into its components. It also suggests how you can check your progress along the way.

Research Essay

1. Select a topic. Choose from the list below or think of another topic and get your teacher's approval.
   - a comparison of the nature and nurture explanations for human behaviour
   - a comparison of your and your parents' socialization
   - a comparison of marriages in three cultures
   - future changes to the workplace
   - a comparison of three formal organizations
   - an analysis of the incarceration rates of men versus women
2. Read the Skill Development in Unit 2 (pages 105 to 107 and 134 to 136). Using these skills, locate, evaluate, and select the information you need. Begin writing up your findings in the form of an essay or research paper.
3. At the halfway point of your project time, complete an interim report. The Interim Report Sheet at right can serve as a guide. After you have answered all the questions, arrange an interview with your teacher to ensure that you are on the right track.
4. Using the answers from your interim report and guidance from your teacher, complete your project.

Interim Report Sheet

Name(s) ______________________

____

What is the topic of your research? ______

____

____

What different theories or viewpoints exist on your topic? ______________________

____

What major findings have you identified? ______________________

____

____

____

What conclusions have you reached so far? ______________________

____

____

____

What unanswered questions do you have? ______________________

____

____

____

What should be your next steps in completing the Summative Project?

____

____

____

____

Survey

1. Select an issue over which people's opinions range. Choose from the list below or think of another issue and get your teacher's approval.
    - What skills are [females/males] better at than [males/females]?
    - What do teenagers think [were/are/will be] the most important socialization agents [ten years ago/now/in ten years' time]?
    - Is the role of the family becoming [more/less] important in Canadian life?
    - Is the nature of work becoming [more/less] rewarding for employees?
    - What are people looking for in group membership? Do they find it?
    - What steps should society take to increase cohesion and reduce violence in Canada?
2. Read the Skill Development in Unit 3 (pages 175 to 177, 207 to 208, and 269 to 273). Using these skills, create and conduct a survey. Begin analyzing your results.
3. At the halfway point of your project time, complete an interim report. The Interim Report Sheet at right can serve as a guide. After you have answered all the questions, arrange an interview with your teacher to ensure that you are on the right track.
4. Using the answers from your interim report and guidance from your teacher, complete your project.

Interim Report Sheet

Name(s) ______________________

____

What is the topic of your survey? _____

____

What is your hypothesis? ______________________

____

What are the independent and dependent variables? ______________________

____

What are the intervening variables? _____

____

What are the target groups of your survey? ______________________

____

What distracter questions have you included? ______________________

____

What results have you obtained so far?

____

____

What conclusions have you reached so far? ______________________

____

What unanswered questions do you have? ______________________

____

What should be your next steps in completing the Summative Project? _____

____

Observation of Group Behaviour

1. Select an aspect of group behaviour that you can ethically observe. Choose from the list below or think of another aspect of group behaviour and get your teacher's approval.
   - Do some groups of teenagers demonstrate more assertive behaviours than others?
   - Are teenagers or senior citizens better at demonstrating socialization skills in interactions with others?
   - How do people's behaviours vary in different social environments?
   - How positive/enthusiastic are the behaviours of employees in various types of work?
   - What differences/similarities are there between the ways that elementary and secondary students interact?
   - What major behaviours do people display in (a) social groups (b) formal organizations (c) bureaucracies?
2. Read the Skill Development in Unit 4 (pages 311 to 313 and 349 to 352). Using these skills, observe and record an aspect of group behaviour. Begin analyzing your results.
3. At the halfway point of your project time, complete an interim report. The Interim Report Sheet at right can serve as a guide. After you have answered all the questions, arrange an interview with your teacher to ensure that you are on the right track.
4. Using the answers from your interim report and guidance from your teacher, complete your project.

Interim Report Sheet

Name(s) ______________________________

____

What is your hypothesis? ______________________________

____

Which group types are being observed?

____

What measurable behaviours are being observed? ______________________________

____

How are you ensuring the observation is being done discreetly? ______________________________

____

What are the independent and dependent variables? ______________________________

____

What are the intervening variables? ______________________________

____

What results have you obtained so far?

____

____

What conclusions have you reached so far? ______________________________

____

What unanswered questions do you have? ______________________________

____

What should be your next steps in completing the Summative Project? ______________________________

____

Unit 2

Self and Others

A number of social forces influence and shape our behaviour. Social scientists from each of the three disciplines have their own approaches to the study of these forces. Anthropologists' concerns include the patterns our culture transmits to us. Psychologists' concerns include the interaction of our inherited traits and our environment. Sociologists' concerns include the influence of family, peers, and other "agents."

This unit will help you combine the insights of all the social sciences to gain a rich understanding of our behaviour and our personal and social development.

UNIT STU

Unit Contents

Overall Expectations

In this unit, you will

- describe some differences and similarities in the approaches taken by anthropology, psychology, and sociology to the concept of self in relation to others
- demonstrate an understanding of the social forces that influence and shape behaviour described by anthropologists, psychologists, and sociologists
- analyze socialization patterns from the perspectives of anthropology, psychology, and sociology

Topics by Discipline

Anthropology

Chapter 4

- An anthropological analysis of self-concept
- Naming traditions and identity formation in different cultures
- The role of gender in influencing our sense o self
- Defining race and ethnicity
- Theories of ethnic identity formation
- Asian self-concept

Chapter 5

- Culture and socialization
- Socialization into gender roles among Canad Sikh women, Nuer women in East Africa, Islamic women in Taliban Afghanistan

Psychology

Chapter 4

- How we protect our sense of self: defence mechanisms
- The influence of names on our sense of self
- Adolescent self-concept
- The two sides of the nature-nurture debate
- The media as a "nurturing" influence
- The Human Genome Project
- The nature of psychological disorders
- Neurotic disorders
- Psychotic disorders
- Gender differences in our brains
- Theories of ethnic identity formation
- Asian self-concept

apter 5

- Ferals and isolates
- The agents of socialization: family, school, peer group, media, religion, workplace, total institutions
- Stages in self-development: the psychosexual theory, the cognitive development theory, the social experience theory, the psychosocial development theory, the moral development theory, the gender-based theory

Sociology

apter 4

- A sociological analysis of self-concept
- Adolescent self-concept
- The influence of context on self-concept and behaviour
- The two sides of the nature-nurture debate
- The significance of the debate to Canadian society
- The Human Genome Project
- Gender's impact on our sense of self
- Gender differences in communication

apter 5

- The concept and components of socialization
- Ferals and isolates
- The agents of socialization: family, school, peer group, media, religion, workplace, total institutions
- Stages in self-development: the psychosexual theory, the cognitive development theory, the social experience theory, the psychosocial development theory, the moral development theory, the gender-based theory

Skill Guide

One of the methods social scientists use to reach conclusions about society is **research investigation**.

In this unit, you can develop the skills needed to do a research essay. These skills are

- Locating and Selecting Information (pages 105 to 107)
- Evaluating and Citing Sources (pages 134 to 136)

Research and Inquiry Skills Learning Expectations

The skill development in this unit will enable you to

- formulate appropriate questions for research and inquiry relating to one or more of the main areas of concern in the social sciences
- demonstrate an ability to locate and select relevant information from a variety of print and electronic sources
- evaluate the relevance and validity of information gathered through research
- demonstrate an ability to organize, interpret, and analyze information gathered
- record information and key ideas from your research, and document sources accurately, using correct forms of citation
- effectively communicate the results of your inquiries

Chapter 4

Forces Shaping Behaviour

Overview of Chapter

Learning Expectations

By the end of this chapter, you will be able to

- identify and assess the major influences that contribute to an individual's personal and social development (for example, heredity, environment, race, gender)
- analyze the role of the mass media in influencing individual and group behaviour
- explain why behaviour varies depending on context and on the individuals involved (for example, at work, within a family, in sports, in a crowd, in a large city or small town)

Open for Debate

Scientists Predict Another Hard Choice for Parents

The time is coming, many scientists say, when parents will pick their children's genes.

From the menu of possibilities, parents might select genes to make their babies resist common diseases and infections, things like cancer, AIDS, heart attacks and Alzheimer's disease. Maybe they would like their children to have fabulous memories or winning personalities or a talent for playing the piano.

"It's not a question of 'if' but 'when' and 'how' this will occur," says Gregory Stock, head of the Program on Medicine, Technology and Society at UCLA's School of Medicine.

"The reason people are fascinated by this whole area is that it will challenge our fundamental thinking about who we are and what it means to be human," says Stock. "We are talking about remaking human biology."

But what part of biology to remake first? Typically the answer is to reduce our tendency to get sick.

Of course, there is no reason to stop with disease protection, the visionaries say. Many genetic "enhancements," as they are called, can also be imagined.

One obvious enhancement is extra brain power. At Princeton, scientists have already created mice—nicknamed "Doogie" after TV's physician prodigy—that are rodent geniuses. They learn faster, remember longer and adapt to changes better than any ordinary mouse.

Even selecting a child's personality in advance might be possible. Experts believe that half of people's personality traits are hard-wired by their genes. Of course, lots of genes combine to create any individual's melange of quirks and temperament. So building a child with, say, David Letterman wit, Mother Teresa compassion and Warren Buffet business sense may not be real easy at first.

Still, scientists are laying the foundation. In mice, at least, they have already tracked down genes that influence many habits, including aggressiveness, overeating and mothering instincts.

Abridged from: Haney, Daniel Q. "Designer Babies." *CNEWS*. [Online]. Available http://www.caldercup.com/CNEWSScience0003/21_babies2.html 21 March 2000.

Think About It

1. How completely is each person's identity controlled by genes? What parts of you might be shaped by other factors?
2. What is your position on changing the genes of infants, assuming we develop the technology?
3. What human rights, legal, or moral issues would arise if scientists had access to your genes?

Section 4.1

Our Sense of Self

Focus Questions

- What is a "sense of self" and how does it develop?
- What factors influence our sense of self?
- In what ways is adolescence a crucial period in the development of self-identity?

Self-Concept: A Sociological Analysis

Our sense of who we are—based on our ideas about our strengths, weaknesses, values, beliefs, hopes, dreams, achievements, and disappointments—is called our **self-concept**. But where does our self-concept come from? Social scientists have a variety of different theories about the development of self-concept. American sociologist Charles Cooley (1864–1929) believed that our sense of self is the result of social interactions with others. In his 1902 work *Human Nature and the Social Order*, Cooley asserted that babies begin to develop their sense of self as they interpret how other people react to them. If babies receive a cuddle, a smile, or verbal approval when they attempt to master a new task like picking up a toy or making vocal sounds, they will repeat the action and feel proud of themselves. Conversely, if babies receive negative feedback or no feedback in response to their actions, they will begin to feel insecure or anxious about themselves. As a result, they will be less inclined to explore the world around them.

Sociologist George Herbert Mead (1863–1931) believed that humans actually have more than one "self." Mead felt that we create different personalities, or selves, depending on the social setting we find ourselves in. In his work *Mind, Self and Society* (published in 1962, several years after his death), Mead called our true self, the **I-self**. The I-self is formed through relationships with our parents and close friends, and is only revealed to those closest to us. We rarely exhibit our I-self in social settings. Mead called our other self the **Me-self**. The Me-self is guided by the rules and expectations of the roles we play. In other words, the Me-self is our public self. Mead felt that our I-self and our Me-self are combined into a total self. This total self behaves according to the social situation and our relationship to the people involved.

Self-Concept: An Anthropological Analysis

Sociologists see the development of the self as a result of the interaction between

Key Concepts

self-concept
I-self
Me-self
culturally constructed concept
enculturation
ego
defence mechanisms
rationalization
displacement
repression
projection
individuality
identity crisis
self-determination
self-enhancers
status set

an individual and others. Anthropologists, in contrast, believe that concepts of the self are **culturally constructed**. This means that a person's culture is the source of the person's ideas or concepts about the world and the people in it. These ideas and concepts will seem obvious and ordinary to the members of the culture, but may be different from the ideas of another culture. The self, anthropologists believe, is an example of one of the concepts each culture constructs uniquely for its members. We can see an example of this in the Mixtec culture.

Anthropologist John Monaghan conducted fieldwork from 1983 to 1986 among the Mixtec cultural group. This group was living in Santiago Nuyoo, in the southern Mexican state of Oaxaca. The Mixtec believe that living things that come into the world at the same time are fundamentally linked to one another. An animal and a human born at the same time will share life experiences and are often said to have a single soul. Each member of Mixtec society discovers his or her *kiti nuvi*, or "animal soulmate," through a local spiritual leader. The Mixtec believe that the discovery is made easier by the fact that the person shares certain characteristics, likes, or dislikes with the animal.

This link between kindred creatures means that the Mixtec concept of "self" is not limited to one individual. Rather, one's self is shared with one's *kiti nuvi*. Those who share a self with more ferocious animals, such as jaguars, stand high in the human social hierarchy. In contrast, the Mixtec believe a smaller *kiti nuvi*, such as a rabbit, will limit a person's wealth and power. The Mixtec concept of self is also used to explain good and bad luck and the nature of dreams.

The Mixtec's ideas about the self contrast with the concept of self in the West. Here we see ourselves as autonomous individuals. We are each responsible for our own destiny.

ASK THE EXPERT

Shirley Fedorak, M.A., lecturer in anthropology at the University of Saskatchewan

What is enculturation?

The way we view ourselves, our world, and others is greatly influenced by our life experiences. We begin to learn the ideas, values, and beliefs of our culture from almost the moment of our birth. This learning process is known as **enculturation**. Many enculturative forces influence our self-concept and world view, including school, peers, church, and the media—especially television.

One of the most important enculturative forces is our family—our parents, grandparents, aunts and uncles, and even our brothers and sisters help shape our opinions and attitudes toward ourselves and others. For example, if we live in a home where all people are considered equal, no matter their origins, beliefs, or physical appearance, then we will grow up feeling more at ease with people from other backgrounds. This is especially important in a country that is a cultural mosaic, like Canada.

Protecting our Sense of Self: A Psychological Analysis

Psychologist Sigmund Freud believed that there are times when our sense of self, or **ego**, faces a crisis. For example, let us say you value honesty and take pride in being an honest person. You recently told a significant lie to someone you care about. How do you make sense of this contradiction between who you believe you are and how you acted? Freud believed that in order to protect our ego against this type of conflict, we use **defence mechanisms**. These mechanisms are unconscious reactions to feelings of frustration, tension, and worry. They alter our view of reality, allowing us to make excuses for our own failures or blame others for our mistakes.

Four Defence Mechanisms

One defence mechanism identified by Freud is **rationalization**. Rationalization is an excuse we invent to explain a failure, loss, error, or our bad behaviour. For example, if we did not get a job we really wanted, we may rationalize our failure by making up an excuse about the person who got the job: "The person only got the job because his uncle works for the company."

Displacement is another defence mechanism identified by Freud. Displacement is when we lash out at someone because we have suppressed anger or frustration from an earlier situation. The person we attack has nothing to do with our anger and frustration. For example, imagine that a friend makes fun of you in front of someone you want to impress. Although you might not feel comfortable lashing out at your friend at the time, you take out your anger later on one of your parents when you return from school. This is a classic example of displacement.

Freud also identified **repression** as a common defence mechanism. Repression is when we push unpleasant urges or thoughts out of our conscious minds and into our subconscious. We are unaware of these repressed thoughts. But they can resurface as physical problems, sarcasm, or unkind behaviour directed at others. For example, a man may find that many of his mother's personality characteristics annoy him. Out of love and respect for his mother, he pushes those negative feelings into his subconscious. Years later, if this man's wife shares some of his mother's characteristics, his repressed feelings may come out in sarcastic remarks made to his wife.

A fourth defence mechanism is **projection**. This is when we see negative traits and feelings in other people that we sense in ourselves but cannot openly admit. If, for example, there is one particular person who "drives you crazy," it is likely because this individual exhibits personality characteristics that you possess, but have worked very hard to hide.

What's in a Name?

Our name is the foundation of our identity. Many of us have been raised in cultures in which our first names have classified us by gender. These names have helped us to develop an awareness of ourselves as unique individuals. Our names

Classic Study

RESEARCHER:
Sigmund Freud, Psychologist

TIME:
1894

SUBJECT:
Ego-Defence Mechanisms

INTERNET RESOURCES

What interesting information can you discover about your own name and the names of those you know? Find out on a "baby naming" site on the Web such as

www.babynames.com or www.babycenter.com

can have a lasting effect on our sense of personal identity. Unpopular or unusual names may make a person feel different. Boys with feminine-sounding names or girls with masculine-sounding names may be teased by other children. Children who are named after someone famous and well-respected may develop strong self-esteem. But they may also develop feelings of inadequacy if they can never measure up to their namesake's legend.

Many Aboriginal cultures have very significant naming traditions. One custom is to give an Aboriginal child a traditional name to honour an ancestor. By giving a baby an ancestor's name, the old name lives again. Another custom involves changing the name after a person experiences a significant event. In an article written by Tara King for the *Seattle Times* on 12 December 1999, Clifford Allen, a full-blooded Nez Perce, describes how his grandfather went through three names in his lifetime. He was known as White Cloud until the Nez Perce War of 1877. When he suffered a war wound at the Battle of the Big Hole in Montana, he became *Husis Owyeen*, or Shot in the Head. After fleeing to Canada, he suffered an eye disfigurement when a bullet glanced off his eye socket. He then became Shot in the Eye. Allen says that many Nez Perce have two names because they live in two worlds. He explains that "in one world we have to have birth certificates and driver's licenses. But ceremonial names are our real names. It is who we are."

Titles and Self-Concept

Psychologist Marlene Mackie has observed that the self-image and status of males tend to be defined by their occupation, while those of females are defined in terms of marriage. Thus, men are called "Mr." whether they are married or not. But many women are asked, "Is it Miss or Mrs.?" That is, are you married or not? To avoid being judged by marital status, some women choose the title "Ms."

RECAP

1. How does Charles Cooley explain the development of our sense of self?
2. According to George Mead, what is the "I-self" and the "Me-self"? How do these two work together?
3. List three reasons why it is important to be careful when selecting a name for a child.
4. Why do some women prefer the title Ms. over Miss or Mrs.?

Adolescent Self-Concept

Adolescents experience many physical, behavioral, and social changes on their way to becoming adults. Consequently, this is a period when an individual's self-concept undergoes considerable change. Psychologist Erik Erikson found that during the period from twelve to eighteen years of age, a teenager's identity changes its form. Erikson believed that the challenge for the adolescent is to develop an identity based on **individuality**. Individuality is the condition of being oneself and understanding who that self is in relation to others. Accordingly, during adolescence, most teenagers spend a lot of time thinking of other people and wondering if other people like them.

Erikson also believed that adolescents have to face an **identity crisis** before they move toward increased self-awareness and independence. These characteristics are achieved only after undergoing an often painful, back-and-forth struggle. On the one hand, the teen has unrealistically high expectations of her- or himself. On the other hand, the teen experiences poor self-concept. During this struggle, most teens experience a reduction in self-esteem and the ability to cope. This is because the transition to a new identity creates a vulnerable self that is subjected to a variety of "dark" feelings. These negative feelings, however, are vital components of the identity formation process.

This confused state of self in middle adolescence was demonstrated by Kidwell et al. in their 1995 study of adolescent identity exploration, published in the journal *Adolescence*. The researchers found that youth who were actively exploring their identity tended to have symptoms such as moodiness, self-doubt, disturbed thinking, impulsivity, conflicts with parents and others, reduced ego strength, and increased physical discomfort.

Although painful, it seems that this identity exploration is the key to the development of self-awareness. And the development of self-awareness is crucial. In their 1997 study, published in Volume 18 of *Remedial and Special Education*, Sharon Field, Alan Hoffman, and Margaret Posch explained that self-awareness is one of the foundational building blocks for **self-determination**. This is the ability to identify and achieve goals based on a foundation of knowing and valuing oneself. The potential for self-determination is directly proportional to the individual's awareness of his or her strengths, weaknesses, needs, and preferences.

Figure 4.1 Negative feelings, stemming from low self-esteem, are natural as adolescents explore their identity.

"Self-Enhancement" in Adolescents and Others

We can all agree that each of us has our own sense of self, our own idea of our strengths and weaknesses. It turns out, however, that we do not always see ourselves objectively, or the same way as others see us. Most of us tend to have a selective memory, and we remember more the positive events involving ourselves. We also develop a system of excuses to explain our failures. In a 1998 study published in the *Journal of Social Psychology*, Jenny Kurman and Yohanan Eshel reported that people have a general tendency to describe themselves more positively than they describe others. They also describe themselves more positively than others describe them. These **self-enhancers** were found to be better adjusted emotionally than those who are more critical of their self-image. This may be because thinking positively has a beneficial effect on our self-esteem. But in this study, not all high self-enhancers were well-adjusted emotionally. The researchers warned that self-enhancement can lead to disillusionment when one becomes aware of gaps between the enhanced self-image and reality. Thus, self-enhancement may contribute to maladjustment.

In Kurman and Eshel's study, adolescents did not suffer from this type of disillusionment. Although the students were somewhat aware of differences between their abilities and their self-evaluations, they disregarded the gaps. The researchers pointed out that ignoring or deflating undesirable information is common practice (although individuals may not be conscious that they do so).

Self-Concept and Behaviour in Different Contexts

Our self-concept, along with the behaviour that results from it, are not static. We show different parts of our personality and different behaviours depending on the situation we find ourselves in. For example, the language you use when talking with your friends outside of school is different from the language you use in a classroom. It is different yet again when you visit an elderly relative or participate in a job interview. Your clothing and other parts of your appearance may also be different in each of these situations.

Does this mean you are a phoney? Not at all. It simply means that you cannot live as an entirely independent being in society. Like all people, you must interact with and depend on others, and this involves learning to adapt to different situations, or "contexts." Individuals who are able to change their behaviour appropriately in each context are much more likely to be a "success."

Each different set of behaviours constitutes a "role." Sociologists refer to the many roles we play simultaneously as our **status set**. One girl's status set may include a daughter to her parents; a sister to her siblings; a friend to her peers; and a catcher to others on her baseball team.

QUESTION:
Is it ever OK to lie to parents or friends?

No matter what the situation or who the person is, there is no room for lies. ... Society today tries so hard to cover up the lies they tell, when they are actually digging themselves in deeper and deeper.

—Shannon Bowman, 17

It's never OK to lie to your parents. You should never lie to close friends. But other people you don't know is fine. ... I personally try never to lie. ... but if I had to lie it would be to people I don't really know or like.

—Mike Bergman, 16

I'd much rather a friend tell me a little "white" lie than to hurt my feelings. I know that when friends ask me about new hair or clothes and trivial stuff like that, I will probably lie and say I like it instead of getting in a stupid fight over it. When it comes to lying to my parents, I can honestly say that once you lie a few times it gets easier. I used to lie all the time, almost every night, because I would bag class and I would have to tell my parents something. Now they know the truth and I'm regaining their trust. So lying, like everything else, is a very complex thing that I think is hard to judge in terms of right and wrong.

—Tonya Alex, 17

The contexts in which she plays these roles may determine certain changes in her personality. She may be calm and controlled as a catcher, outgoing and funny with her friends, and quiet and reserved around her parents. These characteristics are all different parts of her self, but certain characteristics are more likely to surface in certain contexts.

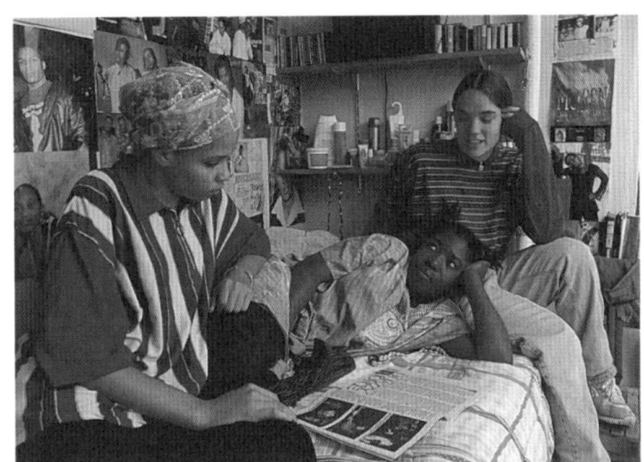

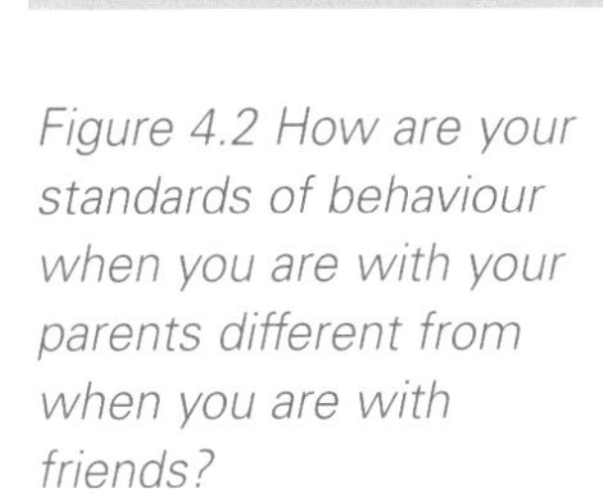

Figure 4.2 How are your standards of behaviour when you are with your parents different from when you are with friends?

RECAP

1. According to psychologist Erik Erikson, what is the primary challenge facing adolescents as their sense of self develops? According to Kidwell's study, what symptoms do adolescents experience while exploring their identity?
2. Give three examples from your own life of how your behaviour changes as you move from role to role.

Section 4.2

The Nature-Nurture Debate

Focus Questions

- What is the nature-nurture debate and why is it important?
- Which side of the nature-nurture debate does the David Reimer case support?
- How is The Human Genome Project important to the debate?

Key Concepts

nature-nurture debate
genes
estrogen
The Human Genome Project
sexual orientation
identical twins
fraternal twins

Studying Personality

One of the biggest areas of controversy that exists in the study of personality is the **nature-nurture debate**. This debate focuses on whether nature (inherited, biological characteristics) or nurture (learned, environmental forces) has more of an impact on personality development.

Nature's Arsenal: Genes

At the time each of us was conceived, we inherited twenty-three chromosomes from the sperm of our biological father and twenty-three chromosomes from the ovum of our biological mother. Those forty-six chromosomes lined themselves up into twenty-three matching pairs. Each chromosome contained thousands of **genes**, each possessing a piece of information that guided our development from embryo to maturity. These genes determined our hair colour, eye colour, hair type, height, and all our other physical characteristics.

The question researchers ask is, Do genes also determine aspects of personality, such as intelligence, sense of humour, and temperament? Or are these personality characteristics determined by environmental factors?

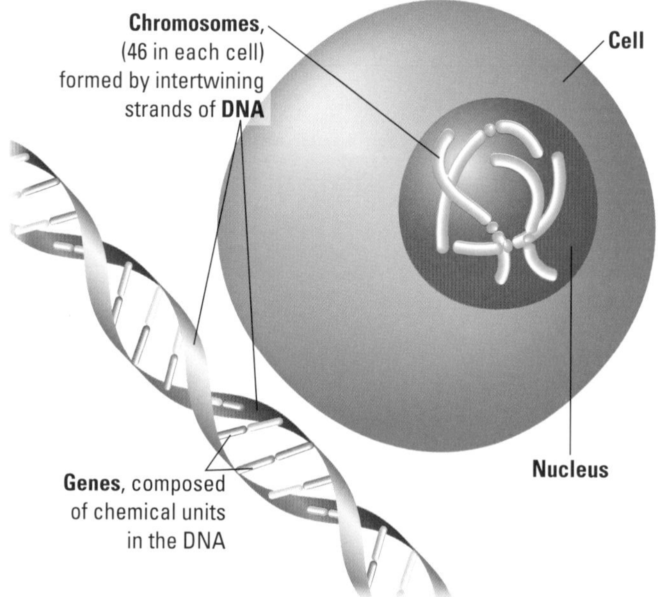

Figure 4.3 Scientists have yet to determine exactly which traits are determined by a person's genes.

Outside Agents: An Array of Factors

There is a rich and varied array of factors in the environment that play a role in personality development. They include the quality and quantity of time a parent spends with a child; the types of toys a child plays with; the amount of television and types of programs a child watches; and the attitudes and values of a child's playmates.

Exactly how these factors might shape a personality over time is the subject of Chapter 5 (see especially pages 123 to 129). For now, we briefly consider the role of one of them—"the media." Two of the most influential elements of the media are television and advertising. Consider this question as you read the facts below: How deeply has my personality been influenced by these media elements?

In September of 1999, the Canadian Pediatric Society (CPS) published a statement. It urged parents and physicians to better monitor children's television viewing habits. Dr. Peter Nieman, a Calgary pediatrician and the principal author of "Children and the Media," believes that it is important to have a powerful position on children's viewing because television has a strong influence on children's development and growth. It is not surprising that television viewing has a powerful effect on children, as the average Canadian child watches twenty-three hours of television a week. Some watch as much as five hours a day. What are the effects of this much television viewing on the development of children?

One negative effect is obesity, both because of inactivity and because of advertising that promotes unhealthy food. Another problem linked to frequent television viewing is an increase in violent behaviour. A third problem is poor academic performance—particularly in the area of reading. Finally, problems with social skills may arise because children are not interacting with other children.

Other critics of television take a more philosophical perspective. Journalist Richard Nilsen is most bothered by television's "secondhandedness" (Nilsen, 1999, J1). Nilsen believes that we need authentic experiences of our own from which to build our lives. He argues that, through television, we get second-hand the experiences of others instead. The more we watch, the less chance we have of fully realizing our own lives. Others share Nilsen's concerns. They believe that audiences wrapped up in the lives of characters on television do not live their own lives.

Another powerful media influence on behaviour is advertising. Part of the power of advertising comes from our society's very high level of exposure to ads. The American Anorexia Bulimia Association (AABA) estimates that the average North American sees or hears about 1500 advertisements a day (AABA, 1997). These ads are intended to, and do, have an enormous impact on behaviour. They encourage materialism and consumerism, creating a "me see, me want" attitude among North Americans. They also promote child sexuality, objectification of women and men, and an unattainable image of

INTERNET RESOURCES

What tips on media literacy can you find at each of the following Web sites?

The CBC: http://cbc.ca/

Media Watch: http://www.mediawatch.com

Canadian Pediatric Society: http://www.cps.ca

Canadian Anorexia-Bulemia Association: http://www.ams.queensu.ca

beauty. For example, in her 1997 book *Losing It: America's Obsession with Weight and the Industry That Feeds on It*, Laura Fraser notes that an average female model is five feet nine and a half inches (177 cm) tall. She weighs 123 pounds (56 kg), wears a size 6 or 8, and generally has too little body fat to menstruate. The average North American woman, on the other hand, is five feet four inches tall (163 cm), weighs 144 pounds (65 kg), and wears a size 12. These advertising images create in many women high levels of self-hate and frustration with their appearance. The AABA notes that 50 per cent of females and 35 per cent of males report dissatisfaction with their body image.

Television and advertising differ from many other factors in the environment in that we can control their impact. We can become "media literate"—that is, aware of and resistant to media influence. For parents, this involves finding out what their children are watching and reading and taking the time to watch and discuss TV programs with them. Parents can also limit the use of television as a diversion or "nanny" and not allow television sets in their children's bedrooms. By being good "television role models" themselves (for example, not watching during supper), media-literate parents can control the negative effects of media on their children's behaviour. For individuals, media literacy involves reducing the amount of time spent watching television. In its place, more time can be spent reading, being physically active, and interacting with others. With respect to advertising, media literacy requires us to keep in mind the following: the goal of advertising is to make us think we are not good enough as we are. We are made to believe that our lives will be better if we look a certain way or buy a certain product. Before making any purchase, we need to ask ourselves, "Is this something I *need*, or something I *want*." And then we have to answer the question honestly!

Case Study: The Boy Who Was Raised a Girl

David Reimer (originally named Bruce), from Winnipeg, Manitoba, was circumcised at eight months. Unfortunately, the surgery went horribly wrong and his penis was destroyed. David's parents decided to "reassign" his sex—two months before his second birthday he underwent castration and cosmetic surgery to construct an exterior vagina. Further surgery would be necessary to fabricate a more complete vagina as the toddler got older.

His parents renamed him Brenda and began to raise him as a girl. Pills containing **estrogen**, the female sex hormone, were prescribed for him at the age of eleven. At this time, his parents approached him about genital surgery, which he refused. When he was fourteen, he was told the truth about his identity and decided to immediately revert to being male. But the damage had been done, and David had suffered terribly as a result of his sexual reassignment.

Even as a small child, his taste in toys, his manner of play, the way he walked, and his appearance always differed from the other girls he played with. As well, he could never be "trained" to urinate sitting down. When he began school, he was treated as a misfit and had few friends. He was socially awkward and became sullen, anxious, and withdrawn. David struggled academically and ended up leaving school altogether and being tutored at home on the advice of his psychiatrist. David made two suicide attempts after learning the truth of his birth.

How can we explain David's experience? Sex reassignment is not common, but it does happen. Some babies are born with ambiguous genitalia, neither fully female nor fully male. Parents and doctors decide whether the child will be "made" into a male or female. In David's case, the recommendation for a sexual reassignment came from Dr. John Money. Money was an influential sex researcher with a Ph.D. from Harvard University, who practised at Johns Hopkins Hospital in Baltimore. Money believed that sexual identity is a result of environmental rather than biological factors—the way a child is treated, the toys a child is given, and the expectations parents have of a child. Money recommended that David's parents, his doctors in Winnipeg, and other adults in his life keep David's true sexual identity a secret from him. He believed keeping David ignorant of his background would help him successfully adjust to his life as a girl. It appears that Money's reputation intimidated David's Winnipeg doctors, who went along with the plan. They continued to do so despite evidence that David's sexual reassignment was not working.

David is now in his thirties, married with three children. John Colapinto has written a book about David's life, entitled *As Nature Made Him: The Boy Who Was Raised A Girl* (Harper Collins, 2000).

---

1. What is sex reassignment and why did David have to have the procedure?
2. What specific problems did David, as Brenda, have while growing up? Why do you think he had those problems?
3. What do you think David's parents did differently when they began raising him as a girl? What might they have done differently if David had been raised as a boy?
4. What evidence does this provide for the nature-nurture debate?

Nature, Nurture, and Canadian Society

The issue of whether nature or nurture is dominant in human development is not just important to researchers. It is an issue that can have enormous influence over the decision-makers who allocate resources to society. If nature controls human development, then corporate and government money should be spent on improving nature. For example, if mental illnesses such as schizophrenia are inherited, then it would make sense to fund screening programs that can alert adult carriers of the disease before they have children. On the other hand, if nurture is the primary influence on human development, then the spending focus should be on the environmental factors most important to development. For example, comprehensive early childhood education programs could be funded for all children to help improve their intelligence. These programs would provide valuable stimulation to very young children as they learn to read, write, do basic math, and participate in the arts and music.

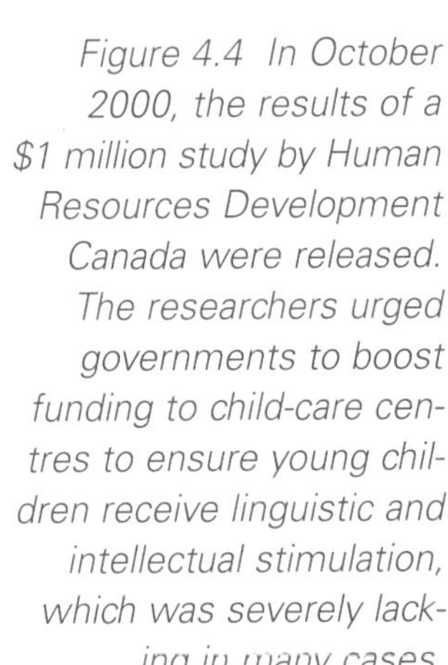

Figure 4.4 In October 2000, the results of a $1 million study by Human Resources Development Canada were released. The researchers urged governments to boost funding to child-care centres to ensure young children receive linguistic and intellectual stimulation, which was severely lacking in many cases.

The nature-nurture debate may be "solved" in the near future when **The Human Genome Project** is complete. Launched in 1989, The Human Genome Project is a multi-billion-dollar research endeavour aimed at identifying the location and function of all human genes. It is an international project, involving scientists from countries such as Canada, the United States, Australia, Brazil, France, Germany, and the United Kingdom. The project is expected to be complete in the year 2004. So far, the results of the project have been staggering. Tens of thousands of genes located in several of our chromosomes have been identified. These genes are linked to several specific disorders, including kidney disease, cancers, leukemia, hypertension, and diabetes. The discoveries so far can help researchers better understand not only these disorders, but also Alzheimer's disease and Down syndrome.

Two people who are not very enthusiastic about The Human Genome Project are Stanton Peele and Richard DeGrandpre. Their article, entitled "My Genes Made Me Do It," was published in the July 1995 issue of *Psychology Today*. Read the excerpt of this article which follows.

My Genes Made Me Do It

Just about every week now, we read a newspaper headline about the genetic basis for breast cancer, homosexuality, intelligence, or obesity. Such news stories may lead us to believe our lives are being revolutionized by genetic discoveries. In many cases, people are motivated to accept research in the hope of finding solutions for frightening problems, like breast cancer, that our society has failed to solve. At a personal level, accepting genetic causes for traits can relieve guilt about behaviour people want to change, but can't.

Meanwhile, genetic claims are being made for a host of ordinary and abnormal behaviours, from addiction to shyness and even to eventual divorce. If who we are is from conception, then our efforts to change or to influence our children may be futile. There may also be no basis for insisting that people behave themselves and conform to laws. Thus, the revolution in thinking about genes has monumental consequences for how we see ourselves as human beings.

Today, scientists are mapping the entire genome—the DNA contained in the 23 human chromosomes. This DNA may be divided into between 50 000 and 104 000 genes. But the same DNA can function in more than one gene, making the concept of individual genes something of a convenient fiction. The mystery of how these genes, and the chemistry underlying them, cause specific traits and diseases is a convoluted one.

The Human Genome project has, and will continue to, advance our understanding of genes and suggest preventive and therapeutic strategies for many diseases. Some diseases, like Huntington's, have been linked to a single gene. But the search for single genes for complex human traits, like **sexual orientation** or antisocial behaviour, or mental disorders like schizophrenia or depression, is seriously misguided.

Most claims linking emotional disorders and behaviours to genes are statistical in nature. For example, differences in the correlations in traits between **identical twins** (who inherit identical genes) and **fraternal twins** (who have half their genes in common) are examined by separating the role of environment from that of genes. But this goal is elusive. Research finds that identical twins are treated more alike than fraternal twins. These calculations are therefore insufficient in deciding that alcoholism or manic-depression is inherited, let alone television viewing, conservatism, and other basic, everyday traits for which such claims have been made.

1. Which areas of human development can we safely say have a biological or genetic basis? For which areas is there debate about their basis in biology (nature) or environment/society (nurture)?
2. Why do the authors question the findings of a biological basis for the latter areas?
3. Why do the authors believe a genetic explanation for behaviour appeals to many people?
4. If scientists prove that genes do control most human behaviour, how should we structure and run society differently?

RECAP

1. Explain in one or two sentences the essence of the nature-nurture debate.
2. Give two examples of environmental factors that make up our nurture. Give two examples of their influence.
3. Describe the type of evidence needed to support the nature side of the debate. Give examples of this evidence for specific cases of the debate.

Section 4.3

Abnormal Psychology

Focus Questions

- Which psychological disorders are linked to a problem with nature? Which are linked to nurture?
- What common myths and stereotypes are associated with mental illness?
- What are the major differences between neurotic disorders and psychotic disorders?

Key Concepts

psychological disorder
stereotyping
neurosis
agoraphobia
phobia
claustrophobia
obsessive-compulsive disorder
psychosis
delusions
hallucinations
antisocial personality disorder
empathy

Understanding Disorders

Simply stated, when someone has a **psychological disorder**, or disease of the mind, she or he finds it difficult to cope with the ordinary stresses of daily life. Such disorders have a variety of causes. For example, some psychological disorders can be caused by an error in nature, such as a chemical imbalance in the brain. Manic depression is one such disorder. Many psychological disorders seem to have a genetic component, in that diseases such as schizophrenia tend to run in families. Other mental illnesses can be caused by problems in the person's environment. For example, serious trauma or abuse, stemming from the environment, has been linked to dissociative disorders such as multiple personality disorder.

In many cases of psychological disorder, a person exhibits behaviour that is only slightly different from what is considered "normal." Only in the minority of cases do mentally ill people exhibit bizarre behaviour. It is these people, however, who are most visible in our society. Few as they are, their behaviour may cloud our understanding of mentally ill people.

People with psychological disorders have long been misunderstood. This has led to **stereotyping**—that is, we assume that all people who are mentally ill share the same characteristics. This is simply not true. The majority of people experiencing mental illness pose no threat to themselves, to others, or to society.

In centuries past, patients with psychological disorders were thought to be possessed by the devil or some other supernatural being. This was the case, for example, during the early Middle Ages in Europe. This belief led authorities to resort to extreme measures in dealing with their patients. People were subjected to all kinds of horrendous "therapies," including castration and transfusions of animal blood. While such brutality began to disappear in the late eighteenth and nineteenth centuries, some of the stereotypes associated with mental illness remain with us today.

Neurotic Disorders

There are two major categories of psychological disorders. The first category is called **neurosis**. People who are neurotic are extremely anxious or tense. They usually react with fear and dread to situations that many others consider non-threatening, such as crossing the street or going to school. People with neuroses may encounter difficulty in life but are generally able to manage their daily affairs. In this section, we look at three types of anxiety disorders: panic attacks, phobias, and obsessive-compulsive disorder.

Panic Attacks

Panic attacks are characterized by fear and intense physical and emotional anxiety. In extreme cases, a person suffering such an attack can pass out. Evelyne Michaels, a writer/broadcaster, had her first panic attack when she was in her mid-twenties. She was working as a television reporter in Toronto. She described her disease in the 1 January 1994 edition of *Chatelaine* magazine.

> I had never felt especially nervous about appearing on camera, but one day, as the crew was setting up for a taped interview, my heart began to race out of control, my stomach became knotted with fear, and my hands were wet and shaking. I felt certain that, if I didn't leave at once, I would faint or even die. I excused myself, saying I wasn't feeling well, and escaped home in a taxi. It was the beginning of a very dark year in my life.

INTERNET RESOURCES

What progress has been made to educate the public about mental illness? What still needs to be done? How well funded is the entire area of mental health? Find out by visiting the Canadian Mental Health Association Web site at

http://www.cmha.ca

> Within a few months, I changed from a happy, independent, outgoing confident person into someone who could rarely leave home because I was terrified of having more attacks. I quit my job to see if an extended rest would help, but the attacks became more intense, soon occurring several times a day. I could go out for short drives if my husband went with me, but the farther from home we got, the worse I felt. So, I stayed home more and more—there, at least, I had no attacks.

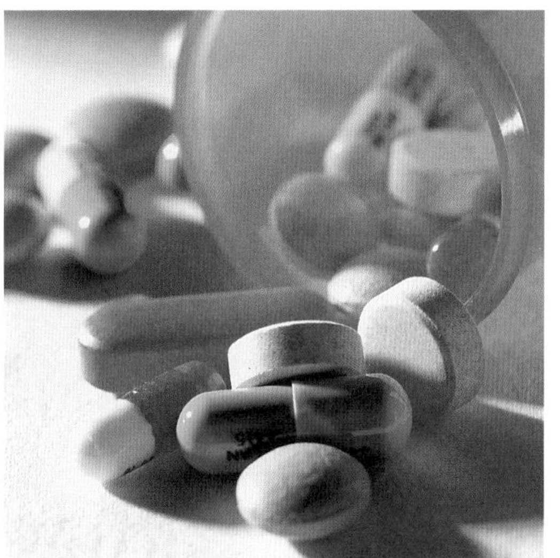

Figure 4.5 Medications for panic attacks include those that block the transmission of the brain protein CCK and those that alter the levels of the brain chemical serotonin.

> For months, the farthest I ventured alone was to a newspaper box one block away. After I saw my fourth doctor in six months, my problem was identified as a panic disorder, along with **agoraphobia**, a fear of leaving home. It took nearly a year of treatment, including medication and therapy, before the condition was under control, and I was able to rejoin the rest of the world.

Panic attacks can strike almost anyone occasionally. Someone who has panic attacks four or more times within a month is considered to be suffering from a panic disorder. Doctors believe that panic disorders affect about 2 to 4 per cent of the population, often starting in early adulthood. In most cases, symptoms abate within a few minutes to a few hours, but leave the sufferer terrified of having another attack. This sets up a vicious cycle of symptoms, fear, and more symptoms.

Many anxiety disorders strike women and men in equal numbers, but more women than men experience panic disorders (with or without agoraphobia). Some researchers estimate that panic disorders are two to three times more common in women. Dr. Cheryl Rowe, an assistant professor of psychiatry at the University of Toronto, says some male cases may go unreported because men are less likely to seek medical help. Women are also more prone to generalized anxiety disorder, which causes prolonged worrying for exaggerated reasons. Why are women vulnerable to these disorders? According to Dr. Rowe, it is because they are more likely to be exposed to abuse, poverty, and powerlessness. This adds to their stress.

Research suggests that anxiety disorders such as panic attacks may be linked to subtle imbalances in brain chemistry. New Canadian research by Dr. Jacques Bradwejn, director of psychopharmacology at St. Mary's Hospital Centre in Montreal, has found that people with a panic disorder are significantly more sensitive to a brain protein—cholecystokinin (CCK)—than other people. "We've recently developed a drug that blocks the transmission of CCK in the brain," he says. The drug is now being tested.

Other experts caution that we should not jump to any conclusions about the causes of these disorders. Psychiatrist Richard Swinson, director of the anxiety disorders clinic at the Clarke Institute of Psychiatry in Toronto, says, "So far, we can't point to any single cause. It's likely that a combination of factors—biological, genetic, psychological, and social—are involved." He estimates that at least 10 per cent of Canadians suffer from one or more anxiety disorders.

For treatment, most experts recommend a combination of therapy and medication. Cognitive therapy can help identify certain thoughts that may trigger or intensify symptoms. Cognitive therapy teaches patients that the symptoms they fear, such as passing out, are exaggerated. The patient can then stop waiting for the symptoms to happen. Behavior therapy helps patients learn how to face the feared situation and accept that they will survive it. For example, a person who has suffered panic attacks on a public bus would be taken to a bus with another person for support. Eventually, after spending time at the feared location with support, the person would be able to manage the situation alone. Tranquilizers are also sometimes prescribed to help control anxiety symptoms when the disorder is at its most active. But tranquilizers are addictive and are prescribed for no longer than six weeks to two months. For longer treatment of up to a year or so, Dr. Swinson recommends antidepressant drugs. These drugs alleviate anxiety symptoms by altering levels of a brain chemical called serotonin.

Phobias

Phobias are another type of neurosis. Simply put, a **phobia** is an irrational, often debilitating fear. When a fear is irrational, it has no basis in reality. Take **claustrophobia**—a fear of enclosed spaces—for example. People suffering from this disorder may honestly believe they are going to suffocate, even though there is plenty of oxygen in the room or area. Phobias can be debilitating in the sense that the person's fear may interfere with their ability to lead a "normal" life. A fear of flying, for example, may prevent a person from accepting a job requiring air travel. In this case, the person's phobia has become debilitating and would require treatment.

Another of many examples of debilitating phobias is social phobia. Social phobia is an intense fear of saying or doing something wrong when around other people. Brenda Richter of Mississauga, Ontario, suffered from this disorder from the time she was a child. The fifty-two-year-old retired nurse says that at certain times in her life she was so debilitated that she could not even talk to friends on the telephone. Her phobia also caused her great anxiety at work, particularly when she encountered very assertive doctors. The part of her work she dreaded the most, however, was meetings. If she had to speak at a meeting, she would literally fall apart. On one occasion, both her arms went completely numb from fear. Despite her social phobia, she did not consult a doctor for diagnosis and treatment until she was forty-six years old.

Treatment for phobias can include exposure therapy, which involves gradually confronting the dreaded situation or object. Relaxation techniques, such as deep-breathing exercises, can reduce anxiety and even cure some phobias relatively quickly.

Figure 4.6 Participants in Northwest Airlines' Program for Anxious Flyers learn about the flight deck during an aircraft tour.

Obsessive-Compulsive Disorder

Obsessive-compulsive disorder (OCD) can be a crippling and difficult-to-treat neurosis. OCD is characterized by behaviour that is obsessed with exactness and symmetry. A person suffering from OCD feels that something awful will happen if he or she does not repeat routine behaviours. Examples of such behaviours include turning the lights off and on twenty times, or checking and rechecking that the doors are locked. These rituals often involve counting, tapping, touching, or ritualized blinking, but often include ordering and arranging as well. One thirty-year-old patient reported that she had to check that the stove was turned off ten or twenty times before leaving the house. She also had counting rituals such as filling and emptying the kettle three times before boiling water. She felt that if she did not do these things she might harm someone. The obsession is the recurring thought, while the compulsion is the uncontrollable behaviour.

The article "Science Puts Love to the Test" (*The Toronto Star*, 14 January 1999) reported on an Italian study comparing the brains of people suffering from obsessive-compulsive disorder with those of students who claimed to be in love. A pattern of brain cells common to both groups was discovered. In particular, the blood of both sets of subjects showed a 40 per cent loss of a specific protein. This protein helps the chemical serotonin travel from one nerve cell to another. The nerve cells that produce the serotonin are concentrated in a particular area of the brain. Serotonin travels from this area to shape awareness of pain, emotions, and sexual behaviour.

OCD affects anywhere from one to two in every hundred people. It can arise from damage to the brain (caused by, for example, an autoimmune infection), head injury, or carbon monoxide poisoning. A 1997 study in Volume 33 of the *Medical Post* found that 11 per cent of children who suffered a traumatic head injury developed OCD symptoms within one year. OCD can also be inherited (passed on by genes) or acquired as a result of environmental factors.

OCD can be treated with drugs that activate serotonin, the brain's neurotransmitter. These drugs may help to suppress symptoms, but can take six to ten weeks to become effective. In most cases, behaviour therapy and psychotherapy are also necessary to treatment. These therapies help sufferers to understand and resist their compulsive actions and to confront their fears.

Figure 4.7 In the 1997 film As Good As It Gets, *the character Melvin Udall exhibits several neurotic symptons. He has phobias about germs (throwing away pairs of gloves and bars of soap after one use, bringing his own plastic cutlery to restaurants) and stepping on sidewalk cracks. His OCD symptoms include daily breakfast at the same restaurant and keeping different colours of M&Ms in separate glass canisters.*

Psychotic Disorders

A more debilitating form of mental illness is **psychosis**. People who are psychotic often lose touch with the real world. They have their own perceptions of reality that are quite different from those shared by most people. For example, a psychotic person may witness a traffic accident and believe that it was caused by her own "bad" thoughts. Some people with psychoses may experience **delusions**—beliefs in something despite all rational evidence to the contrary. Some psychotic disorders also result in people experiencing **hallucinations**—they see or hear something that is not really there.

Antisocial Personality Disorder

Although it is relatively rare, antisocial personality disorder (ASP) can pose a grave danger to others. Most serial rapists and killers are believed to have ASP. **Antisocial personality disorder**, also referred to as sociopathy, is defined in the latest *Diagnostic and Statistical Manual* as a lifelong "pervasive pattern" of rule breaking and violating the rights of others that begins before age fifteen. People with ASP are chronic troublemakers whose symptoms vary greatly in severity: they can be constant money borrowers, pathological liars, white-collar criminals, or, at the most severe end of the continuum, murderous felons. They are impulsive, grandiose, and poor self-observers who do not learn from punishment. They blame others for their problems and see themselves as victims. Their primary hallmark is a striking inability to feel empathy or guilt. **Empathy** refers to the ability to understand or experience the thoughts or feelings of other people. This characteristic is evident in the fact that serial killers often strangle their victims. Strangling requires the killer to be in direct contact with the victim as she or he dies.

Given the often horrendous nature of their crimes, we expect people suffering from ASP to look different from the rest of us. Most often, however, they look like any average person. This, unfortunately, allows them to approach their victims without causing alarm. Canadian serial killer Clifford Olsen, profiled in the case study on page 94, was described as looking and acting relatively normal. Indeed, it is this normal appearance of sociopaths that helps them to elude the police for so long.

People suffering from ASP also have calm and controlled personalities. They seldom lose their tempers; in fact, little seems to bother them. This may be another reason why they appear "normal" and do not arouse suspicion. Yet it may also be the one thing that leads to their capture. Serial killers are calm and controlled because they have an unrealistic belief that they won't be caught. This sense of inevitability may eventually cause them to make a mistake.

According to a national study of psychiatric disorders in the United States in 1999, approximately eight times as many men as women have ASP. No scientific conclusions have been reached as to why. Some theories link the potential for ASP to the Y chromosome or the male sex hormone testosterone. Others link it to cultural influences that encourage violence in men.

Case Study: Clifford Olsen

Clifford Olsen is perhaps the most notorious and reviled criminal in Canadian history. In 1981, Olsen confessed to murdering eight girls and three boys ranging in age from nine to eighteen. He claims that he has actually killed as many as fifty people across Canada and in seven American states. People tend to believe him, but they have no evidence to link him to other murders, and Olsen has not supplied them with any. He is presently serving a life sentence.

Is Olsen a classic sociopath? He certainly appears to possess the characteristics. Olsen claims to have had a normal, happy childhood, yet he admits to being raped by an uncle when he was four years old. By the time he was six, Olsen was stealing property from neighbours' homes. This marked the start of Olsen's life of crime. He has spent most of his life in prison, enjoying short doses of freedom only in 1964, 1972–1973, 1978, and 1980–1981. His lawyer estimates that during these periods, Olsen may have committed one sexual offence and seven property crimes *daily*, as well as one murder *per month*.

Like the classic sociopath, Olsen always looked and acted relatively normal. He lured children into his car by stopping to ask where the local employment office was. He would then scold them for talking to a stranger, present his business card, and offer them a job washing windows for ten dollars an hour. He was always well-dressed and courteous. And the children were not afraid.

Figure 4.8 When journalist Peter Worthington first saw Clifford Olsen at the Kingston Penitentiary in 1990, he was struck by Olsen's lively, vibrant manner, unlike that of other long-term inmates.

---

1. What characteristics of antisocial personality disorder has Olsen displayed?
2. What elements in Olsen's environment (or nurture) might be related to his sociopathy?

The Causes of ASP

The search for causes of ASP gives rise to the usual debate between nature and nurture. An article by Debbie Seaman, published in *Time* magazine on 27 December 1999, reviewed the latest research. Some studies have found links between ASP and insufficient bonding between infants and mothers, an abusive childhood, or an impoverished home environment. But increasingly, research is focusing on biological factors. Studies have shown that identical twins have a dramatically higher chance of sharing ASP than do fraternal twins. Adrian Raine, a neuroscientist at the University of Southern California, found that the brains of people with ASP look different from those of the rest of the population. Specifically, their brains have less grey matter in the prefrontal cortex (the part of the brain that regulates behaviour and social judgment). As well, University of Iowa neurobiologist Antonio Damasio found that early brain injuries affect a person's long-term ability to distinguish between right and wrong. And Thomas Thompson, a forensic psychologist from New Mexico, insists that people with ASP are "hardwired to act out" and "lack free will."

At present, there is no effective treatment for antisocial personality disorder. Though certain medications can curb individual symptoms like aggression and impulsiveness, there are no drugs that can guarantee someone with ASP will stop hurting others. Some psychologists believe that psychotherapy and parent training can help. Others believe that if the behaviour is not caught and dealt with before adolescence, there's little hope of making significant change.

Case Study: A Tale of Two Sociopaths

In 1995, two notorious criminals shocked Canadians with the brutally violent nature of their crimes and their apparent lack of remorse. Paul Bernardo was convicted that year for the sexual torture and murders of Kristen French and Leslie Mahaffy. His ex-wife, Karla Homolka, participated in these crimes.

There is evidence that Bernardo was responsible for at least forty other rapes in the Scarborough area. This includes the rape and murder of Homolka's sixteen-year-old sister Tammy. He has been declared a dangerous offender, and may never be released from prison. He is currently serving a life sentence at Kingston Penitentiary.

Homolka testified against her husband in return for a plea-bargained sentence of twelve years for her part in the crimes. She claimed to be an abused wife who only participated in the crimes because her husband demanded it. Many people are critical of Homolka's plea bargain. They point to evidence on videotapes that shows Homolka as a sociopath in her own right, taking pleasure in the crimes. Homolka is eligible for early release from prison in 2001. In 1999, she applied for a weekend pass from prison to meet her family for a private, prolonged visit. Although her application was denied, the fact that she applied for such a release at all triggered a storm of public outrage.

Should Homolka have been granted this privilege? In the remainder of this case study, two opposing viewpoints are expressed.

Arguing Against Homolka

In a *Toronto Star* article dated 4 November 1999, correspondent Rosie DiManno argued that Homolka should not be granted the privilege of a weekend pass. Her article is excerpted below.

Figure 4.9 Karla Homolka leaves the St. Catharines provincial courthouse after the first day of her manslaughter trail in 1993.

"I revolt at the concept of Karla as a compassionate, courageous and generous woman ... it must be so easy for the former Mrs. Paul Bernardo to reinvent herself behind bars. That persona—the battered, traumatized, horrendously abused spouse—was planted in the public's mind over the summer of '95 by Crown Attorney Ray Houlihan, the man tasked with resurrecting this admitted killer and sexual predator as a credible star witness against Bernardo. All of this was made necessary because police did not find, in time, those grotesque videotapes that would have precluded any 'deal with the devil,' nor necessitated the cooperation of Homolka ...

"She's quick on her feet, our Karla. Intellectually dexterous ... We know that Karla has adeptly bamboozled the system, for years, by promoting herself as a victim, on the same level of violation as the murdered Kristen French and Leslie Mahaffy. We know that Karla has been making an effort to create herself anew, by obtaining a university degree behind bars. We know from Karla's mother that Homolka has also been participating in self-help programs. Perhaps, in a system already philosophically inclined toward a blind faith in rehabilitation, the acquiescence of experts—such as those who testified in court four years ago—is understandable. But what little faith I had in the inexact science of psychology has long since been shattered.

"Karla is a psychopath. She has no conscience. She has no remorse. She adopts personalities to fit the situation, and the battered spouse syndrome was presented to her on a silver platter by the crown at Bernardo's murder trial in the summer of '95. It mattered not, apparently, to the prosecutors, that this construct was an insult and a travesty to all the women who have indeed been traumatized by their despotic mates. If Karla was battered—and there is physical evidence of a vicious beating—she was more compliant masochist than trapped victim. Lord knows she fled the moment she felt Bernardo might kill her too. Homolka has a finely cultivated sense of self-preservation. Karla is an unrepentant sadist. But most of the professionals who have probed her byzantine brain have concluded otherwise. Karla has successfully promoted herself as the victim bride ...

"Karla has always portrayed her vulnerability, her poignant need for acceptance. Her oft-stated version of events has become the accepted premise in too many quarters: that she was under Bernardo's spell, under his thumb, almost from the beginning of their relationship. But what evidence is there of that? Only Karla's word. Her oral testimony in court, the interviews with psychiatrists in hospital before she was sent to prison, the narrative she has spun. In her own words, as written in the hundreds of notes she gave to her husband before and after the big, splashy wedding—which she told the shrinks was all Paul's idea, she never wanted such a spectacle—Karla never so much as hinted at such a miserable existence. She was the one extolling Paul's virtues, she was the one furious at her parents for attempting to delay the nuptials, she was the one aggrieved that Tammy's death had thrown a wrench in her plans for a bridal blast. This was the girl under Bernardo's control?

"There's a big, skeptical world out there where people are not so easily inclined to embrace such a sympathetic scenario. But the public, rightly enraged, has a place in this debate, too. A prison sentence is not just about rehabilitating the offender. It's also society's way to express aversion and contempt for the nature of an offence. There is a place in our system for moral indignation. It's called crime and punishment. It seems we are to congratulate Karla for the great strides she's made, in the face of so much public repugnance. But I revolt at the concept of Karla as a compassionate, courageous and generous woman. This, the same woman who claimed to have gone upstairs to blow-dry her hair after Bernardo strangled Kristen French. This, the same woman who kept the video camera rolling as Bernardo raped 14-year-old Leslie Mahaffy, the child beseeching her for mercy. This is a woman of kindness and valour? Jesus wept."

Excerpted from: DiManno, Rosie. 1999. "The Queen of Cunning." *The Toronto Star*. 4 November 1999.

Arguing in Support of Homolka

The following article, also appearing in the *Toronto Star* on 4 November 1999, was written by Kerry Gillespie and Michelle Shephard. They summarize the arguments of Homolka's mother, Dorothy, in support of granting Homolka an unescorted weekend pass from prison.

"Karla Homolka's mother says her daughter deserves another chance. 'I believe one chance—and if anything happened, then throw away the key. But I know that would not happen,' Dorothy Homolka said yesterday, insisting her daughter feels remorse for her crimes.

"Karla Homolka, 29, has served half of a 12-year sentence for her part in the slayings of Ontario teenagers Leslie Mahaffy and Kristen French. Her ex-husband Paul Bernardo was convicted of first-degree murder for the Mahaffy and French slayings and is now serving a life sentence. The two were also involved in the fatal drugging and rape of Homolka's young sister, Tammy. 'I know the Frenches and Mahaffys went through hell, but people don't think of the hell that our family went through as well,' Dorothy Homolka said. 'I lost a daughter, too.'

"Reminders of Tammy's death and Karla's crimes are constant, she said. Yesterday, Karla Homolka was back in the news again—this time for a federal court challenge she has launched to try to get escorted day passes from the Quebec prison where she is being held. The warden at the Joliette prison for women turned down an earlier request for the passes, which Homolka wanted so she could meet with her family outside the prison. Documents contained in Homolka's appeal application and other prison records offered a rare glimpse Tuesday into her life behind bars. But yesterday, a publication ban was imposed on them. Homolka's prison progress reports are protected by federal privacy laws, Pascal Lescarbeau, Homolka's lawyer, said last night. Homolka's mother says she hopes Karla will win her appeal to give her a chance to visit with her daughter outside the prison walls. 'She still wouldn't be (alone) on the street and people don't realize that.'

Figure 4.10 A photograph published in Canadian newspapers on 22 September 2000 caused a public outcry over what appeared to be the soft treatment Homolka was receiving in prison.

"But for Debbie Mahaffy and Donna French, mothers of the slain girls, the idea of Homolka leaving prison after six years in custody is hard to accept. 'I think the warden is absolutely correct. She's not ready to be out,' Mahaffy said yesterday. 'She needs to do some more work, but I don't know if there is ever enough work that can be accomplished by her. There is no remorse, there's nothing there but attitude,' she said of the handwritten application Homolka submitted to request the passes. 'It's just as if someone has told me my daughter has died all over again.' Mahaffy stayed at home from work yesterday. French carried on, working late, under the caring eyes of co-workers. 'I do feel she is a danger if she's let out,' Kristen's mother said last night. With a letter of reassurance from Corrections Canada that the families will be notified of any decision of Homolka's release, sent just last month, lawyer Tim Danson said yesterday he was dismayed that they had not been notified of the latest developments. And it's learning about it second-hand that hits hardest, French said. 'You're caught off guard and you automatically end up back on the roller coaster again.' But Corrections Canada spokesperson Linda Mariotti said yesterday that victims' families are only informed before an actual release, not a request for a release.

"Homolka has been eligible for parole since 1997. In July, 2001, she will have served two-thirds of her sentence and be eligible for release. And she'll need some partial integration into the community before any release, her mother says. 'She does need to know how she's going to be treated by the public, and I don't think she has an unrealistic view of how she's going to be treated,' Dorothy Homolka said. She says she understands and accepts that the Mahaffy and French families will never be able to forgive Karla. 'I haven't come to terms with the death of my daughter and I haven't come to terms with [Bernardo's] part, so why should the Frenches and Mahaffys come to terms with Karla's part in it?' But she says she has learned, through therapy, to forgive Karla. 'I think the only reason I have, is because I knew—or thought I knew—Bernardo. The control he had over friends—he had the police completely bamboozled and us. So what does a 17-year-old girl have in defence? So she was very stupid. Knowing the type of person she always was and is now, I've come to terms with it.

"'I think she deserves a chance just like everybody else. It was a horrendous crime, but she got her sentence and she's doing it,' she said. Most people just aren't willing to believe anything good about Karla, her mother added. 'It doesn't matter if she comes out and says sorry specifically like that, then it's twisted around.' And while Mahaffy can find no forgiveness for Karla, she has plenty of sympathy for her mother. 'I can't imagine the pain she's gone through, to lose two daughters the way she has.' Karla is taking various self-help courses and doing everything available to her in prison to better herself and learn skills, her mother said. While Mahaffy supports this type of rehabilitation, she is enraged by the availability of these courses to Homolka and not to victims of crime. 'The number of courses . . . I haven't been able to take and they're not available for other victims of crime who have terrible feelings of guilt that they couldn't save their child from the likes of her.'

"Dorothy Homolka says her family is once again bracing for the barrage of threats that come every time her daughter is in the news. 'It's not that I want sympathy from people, just a recognition that Tammy was a victim. They talk about the two all the time and Tammy is left out.' She said she speaks with her daughter once a week and sees her every two months, except during the winter, when the weather makes it too difficult to travel to Quebec. She said she supports her daughter's decision not to move back home."

Excerpted from: Gillespie, Kerry, Shephard, Michelle. 1999. "Dorothy Homolka: Mother Supports Daughter's Campaign." *The Toronto Star*. 4 November 1999.

1. What reasons does Rosie DiManno have for wanting to keep Homolka in jail as long as possible?
2. Why does Homolka's mother Dorothy feel that her daughter deserves a second chance?
3. Which side of this issue do you most agree with? Why?

RECAP

1. What are the two main categories of psychological disorders? What are the major differences between them?
2. Explain how both nature and nurture might contribute to the occurrence of anxiety disorders.
3. Explain how both nature and nurture might contribute to the occurrence of sociopathy.

Section 4.4

Gender and Our Sense of Self

Focus Questions

- How are gender differences distinct from gender roles?
- What difficulties do both men and women face moving into non-traditional gender areas?
- Why is it important to keep challenging our beliefs about appropriate gender roles?

Key Concepts

gender differences
gender roles
corpus callosum
consensus model
glass ceiling
slapstick humour
gallows humour
irony
incongruity

What are little boys made of?
What are little boys made of?
Frogs and snails
And puppy dogs' tails,
That's what little boys are made of.

What are little girls made of?
What are little girls made of?
Sugar and spice
And all that's nice,
That's what little girls are made of.

—Anonymous

Does this childhood poem create gender differences in our society or merely reflect them?

Gender Attitudes

One aspect of our identity that has a significant impact on our sense of self is our gender. Think about it. The first question many people ask following the birth of a baby is, "Is it a boy or a girl?" From that point on, the infant's experience is inextricably tied up with her or his gender.

The **gender differences** that exist between males and females are obvious: males and females possess different physical characteristics and they may have different abilities. In the past, gender differences were used to slot boys and girls into the rigid categories of **gender roles**. Boys were expected to be tough and independent, and not to express their feelings. Girls, on the other hand, were expected to be feminine, emotional, and dependent on others. Until recently, gender roles went beyond simple expectations for behaviour. Ideas about suitable careers, parenting styles, and household responsibilities were shaped by these gender roles. Girls were expected to work either as nurses (but *not* as doctors) or with children (for example, as teachers). Furthermore, it was expected among the middle and upper classes that young women would only work until they got married and had children. It was automatically assumed that they would be the parent to stay home to raise the children and perform the household tasks that would keep the family's life running smoothly (among the lower classes, most women have always had to work regardless of marital status). Boys, on the other hand, had several careers from which to choose. Jobs involving physical strength, such as police work or firefighting, became the exclusive domain of men. It was assumed most boys would marry and have a family of their own, but their careers would not be expected to end with the birth of a child. They would not be expected to come home from work and cook supper for the family.

Times have changed, however, and gender roles are much less rigid today. Rarely does anyone argue that women lack the skills to be excellent engineers, or that men do not possess the qualities it takes to be effective primary school teachers. Yet when males or females try to move into areas that are outside traditional gender roles, they still may face suspicion and open hostility. The following example, excerpted from Volume 15 of *Today's Parent* (1 June 1998), illustrates the bias that exists against men who want to take care of very small children.

Figure 4.11 Some people believe that if more men were employed in early childhood education, the pay would improve, resulting in even more male employment in the field. In 1995, about 35 per cent of primary teachers in Canada were male.

> When David Clarke asked a home daycare agency about becoming one of their caregivers, he got the runaround. Clarke, of Thornhill, Ontario, had been at home full-time with his children for several months, and before that had looked after them part-time for several years due to his irregular work schedule as a restaurant manager. After several requests for an application form, he realized that they were not going to give him one—because he was a man. 'They finally admitted that they didn't want me to go through the trouble and expense of fire and police checks and then not be able to place any children with me.'
>
> Clarke didn't think this was fair and it wasn't—they could have at least given him the application form. However, the agency's concern about not being able to place children with him may have been well founded, and reflects the way our society often regards fathers—second best when it comes to caring for children. This is hardly surprising. Mothers have always been preeminent in this area. So it's going to take more than a generation or two of more-involved fathers to change attitudes.

The Early Impact of Gender

From birth, people respond to babies in a manner that they feel is consistent with the babies' gender. Studies with infants show that the pitch of adults' voices, the way they handle a baby, and the words they choose to describe a baby change depending on the baby's gender. In one study, a male infant is in a room dressed in pink clothing. Both men and women who entered the room picked up the baby gently, talked about how pretty and dainty the baby was, and spoke in a high, soft voice. Then the same baby was dressed in blue clothing, and another group of adults came into the room. This time the baby was described as being big, healthy, and strapping, and the pitch of the adults' voices was much lower.

Figure 4.12 To the extent that boys and girls are treated differently, *from birth, because of gender, it is hard to determine whether gender differences are innate (biological), or a result of the environment (learned).*

Gender Differences in Our Brains

Researchers have found subtle neurological differences between women's and men's brains. These differences involve both the brain's structure and its functioning.

For example, the following tendencies have been noted:

- More men than women are left-handed.
- More men than women favour the right ear when listening; more women then men listen equally with both ears.
- More men than women excel at rotating three-dimensional objects in their heads.
- More women than men prove better at reading the emotions of people in photographs.

Of course, not all men and women fit into these generalizations. Otherwise, women could never read maps and men would always be left-handed. But certain researchers have theorized from these generalizations that, in men's brains, the right hemisphere is dominant.

Another theory, based on such research, involves the **corpus callosum**—a thick bundle of nerves that allows the right half of the brain to communicate with the left. Some researchers hypothesize that the corpus callosum is larger in women than in men. If it is, and if size corresponds to function, then communication between the hemispheres will be easier in women's brains than in men's. This might explain the fact that many females have very good intuition, or the ability to read emotional clues.

Since the size of the corpus callosum varies dramatically with both age and health, we must be careful drawing such conclusions. Autopsies provide little help because brain tissue undergoes dramatic changes in the hours immediately after death. But the following studies do provide some intriguing results.

Neuroanatomist Laura Allen and neuroendocrinologist Roger Gorski of the University of California at Los Angeles studied the corpus callosum by obtaining brain scans from live, apparently healthy people. In their investigation of 146 subjects, published in April 1992, they confirmed that parts of the corpus callosum were up to 23 per cent wider in women than in men. They also measured thicker connections between the two hemispheres in other parts of women's brains. Neuro-psychologist Cecile Naylor, of the Bowman Gray Medical School in Winston-Salem, North Carolina, determined in 1988 that men and women enlist widely varying parts of their brain when asked to spell words. By monitoring increases in blood flow, Naylor found that women use both sides of their head when spelling, while men use primarily their left side. Because the area activated on the right side is used in understanding emotions, the women apparently tap a wider range of experience for their task. However, this effect occurred only with spelling and not during a memory test. Similar studies have confirmed this more equal distribution of women's language

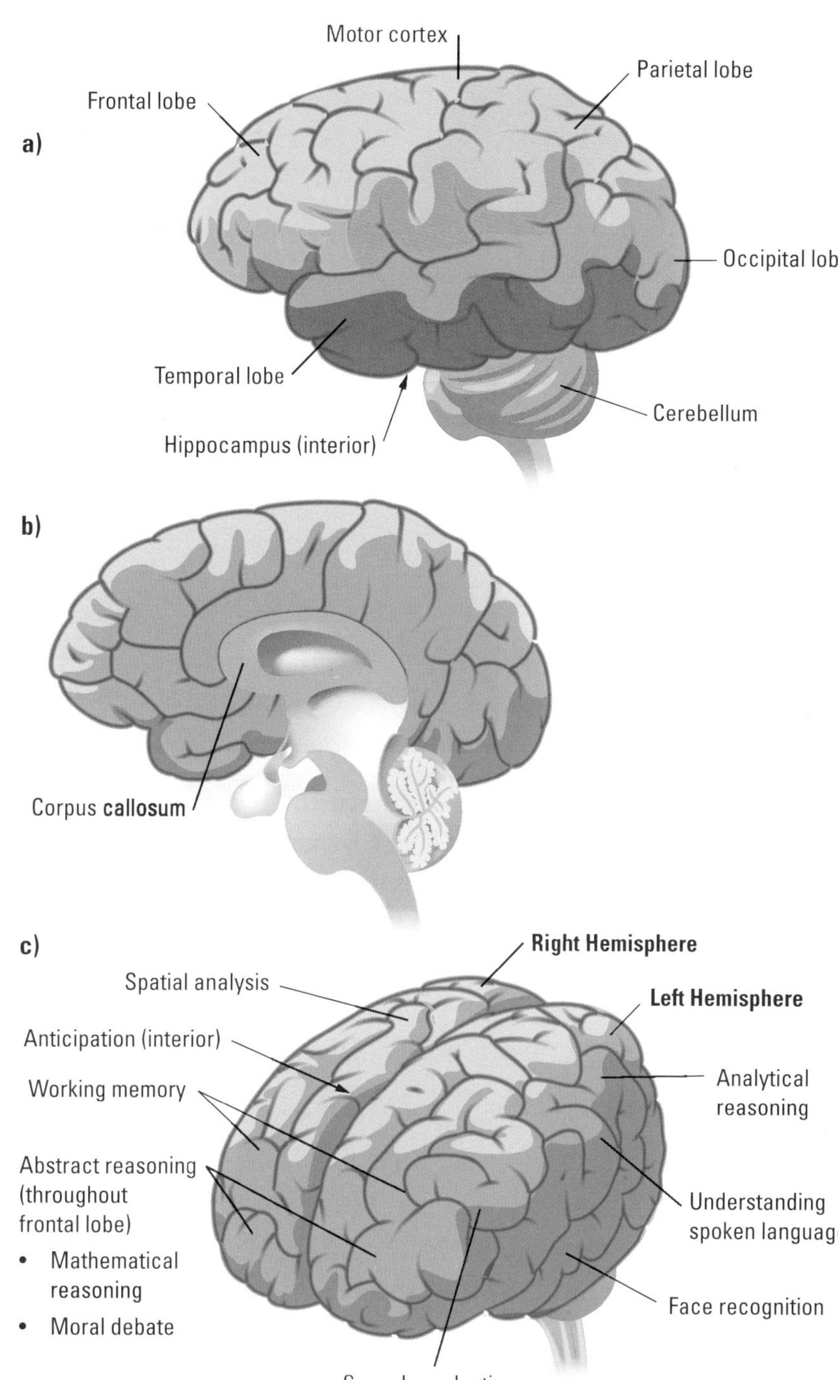

Figure 4.13 a) The parts of the brain. b) Cross-section showing where the corpus callosum connects the two hemispheres. c) Regions where different types of thinking occur.

Figure 4.14 MRI technology makes brain scans and images available to researchers.

ispheres. This ien's left hemi- or injury. archers specu- mmunication between the two sides of the brain could impair a woman's performance of certain visual-spatial tasks. For example, the ability to tell directions on a map without physically having to rotate it appears stronger in those individuals whose brains restrict the process to the right hemisphere. Any crosstalk between the two sides apparently distracts the brain from its job. Sure enough, several studies have shown that this mental-rotation skill is indeed more tightly focused in men's brains than in women's. For example, a German study in March 2000 (Sheppard, 2000, 47) used brain-imaging to confirm that men used the left hippocampus (see Figure 4.13) to navigate through a virtual-reality maze. Women, who completed the task in slower time, tended to use more of the parietal and prefontal areas of both hemispheres (linked to visual clues and reasoning).

The emerging conclusion from these studies is that men's and women's brains are different at several levels, right down to chemical activity and how cells are organized. Psychiatrist and neuroscientist Sandra Witelson, in a 1 May 2000 *Maclean's* article entitled "How We Think," summed up the differences between women's and men's brain thus: "It is like two different automobiles. Each has a motor, a steering mechanism, and brakes. But one is a Volvo and the other is a Lexus—and I'm not for an instant implying which sex is which" (Sheppard, 2000, 47).

Skill Development: Locating and Selecting Information

To produce the *Maclean's* article "How We Think," writer Robert Sheppard had to locate and select information. Locating information involves searching for appropriate sources on a topic. The selection process involves asking questions about the relevance of the information found. Social scientists use these skills to produce research essays in which they develop a position or opinion on a topic.

Let's take an example. Suppose you wanted to locate and select information for a research essay on "The Biological and Cultural Factors Determining Gender Identity and Roles in Canadian Society."

Step 1

A good first source for research is an encyclopedia. Encyclopedias provide concise overviews of topics. Many encyclopedias are available in print and online. Looking up keywords in an encyclopedia directs you to encyclopedia articles. At this starting point in your research, you should select only general articles on the topic. You can always come back to more specific articles once you have developed your understanding of the topic.

- *Example of a print search:* Look up "gender identity" in an *Index* volume of the *Encylopedia Britannica*. You are directed to a main entry, and the other keywords "sex role" and "sexuality" are suggested.
- *Example of an online search:* Access the *Encyclopedia Britannica*'s Web site at http://www.eb.com
  If your school has a subscription, click on "College, School, Library & Business users." If not, click on "FREE for 14 days" to register as a temporary subscriber. Then go back to the "Free Trial Sign-Up Form" and click on "Try a 'sample search'." Enter "gender identity" in the SEARCH screen. The results of clicking on SEARCH are 1727 articles. Click on "enter here" (as a subscriber) and click on "gender identity" to bring up the article. You may also want to bring up hot button articles (for example, sex role), another INDEX ENTRY (for example, human behavioural development), and RELATED TOPICS (for example, personal identity under "more general").

Step 2

Your second set of sources should be books on the topic. Find general books by searching your school library catalogue using broad keywords. Find specialist books after learning basic information and definitions relating to the topic. For example:

- Search the catalogue using "human behaviour" as a broad keyword to find the general book
  Ramachandran, V.S. *Human Behaviour.* San Diego, CA, Academic Press, 1994.
  This source consists of four volumes of alphabetically arranged entries about human behaviour.
- Search the catalogue using "gender identity" to find the specialist book
  Bullough, Bonnie, Bullough, Vern L., Elias, James. *Gender Blending.* Amherst, NY, Prometheus Books, 1997.
  This source deals with subjects as specific as gender identity, transsexualism, and transvestitism.

Step 3

Your third set of sources should be periodicals—popular or scholarly magazines that come out regularly. Writers of periodical articles frequently assume that the reader is familiar with the topic. Examples of periodicals with stimulating social science articles include *Maclean's, Newsweek, Time, Psychology Today, Parenting Magazine,* and *People.* Many periodical articles can be accessed online. For example:

- EBSCO at
  http://search.epnet.com

ProQuest at
http://www.umi.com/proquest
Electric Library at
http://encylopedia.com/home.html
CPIQ (Canadian) at
http://www.galegroup.com/tlist/cpiq_jl.html
Contact your Teacher-Librarian to see which sites the school subscribes or has access to.

Step 4

Search for additional information from electronic sources such as CDs and the Internet. These sources should be carefully selected or narrowed down by asking questions such as:

- Who wrote/published this information?
- For what level does it seem to be designed? (elementary, secondary, college or university, general adult)
- What level of detail and length is provided for my purposes? (too little, about right, too much, far too much)
- How much reference is made to particular social science people, theories, studies, and experiments? (too little, about right, too much, far too much)
- How will this electronic source help to provide a social science focus to the research?
- Which social science (anthropology, psychology, or sociology) does this source best represent? Provide some evidence.

Some electronic sources appropriate for social science research at the secondary school level are Canadian News Disk and SIRS.

Follow-Up

1. Find an encylopedia entry about gender identity/roles or an alternative topic.
   a) Does the entry help to provide a social science focus to the research? If so, how? If not, why not?
   b) What specific information in the entry would you want to find out more about in later stages of your research?

2. Find a general book with information on gender identity/roles or an alternative topic.
   a) What broad keywords did you use to locate the book?
   b) How do you know it is a general book?
   c) Identify the chapter(s) and pages that are relevant to your topic.
   d) Does the book help to provide a social science focus to the research? If so, how? If not, why not?

3. Find a specialist book on gender identity/roles or an alternative topic.
   a) How do you know it is a specialist book?
   b) Identify the chapter(s) and pages that are relevant to your topic.
   c) Which social science (anthropology, psychology, or sociology) does this book best represent? Provide evidence for your answer.

4. Find a periodical article relating to gender identity/roles or an alternative topic.
   a) Identify the periodical title, article title, author(s) (if given), date and edition number, publisher, and place of publication.

b) Does the article help to provide a social science focus to the research? If so, how? If not, why not?
c) Which social science (anthropology, psychology, or sociology) does the article best represent? Provide evidence for your answer.

5. Use an electronic source to find information about gender identity/roles or an alternative topic.
   a) Identify the article, title, author(s) (if given), publisher, and place of publication.
   b) Answer the six bulleted questions in step 4.

Non-Physical Gender Differences

A number of researchers have also conducted research into non-physical gender differences. One type of difference involves speaking style, explored by social scientists researching job promotions. Another difference involves tastes in humour.

Conversational Styles

In her book, *Talking from 9 to 5: How Women's and Men's Conversational Styles Affect Who Gets Heard, Who Gets Credit, and What Gets Done at Work*, Deborah Tannen characterizes the different communication patterns between women and men. She demonstrates that they may be a major factor in the lower incidence of women's promotions to top jobs. One difference Tannen noted was that, in general, women tend to communicate in a more inclusive manner than men do. That is, women tend to want to hear a variety of opinions before sharing their own opinion. Women work from a **consensus model**—allowing everyone to have input in the decision-making process—because they do not want to appear to be bossy and arrogant. However, a woman who asks for the opinions of others before she states her own faces a unique problem. Her boss may interpret this tendency as evidence that she does not know what to do—that she is trying to get others to make decisions for her.

Another difference is that women do not call attention to their accomplishments to the same extent that men do. In most companies, promotion requires not only excellent work, but also the *recognition* of one's work. This may simply

Figure 4.15 Deborah Tannen's research included observing lunchtime activities at companies. She found that men often made a point of getting recognized by having lunch with the highest-level person they could find. Women rarely promoted themselves in this way, often working quietly through their lunch hour instead.

involve making a point of telling your boss, or your boss's boss, what you have done. Women are often reluctant to call attention to their achievements because they feel they would be bragging. The way women choose pronouns is a good example of how women tend not to emphasize their accomplishments. Tannen found that women tend to use the pronouns "we" and "our" when describing their work, while men use the pronoun "I" and "my." For example, men tend to say, "I'm hiring a new manager; I'm going to put him in charge of my marketing division." This makes it sound as if he owns the corporation he works for. In contrast, women tend to say things like, "We have come up with some great ideas on the Rogers Cable deal," even if, in reality, the woman talking had alone done all the work. By trying not to sound arrogant, women downplay their achievements, thus lessening the chances they will be recognized for them. Tannen concludes that it is these gender differences in communication that result in a **glass ceiling**. This term refers to an invisible barrier that some believe keep women from rising to the highest levels of management within corporations.

Sense of Humour

Another non-physical gender difference that may exist between males and females is sense of humour. Studies suggest that more men than women find slapstick humour and gallows humour amusing. **Slapstick humour** involves physical stunts such as walking into doors and pulling a chair out from someone who is about to sit down. **Gallows humour** usually focuses on gory and sick situations such as someone getting killed. Women, on the other hand, tend to prefer jokes based on irony or incongruity. **Irony** is a type of expression in which people say the opposite of what they really mean. **Incongruity** occurs when ideas are put together in an unexpected or illogical way, so that the ideas seem absurd or out of place.

In the following excerpt from his column, humourist Dave Barry discusses differences in sense of humour.

> The first thing you need to understand is that men and women do not have the same definition of the term "a man with a sense of humour." To men, it means "a man who thinks a lot of stuff is funny." Whereas to women, it means "a man who talks and looks kind of like Hugh Grant." This leads to a lot of disagreement between the genders about what is funny. For example, I belong to an organization called the Lawn Rangers of Arcola, Illinois, whose members are dedicated to helping humanity by marching with lawnmowers in parades. The Lawn Rangers are an all-male organization, but sometimes women voluntarily choose to attend our annual meeting. The climactic highlight of the meeting occurs when one of our members gets up on a ladder and performs a routine wherein he ... OK, let's just say that if you were considering a career in proctology, this would definitely change your mind. The women are revolted by this routine, whereas the

men laugh so hard that some of them fall down. (They are not hurt, because they land on men who fell down earlier in the meeting.)

Another example: Recently my wife and I, along with maybe 15 other expectant couples, attended a hospital class on breast feeding. At one point, to illustrate an important issue, the breast feeding instructor walked around the room holding up a cloth model of a breast—kind of like a Muppet—with a little string on the back that the instructor pulled to make the breast change shape. The women looked on with mature, intelligent, concerned expressions. But I made eye contact with a number of men as the Breast Muppet went around, and I can state with certainty that if not for the fact that our wives would hit us, we would have laughed ourselves into a state of dehydration.

My point is that women and men have different senses of humour. This was confirmed last year in a study done by two psychologists from Canada. This study showed that simple, slapstick humour, such as the Three Stooges, appeals to the following two groups of people: 1. People with brain damage. 2. Men. (At this point, the women readers are thinking, "That's only one group!")

And what kind of humour do women like? According to a news article about the Canadian study, women, because of their more sophisticated brains, prefer humour that involves "longer narratives, personal information and memories." The article does not come right out and use the term "Hugh Grant," but it doesn't have to ...

Excerpted from: Barry, Dave. 2000. "Men Have to Work at Humouring Women." *The Kitchener-Waterloo Record*. 18 March 2000.

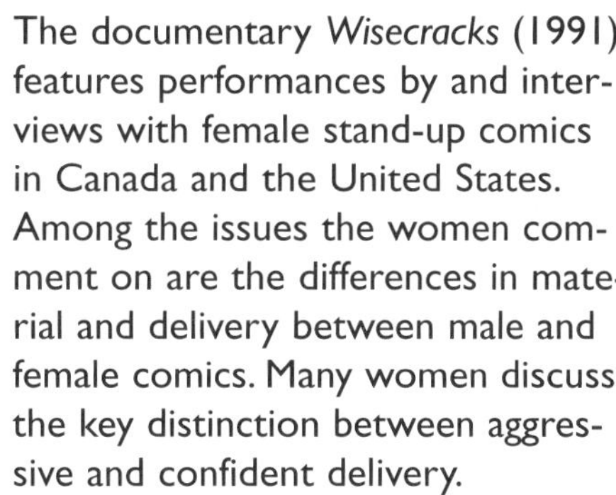

FILM LINK

The documentary *Wisecracks* (1991) features performances by and interviews with female stand-up comics in Canada and the United States. Among the issues the women comment on are the differences in material and delivery between male and female comics. Many women discuss the key distinction between aggressive and confident delivery.

RECAP

1. In what ways are female infants treated differently from male infants?
2. Identify five differences in the way that men's and women's brains function.
3. Identify the differences in women's and men's speaking styles, as observed by Deborah Tannen.
4. According to Dave Barry, what differences exist in the sense of humour of men and women? Do you agree? Explain, giving examples from your own experience.

Section 4.5

Race, Ethnicity, and Our Sense of Self

Focus Questions

- How is ethnic identity formed?
- How do race and ethnic identity influence the way others treat us?
- How do race and ethnic identity influence our own behaviour?

Key Concepts

race
ethnicity
stage models
conformity
dissonance
resistance
immersion
introspection
synergistic articulation
acculturation theory
collectivistic
tiu lien
systemic racism

Defining Race and Ethnicity

The terms **race** and **ethnicity** are often used interchangeably, but they actually have different meanings. Ethnicity describes the relation of an individual to a group with whom the individual believes he or she has common ancestry. This ancestry is based on shared individual characteristics, shared socio-cultural experiences, or both. Terms such as "French," "English," "Greek," or "Jamaican" are used by people to classify their ethnicity. Race, on the other hand, describes the common descent or origin a group shares, often characterized by physical qualities. In the nineteenth century, terms such as "Negroid," "Caucasoid," "Mongoloid," and "Australoid" were introduced by anthropologists to classify human racial types. Members of the Negroid race are descended from Africa and usually have black skin. Members of the Caucasoid race are descended from the region known as the Caucasus and usually have white skin. Members of the Mongoloid race are descended from the region between Lapland (now Finland) and Siam (now Thailand), and usually have yellow skin. And members of the Australoid race are descended from the Australasian area and include large numbers of Aboriginal peoples. Obviously, very few of us define ourselves by these anthropological terms. We usually define ourselves by our skin colour and by the group with which we feel the strongest bond.

In 1997, the American Anthropological Association drafted a statement regarding the term "race." It asserted that the term has no validity as a biological category in the human species. Scientific studies clearly demonstrate that human populations are not unambiguous, clearly separated, biologically distinct groups. Rather, "race" is a set of culturally created attitudes toward, and beliefs about, human differences. These attitudes and beliefs developed during the period of western European exploration and colonization. They ultimately became a body of prejudgments that distort our ideas about human differences and behaviour. The association concluded its statement by saying that present-day inequalities are not consequences of biological inheritance. Rather, they are the result of social, economic, educational, and political circumstances.

Theories of Ethnic Identity Formation

How do concepts of ethnic identity develop? Do they remain constant throughout a person's lifetime? One frequent way researchers have assessed the development of ethnic identity is through **stage models**. These models assume that ethnic identity develops as people resolve conflicts at different stages of their life. The conflict at the lowest stage must be resolved satisfactorily before the next stage can be achieved. In their study of American minorities, Atkinson, Morten, & Sue (1983) proposed that minority identity development follows five distinct stages:

1. **Conformity**. There is conflict between the values of the dominant culture and the values of one's own group. The individual sides with the dominant culture's values.
2. **Dissonance**. The individual becomes confused over the conflict between the dominant culture and her or his own group.
3. **Resistance** and **Immersion**. The individual actively rejects the dominant system and begins to accept her or his own cultural traditions and customs.
4. **Introspection**. The individual questions the values of both the minority and majority culture.
5. **Synergistic Articulation** and **Awareness**. The individual resolves all previous conflicts and develops a cultural identity that combines elements from both cultures.

Don't blame me; work with me

Black community is not to blame for Just Desserts shooting

By Erma Collins

I am still numb: numb that another murder of an innocent bystander has taken place in the city that I have loved and called home for the last 29 years; numb by the frenzied vitriol that has been directed at the entire black community by some members of the public and the media; numb by the fact that many a meeting and conversation has been dominated by expressions of guilt and shame for being black. Yes, I am numb, confused, appalled, sickened, petrified – by all of these things.

I, too, feel grief for the family of Georgina Leimonis. I also understand the feelings of horror that we all have as residents of Toronto. After all, it could have been me or you sitting in that restaurant. If we are not safe from attacks by hoodlums in an upscale restaurant, where else will we not be safe? It is frightening, very frightening.

Equally frightening for me has been the racist idea expressed by some, in various ways, that the entire black community is culpable. As a black person and an active volunteer in the community, I refuse to accept any blame for the actions of the Just Desserts criminals, although I strongly condemn that and other incidents of violence. I absolutely refuse.

Are you, white readers, collectively ex-

up in the system than others for the same crime? Are all criminals treated equally once they are in the system?

All of us, if we can discover how to do it successfully, need to work harder to help parents cope.

Figure 4.16 During a 1994 robbery attempt, three black gunmen randomly killed a white patron at a Toronto café. Some members of the public and media blamed the entire black community for the crime. Articles like the above condemned such racism. What effect do you think this controversy had on the ethnic self-identity of young black men?

Stage models of ethnic identity are criticized by some social scientists as being too simplistic. They overlook the likelihood that a person's ethnic identity evolves and changes over time. Another problem is that an individual may be in more than one stage at a time. Finally, stage theories do not explore the role of racism in the formation of ethnic identity. For example, what happens when a young black person is discriminated against or victimized by members of the dominant culture? How do these experiences affect the formation of ethnic identity?

Some psychologists use **acculturation theory** to understand the development of ethnic identity. Acculturation theory uses various categories or labels to describe how a person integrates her or his ethnic group identity with attitudes toward the larger society.

Sue & Sue offered the labels "traditionalist," "marginal," and "Asian American" in their study of the acculturation of individuals of Asian descent. "Traditionalists" are typically foreign-born and strongly accept parental cultural values. They tend to socialize only with members of their own ethnic group. A "marginal" person rejects Asian values, wants to assimilate into American culture, and tends to socialize with Caucasian Americans. These individuals tend to have little ethnic identity that is associated with Asian culture. "Asian Americans" achieve balance and pride in their ethnic identity by combining traditional Asian values with Western influences.

Acculturation theories have been criticized for defining ethnic identity in oversimplified terms. Such theories do not consider how factors such as generation, age, and gender *within* an ethnic group affect ethnic identity. As well, many individuals find the labels used in these models limiting and demeaning. They fear these models may contribute to stereotypes and overgeneralizations about minority groups. (For example, if a group has noticeable traditionalist members, the entire group might get labelled as "traditionalist." On the basis of this inaccurate label, some people in the dominant culture might discriminate against the group for rejecting the dominant cultural values.)

Asian Self-Concept

In 1996, Christine Yeh and Karen Huang published a study on ethnic identity development among Asian American college students in the journal *Adolescence*. The study identified a number of factors that are unique to Asian culture and distinguish Asian ethnic identity from that of Europeans or North Americans.

For one thing, the Asian subjects were more concerned about how their family or community would judge their actions. The researchers concluded that the process of Asian American ethnic identification is influenced more by external factors than by a person's self-assessments.

Another factor important to the Asian sense of self was described in research reviewed by Yeh and Huang. It is the ability to maintain interdependence between the individual and the community. This factor is in sharp contrast to the tendency in Western self-development to pull away from the family. It results in the **collectivistic** nature of Asian culture, characterized by a strong group identity and concern for others rather than oneself.

This sense of group identity seems to be strongly influenced by the concept of ***tiu lien***, or "loss of face." "Face" in this definition includes the positive image, interpretations, or social attributes that one claims for oneself—or perceives others to ascribe to oneself. If one does not fulfill the expectations of the self, then one loses face.

When one loses face, one feels tremendous shame, because the loss of face will be collectively shared by the family. These feelings are often used as a negative reinforcer in child-rearing.

The social consequence of shame is often exclusion—a particularly painful experience in a collectivistic culture. For example, shaming can involve loss of support and confidence from one's family, community, or social network. In a culture where relationships are crucial to the very existence of the self, the withdrawal of support from the social group may threaten an individual's identity. So the fear of shame, or *tiu lien*, can be a powerful motivating force for conforming to expectations. As such, it may contribute greatly to Asian American ethnic identity development, in which the "social outside" often holds much more weight than the "psychological inside."

REMARKABLE PEOPLE

Lennox Cadore

When Lennox Cadore was a younger man, he wanted an immediate end to racism. Over the years, however, he has come to believe that racism will have to be dismantled like a wall, brick by brick. Cadore was a twenty-eight-year-old outreach co-ordinator with the Etobicoke YMCA when he was interviewed by *Toronto Star* reporter Kelly Gillespie in February of 1999. The interview, entitled "Dismantling the Wall, Brick by Brick," was published on 21 February 1999, and is reproduced below.

"Racism is a wall which will only be broken down over time. You do the things you can yourself to create change. No one person can carry the weight of the world, we have to share the weight. I see it as a long protracted struggle—we all do our part. You break down one brick, two bricks, however many bricks you can in your lifetime, then you pass your chisel to somebody else and that person will keep on breaking it down. It won't happen all in one generation. It probably won't even happen in my lifetime.

"When I was 23 I wanted it to happen now. As I get older I still think it isn't moving fast enough, but concern myself with what I am going to do just to deal with my own life. I can't be out there every day waging a revolutionary war when I have bills to pay, when I want to move forward in my life. I'm not a 23-year-old young blood any more. I'm thinking about a mortgage, a job, car payments, RRSPs.

"Nobody wants to be angry every day. We only live once. I, like everyone else, want to enjoy my life. I do my part to create change. My mere existence creates change. Being in university made people say, 'Whoa what's going on, a black man in university?' I am a role model. If I am able to lead a full life, it will create a situation where people will see me and say, 'Hey, this person must have something going on. Can I learn from this person?' We still have a long way to go when it comes to making people feel included in society. I personally have tried to mesh myself into Canadian society based on my own values. In the context of where I live in Rexdale I feel very comfortable but there's still a sense of disconnection with the rest of society. Even though I've been in Canada for 23 years, I get asked, 'Where are you from?' 'What island were you born on,' is another one I get asked a lot and I say, 'The island of England.' I was born in England, to Caribbean parents. We moved to Canada in 1976. As I grow I become stronger, I don't pay attention to a lot of that stuff any more.

"If you have a problem with me, that's your problem. Why should I deal with your problem? I have my own life to live. I accept there will be **systemic racism** that I'm going to face quite a bit throughout my life but it's just one of the things that I will have to deal with. We can talk about small progresses but we can't be blinded to the amount of distance that we still have left to go. We're living in a city where, in a few years, visible minorities are going to become the majority but if you look at the power structure, corporate Canada or even government institutions, we're not represented. It makes it more difficult for black youth to envision that for themselves.

"I was lucky, I had a lot of opportunities. I've always had positive influences in my personal life. My mother is a solid foundation; my father has always been involved in my life. He was the coach of my school soccer team. I was always seen as a smart kid but not everyone has that. A lot of black youth are unemployed. There's a struggle for young blacks to get the same decent things in life everyone else wants, a house, a car, get married and have children if they want to. It's hard for them to enjoy the privileges society has to offer. A lot of people don't have hope that things could be better. Without hope you don't have the sense of personal responsibility, accountability, motivation. I'd like to be more optimistic about the future and say we're going to make a lot of progress soon, but I've seen a lot of regressive things in the school system—a lot of black youth are dropping out. A teacher in my sister's class said, 'I don't know why I'm teaching you guys—you aren't going to amount to anything.' A friend of mine has his M.B.A., but when he talks about doing his engineering at Waterloo people suggest he do something more practical.

"Racism [disempowers] a society. If you don't believe that your self has any worth then you won't do anything worthwhile. Until we start valuing every single individual we won't be able to realize our full potential. Toronto is truly a global village and we should really be excited about that, not just pay lip service to it. I'd like to see the government and large businesses take up the challenge. Let's really make Toronto, Ontario, Canada, a true model for the world. Let's make it a global village."

Gillespie, Kelly. 1999. "Dismantling the Wall, Brick by Brick." *The Toronto Star*. 21 February 1999.

---

1. Why does Cadore refer to the struggle against racism as a "wall which will only be broken down over time"?
2. Identify some of the ways Cadore feels every individual can work toward reducing racism.
3. Which areas in society does Cadore identify as needing to change?
4. What does Cadore mean when he says that racism disempowers a society?

RECAP

1. What is the difference between race and ethnicity?
2. How does the American Anthropological Association view the term "race"? How does it explain inequalities between different groups?
3. What are the major differences between stage model theory and acculturation theory?
4. What role does shame or guilt play in Asian ethnic identity development? How does this compare with their role in shaping your behaviour within your cultural group? Explain your answer. How is shame or guilt used by your parents as a way to shape your behaviour? Explain your answer.

Activities

Show your knowledge

1. Create a New Vocabulary glossary of the terms and phrases you learned in this chapter.
   a) Record the definition of each term.
   b) Use these terms to create four questions to ask a classmate. Make each question more difficult than the last. Follow the model used for these activities ("Show your knowledge," "Practise your thinking skills," "Communicate your ideas," "Apply your knowledge").
2. Compare how sociologists and anthropologists see the development of the self.
3. Summarize what you know about psychological disorders (pages 89 to 95) in an organizer. Include the names of specific disorders, the general category they fall under, and any suggested treatments.

Practise your thinking skills

4. If it were proven conclusively that personality is most directly affected by nurture, how might each of the following people or institutions change the way children are treated?
   a) parents
   b) schools
   c) toy manufacturers
   d) television and movie producers
5. Record the ways that gender expectations have influenced your life. Consider
   a) the way you were dressed when you were younger
   b) the amount and type of housework you were expected to do
   c) the amount of freedom you have had as a teenager, including your curfew
   d) suggestions/expectations about your future career

Communicate your ideas

6. Journalist Richard Nilson believes that the more time people spend watching TV, the less time they spend living their own lives. Perhaps this same argument could be made for computer games and surfing the

Activities

Internet (as these are largely inactive, solitary pursuits). Write an argumentative paragraph, entitled "Get a Life" or "I've Got a Life," that makes a case for or against people turning off their television sets and computers and interacting more with others.

7. Write a one-page short story where the main character is suffering from an obsessive-compulsive disorder (OCD). Review the symptoms of OCD from page 92 before you write your story.
8. Karla Homolka is due for early release from prison in the year 2001. At that time, she will have served nine years of her twelve-year sentence. Write a letter to the parole board arguing either for or against Homolka's early release.

Apply your knowledge

9. Prepare a "family tree" project that explores the origin of your family's surname. Also investigate whether or not common given names have been handed down over the generations.
10. Locate the latest research into antisocial personality disorder (ASP). Try to determine why eight times as many men as women have ASP. Share your findings with the class.
11. Divide into small groups of males only or females only. Each group should find a partner group of the opposite sex.
    a) With your partner group, decide on a specific type of summer job that both males and females in your group might apply for.
    b) In your individual groups, write a script for what you would consider to be an ideal job interview. Include in the script what you consider to be ideal questions from an employer and excellent responses from the applicant. Also include notes on body language and conversational tone.
    c) Afterwards, compare scripts with your partner group. What differences are there? How do these differences reflect the genders of the scriptwriters?
12. Write a two- to three-page report that describes how ethnicity has influenced your life. Make sure you consider both the advantages and disadvantages you have experienced because of your background.

Chapter 5

Socialization

Overview of Chapter

Learning Expectations

By the end of this chapter, you will be able to

- explain the role of socialization in the development of the individual
- identify the primary and secondary agents of socialization and evaluate their influence
- demonstrate an understanding of anthropological, psychological, and sociological theories that deal with socialization
- evaluate the role of cultural influences in socialization
- demonstrate an understanding of the major questions related to self and others posed by anthropologists, psychologists, and sociologists

Open for Debate

What Causes Eating Disorders?

In July 2000, the Globe and Mail, *a Toronto newspaper, published a column by Dick Snyder entitled "Skinny Girls Are Coltish, A Bundle of Nervous Energy About To Explode. That's Why I Love Them." In an apparent attempt to be humorous, the writer explained why he finds slim women to be attractive and interesting. The article prompted the following reply from a reader.*

Thanks to you my wife is once again safely steered onto that straight and narrow path of fasting, exercising, and purging in search of her elusive concave stomach, emaciated legs and thin wrists. Today, your article has given her that extra little push to skip supper tonight and—why not?—tomorrow's meals as well. Perhaps she'll be fortunate enough to come across a new magazine displaying exactly the body you say is most attractive to men, so that she can post it on the wall for inspiration as she laces up her joggers for her third run of the day.

You may not be ashamed of declaring to the world that you love skinny girls. You may find it intellectually stimulating to deny that the fashion and media industries have anything to do with encouraging eating disorders.

Make no mistake: You and attitudes such as yours encourage my wife's eating disorder. When you use national media to inform all of Canada that skinny girls are perfect, be prepared to shoulder responsibility for the deaths of several girls and women who will desperately be seeking to live up to your published opinion of lovability.

Perhaps, if she is good enough at it, my wife shall be one of them.

Source: Shelley, Robert. 2000. "Starving for Acceptance." *The Globe and Mail.* 17 July 2000.

Think About It

1. Whom does Robert Shelley hold responsible for his wife's disorder?
2. Do you think the media is to blame for negatively influencing some people's self-image? Explain.
3. Do you think people who risk their health to conform to a vision of attractiveness have a brain or biological disorder? Explain.

Section 5.1

What Is Socialization?

Focus Questions

- Which of your important personal characteristics are biologically inherited and which have been learned through your experience?
- How do social scientists define the term "socialization?"
- What evidence would a social scientist give to prove that the times of day we are hungry are determined more by socialization than by our biology?

Key Concepts

socialization
sapienization
primary socialization
secondary socialization
anticipatory socialization
resocialization

Who Am I?

Imagine that you are writing a letter to introduce yourself to a new pen pal. What characteristics about yourself would you include?

Your name probably identifies your gender if it is of European origin (although some European names, like Kim or Robin, are used by both males and females). In addition to your gender, you would probably want your pen pal to know your age and some of your physical characteristics, such as your height, and your hair, eye, and skin colour. You might describe your family and the type of neighbourhood you live in. From there you would perhaps move to some of the things you are good at, such as school, sports, or music. Your introduction might also include the things you like and dislike, the ways you like to spend your spare time, and what qualities you look for in the friends you choose. Having provided this information, you would probably feel that your pen pal would know the basics about you.

Now assume that you were born in the maternity ward of a hospital where attendants made a mistake. You and a baby of the same gender, born at the same time, were misidentified. You both went home with the wrong families, were raised by them, and no one ever discovered the mistake. How many of the things you have described to your pen pal would be the same? In other words, which of the characteristics mentioned previously are biologically inherited and which are learned through your experience? Your eye and hair colour are easy—they are biologically based and would be the same. But, in this different family, would your performance in school, athletics, and music be the exactly the same as they are now?

You have already touched on the nurture versus nature debate in Chapter 4 (pages 82 to 87). This chapter will explore the issue a little more, by examining the concept of **socialization**. Social scientists use this term to describe the lifelong process through which we learn all the knowledge, skills, and attitudes we need to survive and prosper. It is the process through which we become ourselves, in the society we live in.

Studying Socialization

There are various aspects to socialization, and each of the three social science disciplines being examined in this book tends to focus on one particular aspect. Sociologists focus on how people learn the basic rules and attitudes of human behaviour that are considered acceptable in our society (for example, "don't pick your nose"; "treat people of all ethnic backgrounds fairly"). By learning and practising these rules, we will be accepted as full members of society. Psychologists focus more on the development of the human personality, and the acquisition of those personal characteristics that make each individual unique (for example, how well-balanced we are, how self-confident we are). Anthropologists see socialization as the means by which permanent human societies are produced. They use the related term **sapienization** (from *Homo sapiens*, "the human species") to describe what for them are the most important processes of socialization. Anthropologist John H. Bodley, in his book *Cultural Anthropology*, says these are the processes that lead to "a uniquely human way of life centred on marriage, the family, and the household" (Bodley, 2000, 16).

Although each social science discipline takes a different focus on socialization, all of them recognize it as a key process in the development of the individual, as well as a necessary factor in the continuation of society.

Figure 5.1 Socialization in traditional Japanese culture makes it almost impossible to think of a meal without rice. Gohan *(meaning both "rice" and "cooked meal") is the root of the words* asagohan *("breakfast"),* hirugohan *("lunch"), and* bangohan *("dinner").*

Socialization affects virtually every aspect of our lives—even, for example, something as basic as our hunger patterns. You might assume that your hunger is caused solely by biological processes. But social scientists would point out that most North American families eat their evening meal between 5 and 7 p.m., while families in India or Greece often eat between 8 and 10 p.m. We are actually socialized by such patterns to be hungry at certain times of the day, instead of being biologically programmed to be hungry at these times.

Socialization is also closely related to how we perceive the world around us. For example, Kim was raised in southern Canada. Her survival in society has not depended on her knowledge of snow. As a speaker of English, she has only one noun to refer to snow (although she might add adjectives to it to describe snow's condition, such as "wet," "sticky," or "powdery"). But her social learning and her language make it likely that she only sees one thing when she sees snow. René, on the other hand, was raised in the Inuit culture in northern Canada. In this environment, weather conditions are crucial to people's ability to travel and survive. There are accordingly many words for snow in Inuktitut, the Inuit language. There are separate words for falling snow, blowing snow, snow lying on the ground, melting snow, and so on. An important part of Inuit socialization is learning to distinguish snow conditions and use the correct term for each one.

Socialization, as we can see, varies from culture to culture, but the process is vital to all societies.

The Components of Socialization

The socialization process may be divided into a number of components. **Primary socialization** describes the process by which we learn to use language, eat, practise hygiene, deal with our emotions, and understand how to behave as male or female. It comprises the basic understandings we need to function in the society into which we are born. **Secondary socialization** means learning how to function in groups, such as school or church, and how to follow the behaviours society expects of us while acting in group situations. **Anticipatory socialization** is the term used to describe the ability we develop to think ahead and act accordingly. For example, how should we dress for a particular social occasion? How should we address a professor, ski instructor, or a visiting cousin whom we have not previously met? By applying the socialization clues we have already picked up, we should be able to act appropriately in new situations and meet society's expectations. **Resocialization** is the deliberate attempt by society to replace aspects of an individual's socialization with new learnings. In prison, for example, society tries to change inmates' learned behaviours to more appropriate, law-abiding ones.

Socialization and its effects on the individual and society are among the most studied topics in social science. In this chapter, you will find out how socialization occurs. You will learn about how society tries to obtain a certain degree of obedience and conformity from its members. You will also read about some of the significant variations in socialization among world cultures. Throughout, you will be encouraged to think about your own experiences of and understandings about the socialization process.

Figure 5.2 Do you believe school dress codes or uniforms have a socializing influence? If so, which component of socialization is involved?

RECAP

1. On what element of socialization do each of the following social scientists focus?
   a) sociologists
   b) psychologists
   c) anthropologists
2. a) Explain why Inuktitut has so many different words for snow, while English has only one.
   b) Use your answer in *(a)* to explain why the socialization of a young Inuit living in the North differs from that of a young English-speaking person living in southern Canada.
3. How are primary and secondary socialization different?

Section 5.2

Agents of Socialization

Focus Questions

- What agents socialize us?
- What differences are there in the way they influence us?
- Why are these agents so important to us?

Key Concepts

ferals
isolates
norms
manifest function
latent function
peer group
total institutions
degradation ceremony

Growing Up Differently

Have you ever wondered how a person might develop if cut off from normal human contact from an early age? Would such an individual have a personality, show interest in other people, or be able to communicate? We can begin to answer these questions by studying the unusual cases of **ferals** and **isolates**. Ferals are children who have been adopted by wild animals, usually female wolves. Such accounts are considered somewhat unreliable, however. More reliable are the isolate cases—children who have been raised in human households, but were severely neglected physically, socially, and emotionally during their early years.

Anna's Story

In 1938, a social worker was sent to a farmhouse in rural Pennsylvania to investigate a case of suspected child abuse. The social worker discovered a five-year-old girl, named Anna, hidden in a second-floor storage room. She was tied into a chair in such a way that she could not move her arms. Like her legs, her arms were spindly from lack of use. The chair had a potty built into it. It appeared that, from the time she was big enough to use the potty, she had spent her entire life in the chair.

Anna's mother was mentally impaired and unmarried. Having a child out of wedlock was considered a family disgrace at that time, and Anna had been hidden from society. Anna's grandfather was enraged by his daughter's pregnancy. Although he allowed Anna to live in the farmhouse, the daughter thought it best to keep Anna out of sight and contact with anyone.

Local authorities moved Anna to a children's home where extensive tests were done on her. She seemed to be without any of the social skills normally taken for granted. She could not laugh, smile, speak, or show anger. She did not respond in any way to others. Kingsley Davis, the sociologist who studied her, concluded that she had had no socialization and was therefore unable to deal with other human beings.

Genie's Story

In 1970, children's authorities in California discovered a thirteen-year-old girl named Genie. Genie had been kept in a locked room since she was twenty months old. Her father was aggressive, hated children, and had probably murdered two of Genie's siblings. Like Anna, Genie was completely unsocialized. She could not chew her food, speak, stand upright, or even fully extend her arms and legs. On an intelligence test, she scored at the normal level for a one-year-old.

After considerable training, Genie did learn to walk and to speak in simple sentences. But her language was difficult to follow and was never expected to reach normal levels. In 1978, at the age of twenty-one, Genie was sent to a supported home for adults unable to live alone. She was not expected to make any further progress in the development of either her personality or her social skills.

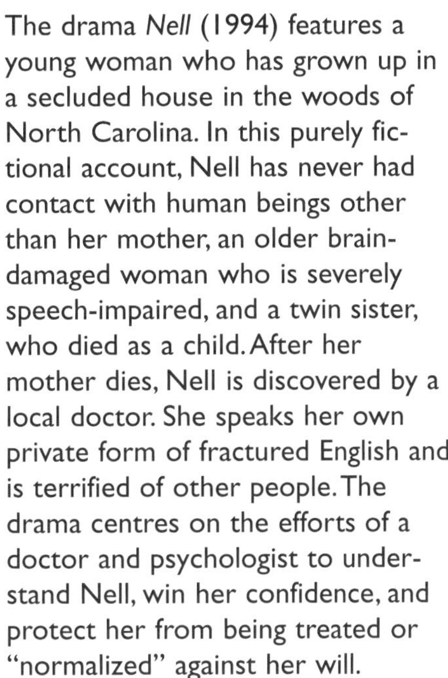

FILM LINK

The drama *Nell* (1994) features a young woman who has grown up in a secluded house in the woods of North Carolina. In this purely fictional account, Nell has never had contact with human beings other than her mother, an older brain-damaged woman who is severely speech-impaired, and a twin sister, who died as a child. After her mother dies, Nell is discovered by a local doctor. She speaks her own private form of fractured English and is terrified of other people. The drama centres on the efforts of a doctor and psychologist to understand Nell, win her confidence, and protect her from being treated or "normalized" against her will.

The Agents of Socialization

Data from isolate cases reveal the importance of socialization at a young age. What isolate children lack is exposure to the "agents" of socialization—the numerous individuals, institutions, and organizations that further the socialization process along. This section looks at some of these agents and their normal effects on us.

Family

For most of us, the family is the first agent of socialization. From it we learn language and communication skills, the normal rules of behaviour (called **norms**), and basic techniques for looking after ourselves. The family is also the first agent

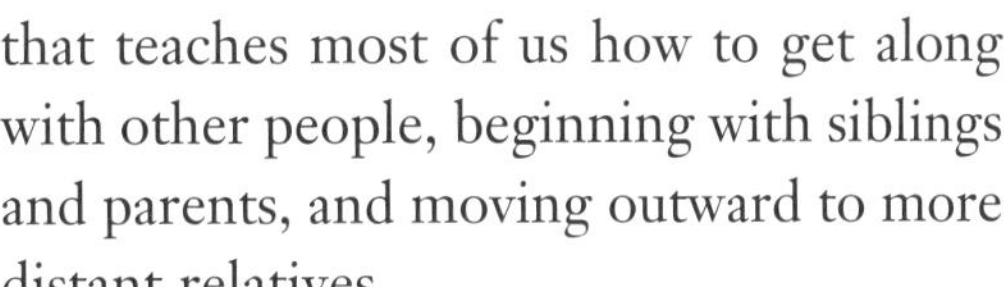

that teaches most of us how to get along with other people, beginning with siblings and parents, and moving outward to more distant relatives.

Since the family teaches us important things about ourselves, it is vital in the development of our personalities. We learn about gender roles—specifically, that there may be some differences in what our society expects of girls/women and boys/men. The family also helps us learn about our own personal qualities. We get some idea about how smart, loved, and trusting we are.

Not all of these perceptions about ourselves may be strictly accurate, however. Later experiences in life may change the image that our family helped us to create about ourselves.

POINT and COUNTERPOINT

Should Physical Discipline of Children Be Outlawed?

The law does not allow one person to hit another person. But section 43 of the Criminal Code of Canada contains an exemption: parents/guardians, teachers, and anyone acting in their place are allowed to use "reasonable force to correct behaviour." Should section 43 be removed from the Criminal Code?

Yes:

Alisa Watkinson, an assistant professor of social work at the University of Regina, launched a challenge against section 43 in 1997. She believes that it violates a child's right to security and to be free from cruel and unusual punishment. (This right is guaranteed by the Canadian Charter of Rights and Freedoms.) Spanking children, she says, is legally and morally wrong. It can damage youngsters' self-esteem and teach them that force is a legitimate tool to get your own way. It can also psychologically damage children, who may grow up to be abusive partners and parents. "We don't allow the beating of wives or criminals—why children?"

Watkinson is a member of the Canadian Foundation for Children, Youth and the Law. This organization is fighting to have section 43 removed. Although the Foundation has not been successful in court so far, it believes the tide of public opinion is turning. The Foundation has vowed to continue its fight to have section 43 removed.

No:

Cindy Silver is a Vancouver lawyer who represents the Coalition for Family Autonomy. This organization supports parents' rights to discipline their children using reasonable force. "If you've tried other methods of discipline with your kids, and they're looking at you and saying, 'Who's the boss?,' there are times with my kids when I just knew that a swat on the bottom would clarify that," Silver says. She adds that existing child protection laws are sufficient to protect youngsters from physical abuse.

Teachers' groups tend to favour the right to use physical interventions with students when necessary. For example, the Elementary Teachers' Federation of Ontario believes that when teachers are forced to break up a fight in the schoolyard, they must be assured that using reasonable force will not leave them open to assault charges. Phyllis Benedict, its president, says, "Interventions by teachers are necessary to protect students from harming themselves or others in potentially violent situations."

Source: Smith, Graeme. 2000. "Parents May Hit Children: Judge." *The Toronto Star*. 6 July 2000.

1. Define the specific actions that you think constitute "reasonable force."
2. Do you think it is acceptable for parents to spank their children? Explain.
3. Make a point-form summary of the arguments from both sides and rank them from most to least valid, in your opinion. Explain your choice of the most valid argument.

School

School is frequently the first agent to make us deal with formal rules. It is also the first place where we are looked after by officials who are not family members.

School teaches us two separate things. The **manifest function**—or visible purpose—of school is to teach us the academic skills we need to prosper in society. These skills help us eventually to find work or become entrepreneurs. The **latent function**—or hidden purpose—is to socialize us to understand and co-operate with strangers, some of whom we may not particularly like.

In many ways, the latent function is the more important. We are taught rules about being on time, being neat, when to speak, and when to be silent. We learn how to speak in a formal manner. We are taught to have respect for authority, found both in our teachers and in the school rules. This prepares us as working adults to show respect for our boss and the rules of the company or organization that employs us. In this way, school is a building block for what is to come later.

School also teaches us about gender roles. It does so in obvious ways (boys and girls must use separate washrooms and change rooms, and young people are often separated for physical and health education classes) and less obvious ways. In the latter case, schools may communicate differences in expectations for boys and girls without intending to. For example, boys' teams may get greater coverage in the daily announcements than girls' teams do. Greater effort may be made to recruit girls to the peer mediation group, on the assumption that girls are "better at that sort of thing" than boys. Our experiences with gender expectations in school, especially these subtle ones, can have a profound influence on us in later life.

Figure 5.3 What aspects of the latent function of school are present in this scene?

Peer Group

A **peer group** is a social group whose members are about the same age and share interests and social position. A classic example is a group of teenagers who all go to the same school, have roughly the same family income, and have a common outlook on life. While younger children tend to form peer groups around neighbourhood friends, teenagers tend to "hang out" with peers who, though they live farther away, are in close contact through school.

Peers give us the opportunity to do things and talk about things that are discouraged in the family. Many teenagers, for example, feel some pressure from peers to smoke as a sign of rebelliousness against families that are opposed to smoking. Sexual attitudes commonly become a topic for discussion in teenage peer groups, and members may express or listen to opinions that would be condemned if expressed in their family. Gender roles may be reinforced in the peer group. Some male teenagers feel pressure to develop their athletic ability, to act cool in all situations, and to seem tough. Females may be pressured to concentrate on their physical appearance, focusing on the effects of diet and skilfully applied makeup, or to adopt mature social concerns such as child poverty or saving the environment. These statements are obviously generalizations; many females become gifted athletes and many males worry about their looks. But, on balance, there appear to be differences in the way many females and many males are socialized by peer groups.

What should families do when there is conflict between family rules and peer values? Many families struggle with this issue during the children's teenage years. Research shows that the conflict can be intense over short-term concerns, such as style of dress and musical taste, over which

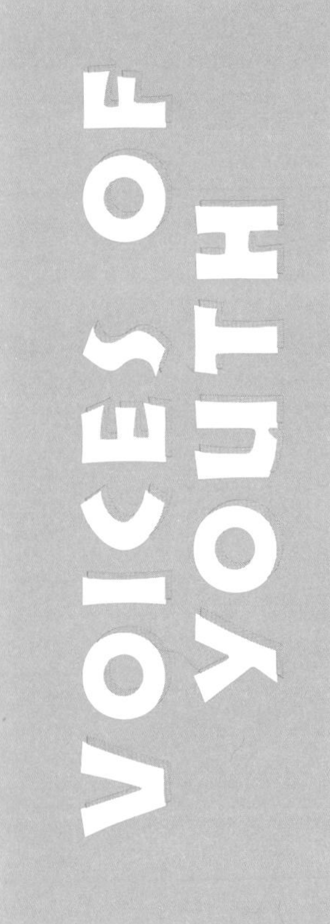

QUESTION:

What were your primary sources of information about sex?

My primary sources of sexual information were my friends. They talk about sex all the time, especially boys. I think boys are obsessed with sex. My mom also told me all the stuff I need to know, because she doesn't want me to make a mistake.

—Iva Sikman, 16

I learned about sex from my friends at first. Then I was also informed by my school in Grade 5, and up until now. I don't really think the information I got from my friends was true, but I trust that what I learned in school was right. In a perfect world, I think that kids should be taught at home and school.

—Joey Weiler, 16

The first source was my friends in Grade 3, and they were all making fun of it and laughing at it. I don't think that they actually knew what it was really like, they just shared what they heard. Then I learned some information from my parents, and when I came to Canada, in health class we found out about sex.

—Stanislava Krajisnik, 15

peers are often more influential. But families have more influence over long-term goals such as going to work, college, or university, and career choices.

Media

We saw in Chapter 4 that the media represent one of the "nurture" factors that influence our behaviour (see pages 83 to 84). Since most of us are exposed to the media from an early age, we can label this "nurture" factor as another "agent of socialization." In the past half-century, movies, radio, television, and popular music have had an increasingly important impact on our expectations from life, our values, and how we see ourselves. What we must remember is that the media function as commercial operations, designed to make money by obtaining as many customers as possible. To obtain these customers, they sometimes present an unrealistic view of life.

For example, police shows on television regularly fit drama, suspense, romance, tragedy, and justice into a fifty-two-minute package. Courtroom movies feature fearless attorneys who battle impossible odds and the corruption of public officials. These characters are armed only with their integrity and cross-examination skills. Being an ordinary police officer or criminal lawyer bears little resemblance to such entertainment.

Advertising, another important media socialization agent, tries to persuade us that we can have it all, even if we have no money. Gender roles are created and reinforced, whether realistic or not. For an example of this, look back at the description of advertised and realistic body images on page 84.

The television viewing habits of young people, shown in Figure 5.4, demonstrate the impact of the media. Many studies have shown that those who watch

ASK THE EXPERT

Why are certain teenagers more susceptible to negative peer pressure than others?

Certain characteristics, either of the teenager or of the situation, make responding to negative pressures more likely. With regards to characteristics of the teenager, younger adolescents and boys are more susceptible to peer pressures than older adolescents and girls. Also, adolescents who are already getting into trouble at home and school often give in to peer pressure to engage in misbehaviour or illegal acts. With regards to the characteristics of the situation, when the pressure involves social issues, adolescents are more likely to respond. When the pressure involves academic or family issues, there is less likelihood of giving in. Overall, adolescents are more likely to respond to pressures from their close friends or those whose opinions they admire than from the peer group in general.

Dr. Jennifer Connolly, professor of psychology at York University

Figure 5.4 Selected television viewing statistics, Canada, 1993–1994

Average total time spent watching TV to age 18	15 000 hours
Average total time spent in school to age 18	1 000 hours
Average weekly time spent watching TV, 18–24-year-olds	males: 16.0 hours females: 19.8 hours
Total number of incidents seen by average person to age 18	violent deaths: 18 000 other violent crimes: 160 000
Percentage of programming by country of origin	USA: 53 Canada: 36 Other: 11

Sources: Henslin and Neslon, 1996, 79. Macionis, Nancarrow Clarke, and Gerber, 1997, 133.

Figure 5.5 What impact has the media had on your socialization? Give examples from movies, television, music, and advertising.

excessive amounts of television are susceptible to stereotyped concepts of gender roles. Even criminal activity has been linked to prolonged television viewing.

Religion

In 1996, around 86 per cent of Canadians indicated that they had some sort of religious faith. About 30 per cent reported weekly attendance at a religious service. For these people, religious institutions influence the socialization process. Those who once belonged to, or were exposed to, a religious group, but not any longer, may also have been socialized by religion.

Religious activities communicate beliefs about gender roles and appropriate sexual conduct. In this way, they often reinforce family socialization. But they also teach responsibility for one another in society—in many religious systems, the rich are responsible for the poor and the well are responsible for the sick.

Another focus of religion is the afterlife. By focusing on what happens after we die, and what we hope to have accomplished by that time, religion raises moral questions such as, "What is a good life?" or "What responsibilities do I have for other people?"

Although religious institutions do not have the same influence on the average Canadian as they did a century ago, deeply moral issues such as abortion and gay and lesbian rights can still take on strong religious tones when being discussed by politicians and others. This suggests that these institutions continue to have an influence on Canadian society.

Workplace

The workplace also contributes to our socialization, especially since so many of us take paid employment at some time in our lives. Ideally, the messages about punctuality, appropriate dress, and respect for authority we learned in school will already have been learned as we enter the workplace. We will then have to learn specialized language, procedures, rules, and codes as they relate to our job. We will be expected to commit ourselves to the success and growth of our employer. We will also have to learn proper ways of dealing with colleagues, customers, and competitors. Team-building exercises are a common method used by many employers to instill the values needed to act appropriately within the workplace—in other words, to socialize employees.

Total Institutions

Total institutions are intended to wipe out the results of prior socialization, replacing them with a new socialization process. Total institutions may be legitimate government agencies, such as "boot camps" for young offenders that try to wean inmates away from criminal activity. Or they may be destructive religious cults that try to make members entirely dedicated to the wishes of their leaders. In either case, there is an emphasis on removing individuality and replacing it with a common group identity. Common methods to accompish this are giving people identical clothing and haircuts; and enforcing strict rules about daily activities, such as when to get up and when to go to bed.

Classic Study

RESEARCHER:
Erving Goffman, Sociologist

TIME:
1961

SUBJECT:
Total Institutions

Asylums as Total Institutions

Erving Goffman's 1961 book *Asylums: Essays on the Social Situation of Mental Patients and Other Inmates* originated the study of total institutions. In Goffman's definition, these institutions cut members off from the rest of society and place them under the total control of the officials who run the institutions. He noted that many such institutions use a **degradation ceremony**—the institution's members are forced to take part in an embarrassing ritual before others. A good example of this occurred at Alcatraz, a federal prison for men in California. On admission, new inmates were forced to strip, take a shower, and then walk naked, in front of all the guards and inmates, to their cell, where their prison uniform was waiting. Such ceremonies were designed to weaken a person's current identity so that a new one could be put in its place.

Figure 5.6 Which characteristics of total institutions identified by Goffman are visible at this young offender boot camp operated by the Ontario government?

Goffman pointed to three characteristics of total institutions. First, all aspects of daily life are closely supervised by staff. Second, members have no choice regarding food, sleeping arrangements, daily activities, and the like. Third, there are formal rules about virtually all aspects of the daily routine.

Several decades have passed since Goffman made his observations. In many present-day total institutions, degradation ceremonies have been abolished. But the three characteristics identified by Goffman remain in place. In Chapter 6, we will return to the concept of total institutions.

RECAP

1. Which agents of socialization are the most important during our infancy and early childhood? Why?
2. Which agents are the most important during our adolescence? How do their messages differ from those we received as young children? Why are they different?
3. What evidence have you seen in this section that socialization is a lifelong process?

Section 5.3

The Process of Socialization

Focus Questions

- What do this section's theories of socialization have in common?
- How are they different from one another?
- Which theories do you think come closest to the truth? Why?

Key Concepts

self
Oedipus complex
Electra complex
citations
looking-glass self

Stages in Self-Development

In Chapter 4, we identified some of the major influences on our personal and social development. These included social interactions (pages 75 to 81); "nature" and "nurture" (pages 82 to 99); gender (pages 100 to 109); and race and ethnicity (pages 110 to 114). In this chapter, we have looked more specifically at the social interactions and factors in our "nurture" that socialize us—that is, that teach us society's rules and help us develop our personality. Our focus now is on exactly *how* this personality develops. What are the stages an individual goes through, from the raw material of personality at birth, to emerge with a **self**?

Social scientists recognize that this process of "self-emergence" sets us apart from all other organisms. Although we share with other animals some biologically rooted drives, such as hunger and thirst, our existence is made up of far more than just instinct and biology. The theories we look at in this section try to break down into stages this uniquely human process of absorbing our experiences to become complete selves.

The Psychosexual Theory

The work of Austrian psychologist Sigmund Freud (1856–1939) was introduced in Chapter 2. There we overviewed Freud's theory of the human mind. Freud divided the mind into a conscious and an unconscious part. He further divided the unconscious part into the id, the ego, and the superego (see page 26 to refresh your memory). In Chapter 4, we briefly mentioned the role of the ego and its defence mechanisms in protecting our sense of self (see page 77). In this section, we look at how the self emerges through stages proposed by Freud.

According to Freud, we are born with an impulse to seek pleasure and avoid pain. This impulse is part of the id. Sometimes this impulse can be in direct conflict with the ego, which encourages us to obey the expectations of family and society. So, at various stages in our life, the id and ego battle each other. Our personality is formed as one or the other (the id or the ego) predominates. If the id consistently wins, our personality veers to an extreme. We tend to be selfish and inconsiderate, concerned only with our own pleasures. If the ego is the consistent winner, our personality veers to an opposite extreme. We may be extremely considerate of other people and concerned with others less fortunate than ourselves. But at the same time, we may be cool and distant in our personal relationships. A combination of id and ego victories at various stages results in a personality between these two extremes. We can see how this works more clearly in an organizer outlining the first five stages of Freud's development classifications.

As Figure 5.7 shows, personality development in Freud's theory largely depends on how we deal with toilet and sexual functions. If we deal with them with feelings of acceptance and openness, we become happy, confident, and successful people. Those who have feelings of guilt and shame toward these functions become nervous, self-doubting, and insecure.

Freud's ideas have become less accepted now than they were in his time. One reason for this is a shift in social scientific thinking. The notion that human behaviour is driven by inborn and unconscious motivations is now largely unpopular. Instead, today's social scientists place much more importance on external social factors in socialization. Feminist social scientists are especially critical of Freud, pointing to Freud's belief that what is male is "normal." His writings indicate that he regarded females as inferior.

Figure 5.7 Stages of Freud's psychosexual theory

Stage	Age	Id's pleasure focus	Signs in adulthood that the id won
1. Oral	birth–18 months	• oral gratification • sucking breast/bottle • placing things in mouth	• overeating • smoking • nail-biting
2. Anal	18 months–3 years	• bowel pleasure • resisting toilet training	• meanness • resentment of authority • obsessive neatness
3. Phallic	3–6 years	• awareness of sex organs • love-hate relationship with same-sex parent (**Oedipus complex**—boys, **Electra complex**—girls)	• selfishness • manipulativeness • poor opposite-sex relationships
4. Latency	6 years–puberty	• same-sex friends, few opposite-sex friends	• lack of close friends
5. Genital	adolescence	• dating and marriage • sexual energy	• guilt about sexuality • feelings of inadequacy • poor sexual relationships

The Cognitive Development Theory

Jean Piaget (1896–1980) was a Swiss psychologist. His studies on children's development are still regarded as important. Piaget observed that children go through a series of chronological development stages. He believed that the self emerged step-by-step as a person mastered each stage. His 1926 book *The Language and Thought of the Child* summarized his findings.

Piaget theorized that babies come into the world incapable of surviving on their own. They acquire the ability to survive

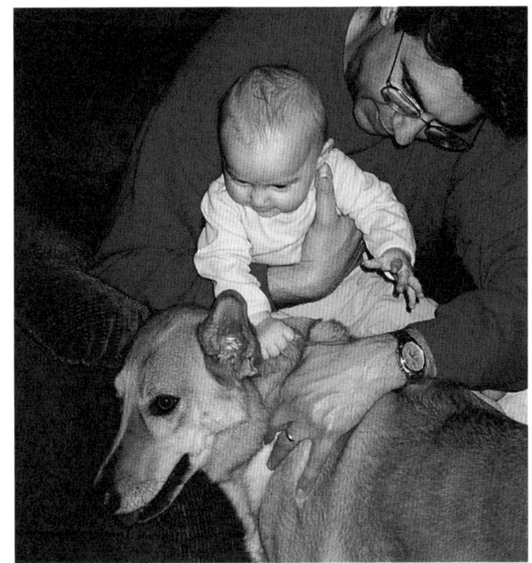

Figure 5.8 In the sensorimotor stage, infants explore their environment largely through touching and acting on objects. Later, they develop the ability to think about, or represent, objects in their minds.

Figure 5.9 Piaget's stages of cognitive development

Stage	Age	Characteristics (concluded from experiments)
1. Sensorimotor	birth–2 years	• learn by touching • egocentric (see selves as centre, do not understand that a situation may look different to others) • understand that something exists only when they can see it
2. Pre-operational	2–7 years	• understand symbols • understand that something exists even when they cannot see it • understand concept of "dog" or "cat" when they cannot see one • cannot appreciate that the other child may have been right and they may have been wrong
3. Concrete operational	7–11 years	• have logic • understand that a set of objects (e.g., seven marbles) still has the same quantity (seven) even when arranged in a different pattern • understand that two glasses of different shape can contain the same amount of water • understand principles of measurement and size
4. Formal operational	11 years +	• can think abstractly • can refer to something "on my right-hand side," or "on my left-hand side. (contrast with egocentrism of stage 1) • can see that the other person may have been right and they may have been wrong

INTERNET RESOURCES

Do you want to find out more about Piaget's work and experiments? Visit a University of Geneva site at

http://unige.ch/piaget/PiagetGB.html

Click on "Biography" for an overview of Piaget's life and achievements. "Publications" lists several books on Piaget's ideas. Each book's table of contents is included. Look at the contents of the book *Piaget Today*. What directions are being taken by current research?

independently by adapting to new situations as they grow and develop. As they adapt, they must also organize their learning in a way that makes sense to them. This process is limited by the natural development of the human brain in the early years. He divided these years into four stages.

Piaget's work has been the subject of much research. Some of it, such as that of Kohlberg and Gilligan in the 1970s, has shown that some 30 per cent of thirty-year-olds have never reached the formal operational stage. This has led social scientists to refute Piaget's suggestion that all people progress through his stages at the same rate. Still, Piaget is recognized and respected for showing that our cognitive and social development is orderly and predictable. Socialization and self-emergence proceed in stages as the human brain develops.

Skill Development: Evaluating and Citing Sources

In the above "Internet Resources" feature, information is available from both the site itself and the books recommended at the site. To use these sources in a research essay, you must evaluate their validity. If they are valid, and you use them, then you must cite them appropriately.

Social scientists can usually rely on the validity of published books and periodicals. Because these sources are expensive to produce, publishing companies stake their reputations on the material's validity and freedom from bias.

How do you judge the validity of a Web site source?

Step 1

Make an initial judgment about the site based on its address suffix (if it has one). The following suffixes are clues about the site:

- —.edu: a US educational institution site (for example, the University of North Carolina's home page is http://www.unc.edu)
- —.org: a US registered organization site (for example, the Public Broadcasting system's home page is http://www.pbs.org)
- —.com: a US commercial operation site (for example, a leading book retailing site is http://www.amazon.com)

- —.ca: a Canadian site (for example, an educational institution such as the University of Western Ontario at http://www.uwo.ca or a commercial operation such as Air Canada at http://www.aircanada.ca)

Addresses with the dot-edu and dot-org suffixes are generally reputable. But it is still important to check the organization's reputation in the field before accepting the information contained at the site.

Step 2

Do a more thorough test of the site. This is especially important for dot-com and dot-ca addresses and addresses with no suffix at all.

Judging the Site for Validity

If a site is valid, you should be able to answer easily the first two questions. You should be able to answer "yes" to most of the remaining questions.

1. Who/what is the source of the page?
2. Is the site created by an individual, group, or organization?
3. Are the author and the author's credentials clearly identified?
4. Are links provided to other sources that can be contacted for confirmation or more information?
5. Does the author provide a bibliography and/or citations to confirm the accuracy of the information?
6. Is the intent of the page to inform or educate, rather than to entertain the reader?
7. Does the page seem to be free from open bias, and confirm information from other sources?
8. Has the site been updated recently?

Modified from: Memorial University of Newfoundland. *Internet Validation Project.* [Online]. Available http://www.stemnet.nf.ca/~dfurey/validate/students.html 29 September 2000.

Step 3

Record the relevant information from all sources, including **citations**. Citations tell the reader where your information comes from. They prove to the reader that you have actually done the research, and they demonstrate your academic honesty.

- Citation from within the essay:

> Children who are trained in a relaxed climate of praise for their successes are likely to become confident and creative adults (Hall and Lindzey, 1970, 51).

- Bibliography citation form for a book:
  Last Name, First Name. Date. *Source Title*. Place. Publisher.
  For example:
  Hall, Calvin S., Lindzey, Gardner. 1977. *Theories of Personality.* New York. John Wiley and Sons. 1977.
- Bibliography citation form for an article in a book:
  Last Name, First Name. Date. "Article Title." In First Name, Last Name, eds. *Source Title*. Place. Publisher.
  For example:
  Smith, Dorothy. 1985. "Women's Inequality in the Family." In Allan Moscovitch, Glenn Drover, eds. *Inequality: Essays on the Political Economy of Social Welfare*. Toronto. University of Toronto Press.
- Bibliography citation form for an article in a periodical:
  Last Name, First Name. Date. "Article Title." *Periodical Title*. Volume and Edition Numbers OR Date.
  For example,
  Rymer, Russ. 1992. "The Annals of Science: A Silent Childhood." *New Yorker.* 13 April 1992.

- Bibliography citation form for an electronic source:
  Author. *Title*. [Online]. Available
  OR "Article Title." *Source Title*. [Online]. Available
  http://address/filename
  Date of document or date of download if document date not provided.
  For example:
  "Sigmund Freud." *The Columbia Encyclopedia*, 3d ed. [Online]. Available
  http://www.encyclopedia.com
  30 September 2000.

Follow-Up

1. Imagine you are researching the genetic modification of food by biotechnology companies. You find information at a dot-com site.
   a) What validity problems might arise?
   b) Might these same problems arise at a dot-ca site? Explain.
2. Use a search engine to find an electronic document about one of the stage models for socialization presented in this section.
   a) Use the eight questions on page 135 to evaluate the site and document.
   b) Present a brief summary of the document and your validity findings.
3. Find three valid electronic documents about one of the stage models for socialization presented in this section. Make a bibliography of these three sources, using the correct citation form. If the sites refer to books and articles, add these to your bibliography, citing them correctly.

The Social Experience Theory

Charles Horton Cooley (1864–1929) and George Herbert Mead (1863–1931) were colleagues at the University of Chicago. They asserted that the self did not exist at birth, was not part of the body, and was not controlled by biological drives. Self-development, they believed, was based on how we think others see us. Cooley coined the term the **looking-glass self** to capture this idea that we view ourselves as having the features we think others see in us.

Mead suggested that the self has two parts. These two parts were briefly introduced in Chapter 4 (see page 75). There is the subjective part (the "I"), which initiates social actions, such as starting conversations or asking for a date. The other part is the objective part (the "Me"), in which we play the role of the other person. The Me-self forms impressions about the I-self based on the responses of the other person. For example, if the other person accepts the date, the Me-self is moulded positively. If the other person says "no," the Me-self is moulded negatively.

Mead and Cooley believed that children's social experience was vital to their development of the Me-self. An important part of this experience is participating in role-playing games (for example, pretending to be a parent or a police officer).

Just as Freud's psychosexual model has been criticized for downplaying the social element, Mead and Cooley have been criticized for downplaying the biological. But their demonstration of the importance of social experience is valued.

The Psychosocial Development Theory

Erik Erikson (1902–1994), a German-American psychologist, has made a unique contribution to our understanding of human development. His book *Childhood and Society* (1950) presented his theories about how the self develops. They are summarized as follows.

The typical human life is divided into eight chronological stages. In each stage, the subject faces a conflict between personal wants and family or societal expectations. The self emerges as we—successfully or unsuccessfully—resolve each crisis point of conflict. The more successful the resolution, the more ready a person is to move to the next stage. The individual who has successfully resolved all eight conflicts will, in old age, be a complete self who regards life with a sense of pleasure. The individual who has not

Figure 5.10 Erikson's stages of psychosocial development

Stage	Age	Experiences promoting positive socialization	Experiences hindering positive socialization
1. Trust v. mistrust	birth–1 year	parental care of physical and psychological needs	lack of physical care, uncertain parental love
2. Autonomy v. shame and doubt	2 years	encouragement of independence, clear discipline	criticism, lack of encouragement, overprotective discipline
3. Initiative v. guilt	3–5 years	encouragement of child's interests, parental pride and confidence	criticism of child's failures
4. Industry v. inferiority	6–12 years	guidance and praise of academic and social development	too high or too low expectations for success in school
5. Identity v. diffusion	adolescence	strong role models to promote self-esteem and life goals	lack of role models, social demands causing inner turmoil
6. Intimacy v. isolation	young adulthood	healthy identity, concern for others, involvement in caring relationships	overemphasis on self over others, fear of being hurt through bad relationships
7. Generativity v. isolation	adulthood	making good personal decisions, success, enjoyment of work, concern for growth of others	lack of concern for others, being self-centred, becoming despairing
8. Integrity v. despair	old age	self-confidence, having led a complete life, sense of satisfaction	depression, lacking fulfillment, sense of failure

successfully resolved many of these conflicts is likely to be haunted by a sense of lost opportunities. It is common for that person to feel, "I wish I had my life over again to avoid these mistakes."

Like Freud and Piaget, Erikson relied on chronological, age-related stages to explain the emergence of the self. Critics suggest that the model is too rigid, because not all individuals go through the stages at the same pace or with the same completeness. But the simplicity and logic of Erikson's model have made it one of the more popular and long-lasting ones.

The Moral Development Theory

Lawrence Kohlberg, an American psychologist, disputed G.H. Mead's assumption that the self develops mainly through social experience. Intrigued by the findings of Piaget, he concluded that our ability to judge the morality of actions evolves through stages as our brains develop. His 1966 study summarized his findings. A simplified version appears below.

- *The Preconventional Stage*: This is the stage of young chiildren's moral reasoning. They decide on an action solely on the basis of whether or not it is in their direct personal interest. They believe that rules are rules, never to be varied. They should obey rules because they could be punished if they don't.
- *The Conventional Stage*: We move into this stage in our teenage years, at which time we give up some of our childish selfishness. We acknowledge the needs of others. We recognize that right and wrong need to be consistent with society's norms. We believe our behaviour should broadly correspond to those norms. We accept that rules may vary according to particular circumstances, but that generally they should be followed. Otherwise, society will break down.
- *The Postconventional Stage*: As adults, we move beyond blind acceptance of society's norms, and wonder if they are they ethically justified. Is it right for a parent to break into a store to steal food for a starving family? The preconventional child will say, "No, you could get into trouble for that." The postconventional adult will argue that it is a greater crime to let a family starve than to steal food.

Like Piaget, Kohlberg suggested that our development occurs in fairly predictable stages. We move through them as we deal with moral and ethical issues and as our brains and experience grow. The same criticisms levelled at other stage models also apply to Kohlberg's findings. Another serious criticism is that all the subjects of his research were boys. Some claim he made a serious research error in generalizing the results of these male subjects to all humanity.

The Gender-Based Theory

You have already read in Chapter 4 that their gender affects how babies are treated (page 102). You have also learned about gender differences in general (pages 100 to 109). Carol Gilligan, a psychologist at Harvard University in Massachusetts, explored gender differences in moral development. She began her studies by critiquing Kohlberg's research method, which relied exclusively on boys.

In her book *In a Different Voice* (1992), Gilligan concluded that male moral development occurs from a justice perspective. This means that males consider formal rules and abstract principles to be important in defining right and wrong actions. Females, on the other hand, have a "care and responsibility" perspective. They judge actions based on how those actions affect personal relationships and loyalties. In this theory, Gilligan claimed a boy might see stealing as wrong because it is "against the rules," and he might want the thief to be punished. A girl is more likely to wonder why a person would steal, and she would want to help such a person. Kohlberg believed that the abstract, rules-based approach of males is superior to the person-based female approach. But Gilligan challenged this idea, pointing out that caregiving and support are key norms in any civilized society.

Critics have suggested that Gilligan's findings are valid, but do not tell us why the differences exist. Is it because females are biologically different from males, or is it because they have been differently socialized? Gilligan suggested that it is largely a matter of socialization, but there is obviously room for the other solution in this discussion.

Figure 5.11 Gilligan supported her theory with research of children at play. Boys tend to like games with intricate rules and to argue passionately over disputes. Girls tend to bend the rules or quit playing to protect the feelings and relationships in the group.

RECAP

1. What is the key to successful socialization according to each of the theories presented on pages 131 to 134 and pages 136 to 139?
2. Which of the theories are based on the assumption that there are predetermined biological stages in our socialization? Give examples.
3. Which of the theories are based on the assumption that our socialization is determined almost exclusively by our social experiences? Give examples.

Section 5.4

From Culture to Culture

Focus Questions

- What changes in socialization are Canadian Sikh women and men undergoing?
- How can both women and men be "husbands" in Nuer culture?
- How has the Taliban regime in Afghanistan changed women's lives?

Key Concepts

dastaar
pastoralist
bride-wealth
genitor
pater
Taliban
fundamentalist
burqah

Culture and Socialization

So far in this chapter, you have examined what socialization is; how it works; and what its effects are. You have looked at socialization mainly from the viewpoints of psychologists and sociologists. But anthropologists also have important contributions to make to our understanding. Anthropologists look at the emergence of the self as it relates to the culture of the society. Anthropologists focus on variations in socialization from culture to culture and their effects on the individual.

This section looks at the following aspect of socialization from the anthropological viewpoint: how do females learn the gender expectations of their society? We present three different case studies, each showcasing a different culture, to show the variety of results that can develop.

Case Study: Sikh Women in Canada

The traditional centre of the Sikh religion is the Punjab region of northern India. There are about 16 million Sikhs around the world. The largest groups outside India live in Great Britain, the United States, and Canada. About 60 000 Sikhs currently live in Canada. Sikhs are perhaps most visible because of the turbans worn by Sikh men to cover their uncut hair. Not cutting one's hair is a sign of commitment to Sikhism.

Traditional Sikhism took a fairly conventional approach to gender roles. Males were expected to provide for the family, while females were supposed to look after the family. Women were generally not expected to play a significant role outside the family. But these roles were not based on anything inherent in the religion itself. In fact, Sikhism's founder Guru Nanak (1469–1539) made a point of not making distinctions between people. Guru Nanak suggested not only that females and males were equal, but also did not distinguish between people of different caste, which went against common belief in India. After Guru Nanak's lifetime, however, specific gender roles did tend to develop among followers of the religion.

Sikh Women in Canada

Sikh women born and raised in Canada receive somewhat conflicting cultural messages. Older Sikhs, especially those born in India, tend to support traditional gender roles. Younger Sikhs support less rigid roles; their exposure to the prevailing culture in Canada backs them up.

Many young Sikh women regard themselves as feminists and see no conflict in this position. In the words of Rajvinder Kaur, a law student:

> I think that Guru Gobind Singh [one of the early Sikh leaders] was a staunch feminist! People always get scared when I use that word. I think that my personal definition of feminism is anybody who is committed to and believes in the inherent equality between the genders (Mahmood and Brady, 2000, 44).

Figure 5.12 Palbinder Kaur Shergill, a parliamentary candidate in British Columbia when this photo was taken, wears a turban.

Hair and Socialization

Hair is very important in Sikh culture. One of the basic principles of Sikhism is that neither males nor females should cut their hair. Men often wind their hair on top of their head and bind it tightly with a **dastaar,** or turban. Women often plait their hair and wear it down their backs. This distinction between the practice of men and women is culturally based; there is nothing in the Sikh religion itself requiring these differences. So some young Sikh women are starting to wear turbans, which has shocked some older, traditional Sikhs. But others are supportive. As one young woman says:

> Grown men of various ages have come up to me and told me that they love my turban. Some have said that my turban looks very attractive, and some have even said that I am beautiful. The interesting thing to note is that none of these men were East Indian. They were white, black or oriental. It's true that some East Indian men think that women do not look good in turbans; that it isn't feminine. It just goes to show you how our ideas on beauty are so culturally based (Mahmood and Brady, 2000, 58).

Marriage Expectations

Another cultural item that is changing among Sikhs is the arranged marriage. In earlier times, it was possible for a Sikh couple to get married without ever really knowing much about each other. The two families made the spouse selection and arrangements. Today, it is more common for Canadian families to introduce their daughter or son to a candidate they feel is a suitable match. They then let the two people decide for themselves. In the words of Sukhminder Kaur , a young single woman:

> I believe that parents should be the key players in the marriage, but at the same time the woman should have some say. It's like if a friend says, "Hey,

there is this guy and he is really good-looking and smart and maybe you should get to know him." I could see my parents doing that. And if that is an "arranged marriage," then I am all for it because it is just another way of meeting someone. And what if that is the perfect person? (Mahmood and Brady, 2000, 80)

Sikh girls and women living in Canada are being socialized differently than their counterparts in India. They are examining gender roles and modifying more traditional approaches. As a result, Sikh women's and men's socialization processes, as well as their sense of self, are undergoing major change.

Source: Mahmood, Cynthia, Brady, Stacy. 2000. *The Guru's Gift: An Ethnography Exploring Gender Equality with North American Sikh Women*. Mountain View, CA. Mayfield Publishing Company.

1. Describe two ways in which a Sikh girl may be socialized differently from a Canadian girl of European background.
2. Describe two ways in which a Sikh girl in Canada may be socialized differently from a Sikh girl in India.
3. How do you account for Canadian Sikh women's practice of wearing turbans?

Case Study: Women in East African Pastoralist Cultures

The Nuer people of sub-Saharan East Africa have a highly developed economic and cultural system. The system is largely based on cattle—all wealth is measured in cattle (which provide milk and meat) and all cultural transactions are related to cattle. These cultures are described as **pastoralist**, or based on animal herding.

Marriage decisions involve the families of the two participants. Talks are held to decide the transfer of cattle from the bride's to the groom's family. This is called **bride-wealth**, and legitimizes the marriage and the children it will produce. There is a strict list of family members who must receive a share of the transferred cattle. Some of them—such as grandparents—might already be dead. Once the marriage has been completed, the bride and groom live in a simple nuclear family, headed by the husband.

This picture of marriage and family may suggest that women play no important role in Nuer culture. In fact, many other domestic arrangements are possible. For example, a woman who is unable to bear children may become a "husband" by marrying another woman. The wife takes a male lover (the **genitor**) and bears children. The female "husband" is regarded as the children's *legal* father (the **pater**). The genitor plays little role in the raising of the children, who are not regarded as part of his family. When the child of such a marriage eventually marries, normal bride-wealth practices are followed. The fact that there are two female parents is irrelevant. All bride-wealth goes to the pater's family and none to the genitor's. The Nuer place greater importance on paternity, in a legal sense, than on biological parenthood.

Women have some freedom when it comes to their domestic relationships. For example, widows often do not remarry. They may live with lovers and have children with them. But such children always belong to their dead father, who will always be their pater. A woman may also move in with a lover while she is still married. But her husband will still be the pater of any children that result from this relationship. The bride-wealth originally paid to the husband's family ensures that all of the wife's children will belong to her husband.

Males and females are not totally equal in Nuer culture. Bride-wealth tends to favour men, giving them the right to paternity even when they are not biological fathers (though women acting as husbands also have this right). Paters also claim cattle when their wives' daughters marry.

The bride-wealth system helps to maintain economic equality between all family units in pastoralist cultures. Women and men are therefore motivated to maintain their dependence on each other for the sake of stability. So, even though women and men are not equal, their interests are remarkably similar.

Source: Bodley, John H. 2000. *Cultural Anthropology*, 3d ed. Mountain View, CA. Mayfield Publishing Company.

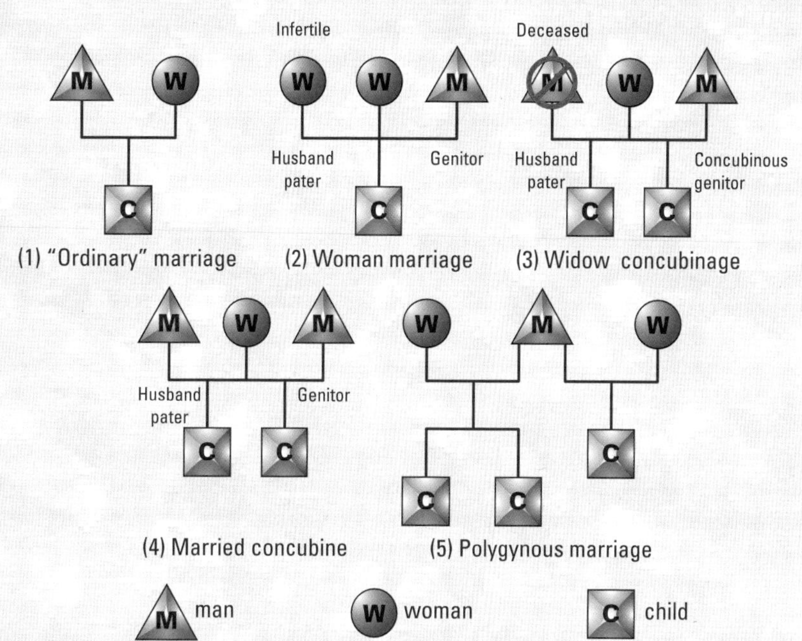

Figure 5.13 Anthropologist E.E. Evans-Pritchard identified ten Nuer forms of marriage (Bodley, 2000, 103). Those labelled (1) *to* (4) *are described in this case study. For more information on* (5), *Polygynous marriage, see Chapter 6, pages 182 to 184.*

1. Describe the bride-wealth system.
2. Describe one other unique feature of Nuer culture. Explain how this feature affects the role of women.
3. Do you think that men dominate women in Nuer culture? Explain your answer.

Case Study: Islamic Women in Afghanistan

Islam is one of the great religions of the world. It is the dominant religion in North Africa, as well as in the area stretching from the Middle East to Pakistan and Afghanistan. The tenets of the religion are believed to have been revealed to the Prophet Muhammad (570–632). In Islam, Allah is regarded as the one, true God, and Allah's message is believed to be found in a sacred scripture called the *Qu'ran* (Koran).

The *Qu'ran* has been subject to varying interpretations. In one interpretation, women are morally and legally inferior to men. Many Muslim customs (customs of Islam) seem to reinforce this interpretation. For example, daughters inherit less than sons. Women may have only one husband at a time, while men may have up to four wives at a time.

In some Islamic countries (for example, Egypt and Jordan), women can receive higher education and work as professionals. They must dress modestly, but can go out in public in Western clothing. In Afghanistan, however, women are prevented from playing virtually any role outside the home. They must be totally covered when out in public, and must be accompanied by a male relative.

Women in Afghanistan were relatively free until 1994, when the **Taliban** gained power. The Taliban are Islamic **fundamentalists**. They claim that their decrees, based on their own, sometimes mistaken, interpretations of Islamic law, are the only legitimate applications of the *Qu'ran*'s edicts. Educated, urban women have been forced to make the greatest changes as the culture of the Afghani state changed. Women who worked as teachers, doctors, and lawyers have been forced to give up their jobs (a few practise as doctors in women's hospitals). No education is available for women or girls. At home, women must be invisible from outside, so windows are curtained. Even though begging is a violation of Taliban law, it is common to see women, alone or in groups, begging on the street. In order to go out in public to beg, women must wear a **burqah**. This is a head-to-foot garment with a gauze covering over the wearer's eyes. When someone gives these women money, they may offer only the briefest of "thank yous." Speaking to strange men—especially without a male relative present—is not permitted.

Figure 5.14 A young girl peers out from a group of Afghani women wearing traditional burqahs.

Gender expectations in Afghanistan are unvarying and strictly enforced. Women and men are publicly whipped for transgressions (women are whipped through their burqahs). So violent are these whippings that they leave the victims injured for months afterwards.

Sources: Vollmann, William T. 2000. "Across the Divide." *New Yorker*. 15 May 2000. Orr, David. 2000. "Afghans Look to Escape Oppression." *The Globe and Mail*. 9 June 2000.

1. What is a burqah? In what way is it symbolic of the restrictions facing women in Afghanistan?
2. What factors in Afghanistan's culture and history have had the most influence on female socialization?
3. Why do many Canadians consider Afghani women to be oppressed? Do you think this judgment is solely based on a cultural bias, or is something more involved in making it? Explain.

Activities

Show your knowledge

1. Define these terms:
   a) primary socialization
   b) secondary socialization
   c) anticipatory socialization
   d) resocialization
2. What are five important things that we must learn or discover during the socialization process?
3. What are the major contributions to the socialization process of each of the following?
   a) the family
   b) school
   c) the peer group
   d) media
   e) religion
   f) the workplace
4. What statistics in the "Media" section (pages 127 to 129) show that young people spend a lot of time watching television? What statistics show that much of this programming is violent in nature? How much of this programming is Canadian? How much is American?
5. Create an organizer to show what each theorist (pages 131 to 134 and pages 136 to 139) believes is the key to successful socialization.
6. Identify and describe one aspect of
   a) Canadian Sikh culture
   b) Nuer pastoralist culture
   c) Taliban culture in Afghanistan

Practise your thinking skills

7. At the top of a piece of paper, make a horizontal scale labelled with the numbers 1 to 10. (Note: On this scale, "1" will represent "totally coming from biological inheritance"; "10" will represent "totally coming from the socialization process"; "5" will represent "coming equally from biological inheritance and socialization.") Place the following items on the scale. On a separate piece of paper, give reasons for your choices.
   a) being right- or left-handed

Activities

b) being good at playing a musical instrument
c) being good at making puns
d) being genuinely concerned with trying to help others solve their problems
e) being close to your ideal body weight
f) being able to work for long periods of time without a break
g) physically resembling one of your parents
h) liking to read long novels
i) understanding your personal needs and addressing them
j) wanting to find a soulmate to spend the rest of your life with

8. Do you think that watching too much television, especially of a violent nature, negatively affects young people's socialization? Give reasons for your answer.
9. In a small group, discuss each of the following hypotheses. State whether you think each one is correct and your reasons for your opinion.
   a) Teenagers choose their friends based on similarities of values and attitudes.
   b) Parents who are aware of their teenagers' values and attitudes have greater influence over the friends they choose.
   c) Adolescents who take drugs and drink alcohol are more likely to come from families that do not take drugs and drink alcohol.
   d) Adolescents who have families with high levels of bonding are more likely to have friends who take drugs.
   e) High self-esteem and self-confidence help adolescents resist negative peer pressure.
   f) Over 80 per cent of adolescents who tried illegal drugs report that they did so because of peer pressure.
10. How would each of the theorists from pages 131 to 134 and pages 136 to 139 explain the following?
   a) Some people like their families and others do not.
   b) Some people do well in school and others do not.
   c) Some teenagers join violent gangs and others do not.
   d) Some people commit crimes and others are law-abiding.
   e) Some people have successful careers and others have difficulty keeping a job.
   f) Some people have children who love them and others have children who hate them.

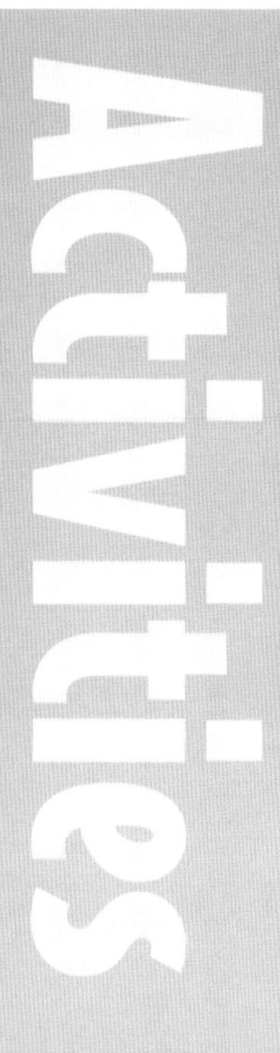

g) Some people are happy and content in old age and others are bitter and complaining.

11. In which of the three cultures examined (pages 140 to 144) do women have the greatest freedom? In which do they have the least freedom? Use specific examples to support your position.

Communicate your ideas

12. Compare the choices on your horizontal scale from Activity 7 with those of a classmate. Discuss why the two of you have placed the items where you have. Make any changes you think are necessary.
13. Research one of the hypotheses from Activity 9. Report your findings to the class.
14. Research a total institution. Possible institutions are a military boot camp, a federal penitentiary, a religious cult. Find out
    a) its major features
    b) how successful it is in its objectives and in resocializing its members
    c) reasons for its success or lack of success

    Report your findings to the class.
15. Research the life and work of one of the theorists on pages 131 to 134 and pages 136 to 139. Create a display featuring the theorist's background, interests, writings, and findings. Present your display to the class, stating and giving reasons for whether or not you regard the researcher's theory as useful and accurate.
16. Research the position of women in a particular culture. Answer the following questions carefully. As you encounter situations different from those of your own culture, avoid describing or judging them by the standards of your own culture.
    a) What are some of the difficulties they face?
    b) How have they managed to change their position in the culture?
    c) How does their position in the culture compare with the position of women in Canadian culture?

    Present your findings to the class.

Apply your knowledge

17. Add ten characteristics similar to the list in Activity 7. Ask five classmates to rank them on the horizontal scale. Do the same with five

Activities

non-classmates. What do you observe about your subjects' viewpoints on the importance of biological inheritance versus socialization?

18. Imagine you are starting your own service company (for example, a fast-food restaurant, variety store, or doughnut shop).
    a) Make a short list of values that your company stands for (for example, "Total customer satisfaction, or your money happily refunded").
    b) Create a team-building plan. The plan should encourage employees to accept the values of the company and put them into practice.
    c) How successfully do you think an entrepreneur could do this in real life? Give reasons for your answer.
19. Choose yourself or a friend as a subject. Examine the subject's socialization process. Which of the theories on pages 131 to 134 and pages 136 to 139 is the best explanation for the development of the person's self? Why? Discuss your conclusions with a classmate. (Note: Be careful to respect the subject's privacy during your discussion.)
20. Imagine you have been asked to write a report for the government of Canada about ways to increase gender equality.
    a) Research this topic and then make a list of recommendations to achieve greater gender equality. Be sure to consider the following headings:
        - education
        - families
        - jobs
        - media
        - law
    b) Make a copy of the following organizer. Complete it with your recommendations and findings.

How to Achieve Greater Gender Equality in Canada

Heading	Current situation	Recommendations
Education		
Families		
Jobs		
Media		
Law		

Unit 3

Social Structures and Institutions

Education, marriage, health care, the prison system, policing—all these are social institutions common to many different cultures. They are necessary to almost all societies, but they may function differently from culture to culture. These institutions and structures also change within a society. This has been especially true of work and education in Canada.

This unit will help you to understand these institutions and structures and to respond to the challenges they pose.

U N I T S T U

Unit Contents

Overall Expectations

In this unit, you will

- identify social institutions common to many cultures
- compare how selected social institutions function in a variety of cultures
- demonstrate an understanding of recent structural changes in work and education and of the impact these changes have on Canadian society

Topics by Discipline

Anthropology

Chapter 6

- Social control in Canada and Africa
- Changes in Canadian marriage
- Marriage in Hutterite culture
- Marriage as a cultural universal
- Monogamy among the Mixtec and in India
- Polygamy in Africa and Tibet
- How politics and technology affect marriage
- Changes in the Canadian family

Chapter 7

- A brief history of economic systems
- The purpose of work

Chapter 8

- School discipline
- Violence in schools
- Multicultural and Aboriginal education in th 1970s and '80s
- Home-schooling

Psychology

Chapter 6

- Romance in Euro-Canadian marriage

Chapter 7

- The economy of the future
- Reasons for workplace conflict
- Reducing workplace conflict
- Conflict-management styles

Chapter 8

- Why students drop out
- Violence in schools
- Progressive reforms of the 1960s

Y GUIDE

Sociology

hapter 6

Characteristics and purposes of social institutions
Total institutions
Social control
Issues in Canadian criminal justice
Marriage as a social institution
Changes in Canadian marriage
Forms of polygamy
Monogamy and social values
How politics and technology affect marriage
Changes in the Canadian family

hapter 7

What is the economy?
A brief history of economic systems
The post-industrial economy of the information age
The informal economy
The purpose of work
Canada's economic sectors
The post-industrial labour force
Technological, economic, and employment trends in the "new economy"

hapter 8

School discipline
Why students drop out
The functionalist approach to education
The conflict approach to education
Traditional versus progressive philosophies
Traditional curriculum in the 1950s
Progressive reforms of the 1960s
Multicultural education in the 1970s and '80s
The *Ontario Curriculum*
Distance learning
Home-schooling
Charter schools
Corporatization

Skill Guide

One method social scientists use to investigate society is the **survey**.

In this unit, you can develop the skills needed to do a survey. These skills are

- Creating a Survey (pages 175 to 177)
- Interpreting Survey Results (pages 207 to 208)
- Presenting Survey Results (pages 269 to 273)

Research and Inquiry Skills Learning Expectations

The skill development in this unit will enable you to

- demonstrate an understanding of a research method for conducting primary research
- describe the steps involved in a social science research and inquiry method
- use a social science research method effectively and ethically
- demonstrate an ability to organize, interpret, and analyze information gathered
- evaluate the relevance and validity of information gathered through research
- effectively communicate the results of your inquiries

Chapter 6

Social Institutions

Overview of Chapter

Learning Expectations

By the end of this chapter, you will be able to

- identify social and civil institutions in Canadian society and analyze the roles they play in society
- compare how selected social institutions (marriage, the criminal justice system) function
- describe the social institution of marriage in three diverse cultures
- demonstrate an understanding of the ways in which social institutions change over time from a social science perspective

Open for Debate

Russia's Social Institutions Fail to Prepare Youths for Society

When he was arrested with his three older brothers for kicking a tramp to death, 10-year-old Volodya Yakovlev was still a round-faced kid from a problem family in deprived outer Moscow. Despite his confession, Volodya's innocent smile and sweet treble voice made the 1994 crime seem unbelievable. Police and courts blamed his oldest brother, who was then 14, for instigating the violence. Volodya was not punished, although he was later separated from his mother and sent to a state children's home.

Now, however, after three years of brutalizing "care" by local authorities, Volodya has started to look like a hardened criminal. Tall, gangling, shaven-headed and perpetually grinning, he boasts between cigarettes about his lock-picking expertise, thefts, truancy and multiple arrests. His future? More crime, he says. At 13, it's too late for anything else. "Jobs? No way. And I won't be bothering with military service, either," Volodya says in brutal street speak. "There's nothing to do. The army wouldn't take me with my record. Anyway, there's nothing to steal there."

The story of Volodya Yakovlev bears chilling witness to the way Russia's grim social institutions—orphanages, children's homes, reform schools, the army and, later, prisons—fail in their stated aim of creating order in society. Instead, a mix of official neglect and excessive severity at these institutions actually encourages the formation of an angry and alienated underclass, with no way of surviving except through crime and violence. Social workers and human rights activists are unanimous in saying that the best way to get rid of Russia's criminal underclass is not to attack the violent victims of society who make it up—but the state officials whose negligence and greed create it. They accuse the *chinovniki*, the self-serving class of invisible bureaucrats who channel funds from budgets to institutions, of cynically perpetuating an abusive system that does little to correct wrongdoing or foster civic virtues—for no other reason than to line its own pockets.

For children such as Volodya, one step into this system can become a life sentence. Horrifying statistics cited by activist Boris Altshuler, head of a children's rights program, reveal that the 200 000 youths in state homes are likelier than others to inflict violence in the future.

"Every year, 15 000 to 17 000 of these kids are released into the real world at 18. But they're completely institutionalized. They can't handle normal life," Altshuler says. "So, in their first year of freedom, 5000 of these kids go to prison, 3000 become tramps and 1500 commit suicide."

Abridged from: Bennet, Vanora. 1998. "Russia's Social Institutions Fail to Prepare Youths for Society." *Los Angeles Times*. 22 September 1998.

Think About It

1. What social institutions does the author blame for creating angry and alienated youth?
2. What role might the family and friends of Volodya have had on his behaviour?
3. Do you think the situation described could happen in Canada? Explain your answer.

Section 6.1

Social Institutions Are All Around Us

Focus Questions

- What are social institutions?
- What are the characteristics and purposes of social institutions?
- At what point do social institutions turn into total institutions?

Key Concepts

personal institutions
impersonal institutions
entrenched
total institution
conformity
institutionalization

What Are Social Institutions?

Our focus in the last unit was twofold: the forces that influence and shape human behaviour (Chapter 4), and how we are socialized into our beliefs and behaviours (Chapter 5). The forces that we have considered in these chapters are either *in ourselves* (for example, "nature," or heredity, and gender) or *in others* (for example, the agents of socialization). The "others" who influence, shape, and socialize us are parts of a larger entity we call society. Our focus on this unit is how these influences fit into our society as "social structures" and "social institutions."

Social institutions are all around us. Churches, schools, government, media, the family, peers, the military, and the legal system are all examples of social institutions. Social institutions play an important role because they shape values and beliefs, maintain order, and help society to function efficiently. Some social institutions, like the family, are **personal** because they affect individuals' lives intimately. Others, like the government, are **impersonal** because they involve the activities and behaviours affecting large groups of people.

Characteristics

Social institutions share a number of characteristics. They have usually existed for a long period of time. They have well-established, or **entrenched**, patterns of functioning known as a structure. Because of these entrenched patterns, change usually occurs slowly in social institutions. Most social institutions have a specific purpose, and their members are joined together by shared values and beliefs.

One example of a social institution is our legal system. It fits the definition because it supports and enforces the behaviours our society generally agrees should be promoted and obeyed. Its structure is based on the Criminal Code of Canada, which outlines all of the behaviours considered to be criminal in our society. The police, who are responsible for enforcing criminal laws, are one of the many parts of the legal system's structure. Another part is the court, or judicial, system, which must determine the guilt or innocence of accused persons and proclaim the relevant sentence.

Purposes

Social institutions serve many purposes. One purpose is to act as an agent of socialization. As we have learned, socialization is a complex process whereby people learn their group's or society's acceptable ways of thinking and behaving. As a social institution, the legal system teaches us about acceptable behaviour from a legal perspective. For example, in Canada, if you are the victim of a theft, you cannot retaliate by stealing something in return. The legal course of action is to call the police, who will investigate the theft in the hope of bringing criminal proceedings against the thief on your behalf.

Another purpose of social institutions is to maintain order and security. If we all did whatever we wanted to do, whenever we wanted to do it, society would be chaotic. In fact, society would be more dangerous if there were no rules or laws to guide us. All of our social institutions, whether they are our families, our schools, or our legal system, contribute to maintaining social order, stability, and security.

"Total" Social Institutions

During the 1950s, one of the major areas of study of Canadian-born sociologist Erving Goffman was mental institutions. From this work, he noted how a social

ASK THE EXPERT

Dr. Vincent Sacco, professor of sociology at Queen's University

Do sociologists agree that social institutions promote the common good?

No. Sociologists have long debated whether social institutions are the source of, or the solution to, human misbehaviour. This debate hinges on our assumptions about human nature. In one view, people commit deviant acts largely because social institutions force them to do so. For example, wife assault might result from a structure of family life that gives some family members too much power over others. The other side to this argument is that humans naturally tend to behave in narrowly self-interested ways. Left to our own resources, the temptation to lie, cheat, and steal is hard to resist. Social institutions, rather than being the great corrupters of people, are the major reason why people conform to society's rules. Thus, the family, the school, and the workplace are settings in which we learn the importance of co-operation and the costs of wrongdoing. Advocates of this view link serious social problems such as delinquency and addiction to schools that don't teach, families that don't nurture, high rates of unemployment, and churches with many empty pews. Based on the evidence, both perspectives have some validity.

institution can become a **total institution**. This occurs when people in the institution are isolated from the rest of society and manipulated by administrative staff. In Chapter 5, we introduced some of the characteristics of total institutions in our discussion of agents of socialization (see pages 129 to 130). In review, these characteristics include the following:

- All aspects of daily life and all daily tasks are planned and monitored without any input from the residents.
- All aspects of life—work, play, and sleep—are carried out under one roof in a place completely isolated from the outside world.
- A privilege system operates in which residents can earn small rewards and preferential treatment by complying with the rules.

The goal of total institutions is resocialization—radically altering residents' personalities through deliberate manipulation of their environment. Resocialization is a two-part process. First, the staff of the institution tries to erode the residents' identities and independence. Strategies to erode independence include forcing individuals to surrender all personal possessions, get uniform haircuts, and wear standardized clothing. Independence is eroded by subjecting residents to humiliating and degrading procedures. Examples are strip searches, fingerprinting, and assigning serial numbers or code names to replace the residents' given names.

The second part of the resocialization process involves the systematic attempt to build a different personality or self. This is generally done through a system of rewards and punishments. The privilege of being allowed to read a book, watch television, or make a phone call can be a powerful motivator for **conformity**. Conformity occurs when individuals change their behaviour to fit in with the expectations of an authority figure or the expectations of the larger group. In the most punitive of total institutions—prisons and mental hospitals—the duration of confinement often depends on how well rules are followed. This makes the pressure to conform tremendous.

Goffman pointed out that no two people respond to resocialization programs in the same manner. While some residents are found to be "rehabilitated," others might become bitter and hostile. As well, over a long period of time, a strictly controlled environment can destroy a person's ability to make decisions and live independently. Known as **institutionalization**, this negative outcome of total institutions prevents an individual from ever functioning in the outside world again.

POINT AND COUNTERPOINT

Is the Canadian Military a Total Institution?

There is no question that a person who joins the military will undergo changes. Do these changes "resocialize" the recruit? Would this or other factors qualify the military as a total institution? What do you think?

Yes:

- The military is almost entirely independent from other institutions. For example, it sets and enforces its own regulations, and members who commit an offence face a military tribunal rather than a criminal court trial.
- Recruits face intense psychological pressure to stay. There may also be financial pressure—recruits may have to repay the army for their education and training.
- Basic training strips recruits of their identity by changing their physical appearance and eliminating privacy.
- Basic training forces conformity to the group through a strict routine, initiation and hazing rituals, and group activities.

No:

- Although largely independent, the military still falls under the control of the federal government.
- Recruits are free to leave the armed forces at any time; despite pressures to stay, there is no coercion.
- Basic training is not intended to be a resocialization process. Rather, it is a necessary learning program in teamwork and successful soldiering skills.
- Basic training is not intended to force such conformity that recruits' identities are stripped. Rather, it teaches recruits never to challenge orders so that larger group goals can be accomplished.

1. Which of Goffman's characteristics of a total institution do you think apply to the military?
2. How would the absence of the characteristics you listed in Question 1 affect the military? Would these effects be positive or negative? Explain.
3. Why might the military need soldiers to conform?

RECAP

1. What are the characteristics and purposes of social institutions?
2. How do social institutions differ from total institutions?
3. Why is it impossible to guarantee successful resocialization within a total institution?

Section 6.2

Criminal Justice Systems

Focus Questions

- What is the role of the criminal justice system in Canada?
- Is punishment an effective way of changing behaviour?
- How can society play a role in reducing crime?

Social Control

One need all societies share is for their members to conform, at least to some extent. Social control mechanisms are the methods used to ensure that individuals behave in acceptable ways. When individuals behave unacceptably—"breaking the rules"—a system of criminal justice takes over. In Canada this system is a formal institution. In other societies, the system may be much more informal.

Canada: A Formal System

The Criminal Justice System (CJS) in Canada is one of this country's largest and most expensive institutions. The CJS has three components, each with its own role and responsibilities. They are law enforcement agencies, the courts, and correctional agencies and institutions.

The main functions of law enforcement agencies are to protect society, to prevent crime, and to apprehend and arrest criminals. Law enforcement, the "front line" of the CJS, is accomplished by the police. All municipalities must have sufficient police to maintain law and order. To do this, they can create their own forces. Some take the alternative route of establishing a contract with the Royal Canadian Mounted Police (RCMP) or the provincial police (in Ontario and Quebec). Canada has approximately one police officer for every 475 people.

The Canadian court system processes people charged by the police with a criminal offence. It is **adversarial**. This means that lawyers, representing the defendant on one side, compete in court with the Crown (prosecution) to "win" the case. Critics of this system argue that the search for truth is often overshadowed in the fight to win a case. Supporters of the adversarial system believe that it is the only way to ensure a decent defence for suspects. In Canada, defendants who cannot afford a lawyer can have one appointed to them at taxpayers' expense. This provision is designed to help ensure that no person is convicted without a fair trial.

Correctional agencies and institutions have three functions. The first is punishment of the offender, once convicted by the court. Punishment fulfills society's need and/or desire for **retribution**—that is, for inflicting suffering on the offender

Key Concepts

adversarial
retribution
deterrence
specific deterrence
general deterrence
rehabilitation
patrilineal
Kpelle *moot*
low self-control

INTERNET RESOURCES

By examining their Web sites, identify which of the three functions of correctional institutions each of the following organizations supports. Provide evidence from each Web site for your conclusions.

Canadian Association of Elizabeth Fry Societies
http://www.elizabethfry.ca/

CAVEAT Canadians Against Violence
http://www.caveat.org/

The John Howard Society of Canada
http://www.johnhoward.ca/

Victims of Violence
http://www.victimsofviolence.on.ca/

comparable to the suffering caused by the offence. Retribution, a popular concept among many, has its roots in the biblical concept of "an eye for an eye." Punishment is also intended to achieve **deterrence**. Deterrence is the use of fear to discourage or prevent criminal behaviour. When punishment teaches the individual offender that "crime does not pay," and the offender does not commit further crimes out of fear of punishment, **specific deterrence** has occurred. Many people also believe that punishment results in **general deterrence**. In that case, other members of society, fearing the punishment meted out to an offender, decide against breaking the law.

A second function of correctional agencies is **rehabilitation**. Rehabilitation consists of actually reforming or improving an offender. As a result, the person chooses not to offend again—not out of fear of punishment, but out of a new acceptance of society's values. Since most offenders do not stay in prison forever, and neighbourhood residents do not want untreated ex-convicts among them, most Canadians agree that rehabilitation is necessary. But rehabilitation programs cost money, and the taxpayer is the ultimate source of this money. According to surveys, most Canadians currently have the perception that prisoners "have it easy" (Adams, 1990, 2–5; Angus Reid Group, 1996, 3). They are reluctant to allow the government to spend any additional taxpayer funds on the penal system. Although non-governmental organizations such as the John Howard and Elizabeth Fry societies provide programs serving prisoner needs, less than half of the general prison population receives counselling or treatment. Less than one-third of sex offenders receive any sort of rehabilitation.

The third function of correctional agencies is to protect the public. Jailing violent offenders keeps the public safe from them, at least temporarily. This function is important when there is a social climate of fear of crime and criminals. According to a spring 2000 Statistics Canada report, this fear is prevalent in Canada. The fear of being victimized is at high levels, even though the rates of all types of crime in Canada are dropping. A powerful trigger for fear is the recurrence of crime by offenders paroled from jail. In response, organizations such as CAVEAT (Canadians Against Violence Everywhere Advocating Its Termination) have formed. CAVEAT and other groups work hard to restrict the possibilities of parole and bail for serious offenders.

Informal Systems

In most Western societies, Canada included, people lead largely anonymous and independent lives. Most of the people we interact with are not close to us. The contact we have with them is usually one-dimensional. Imagine, for example, your life in a few years' time. You live on your own. Neither your landlord nor the person who runs the local convenience store is a relative or good friend. Your contact with these people is severely restricted—paying the rent in the one case and making small purchases in the other. Basically, our society is highly impersonal and fragmented. Our criminal justice system follows suit: it is impersonal and functions independently from the rest of society. Following its own rules, it assumes a "winner-take-all" attitude—either the prosecution or defence wins, the other side loses, and no consideration is given to how people's relationships are affected.

Other cultures may have a very different social structure. Social relationships are multi-dimensional and complex. A landlord usually *is* a relative and may well be a neighbour too. Social relationships with landlords, and with virtually all others in society, last a lifetime. Maintaining good relations with all is of paramount importance. In such cultures, the legal

Figure 6.1 The Aboriginal healing circle is an example of an informal justice system. In handing down sentences, the circle focuses on healing the victim, the offender, and the community.

system tends to have more informal elements than Western systems do. It also tends to prioritize harmonious community relations.

Aboriginal systems of justice can be classified as "informal." In many systems, the emphasis is on healing offenders, righting the conditions that led to the offence, and integrating the offender back into the community. The focus is on social harmony.

The Kpelle culture of Africa provides another example. The Kpelle live in central Liberia and the adjoining regions of Guinea. They are a **patrilineal** society, which means that property and inheritance are passed through the male line. The Kpelle number approximately 175 000.

In 1957 and 1958, anthropologist James L. Gibbs conducted a field study of the Kpelle's legal system. The court system is divided into two branches: the "formal" court and the "informal" court, or *moot*. The official court handles cases of assault, possession of illegal charms, and theft involving unrelated litigants. Some marital disputes are brought before the formal court, but they usually are not resolved well. The harsh tone of the court tends to drive spouses further apart rather than reconciling them.

The **Kpelle *moot*** is an informal airing of a dispute that takes place before an assembled group. The group includes the complainant, the "accused," neighbours, and other family members. The *moot* is presided over by a mediator selected by the complainant. The mediator is a kinsman who usually holds an office such as town chief. As such, he has some skill in dispute settlement. The following transcript illustrates the open nature of the moot and the way in which disputes are resolved.

> Wama Nya, the complainant, had one wife, Yua. His older brother died and he inherited the widow, Yokpo, who moved into his house. The two women were [classified as] sisters. After Yokpo moved in, there was strife in the household. The husband accused her of staying out late at night, of harvesting rice without his knowledge, and of denying him food. He also accused Yokpo of having lovers and admitted having had a physical struggle with her, after which he took a basin of water and "washed his hands of her."
>
> Yopko countered by denying the allegations about having lovers, saying that she was accused falsely, although she had in the past confessed the name of one lover. She further complained that Wama Nya had assaulted her and, in the act, had committed the indignity of removing her headtie, and had expelled her from the house after the ritual hand-washing. Finally, she alleged that she had been thus cast out of the house at the instigation of the other wife who, she asserted, had great influence over their husband.
>
> Kolo Waa, the Town Chief and the brother of Yokpo, was the mediator of the *moot*, which decided that the husband was mainly at fault, although Yua and Yokpo's children were also in the wrong. Those at fault had to apologize to Yokpo and bring

gifts of apology as well as local rum for the disputants and participants in the *moot* (Gibbs, 1963).

Gibbs, who was present at the *moot*, identified factors that contributed to the long-term reconciliation of the problem. First, the proceedings, although "spirited," remained orderly and open—any person present was allowed to speak at any time. This allowed for all parties to feel they had been "heard" on the issues at hand. They also felt they had an impact on the final resolution of the dispute. A second, perhaps more important, factor was that the faults of *both* parties were pointed out. This allowed the party at fault to save face. Though Wama Nya was found to be in the wrong, he was not singled out and labelled as deviant.

Issues in Canadian Criminal Justice

The Canadian criminal justice system contains many features of which we can be proud. Examples include protection from unfair search and seizure, the right to a fair trial, and the right to be tried within a reasonable period of time. But disturbing issues have arisen involving several facets of the system. In this section we look at three of them: the power of the police, the numbers of prisons, and the value of attempting rehabilitation. At the end of this section, you have an opportunity to judge Canada's criminal justice system. Does it need to be tougher and mete out harsher penalties? Or should we seek alternative methods of dealing with crime?

QUESTION:

Do the police treat teenagers fairly?

I have been to a couple of demonstrations where the police were called in to keep their eye on the situation. They were very fair. The demonstrations were peaceful so the police did not interfere. The only people they treated unfairly were the ones who treated the police poorly.

—Mirjana Radulovic, 17

I think that the police are like other adults, and judge teens on their looks. I think that teens are arrested more easily than adults. If you're with a group of four or more people you are likely to get stopped by street police, just so they can ask you where you're going, where you're coming from, and what you're doing.

—Chris Wickens, 17

The punishments the police give teenagers are usually the same given to adults. The police do let you off on warnings, though, for less serious crimes. Teenagers seem to have a fear of police and other authority figures and mouth off to them, which doesn't really help their cause.

—Ashley Houston, 16

The Power of the Police

We stated earlier that the ratio of police officers to citizens is about 1:475. Since police forces can be thinly spread, officers must judge carefully when and how to intervene in situations. In their book *Sociology* (1997), John J. Macionis, Juanne Nancarrow Clarke, and Linda M. Gerber cite studies of police behaviour (Smith and Visher, 1981; Smith, 1987). One study specified which factors influence the actions of police. The first was how serious the police perceive the situation to be. More serious situations tend to result in an arrest. The second was what the police believe the victim wants. The third was the amount of co-operation the suspect offers. Unco-operative suspects tend to get arrested. The fourth factor was the police's history with the suspect. Prior negative contact tends to result in an arrest in the present situation. This factor can be related to a finding by Schellenberg in a study published in the journal *Work and Occupations* (1996). Police, when considering making an arrest, are less likely to check a suspect's record on their patrol car computer line if they know the individual personally (that is, have had prior positive contact), or otherwise feel the individual is trustworthy. Fifth, the presence of bystanders increases the chance an arrest will be made. And sixth, all else being equal, police are more likely to arrest people of colour than white people.

The Smith and Visher studies were conducted in the United States. But their findings, especially as regards the sixth factor, seem to apply equally to Canadian police behaviour. Several provincial task forces and commissions throughout the 1990s published statistics on the overrepresentation of non-white offenders in Canadian prisons. They included the Commission on Systemic Racism in the Ontario Criminal Justice System and the Public Inquiry into the Administration of Justice and Aboriginal People. It was

Figure 6.2 Some studies of police behaviour in the United States suggest that, all else being equal, suspects of colour are more likely to be arrested than white suspects.

reported that, in Ontario, black people are imprisoned at five times the rate for white people. Aboriginal peoples are imprisoned at three times the rate. A 1991 Alberta task force found that Alberta police treated minor offences in public places more strictly if committed by Aboriginal peoples than by non-Aboriginal people.

Are there cases of abuses of police power? Are they widespread? Is there systemic racism in law enforcement agencies? These are issues being studied and debated in the legal world and in the wider society.

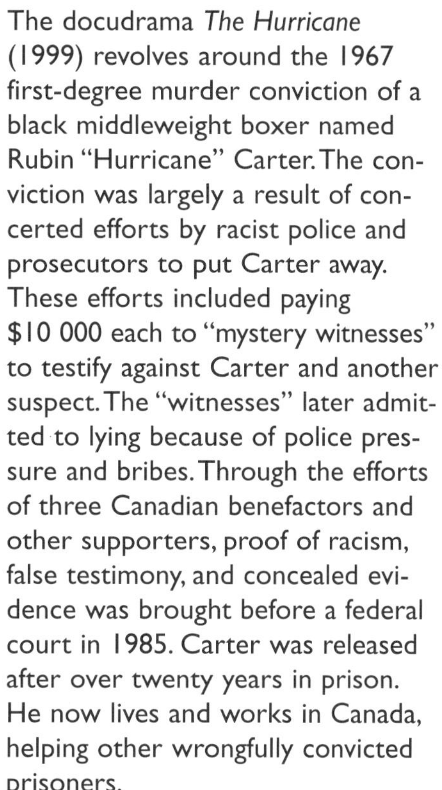

FILM LINK

The docudrama *The Hurricane* (1999) revolves around the 1967 first-degree murder conviction of a black middleweight boxer named Rubin "Hurricane" Carter. The conviction was largely a result of concerted efforts by racist police and prosecutors to put Carter away. These efforts included paying $10 000 each to "mystery witnesses" to testify against Carter and another suspect. The "witnesses" later admitted to lying because of police pressure and bribes. Through the efforts of three Canadian benefactors and other supporters, proof of racism, false testimony, and concealed evidence was brought before a federal court in 1985. Carter was released after over twenty years in prison. He now lives and works in Canada, helping other wrongfully convicted prisoners.

The Number of Prisons

In the late 20th century, prisons became the fastest growing segment of the US economy. In the same period, the large operational costs of correctional agencies became an issue in Canada. Between 1987 and 1997, the total correctional population in Canada (federal, provincial, probation, and conditional release) increased by 44 per cent (Canadian Centre for Justice Statistics, 1997). Between 1950 and 1997, Canada's inmate population rose approximately 2.5 times (Linden, 2000, 68). In 2001, about 34 000 people in Canada can be found in prison at any given time. This represents an adult population prisoner rate of 115 per 100 000 of population. Such a rate is much higher than the rate found in Western European nations, but lower than the rate in the United States.

What are the costs of maintaining prisons for these numbers of people? Reports of the average cost of keeping an offender in a federal penitentiary range from $50 000 to $65 000 a year. In contrast, the yearly cost for an offender in a halfway house is about $33 000. Much less expensive still is the cost of supervising an inmate on parole—$9000 per year (Solicitor General Canada, 2001).

Given this cost breakdown, how is money actually being spent? In 1995–1996, 77 per cent of the total correctional caseload were outside of prisons, under community supervision. However, only 12 per cent of all correctional spending went toward funding community supervision services. The case study that follows argues for making these services a greater priority in Canada.

Case Study: Prison versus Programs

The following article argues in favour of closing prisons and expanding rehabilitation programs.

"Reason must prevail over emotion, the government told us, as it ordered hospital closings. It is a waste of resources to keep high-cost institutions running, when patients can recover at home. Prudence must triumph over passion, it told us, as it ordered school closings. It is a drain on the public purse to run half-empty inner city schools when families are moving to the suburbs. If the government really believes its own rhetoric, it should now start closing prisons.

"The crime rate has fallen steadily for the last six years. Murders, robberies and assaults—the type of crime from which society needs protection—have showed the steepest decline. The incarceration rate is also beginning to drop. [In 1997], there were 32 917 adult offenders in penal institutions on any given day, down 3 per cent from the previous year.

"Rationalizing prisons could yield significant savings. It costs $1.9 billion a year to keep Canada's 52 penal institutions open—an average of $56 800 per inmate. Yet governments across the country, with the honourable exception of Alberta, are in no hurry to close jails. On this issue, it seems, logic is no match for feelings.

"Any objective look at the evidence suggests that Canada will need fewer penal institutions in the years ahead. The baby boom generation is aging. With fewer people in the 18-to-40 age range, which accounts for 70 per cent of serious crime, it follows that fewer jails will be needed. Courts are increasingly handing out conditional sentences, which allow a low-risk offender to admit responsibility, provide restitution, and perform community service. This trend is likely to intensify as more judges become comfortable with Bill C-41, the Sentencing Reform Act, which encourages them to consider alternatives to incarceration. And these alternatives appear to work. Jurisdictions that have tried conditional sentencing have noticed a drop in recidivism. They have also found offenders get more help dealing with substance abuse and mental illness outside the prison system.

"So what is stopping our policy-makers from closing prisons and saving money? Two things: their attitudes and our perceptions. Most governments in this country got elected on strict law-and-order platforms. They promised to crack down on young offenders, hand out tougher jail sentences and keep the streets safe. To turn around, now, and admit that crime isn't really out of control and locking up offenders isn't always the best approach, would be embarrassing.

"The second factor standing in the way of closing prisons is public fear. Despite six consecutive drops in the crime rate, 77 per cent of Canadians believe the streets are becoming more dangerous, and their homes and communities more vulnerable. We in the media reinforce this impression by describing acts of violence in great detail, without devoting much attention to the causes of crime. We report crime statistics without explaining—or understanding—why a disproportionate number of blacks and Aboriginal Canadians end up in jail. We document the failures and shortcomings of our justice system, while overlooking the programs that are working.

"Our politicians, in turn, exploit people's fears to win votes rather than daring to challenge conventional wisdom. It is much safer to promise more cops and more jails than to tell people their concerns are exaggerated. It is far easier to vilify young offenders than to tackle the poverty, domestic abuse and drug use that often lead to crime.

Abridged from: "Fear Imprisons Debate on Jail Issue." 1998. *The Toronto Star*. 28 November 1998.

1. Why does the author argue that we should be reducing the number of jails in Canada?
2. What is stopping policy-makers from closing prisons? Explain your answer fully.
3. Why do Canadians continue to believe the streets are becoming more dangerous, despite evidence to the contrary?

Rehabilitation or Radical Reform?

In *Sociology* (1997), Macionis et al. present the controversial work of Travis Hirschi. This sociologist proposes the abandonment of the current criminal justice system. He argues that prisons only protect members of the public from offenders for a short period of time. But they do little to reshape offender's attitudes or behaviours in the long run. Rehabilitation cannot occur when someone is locked up with criminals for months or years on end. Rather, incarceration simply strengthens criminal attitudes and skills. It also severs whatever social ties inmates have with the outside world. This actually makes it *more* likely that individuals will commit further crimes upon their release.

Hirschi's alternatives to the present system are based on a careful analysis of the characteristics of criminals. He points out that criminal behaviour is strongly correlated with age. Crime rates are high among people in their late teens and early twenties, and they fall steeply among older sectors of the population. In light of this fact, public sentiment demanding stiffer sentences appears misguided. The eventual result of passing such sentences is a prison population in which the great majority have aged beyond their peak crime years. Thus, the bulk of taxpayers' prison funding is going toward warehousing a diminishing crime threat. Hirschi argues that we must intervene in the lives of young people *before* they break the law. This intervention includes restricting the unsupervised activities of teenagers. Directing resources in this way will help reduce teenagers' access to guns, drugs and alcohol, cars, and each other.

Hirschi's analysis has also uncovered a strong link between criminal behaviour and **low self-control.** A person with low self-control requires instant gratification of all desires. The person cannot understand the long-term consequences of her or his actions. Hirschi argues that teaching children self-control at an early age could do much to reduce crime. This trait must be taught by parents, not governments. Therefore, Hirschi is an advocate

INTERNET RESOURCES

Find statistics to show how age relates to crime at

http://www.statcan.ca/english/kits/

Click on "List of all Education Resources." In "Canadian statistics," click on "Justice and crime" and proceed from there.

Find evidence to show how family characteristics relate to children's behavioural problems at

http://www.statcan.ca/Daily/English/981028/d981028.htm#ART1

of strong—preferably two-parent—families. He believes we need to target extra funds and assistance to seriously dysfunctional families. He points out that preventing teenage pregnancy would alone reduce crime rates in the long term more effectively than all current criminal justice programs combined.

Hirschi's work has been criticized for being overly simplistic. For example, having low self-control in matters such as smoking is unlikely to have any relationship to criminal activity. Also, many educated people who commit white-collar crime have lived lives of considerable self-control—otherwise, they would not have achieved an advanced education.

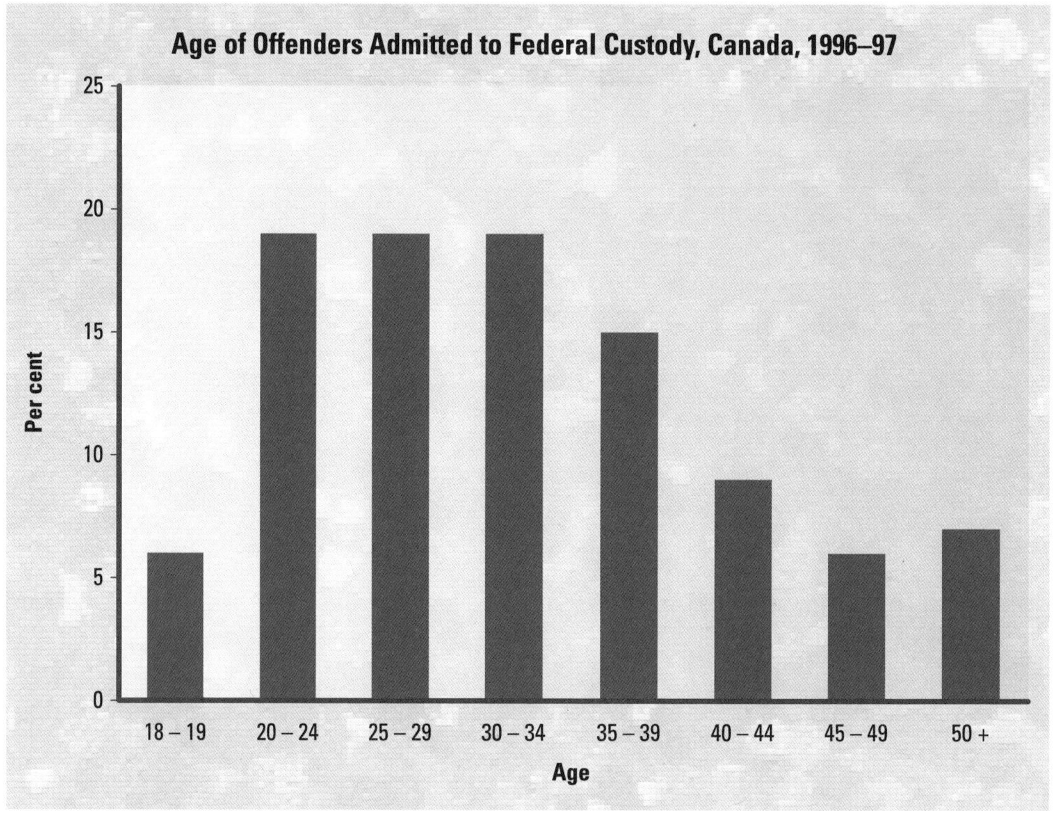

Figure 6.3 Do the statistics in the bar graph support Hirschi's argument? Explain.

Source: Adult Corrections Survey, Canadian Centre for Justice Statistics, Statistics Canada, 1997.

POINT AND COUNTERPOINT

Should Canada's CJS Be Tougher?

More than three-quarters of inmates in Canadian prisons are repeat offenders. How can this problem be solved? Should penalties be harsher?

Yes:

- Stiffer sentences for existing crimes would make the CJS more of a deterrent. For example, a stiff life imprisonment sentence of twenty-five years or more ensures that an offender is never released. This deters both the offender and others.
- Countries with extremely harsh justice systems, such as Singapore, have extremely low crime rates. These countries are not afraid to swiftly punish even minor offences by practices such as caning.

No:

- Punishment itself has an unpredictable impact on behaviour. Some people improve their behaviour in response to punishment. Others may behave even more inappropriately to "get back" at their punishers. Still others learn to be more aggressive and violent while in prison.
- In a tougher system, individuals may hide their inappropriate behaviour to avoid further punishment. In this case, they may appear to be reformed, but may not be at all.

1. Recall the three functions of prisons: punishment (retribution and deterrence), rehabilitation, protection. Would a tougher CJS make prisons more or less effective in fulfilling each function? Explain.
2. If our system is not toughened, how should it change?
3. What is your opinion on this question? Write a letter to the federal Minister of Justice explaining your position and suggesting a course of action.

RECAP

1. What factors determine whether a society will have a formal or an informal legal/justice system?
2. What are the three main components of the criminal justice system in Canada? What is the purpose of each?
3. Describe Hirschi's two main alternatives to the current CJS. Do you consider these alternatives to be valid? Explain.

Section 6.3

Marriage in Canada

Focus Questions

- Why does marriage continue to be a popular institution?
- Why do most people in mainstream Canadian culture base their decision to get married on "romantic love"?
- Why is it hard to define a "typical" Canadian wedding?

Key Concepts

free-choice marriage
romantic love
phenylethylamine
mainstream
acculturation
communal
distracter questions

A Popular Institution

Marriage is a very popular and enduring social institution. This might surprise some Canadians who know how high the divorce rate is in our country. With about 40 per cent of marriages ending in divorce, would it not be natural to assume that marriage as an institution is in trouble? The answer is simply no. It is true that divorce rates began to climb after divorce laws were liberalized in 1968. But these rates peaked in 1987 and have been declining since. As well, the remarriage rate in Canada is an astonishing 35 per cent. This rate indicates that, even after a negative marriage experience, people are more than willing to try again.

Marriage in mainstream Canadian and North American culture is based on **free-choice** love matches. The term "free-choice" does not mean that all individuals can always form the attachments they would like. What it does mean is that the job of seeking and developing relationships is ours rather than that of a third party.

One of the means through which to achieve a free-choice love match is dating. Those who practise dating are socialized into the behaviours of being part of a couple. Some people have a more casual view

Figure 6.4
Divorce rates in Canada

Year	1921	1941	1961	1968	1969	1981	1985	1986	1987	1990	1994	1995	1997
No. of divorces	558	2462	6563	11 343	26 093	67 671	61 980	78 304	96 200	80 998	78 880	77 636	67 408
Rates per 100 000 pop.	6.4	21.4	36.0	54.8	124.2	271.8	253.6	298.8	362.3	295.8	269.7	262.2	223.0
Rates per 100 000 married couples	n/a	n/a	n/a	n/a	n/a	1174.4	1103.3	1301.6	1585.5	1311.5	1246.3	1221.9	n/a

Source: Statistics Canada.

of dating, seeing it more as recreation or an end in itself. In many cases, dating one or more people over a number of years results in finding a "true love." This concept of true love, also known as **romantic love**, involves the selection of a partner based on the following characteristics: physical attraction, shared values and goals, and compatible personalities.

Psychologist Robert Sternberg's "triangular theory of love" (1986) fits romantic love into a larger picture of love. He breaks love down into three components: passion, intimacy, and commitment. He defines passion as "the drives that lead to romance, physical attraction, sexual consummation, and related phenomena." He defines intimacy as "feelings of closeness, connectedness, and bondedness in loving relationships." He defines commitment as "the decision that one loves someone else and...the commitment to maintain that love" (Sternberg, 1986, 119). As Figure 6.5 shows, romantic love is one of several different kinds of love, each with its own components.

Free-choice marriages based on romantic love have their critics. Some people would argue that love can blind us to the faults of our future mate, resulting in a bad choice. The research of Berscheid and Hatfield (1978) supports this claim. They found that we tend to fall in love with others, not necessarily for who they truly *are*, but for who we *want* them to be. It is not surprising, therefore, that many people feel they have fallen *out* of love after a few years of marriage. With romantic love at the root of a marriage, the relationship can crumble as the passion declines.

Kind of love	Passion	Intimacy	Commitment
Non-love	—	—	—
Liking	—	+	—
Infatuation	+	—	—
Empty love	—	—	+
Romantic love	+	+	—
Companionate love	—	+	+
Fatuous love	+	—	+
Consummate love	+	+	+

Figure 6.5 Sternberg's eight kinds of love

These same critics would argue that, because we make these errors, marriage is too big of a decision to be made by one person alone. Family and friends should have input into the selection of a person's marriage partner. Since these people are outside the relationship, they are not swayed by the emotion of love and can be more objective.

Diane Sollee is the head of the Coalition for Marriage, Family and Couples Education in Washington. She is a firm believer in the value of the extended family's contacts and resources. She argues that applying these resources, in a way similar to an "arranged marriage," is by far the best way to meet a suitable mate.

Psychologist Debbie Then points to Hollywood as an example of how meeting others through intimate contacts is a common route to marriage. Dr. Then believes that Hollywood is actually one big extended family because actors move in similar circles and frequently cross paths. For example, model Christie Brinkley met her husband, architect Peter Cook, through a friend. Actor and activist

Sharon Stone met her husband, editor Phil Bronstein, through her producer. And actor David Duchovny met his wife, actor Téa Leoni, through their agent. Dr. Then admits that it might seem odd to look to Hollywood, where divorce rates are notoriously high, to study "arranged marriages." But she notes that even in Hollywood, the marriages that last the longest are those where couples met through a mutual friend or family member. So if your parents or friends dislike the person you are in love with, do not dismiss their concerns out of hand. Their predictions of problems to come may well be accurate.

The Role of Romance

The experience many of us call "falling in love" actually consists of a number of physical symptoms. When we are near the person, our heart rate usually increases, our hands may become clammy, and our speech and laughter patterns often change. Some researchers believe that a chemical in the brain called **phenylethylamine** is responsible. When this chemical is activated, it runs through the body and creates the physical sensation of romantic love. Research done on "love addicts"—people who continually fall in and out of love—has revealed how this chemical operates. In some cases, when such "addicts" are not involved in a relationship, they binge on chocolate. Chocolate contains the same chemical—phenylethylamine—that creates the physical symptoms of "love." These patients seemed to need to stimulate the level of this chemical in their brain. So if they are not currently in love, they increase the phenylethylamine in their system by eating large amounts of chocolate.

Figure 6.6 Phenylaline, here photographed under a microscope, is an amino acid that the body converts into the chemical hormone phenylethylamine (PEA, also called the "love molecule"). The production of PEA in the brain can be triggered by eye contact or hand-touching when "in love." PEA is also one of around 300 chemicals in chocolate.

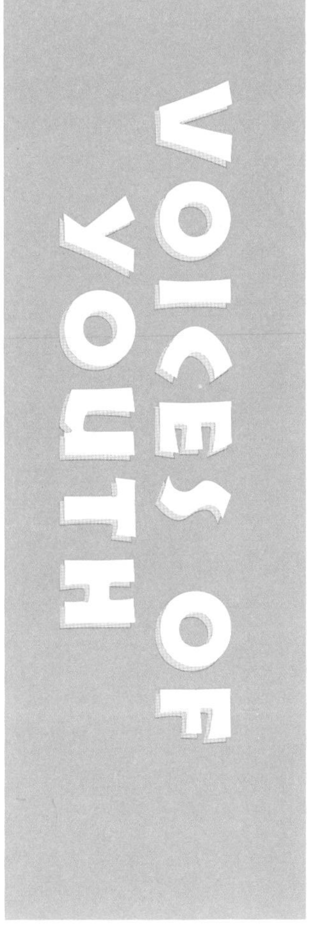

QUESTION:

Is it wrong to kiss on a first date?

I think that you shouldn't kiss on a first date. Although some people may take that the wrong way and think you don't like them, I wouldn't want to go out with someone just for the physical aspect anyway. When you don't kiss, I think it can tell the other person that you respect who and what they are.

—Brad Guldemond, 17

I wouldn't say kissing on the first date is wrong, but I don't think I would do it myself. I think it would be moving too fast physically and not emotionally. I feel it is important to have a good friendship with someone before getting too involved physically.

—Joe Bauman, 16

I feel that kissing on the first date is fine if the chemistry is there. I feel that it does have to be special, and that you don't go around just kissing everybody. I know for me that the buildup to the kiss is the hardest thing, because I wouldn't make the first move—you just never know what the guy is thinking.

—Mandi Eby, 16

I see absolutely no problem with kissing on a first date. If the mood is right and you can feel that the physical attraction is mutual, then by all means go for it. But sometimes it can be better to wait and let the attraction grow stronger.

—Heather Slade, 17

Canadian sociologist John Lee believes that romantic love serves a psychological need in humans. Lee theorizes that we have a psychological craving to be loved. The loving relationships we develop foster our self-esteem. Lee says our psychological need for love is especially strong in a society that is becoming more urbanized and alienating. In such a society, people look for a mirror image of themselves to fill the empty feeling of being alone. People want a relationship that is supportive of who they are.

Lee's work is supported by studies conducted by American researcher Bernard Murstein (Murstein, 1995). He suggests that, contrary to popular opinion, opposites do *not* attract. Murstein's research found that people tend to date people who are similar to themselves in physical attractiveness, academic achievement, and personality. Although we may dream of finding someone who is better looking or more intelligent than we are, in the end we choose someone who is similar to ourselves.

A Changing Institution

In the early nineteenth century, marriage in Canada was usually governed by economic factors. After industrialization developed later in the nineteenth century, economics declined as the prime consideration. Young people were encouraged to find a partner of similar economic and social background. This was usually accomplished by family members introducing prospective marriage partners to each other. Courtships were monitored by the family and the community, with couples spending time together in chaperoned situations (that is, an older adult was always present, preventing the couple from being alone together).

In the 1920s, young people challenged the restrictions of these traditions. The concept of dating was born.

Today, it is hard to describe a "typical" Canadian wedding. In **mainstream** Canadian culture—that is, according to the customs of the majority of Canadians—couples have three choices. They can go to a local courthouse for a private, non-religious ceremony. They can have a small and intimate gathering at their home. They can have a large wedding with all the trimmings. The latter type of wedding usually involves the bride being dressed in a white gown and the groom wearing a tuxedo. There are several attendants for the bride and groom, and they are usually involved in a rehearsal before the big day. The ceremony is performed in a place of worship, and a reception follows that involves a large meal and a dance. A traditional wedding like this, with 100 guests in attendance, can cost anywhere from $10 000 to $35 000.

While marriage ceremonies have become more varied over the years, so have people's opinions on what kinds of unions should enjoy the rights of marriage. Changes in public support for same-sex marriages can be tracked in Figure 6.7.

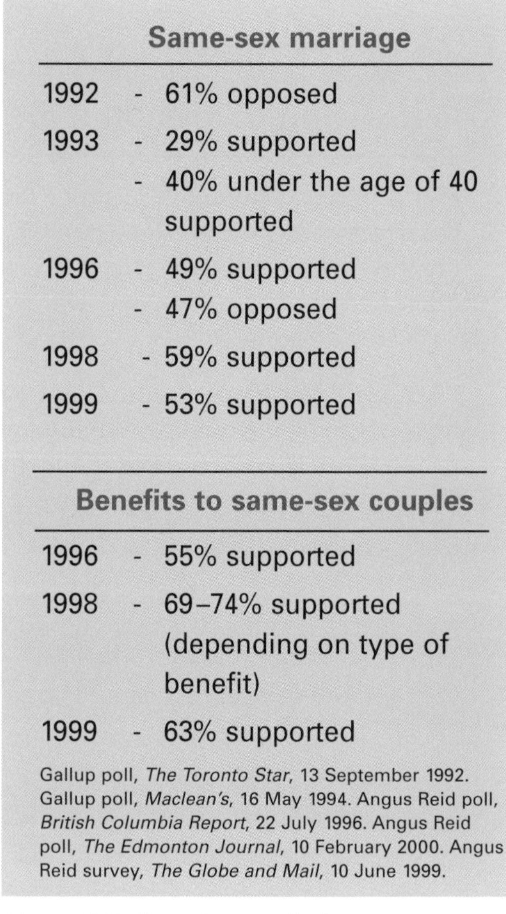

Same-sex marriage	
1992	- 61% opposed
1993	- 29% supported - 40% under the age of 40 supported
1996	- 49% supported - 47% opposed
1998	- 59% supported
1999	- 53% supported

Benefits to same-sex couples	
1996	- 55% supported
1998	- 69–74% supported (depending on type of benefit)
1999	- 63% supported

Gallup poll, *The Toronto Star*, 13 September 1992. Gallup poll, *Maclean's*, 16 May 1994. Angus Reid poll, *British Columbia Report*, 22 July 1996. Angus Reid poll, *The Edmonton Journal*, 10 February 2000. Angus Reid survey, *The Globe and Mail*, 10 June 1999.

Figure 6.7 Canadians polled on same-sex couples

In the late twentieth century, same-sex unions became partially recognized. The main form this recognition took was legislation extending to same-sex couples more of the benefits and obligations that opposite-sex couples have. Any recognition beyond this level remains a controversial issue for Canadians. For example, in 1994, an Ontario law (Bill 167) expanding the definition of "spouse" to include same-sex partners was narrowly defeated.

Case Study: Would You Marry Someone You've Never Met?

The following article appeared on 11 February 1999 in the *Toronto Star*. Sociologists and psychologists wonder: Do the incidents described reflect changes in our culture?

"It was quite the wonderful wedding. The beautiful bride wore a lovely white dress, the handsome groom was impeccable in full morning dress, the guests were cheerful and congratulatory. And the bride and groom were excited at finally meeting each other for the first time.

"Er, do what? No, it wasn't an arranged marriage in the cultural sense. It was more an ultimate blind date, except that the couple got married at their very first meeting. And although it was a legitimate marriage ceremony, it was also the ultimate publicity stunt, organized by an English radio station and covered widely in the English newspapers. The station held a contest to find the ultimate blind date with their prize being a luxury wedding, a glitzy honeymoon, a free apartment with a canal view and free use of a car. Even the wedding rings were provided by a sponsor—as was everything else, from clothing, to food, drink, and flowers. Greg, 28, and Carla, 23, were chosen from more than 200 applicants, and after the ceremony they said that the first thing they wanted to do was 'get to know each other.' Which, to put it mildly, is very understandable.

"Will it last? The smiling couple said they're going to prove everyone who said they would soon split up wrong and then left for their Caribbean honeymoon. My only thought was: How do you explain to other people you meet at the resort that you've only just met your spouse?"

Abridged from: Gibson, Valerie. 1999. "Never Met? Say 'Hello' and 'I Do.'" *Toronto Star*. 11 February 1999.

Although few Canadians are familiar with the British television show described above, most are familiar with the notorious show "Who Wants to Marry a Multi-Millionaire?" The program ran on the Fox network in February 2000. The show saw Rick Rockwell, a stand-up comic, select Darva Conger, a nurse, to be his bride. At the end of the show, Rockwell and Conger, who had never met or spoken, were married and then left on their honeymoon. Shortly after their return, Conger filed for an annulment. It turns out that Rockwell's claims to "multi-millionaire" status were dubious at best. Furthermore, a former girlfriend had filed a restraining order against Rockwell. Conger, however, has not returned the new vehicle or the $35 000 wedding ring she received from Rockwell. She posed nude for the August issue of *Playboy* for a reported fee of $500 000. In defence of her fee, she claimed hard times after being fired from her job as a nurse.

1. If you lived in an isolated, traditional culture in another part of the world, what would you think about Western culture and values after hearing about these "instant" marriages?
2. What do you think are the goals and motivations of individuals who get involved in instant marriages?
3. Do these contests and programs make a mockery of the institution of marriage, or are they just good entertainment?

Marriage in Hutterite Culture

Over generations, the families of immigrants to Canada usually adopt the practices of the mainstream culture. For example, if an immigrant couple moved to Canada several decades ago and raised children in Canada, the couple's grandchildren would probably have a "Canadian" wedding. This process of adopting the customs of the country in which you live is called **acculturation.** There are some cultures, however, that choose to maintain their own distinct way of life within Canada. They do not adopt mainstream values. One such cultural group is the Hutterites.

The Hutterites first came en masse to Canada from the Ukraine in 1918. Today, they practise a traditional, largely self-sufficient farming lifestyle in Alberta, Saskatchewan, and Manitoba. Although their farms make use of some technological developments from mainstream culture, they adhere to their traditional social practices. Hutterite children are socialized into specific roles based on gender. Both males and females are expected to marry in their late teens or early twenties. Teenagers are closely monitored by their parents. Dating is restricted, and sex outside of marriage is strictly forbidden. Marriages are often arranged by parents or other community members, who select another member of the community as a suitable spouse. Once a spouse has been chosen, the potential groom and his father travel by horse and buggy to the future bride's colony. They formally ask for the consent of the bride and her family. If it is given, the bride and her family travel to the groom's colony for the marriage ceremony the following week. The bride then stays in the groom's colony, where they begin their life together.

Figure 6.8 Married women do communal chores together in Hutterite colonies.

Hutterites live a **communal** lifestyle, which means that all members live together and farm together. Any profits made by individual families are divided equally among members of the larger community. Newly married couples live in an apartment in a longhouse, where they share cooking and laundry responsibilities with the other occupants. Birth control is prohibited, and women are expected to become pregnant within one year of marriage.

The social institution of marriage plays a very important role in passing traditional values on to children. These values have been crucial to the continued survival of the Hutterite culture.

- Seventy-five per cent of marriage ceremonies in 1997 were conducted by a member of the clergy; the remainder were solemnized by civil officials such as judges, justices of the peace, and clerks of the court.
- Ontario had the highest level of religious marriages, with nearly all marriage ceremonies (94 per cent) conducted by clergy of various faiths.
- Religious ceremonies were also common throughout the Maritime provinces, ranging between 80 and 86 per cent.
- Civil marriages were most popular in the Yukon (71 per cent) and British Columbia (56 per cent).
- Eighty-two per cent of weddings in which both spouses were marrying for the first time were conducted by clergy.
- Only 58 per cent of weddings in which both spouses had been previously divorced were conducted by clergy.

Source: Canadian Social Trends, *Spring 2000, Ottawa: Statistics Canada.*

Figure 6.9 Some fast facts on religious marriages

Skill Development: Creating a Survey

In order to obtain information such as the "Fast Facts" above, Statistics Canada conducts surveys. A survey is a set of questions designed to give social scientists specific information in a usable format. The questions are carefully designed, giving respondents a choice of answers. Surveys are used by social scientists to study people's attitudes and behaviour. They may be conducted on a wide range of people, to represent all members of society. Alternatively, particular groups within society may be investigated.

Let's take an example. Suppose you wanted to find out the following as it applies to high-school students:

- What is the relationship between academic performance and hours spent working at a part-time job?

Step 1

First, formulate a hypothesis based on the question you want answered. The hypothesis must be specific. Your survey results will either support/prove the hypothesis, or reject/disprove it.

- Sample hypothesis: Students who work more than sixteen hours a week have lower academic performance than those who work less than sixteen hours a week.

Step 2

Identify the questions you would need a person to answer to prove or disprove the hypothesis.

- Sample questions (round 1):

  1. *Do you have a part-time job?*
  2. *How many hours a week do you work?*
  3. *What is your level of academic performance?*

Adjust your questions in a second round if they are not specific enough. Do this by imagining the possible responses. For example, Question 2 might be hard to answer if the hours vary. It could be adjusted to

- Sample Question 2 (round 2):

2. *"How many hours a week do you work on average?"* or *"How many hours did you work last week?"*

Question 3 also might be hard to answer. It could be adjusted to

- Sample Question 3 (round 2):

3. *"What was your overall average last semester?"* or *"What was your overall average last year?"*

Step 3

Make up multiple-choice answers for your questions. Otherwise, if you allow respondents to write in their answers, you might not get usable results. For example, some might answer Question 3 with a letter grade, while others might answer with a percentage number. By giving respondents a series of choices, you make the job of interpreting the results much easier.

- Sample choices for Question 3:

a) less than 50 per cent
b) 50–59 per cent
c) 60–69 per cent
d) 70–79 per cent
e) 80 per cent +

Step 4

Add **distracter questions** to obscure the true purpose of the survey. If the purpose of the survey is obvious, respondents might not answer as objectively as possible. In the sample survey on page 177, six of the nine questions are distracters.

Follow-Up

1. Explain the role and importance of each of the following in creating survey questions:
   a) specific information
   b) a format that is usable
   c) a choice of answers
   d) distracter questions

2. Rewrite each of the following questions, together with possible answers, so that they would provide us with specific information in a usable format:
   - What do you like to do outdoors?
   - Do you think that the legal system is too soft on young criminals?
   - How important are good friends?
   - Is it important for a happily married couple to have similar interests?
   - Are looks more important than intelligence when choosing a mate?

3. With a partner, pick one of the following hypotheses:
   - There is a link between the way teenagers dress and the type of music they like to listen to.
   - High-school students who like to read a lot do better in languages and the social sciences than those who do not.
   - Teenagers who watch a lot of television or movies are likely to have fewer friends than those who watch less.

Personal Survey

1. How many rooms are there in your home, counting all bathrooms and bedrooms?
   (a) less than 4 (b) 5–6
   (c) 6–7 (d) more than 7
2. Do you have part-time job?
   (a) yes (b) no
3. If you answered "yes" to Question 2, are you required to wear a uniform in your job?
   (a) yes (b) no
4. What is your favourite subject area in school?
   (a) languages (b) arts
   (c) social science (d) math/science
   (e) technology (f) other
5. How many CDs do you own?
   (a) less than 10 (b) 10–20
   (c) 20–30 (d) more than 30
6. If you answered "yes" to Question 2, how many hours on average do you work in a typical week?
   (a) less than 5 (b) 6–12
   (c) 12–15 (d) 16–20
   (e) more than 20
7. How do you feel about the following statement? "The depic-tion of violence in the media increases violent behaviour among teenagers."
   (a) strongly disagree (b) disagree
   (c) neutral or unsure (d) agree
   (e) strongly agree
8. What was your average percentage in all the courses you took last year?
   (a) less than 50 per cent (b) 50–59 per cent
   (c) 60–69 per cent (d) 70–79 per cent
   (e) 80 per cent +
9. How many people do you regard as your really close friends?
   (a) less than 2 (b) 3–4
   (c) 5–8 (d) more than 8

Imagine that you are doing a survey to prove or disprove the hypothesis you have chosen.

a) Create eight survey questions, together with possible answers, that meet all the necessary criteria described above.
b) Compare your survey questions with those of another pair of students (working on the same or a different hypothesis). What changes would you make to the two sets of questions and answers?
c) What have you learned about survey questions and answers from this exercise?

RECAP

1. In what ways is love a chemical (or biological) experience rather than simply an emotional experience?
2. Is the institution of marriage alive and well in Canada? Explain.
3. What are the advantages and disadvantages of free-choice marriage?

Section 6.4

Marriage in Diverse Cultures

Focus Questions

- What various forms of marriage exist throughout the world?
- What are the major differences between Western and non-Western attitudes toward marriage?
- Which form of marriage has the greatest benefits for men, and which has the greatest benefits for women?

Key Concepts

monogamy
polygamy
polygyny
polyandry
arranged marriage
endogamy
caste lines
fraternal polyandry

A Cultural Universal

Marriage is a cultural universal, which means that it exists everywhere. However, particular forms of marriage and family structure vary throughout the world.

In North America, the only legal form of marriage is **monogamy**, where one woman is married to one man at a time.

In the majority of the world's cultures, however, **polygamy**, or plural marriage, is permitted. There are two types of polygamous marriages. **Polygyny** is a marriage where one man has more than one wife.

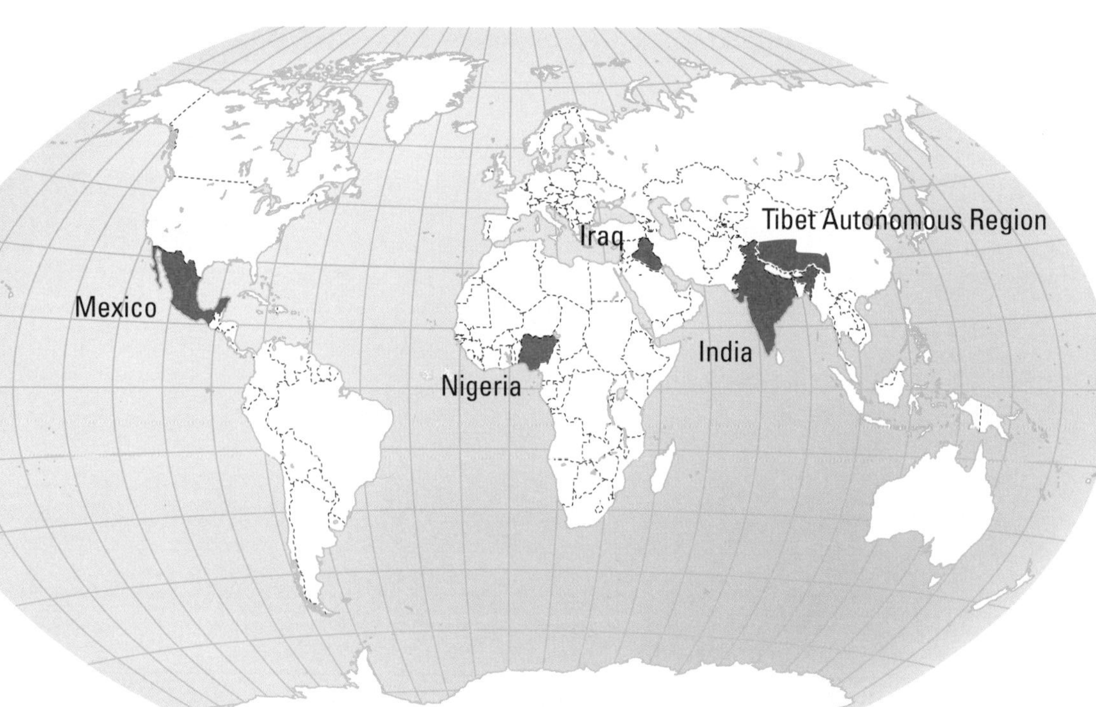

Figure 6.10 Marriage practices of cultures living in these highlighted and labelled regions are described on pages 179 to 189.

Polyandry is a marriage in which a woman has more than one husband. One common misconception in the West is that polygamy is practised because of the high sex drive of the person with several spouses. In reality, however, polygamy is related to issues of property rights, access to resources, and the sharing of daily work. In fact, the Koran, the sacred text of the Islamic faith, allows plural marriage only if the husband can provide for all his wives equally. Supporters of polygamy argue that it is a much better form of marriage than monogamy. They point to the high rates of divorce of monogamous marriages and emphasize the negative effects of divorce on children's psychological and economic well-being.

Whether monogamous or polygamous, free-choice or arranged, the institution of marriage throughout the world serves a number of important functions.

Monogamy

Earlier in this chapter, we looked at the role of romantic love in many North American marriages. When we look at monogamous marriages in other parts of the world, we see that romantic love often operates much differently in the marriage than it does here. On pages 179 to 180, we find that economics and other practical considerations are foremost in Mixtec marriages. On page 180, we find that romantic love is viewed as a by-product of arranged marriage, as this custom is practised in India. We see a new form of arranged marriage in the case study that begins on page 181.

Mixtec Marriage

The Mixtec are an indigenous group living in southern Mexico, with a population of approximately 400 000. Anthropologist John Monaghan learned much about Mixtec marriage practices during three years of fieldwork among the Mixtec. Many of his observations can be found in his book, co-authored with Peter Just, *Social and Cultural Anthropology: A Very Short Introduction* (2000).

As in Canadian mainstream culture, Mixtec marriages are monogamous. Romantic love, however, plays a very small role in the selection of marriage partners. Marriage is seen as an *economic* arrangement involving the transfer of wealth between the parties involved. The Mixtec also believe that any household that does not contain an adult female and an adult

Figure 6.11 Mixtec culture highly values households with both one adult male and one adult female. Therefore, remarriage takes place quickly after the death of a spouse.

male is destined to fail. As a result of this belief, remarriage occurs very quickly after the death of a spouse.

Arranged Marriage in India

India, like other developing countries, has undergone extensive social change in the past fifty years. Yet the centuries-old practice of **arranged marriage** has remained largely in place. In an arranged marriage, also known as **endogamy**, parents select who their child will marry. A person does not choose a partner for her- or himself. Indian sociologists estimate that about 95 per cent of marriages in the country are arranged.

In their book *Sociology: A Down-to-Earth Approach* (1996), James Henslin and Adie Nelson analyze marriage. They adopt the common sociological principle that a group's marriage practices match its values. For example, the freedom of choice in mates in North American marriages matches the North American values of individuality and independence. Similarly, arranged marriages reflect the Indian value of children deferring to parental authority. To Indians, mate selection is far too important a matter to trust to an inexperienced young person. Young people are socialized to adopt this view. They are trained to see adults as having cooler heads and superior wisdom in this matter.

Figure 6.12 The Hindu bride and groom at this arranged wedding met and spoke to each other for the first time during their marriage ceremony.

Indian values regarding love, specifically those of Hindu tradition, are also reinforced by the practice of arranged marriage. For many Indians, love is a peaceful emotion based on long-term commitment and devotion to family. Indians typically believe love is something that can be "created" between two people under the right conditions. One of those right conditions is marriage. A third cultural value seen in Hindu marriages involves social class. Social classes, or **caste lines**, are reaffirmed in that Hindu marriage partners may not marry outside their caste. (It should be noted that the Hindu Marriage Act of 1955 did away with all caste restrictions for *civil* marriages. The restrictions hold, however, for religious marriages.)

As we have just seen, the predominant cultures in India and North America cultures have produced opposite approaches to love and marriage. For Indians, marriage precedes love. For North Americans belonging to Euro-Canadian and Euro-American cultures, love precedes marriage.

Case Study: An Arranged Marriage in Canada

The letter in this case study presents a young Indian-Canadian Muslim woman's thoughts on marriage. There is no requirement in the religion of Islam that marriages be arranged. However, dating is not allowed, so many Muslims use an intermediary to find a spouse. Although the letter is fictional, it describes a situation common to many young Muslim women in Canada.

---

27 January 1995

As salaamu Alaikum
Dear Mariam,
I can hardly believe that in a few weeks I am going to be a married woman. Although I've only known Ahmad for a short time and we've never dated in the Canadian sense of the word, I feel very confident that he is a good choice of a husband. After all, it is my choice to marry him; my parents only arranged for our meeting.

My friends at work don't really understand what an "arranged marriage" means these days. They think that Ahmad's parents and my parents got together when we were born and said, "Khadija and Ahmad must be married even if they hate each other. They will learn to love each other." In fact, the whole process has been guided by Islamic law, continuously based on my approval and consultation. My parents acted as my spokespeople to make sure that I didn't get hurt or have to go through any unnecessary hassles.

I was the one who expressed an interest in getting married, and I wanted to make sure that my husband was going to be primarily a good Muslim who would create with me a loving, happy family based on the Islamic ideals that are very important to me. By meeting Ahmad's family, I was able to see how he behaved with his family, and I already feel welcomed by his parents into their family. They have shown me how much they respect me, and I hope that I have returned the feeling of respect to them.

My friends at work also thought that Ahmad and I were not allowed to talk to each other. Although we never "went out" on dates without a family chaperone, we did get plenty of time to speak privately, both on the telephone and in person. Often his older sister and her husband would invite us over to their house for dinner. They would let us talk by ourselves in the living room. It was during these conversations that Ahmad and I were able to talk about our expectations of each other as husband and wife. We discussed everything possible, like our careers, children, finances, where to live, how to share the housework, values, religion, politics, extended family, and long-term plans. It was easy to discuss these things honestly because at that point we had no emotional ties to one another.

I know this sounds kind of clinical and rational. Obviously, there had to be some physical attraction for me to really feel I could marry him. I feel that my "introduced marriage" is good because I became attracted to the important things about Ahmad—not what kind of car he drives or whether he likes comedies more than adventure movies. Also, I guess I don't believe that you have to date a lot of different people to make an informed decision about marrying someone.

When people talk about "arranged marriages," they usually say that you don't fall in love then get married. Instead you get married and then fall in love. To me, love is not an emotion that happens in an instant and then subsides—that is attraction. To me, marital love is a lifelong commitment. I am confident that Ahmad has made the commitment, as I have, to ensuring our lifelong happiness and security by trying to have the patience to deal with the adversities that life inevitably brings.

My friends think that I have missed out on all the fun by not dating and that this "arranged marriage" is the end of my life. That seems strange to me because I feel like the fun is just beginning.

Walaikum as salaam,
Khadija Ali

1. How is Khadija Ali's marriage different from the arranged-marriage customs described on page 180?
2. How do Indian and Euro-Canadian attitudes toward love and marriage differ?
3. What are the advantages and disadvantages of parental involvement in marriage?
4. If your parents were selecting a marriage partner for you, what qualities would they look for? How would their list of qualitities differ from your own?

Forms of Polygamy

As mentioned on page 178, polygamy is permitted in a majority of the world's cultures. However, as H. E. Fisher pointed out in his book *Anatomy of Love: The Natural History of Monogamy, Adultery, and Divorce* (1992), monogamy can be considered a "norm." It seems that monogamous patterns assert themselves even in cultures where polygamy is permitted.

We also read on pages 178 and 179 that polygamy takes the form of either polygyny (one husband, multiple wives) or polyandry (one wife, multiple husbands). Of the two, polyandry is the rarest. It is found in less than 1 per cent of the world's cultures and is always found in combination with polygyny. In this section, we look at polygyny in Africa and then focus on two cultures in which the rarer polyandry is found. As you will read, the specific ways polyandry is practised in Tibet and Nigeria vary considerably.

Polygyny in Africa

Anthropologist Niara Sudarkasa has conducted research on the polygynous marriages of the Yoruba of Nigeria. She reported in a 1988 article entitled "African and Afro-American Family Structure" that a fairly typical living pattern exists. Within the family home, the husband and his wives each have a separate room and their own household items. Each family has a senior wife who plays a very important role as a confidant to the other co-wives. The senior wife is also an intermediary between the co-wives and the husband. The wives of the husband co-operate in economic activities and frequently look after each other's children. A distinction is made between the children of different mothers—each mother, with her children, makes up a subunit within the family.

Anthropologists such as Sudarkasa debate whether African men and women equally value polygamous marriages. Most research indicates that men value polygyny more highly than women. Some evidence, however, shows that African

Figure 6.13 There are two wives in this Kikuyu family. What are the advantages and disadvantages of such a family structure?

women value polygynous marriages for the companionship of co-wives. Polygyny gives wives peers with whom they can share the housework, husband care, and child care. Sudarkasa believes that most African women would prefer being a co-wife to bearing children outside of marriage or to being a childless unmarried woman. Both of the latter options would be "abnormal" in most African societies. In one study conducted in western Kenya, most women expressed the opinion that senior wives should be allowed to select the second and subsequent wives (Kilbride, 1999, 203). Since husbands are away from home frequently, this would ensure that the co-wives were compatible.

In some African countries today, polygyny is on the decrease. This is due, in large part, to the fact that more women are receiving post-secondary education and embarking on careers. Professional women are rejecting marriage altogether (Kilbride, 1999, 206). They feel men are unsupportive of their desires for a career, an independent lifestyle, and an advanced education. As well, women feel that too many Kenyan men involve themselves too frequently with mistresses. They also disagree with a long-standing African tradition that says men have the "right" to beat their wives. In this new era, many educated African women seek out a man only when they are ready to have a child. This usually occurs when they are in their thirties.

Fraternal Polyandry in Tibet

Fraternal polyandry is a type of marriage in which two, three, four, or more brothers jointly take a wife. The eldest brother usually has the greatest authority in the marriage, and he is usually the one who manages the household. But all brothers share in the work and participate as sexual partners. Children of the marriage are treated equally, and there is no attempt on the part of the adults to link the children to their biological fathers. The children, in turn, consider all the brothers as their fathers.

Anthropologist Melvyn Goldstein notes that fraternal polyandry is not uncommon in Tibetan society. In a 1987 article in *Natural History* (vol. 96, no. 3), he reported that the Tibetans' own explanation for choosing this type of marriage is based on economics. This type of marriage prevents the division of a family's wealth and property. This ensures that all family members enjoy a higher standard of living. As the husbands benefit from this consolidation of wealth, the wife is assured of a sound economic future. She has a number of men to help provide for her and her children.

Tibetans also believe that this form of marriage reduces family conflict. If three brothers were to take three separate wives, there would be many more heirs to the family property. If the eldest brother were to have only one female child, and the youngest brother were to have a male child, conflict would be inevitable. Although the female child's father is the elder, there would be great pressure for the youngest brother's male child to inherit the family property.

Fraternal polyandry benefits Tibetan society by limiting population growth. As Figure 6.14 shows, repeating the practice

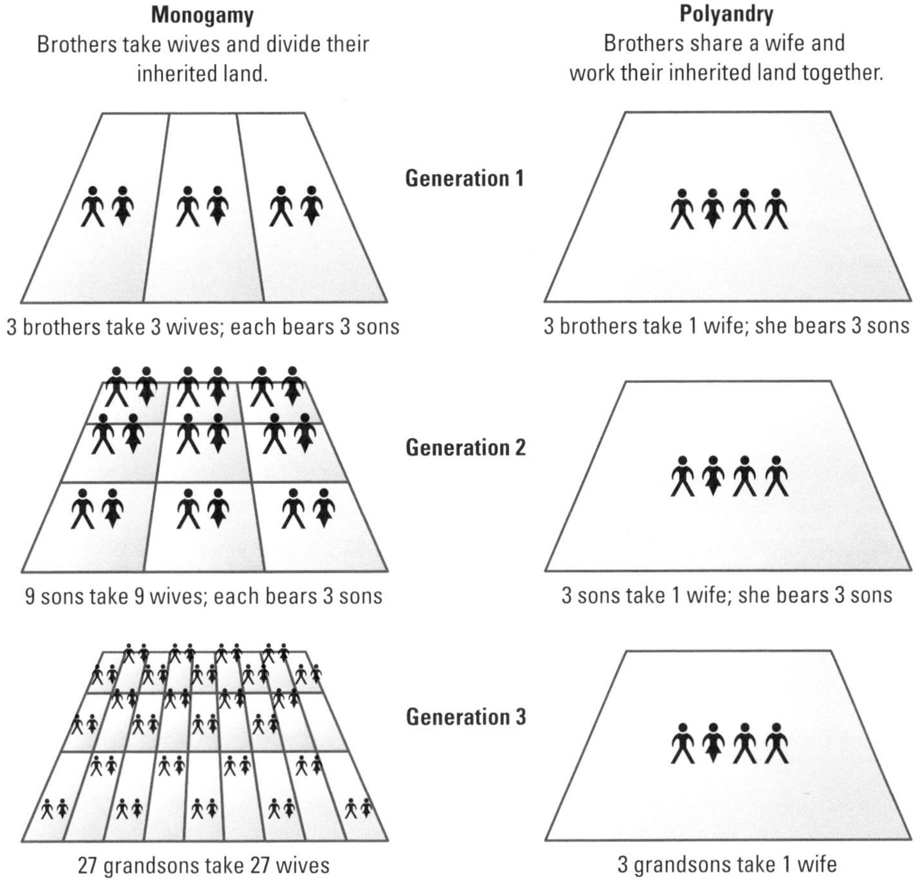

Monogamy
Brothers take wives and divide their inherited land.

Polyandry
Brothers share a wife and work their inherited land together.

Generation 1

3 brothers take 3 wives; each bears 3 sons

3 brothers take 1 wife; she bears 3 sons

Generation 2

9 sons take 9 wives; each bears 3 sons

3 sons take 1 wife; she bears 3 sons

Generation 3

27 grandsons take 27 wives

3 grandsons take 1 wife

Figure 6.14 Population growth patterns in monogamy and polyandry

of three brothers taking one wife results in zero population growth. If, however, three brothers take one wife each, and each bears three sons, the population grows exponentially over generations. Why is population growth a problem? Tibetan communities, dependent on farming, have very little suitable land available to them. Moreover, most Tibetan communities do not have reliable sources of irrigation. Thus, population growth puts huge pressure on resources.

Despite these economic advantages, Tibetans practising fraternal polyandry do face some problems. One is the unequal power distribution among brothers. The eldest brother enjoys the greatest authority within the household. His younger brothers have to subordinate themselves to his will and have very little hope of improving their status. Another problem that can arise is tension and conflict over sexual favouritism. The wife normally sleeps with the eldest brother. But they both are responsible for ensuring that the other males have opportunities for sexual access. This access is usually assured by the fact that all brothers are rarely home at the same time—the Tibetan economy requires males to travel frequently to trade and sell goods. But if travel patterns change, or if the wife clearly favours one brother over the others, conflict can result.

"Double Marriage" in Nigeria

The following excerpt is from an article entitled "African Polygyny: Family Values and Contemporary Changes." It describes a tradition of polyandry followed by the Irigwe of Benue-Plateau State in Nigeria.

> Most women have at least two marriages in this community. The first type, the "primary marriage," is arranged by parents prior to the couple's adolescence. "Second marriage" is arranged later by the couple itself. When a woman leaves her primary husband and goes to a secondary husband, she leaves behind everything except the clothes and jewelry she is wearing. She may be fetched back by her former husband, or she may decide to stay and take up residence with her new husband, who then provides her with a house and everything she needs for housekeeping. The traditional Irigwe marriage system has no divorce. A woman's prior marriages are not terminated by her switching residence to another spouse. At any point in time, she may return to any of her spouses and resume residence with him. Paternity is settled by consensus, and a husband competes with his wife's other husbands for the paternity of the child she bears (Kilbride, 1999, 201).

REMARKABLE PEOPLE

Niara Sudarkasa

A renowned anthropologist, Dr. Niara Sudarkasa is an authority on several topics. They include the roles of African women, Yoruba trade and migration, and African and Afro-American family structure. She was the first woman to serve as president of Lincoln University in Pennsylvania.

Sudarkasa began her anthropology studies after graduating from Oberlin College, Ohio at the age of eighteen. By the age of twenty-five she had earned master's and doctorate degrees in anthropology from Columbia University, New York. She was an assistant professor at New York University (1964–1967) and at the University of Michigan (1967–1970). While at Michigan, she rose to associate professor (1970) and full professor (1976).

Sudarkasa has conducted field research in Ghana, the Republic of Benin, Nigeria, the Caribbean, and the United States. She has also travelled to twenty-seven African countries.

Her other achievements include directing the Center for Afro-American Studies and conducting studies for the Center for Research on Economic Development. She also served as associate vice-president for academic affairs at the University of Michigan until 1986. She is one of five Americans representing the US on the fifteen-member Trilateral Task Force on Educational Collaboration linking the US, Canada, and Mexico. Dr. Sudarkasa has been awarded twelve honorary degrees from US and African universities. She is one of seventy-five women included in Brian Lanker's *I Dream A World: Portraits of Black Women Who Changed America.*

1. Dr. Sudarkasa lectures widely on the extended family. She considers it to be the most humane of all social institutions. Does what you have learned about family structures in other cultures support this view? Explain.

Changing with the Times

The marriage institution in Canada has undergone considerable change, summarized earlier in the chapter (see pages 171 to 172). The marriage institution in other cultures is also changing. One reason for change is political—events such as wars and economic sanctions can dramatically affect people's standard of living, putting pressure on marriage customs to adapt to new circumstances. Another reason for change is the spread of technology, such as the Internet, around the world. Internet Web sites attract hundreds of thousands of people with similar interests who would not meet in any other way. Relationships and even marriage arrangements can develop quickly and over long distances. The following two case studies present examples of such change in Iraq and the Indian-Canadian community.

The context for the first case study is the aftermath of the Gulf War between Iraq and the United States. War between the two nations began in January 1991 and ended scant weeks later (a ceasefire took effect on February 28). Although the bombing ended over ten years ago, United Nations economic sanctions continue. These sanctions affect every part of Iraqi life—including marriage.

Case Study: Mass Weddings in Iraq

The following article appeared on 12 August 2000 in the *Kitchener-Waterloo Record.*

"[In Baghdad], Nada Omran and Fathi Jabran chose to share one of the most important days in their lives with dozens of strangers. It was the only way the two government workers could afford to get married. With [United Nations] trade sanctions pinching every facet of life in Iraq, the government sponsors mass weddings as a way to put marriage in reach of Iraqis who might otherwise have to save for years to pay for white gowns, cakes, and reception bands.

"'We have been waiting for this dream to come true for two years,' said Omran, 26, holding Jabran's arm as the two stood in the Baghdad park after their recent mass wedding. 'We do not want to think of what will happen after the honeymoon...we will manage one way or another,' said Jabran, 29.

"Although an international coalition forced Iraq to retreat from Kuwait, the strict sanctions are being kept in place until UN inspectors certify that Iraq is free of weapons of mass destruction. Lack of trade is slowly strangling the economy. A decade ago, one Iraqi dinar bought more than $3 US. Today, it takes 2000 dinars to buy $1.

"Civil servants on fixed salaries have been especially hard-hit by inflation, slipping from middle class into poverty. It is not unusual to find university professors moonlighting as taxi drivers or doctors dealing in second-hand furniture. Families have lost their homes. Children are sent out to beg on street corners or take jobs sweeping up shops or washing dishes in restaurants.

Figure 6.15 A group of brides and grooms pass by a portrait of President Saddam Hussein as they walk to their mass wedding of over 400 couples in the summer of 2000.

"Many young Iraqi men—up to 2 million, by some estimates—have migrated abroad to seek work. The young women left behind sometimes have trouble finding someone to marry. The ones who do run into other difficulties. Furniture prices and apartment rents are so high it is almost impossible for a new couple to set up their own household. Some families take up collections among relatives to cover wedding expenses.

"Fearing social problems could result from deferred marriages, the government of President Saddam Hussein began mass weddings in 1996, and has sponsored 454 since. Sponsors lend wedding gowns and suits and the government pays for cakes and hotel bills for a three-day honeymoon. Famous singers performed for free during the reception for Omran and Jabran's wedding."

Source: Faleh, Waiel. 2000. "Mass Weddings Help Couples Navigate Sanctions Against Iraq." *Kitchener-Waterloo Record*. 12 August 2000.

1. What impact have continued economic sanctions had on the Iraqi economy?
2. How have these changes affected the wedding practices of Iraqi citizens?
3. Why do you think the government started sponsoring mass weddings? What "social problems" do you think the government was worried about?

Case Study: Indian Marriages Go High Tech

The following article appeared on 24 March 2000 in the *Calgary Sun*.

"Searching for the perfect mate is never easy.

"But for some Indian men and women, where an arranged marriage or endogamy is the traditional course, the solution could be as close as the click of a mouse. A unique new Calgary-based website—www.weddingsindia.net—is drawing about 250 000 hits a month. 'We're one of the first of our kind in the North American market,' says Anurag Dhand, Director of Strategic Developments, of the website which helps 'arrange your marriage' through the use of free Indian matrimonials on the Net. 'If you're an Indian or Pakistani from India or anywhere else, our matrimonial service can help you find a bride or groom of any religion.' That includes Hindu, Sikh, Muslim, Christian, Punjabi, or Tamil.

"Once you determine your search terms, the website does the rest, selecting a list of suitors for you to choose from. Dhand says prime marriage material would include the following features: Age 25-36, high educational level, non-smoker, non-drinker, employed, from a good family, pleasing appearance, and strong goals. 'Most people are looking for a familiar network,' he says.

"Parents and family members are vital in providing objectivity in order to properly assess a potential life-partner, agrees Dr. George Kuriam, professor of sociology at the University of Calgary. 'There's no such thing as a perfect match,' he says. 'It's a matter of compromise, and give-and-take. People should respect each other's personalities.' That means becoming more tolerant of each other and appreciating your mate's good qualities, instead of dwelling on their less desirable traits. 'Total freedom of choice doesn't work,' says Kuriam, who married in 1964, a union sanctioned by his family. 'That's evidenced by the high divorce rates in North America.'

"By comparison, in India, couples divorce at the rate of 'less than 25 per cent.' Kuriam believes arranged marriages will endure only in a 'modified sense,' in urban society. Despite his predictions, if www.weddingsindia.net's traffic is any indication, endogamy in the Indian community will persevere. The popularity of Dhand's website continues to grow. 'To date, our advertising has been all word-of-mouth.'"

Abridged from: Isaac, Jennifer. 2000. "Wed Through the Web." *The Calgary Sun*. 24 March 2000.

1. Identify three ways in which traditional endogamy in India has changed. Support your answer with examples.
2. How do Indian and North American attitudes toward love and marriage differ?
3. What are the advantages and disadvantages of parental involvement in marriage?

RECAP

1. What are the differences between monogamy, polygyny, and polyandry?
2. What varying attitudes do women in Africa have toward polygyny? Give a detailed account of why each attitude exists.
3. Choose a marriage practice not followed in mainstream North American culture. Describe three benefits it has. Speculate on why it is not widespread in North America.

Section 6.5

The Changing Family

Focus Questions

- What factors have caused the birth rate in Canada to fluctuate in the twentieth century?
- In what ways did the Divorce Act of 1968 change the nature of the Canadian family forever?
- What current trends are affecting the Canadian family today?

Key Concepts

conscription
baby boom
nuclear family
"no-fault" divorce
blended families
common-law relationships

Classic Study

RESEARCHER:
Harry Harlow, Psychologist

TIME:
1957 onward

SUBJECT:
Mother Love

The Most Important Institution

There is no social institution that is more important, or has undergone more change, than the family. The family is important because it provides the love and nurturing crucial for children and adults to thrive. It is also the major agent of socialization for children. Ideally, it teaches hygiene and other life skills, manners, and communication skills. It also instills characteristics needed for social success, such as the ability to share, be patient, and solve problems. A happy, high-functioning family provides all of its members with strength, stability, and security. Such a family is the one safe place its members can turn to when in trouble.

A Mother's Love

Starting in 1957, psychologist Harry Harlow conducted a series of experiments with rhesus monkeys. He wanted to determine the importance of a mother's love during an infant's life. In one set of experiments, Harlow placed an infant monkey in a cage with two non-living "surrogate" mothers. One was made totally of wire but had a rubber nipple in its chest that provided milk. The other "mother" was covered with soft terry cloth but did *not* have a nipple and so did not provide milk. Harlow and his team found that infant monkeys would spend twenty-two hours a day on the cloth "mother." Apparently, the infants required the warmth and comfort provided by the cloth mother. This was more important than the nourishment provided by the wire "mother."

Charting Family Change

Early settlers to Canada came from northern and western Europe. Following their cultural traditions, young couples established independent households soon after they married. To make this possible, young men worked and saved money for many years before they married. The average marriage age was twenty-eight for men and twenty-five for women.

During the nineteenth century, the majority of Canadian families lived on farms. Having a lot of children was the norm so that more hands could help with the daily chores. This need coincided with religious beliefs that supported procreation in families. Also, effective contraception was generally lacking. As a result, the average number of children born to a woman in 1851 was 6.6.

The Family of the Early 1900s

By the late 1800s, economic opportunites created by industrialization pulled many families into cities. Even children found jobs in factories, working long hours in unsafe conditions. By the 1920s, however, child labour laws had been introduced that limited the number of hours children could work. Mandatory school attendance laws further freed children from the drudgery of factory work. These changes resulted in a decrease in family size. By 1901, women gave birth to an average number of 4.6 children. By 1921, the average had fallen to 3.5 children.

During this time period, society frowned on divorce, and divorce laws were very restrictive. In fact, divorce was granted only when proof of adultery was provided. As a result, the divorce rate in 1901 was only 3 per 10 000 marriages. Single-parent families did exist, and remarriage did occur, but both were mostly a result of the death of a spouse. Health conditions were poor, maternal mortality rates were high, and fatal outbreaks of disease were frequent. Young widows or widowers almost always had to remarry to ensure the financial support of young children.

Figure 6.16 This couple celebrated their marriage in British Columbia in 1906. During the first half of the twentieth century, marriages in Canada did not often end in divorce.

The Family of the 1930s

When the Great Depression hit, high rates of unemployment made it impossible for many to marry. Marriage rates decreased dramatically between 1928 and 1932—from 7.5 to 5.9 per 1000 population. The number of children born during the Depression also declined. For most of the 1930s, the birth rate was fewer than 3 children per woman. As many as 20 per cent of women had no children at all. By 1937, the total fertility rate had dropped to only 2.6 children per woman.

The Family of the Baby Boom (1946–1966)

When Canada entered the Second World War in 1939, government spending stimulated the economy. This prosperity coincided with the threat of **conscription**—single men being forced to join the Canadian forces. As a result, many couples rushed to the altar. By 1942, the marriage rate had jumped to 10.9 marriages per 1000 population. High marriage rates led to the phenomenon known as the **baby boom**. This term refers to a period when family size began to increase, reversing a century-long decline in fertility rates. The birth rate continued to climb until it reached its peak of 3.9 births per woman in 1959.

The other major change during this period was the structure of the family itself. Families began to consist primarily of a wife and husband and their biological children. Fewer relatives and extended family members lived under the same roof. In this **nuclear family**, the wife usually maintained the home and cared for the children. The husband was typically employed for wages outside the home.

Changes to the Divorce Act

Before 1968, most Canadians viewed marriage as a lifetime commitment. Unhappiness in the marriage did not constitute a strong enough reason to end it. But changes to the Divorce Act made it possible to get a **"no-fault" divorce**. This meant that "grounds" for divorce (that is, adultery or cruelty) no longer had to be proven. All that was required was for a couple to be separated for a period of three years. In 1986, the separation period was further reduced to one year. After the introduction of the Divorce Act, the divorce rate climbed steadily. It reached a record 362 divorces per 100 000 population in 1987. Since then, however, the divorce rate has been declining, down to 223 per 100 000 in 1997.

During the 1960s, fertility rates began to decline, and that trend continues to this day. One reason for the drop in fertility is that contraception became more effective and available. This allowed couples to limit the number of children they had. To some extent, it also allowed them to time the birth of their children. As well, the greater numbers of women entering the workforce tended to want smaller families. By 1997, the fertility rate had dropped to 1.6 children per woman, the lowest recorded rate in Canada's history.

The Canadian Family in the Twenty-First Century

Remarriage has become a fact of life in Canada. In 1997, a full one-third of marriages were a remarriage for one spouse or the other. Men are more likely to remarry than women. In some cases, this happens because an ex-wife, granted custody of children, has a harder time finding another spouse. Another factor is that men tend to marry younger women, creating a larger marriage pool for men.

The **common-law relationship**—living together without getting legally married—is another fact of life for Canadian families. By 1996, 12 per cent of cohabiting couples (about one in eight) were common-law. Statistics Canada predicts that, if current growth rates continue, common-law relationships will equal marriages by 2020. Despite their popularity, common-law relationships are less stable than legal marriages. Fifty per cent of common-law relationships dissolve within five years. Those that lead to marriage are still more likely to end in divorce (as compared to relationships where the couple married without living common law).

A growing number of young adults live with their parents. This growth can be linked to economic uncertainty and a greater need for post-secondary education in order to get a job. By 1996, 23 per cent of young women aged twenty to thirty-four lived at home, up from 16 per cent in 1981. Over the same period, the percentage of young men in the same age group residing in the parental home rose to 33 per cent from 26 per cent (Boyd and Norris, 1999, 2).

Figure 6.17 Blended families are formed when people with children from previous relationships marry. These families may experience high stress levels as they work out how to live together.

Other more general trends have also been established in Canadian families. The number of families that include extended family members has risen—from 150 000 in 1986 to about 208 000 in 1996. This is still a small total overall, but the proportionate increase over ten years is quite remarkable. This type of household grew *twice* as fast as other family types. As well, same-sex unions are gradually winning political recognition in some circles (see page 172). However, it is not known whether such unions will ever have legal rights similar to those of heterosexual couples.

RECAP

1. Why did couples tend to marry late during the settlement period of Canadian history?
2. Identify three factors linked to a drop in the birth rate at the turn of the century.
3. Identify three major changes that occurred in the post-war period.

Activities

Show your knowledge

1. Create a New Vocabulary glossary of the terms and phrases you learned in this chapter.
   a) Record the definition of each term.
   b) Use these terms to create four questions to ask a classmate. Make each question more difficult than the last. Follow the model used for these activities ("Show your knowledge," "Practise your thinking skills," "Communicate your ideas," "Apply your knowledge").
2. Why is it necessary to have social institutions in society?
3. How do attitudes toward marriage in a culture such as the Mixtec differ from those in North American culture?
4. Explain why the family is thought to be the most important social institution.

Practise your thinking skills

5. Mahatma Gandhi said that the problem with the concept of "an eye for an eye" is that it leaves everyone blind. What did he mean by this comment? Why do you think most human beings demand retribution?
6. Which of the three purposes of correctional agencies do you think is best met in our criminal justice system?
7. What do you think is the weakest aspect of our criminal justice system?
8. Why is it important to study the social institutions of cultures other than our own?
9. List at least three institutions in Canadian society that you consider to be total institutions. Explain your choices fully.
10. Choose two love songs that describe romantic love. How do the lyrics promote the idea that Mr. or Ms. Right is out there waiting for us? What other parts of popular Canadian culture encourage romantic love?
11. Do you agree that love can blind us to the negative aspects of our partner's personality? Have you ever had a friend who was involved in a relationship that you knew was going nowhere? If so, how did your friend react when you tried to talk to him or her about it?
12. In Sternberg's triangular theory
    a) in what order do you think the components of love combine to result in a Euro-Canadian free-choice marriage? Explain.
    b) in what order do you think the components combine to result in an arranged marriage? Explain.

13. Why do you think no divorce exists in Irigwe culture (see page 186)? How would the institution of marriage and other aspects of our culture change if no divorce was allowed here?
14. Why do you think common-law marriages are less stable than legal marriages?

Communicate your ideas

15. Write a short opinion piece that argues whether or not punishment is the most effective way of changing criminal behaviour.
16. Create two charts that range from 1850 to the year 2000. On one chart, plot changes in Canadian marriage rates. On the other, plot changes in fertility rates.
17. Create a "Point and Counterpoint" feature around the following question: Was Canada's Divorce Act of 1968 a negative or positive development? At the end, explain your own viewpoint in detail.
18. Write a letter to a friend who lives in a culture quite different from that of Canada. In your letter, describe a "typical" Canadian wedding. Do your best to explain why each of the traditions and rituals occurs.

Apply your knowledge

19. Record the ways that your high school tries to encourage productive behaviour in all its students. Include both the ways productive behaviour is rewarded and the ways that unacceptable behaviour is punished.
20. Select one social institution not discussed in this chapter. Possibilities include the peer group, the media, government, and religion, among others.
    a) Describe the characteristics of the institution.
    b) Explain the role of the institution.
    c) How much influence has this institution had on your life?
21. What social institution or institutions have had the greatest impact on your life? Provide examples in your answer.
22. Choose a cultural group outside mainstream Canadian culture that you have not read about in this book (for example, Mormons, Mennonites, Buddhists). Research and describe the group's marriage ceremony. Use all appropriate "Key Concepts" from the chapter in your description.

Chapter 7

Work Structures

Overview of Chapter

Learning Expectations

By the end of this chapter, you will be able to

- analyze the structural changes that are occurring in the world of work within Canada
- identify current trends in Canadian employment and unemployment patterns and analyze the influence these trends have on individuals, groups, and communities
- describe the structural ways in which conflict is addressed in the workplace

OPEN FOR DEBATE

A Lesson in Finding Work

Finding summer work is tough enough for anyone, but for high school students, many of whom are first-time job seekers, it can be a confusing and overwhelming struggle.

Nancy Schaefer, director of the non-profit Youth Employment Service, says even though the majority of jobs are filled by the spring, there are still vacancies for younger students who are persistent and can find out where to look and whom to contact. Most young job hunters face the same problem, she says—lack of experience.

That's why Schaefer, with input from the non-profit agency's staff and student clients, wrote *Good Job—A Young Person's Guide to Finding, Landing and Loving a Job*.

The free book, available for reference at many student job placement centres, covers just about every question a student could possibly have when looking for a job.

It starts by posing three simple questions designed to help students decide what they really want to do for work:

- What are you interested in?
- Why?
- What are you already good at?

It is best to tailor your resume to fit the job, says Schaefer. For example, if applying for a job working with children, any babysitting experience should be highlighted before any unrelated past work.

Along with your resume, make sure you write an upbeat cover letter stating you're the best person for the job, that you can do it and really want to.

No matter how hard it seems, with the right support students can find a good job, if not the job of their dreams, Schaefer says.

Abridged from: Harvey, Robin. 2000. "A Lesson in Finding Work." *The Toronto Star*. 20 June 2000.

Think About It

1. Summarize Nancy Schaefer's point of view and attitude toward finding work. Do you agree or disagree with this outlook? State your reasons.
2. Discuss with classmates what common job-hunting and part-time/summer job experiences you share.
3. "You don't get a job without experience, but you can't get experience without a job." Come up with a practical solution to this timeless puzzle.

Section 7.1

The Evolution of Work

Focus Questions

- What role has technology played in the historical development of the modern economy?
- What role have humans played in the historical development of the modern economy?
- How have humans been affected by the economic changes that have resulted in the modern economy?

What Is the Economy?

Just like the criminal justice system and the family, the **economy** is a social institution. It organizes the production, distribution, and consumption of goods and services within a society. It does this in an established, predictable way. **Production** refers to the creation of goods and services. **Distribution** is how the goods and services are delivered. We describe the use of goods and services as **consumption**.

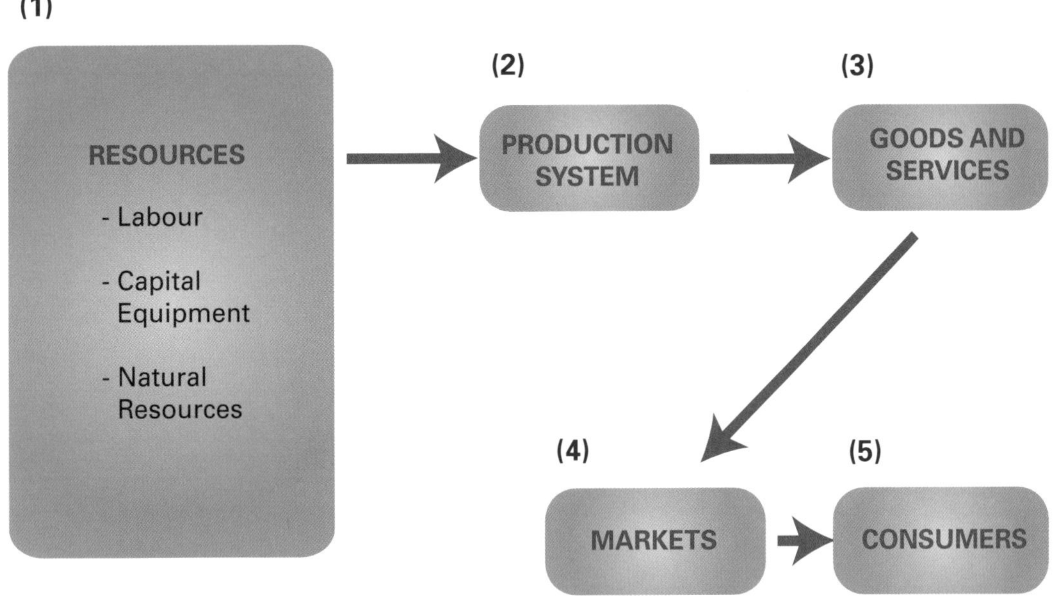

Figure 7.1 In Canada's economic system (1) resources are (2) ***produced*** *into (3) goods and services. Goods and services are* ***distributed*** *through (4) markets to (5)* ***consumers****.*

Key Concepts

economy
production
distribution
consumption
surplus
subsistence economy
division of labour
Industrial Revolution
mechanization
wage labour
labour unions
post-industrial economy
Information Revolution
Y2K bug
global economy
convergence

A Brief History

Canada's economy today is part of a complex global web of interdependent relations. Producers are related to consumers, employers are linked to employees, governments are connected to citizens, and nations are related to each other. But this web is a relatively new development. It has taken centuries of technological innovation and social change to bring about the modern state of the economy.

Hunting and Gathering Societies

Early human societies consisted of small nomadic groups of about twenty to fifty related people. They lived off the land, hunting and gathering what they could find. They moved from place to place as they used up their food supply. Production, distribution, and consumption were all part of family life. "Work" consisted primarily of doing what had to be done to ensure the survival of the group. Because these early societies produced little or no **surplus** (extra or leftover goods), they are said to have had a **subsistence economy**. In such a system, workers produce only what they immediately consume.

The Agricultural Revolution

Between five and ten thousand years ago, people learned to breed animals and cultivate plants. This development brought revolutionary changes to human society. Agriculture made the food supply more dependable, resulting for the first time in a **surplus** of food. This surplus allowed human groups to become much less nomadic and encouraged permanent settlements. It also allowed groups to grow in size and led to what social scientists call a specialized **division of labour**. Freed from the demands of food production, some enterprising individuals made handicrafts. They designed tools and weapons, did carpentry, made leather crafts, and constructed buildings. Trade was stimulated by the surplus of goods created by these handicraft workers. To make it easier to exchange goods and services, villages and towns emerged.

Throughout this period, human labour, or "work," became more and more specialized. It was now being done for something more than just mere survival. It was also more often being done away from the worker's immediate family. Futurist Alvin Toffler calls this the "first wave" of human development.

The Industrial Revolution

In the mid-eighteenth century, new inventions such as the flying shuttle (for cutting cotton), the spinning jenny (for feeding yarn), and the steam engine (for transportation) appeared in England. These technological changes produced the **Industrial Revolution**, a turning point in human history. The cotton industry was the first to be transformed by machine production. Other industries followed suit, resulting in an extraordinary increase in goods and services. The Industrial Revolution brought with it four very significant innovations that ushered in the modern economy:

1. **Mechanization.** Before the Industrial Revolution, the energy needed for the production of goods was provided by people, animals, water, and

wind. In the 1760s, English inventor James Watt introduced steam-powered machinery, increasing production a hundred times over. A surplus of goods and wealth never witnessed before was almost instantly created.

2. **Centralization, Specialization,** and **Mass Production.** Prior to industrialization, handicrafts were produced by the cottage industry system. Workers fashioned a limited number of products from beginning to end in workshops within or close to their homes. The new industrial economy shifted most jobs into centralized steam-powered factories. Workers found themselves mass-producing raw materials into cotton goods and other saleable products. Quite often they repeated a single specialized task over and over, playing only a small part in the production of the finished good.
3. **Wage Labour.** The industrial economy brought into existence a new "working class" that sold its labour for wages. These workers were employed in factories where the pace of work was dictated not by the needs of the day and season, but by machines and clocks. Conditions in the early factories were dismal—men, women, and children worked alongside each other for up to sixteen hours a day. The employer-employee relationship, once based on a long-term personal connection and loyalty, was now impersonal. More often than not, it was based on exploitation of the workers by the new factory owners. Many of these employers amassed vast fortunes while workers toiled in poverty.

Workers eventually formed **labour unions** in an attempt to improve wages and working conditions. Labour unions, as well as church groups, continue to represent their members' collective interests. At times, both unions and church groups have been at the vanguard of the struggle for social justice.

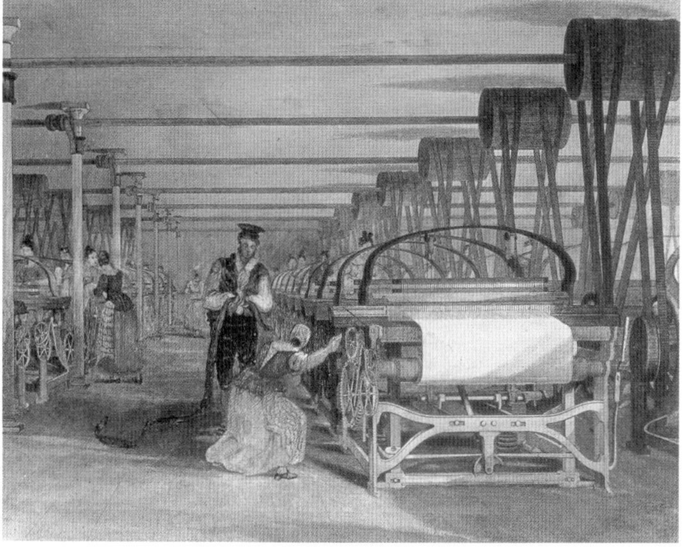

Figure 7.2 The invention of steam-powered machinery (left) *helped create the factory system of the Industrial Revolution* (right).

4. **Standard of Living, Quality of Life,** and **International Trade.** At first, the economic benefits of industrialization were shared very unequally among factory owners and workers. Children as young as seven felt obligated to work up to fifteen hours a day to support the family. In 1832, a parliamentary committee in London investigated factory textile conditions. Their findings, published as the Sadler Committee Report, resulted in the Act of 1833. This act limited hours of employment for women and children. Along with reforms came industrial economic expansion. Eventually, surpluses were created, and the national wealth raised the standard of living and quality of life for most people. These surpluses also stimulated extensive trade between the nations of the world.

By 1900, the Industrial Revolution had spread to other parts of Europe and North America. The Canadian experience of the revolution was similar to the English one, with a modern economy instituted as a result of industrialization's innovation.

During the twentieth century, industrial markets continued to expand, and standards of living continued to rise. Governments in most industrial nations worked to improve labour conditions and raise wages. Extended public schooling and political rights for citizens accompanied the economic changes. Industrialization, which Toffler labels as the "second wave" of human development, continues to run its course in today's developing nations.

Figure 7.3 Labour force by industry, Canada, selected years

	1911	1931	1951	1971	1991	1999
Goods-producing sector	**66.0**	**58.9**	**52.4**	**37.4**	**26.8**	**26.1**
Agriculture	35.3	30.0	15.8	6.1	3.4	2.8
Forestry, fishing, mining, oil, and gas	5.1	4.5	5.4	3.0	2.1	1.8
Utilities*	n/a	n/a	n/a	n/a	n/a	0.8
Construction	7.6	6.7	6.1	6.8	6.6	5.3
Manufacturing	18.0	17.7	25.1	21.5	14.7	15.3
Services-producing sector	**34.1**	**41.1**	**47.5**	**62.7**	**73.2**	**73.9**
Trade	9.9	11.3	14.3	16.0	17.2	15.5
Transportation*	7.3	8.0	10.0	8.4	7.5	5.1
Services**	13.9	18.7	17.9	30.2	40.7	48.0
Public administration	3.0	3.1	5.3	8.1	7.8	5.3

Note: Some columns may not add up to 100 due to rounding.

* There have been changes in classification within these categories. Pre-1999, utilities are included under transportation.

** By 1999, services can be broken down into finance, insurance, real estate, leasing, professional, scientific, technical, management, administrative/support, educational, health care, social assistance, information, culture, recreation, accommodation, food, and other.

Sources: Leahy, 1983; Statistics Canada, 1986, 1998, 2001.

The Post-Industrial Economy of the Information Age

By the middle of the twentieth century, the economies of Canada and most other advanced industrial nations were becoming post-industrial. In a **post-industrial economy**, the provision of services has become far more important than manufacturing. The three characteristics presented on this page and the next form the essence of post-industrial economies.

A Prominent Service Sector

As Figure 7.2 shows, about 74 per cent of the 1999 Canadian labour force was involved in some kind of service work. These service jobs included clerical work, teaching, health care, information processing, banking and commerce, and sales. By comparison, approximately 15 per cent of working Canadians were employed in the manufacture of goods. Less than 5 per cent were involved in industries that extract natural resources (agriculture, forestry, fishing, mining, and gas).

An Information Revolution

The technology that got the industrial economy going was steam-driven and later electricity-driven. The post-industrial economy is propelled by the technologies of the **Information Revolution**: the computer, the Internet, and other innovations in communications. Automated machinery and robotics have steadily reduced the role of human labour in production and manufacturing. Upcoming generations of workers, no longer needed in great numbers in manufacturing, must find their places in the new information-based economy. Proficiency with computers, whether it be in design, communication, or programming, is a must.

Why is the word "revolution" used to describe the prominence of information and computer technology in the post-industrial economy? One reason is that computers have gradually taken over not only economic activities, but also countless other aspects of our lives. Never was this fact more dramatically demonstrated than on 31 December 1999. Millions of people all over the world counted down the seconds to midnight with conflicting feelings of excitement and anxiety. For almost two years, they had heard the warnings of forecasters about the **Y2K bug**. This was a program/design flaw that might have caused the world's computer systems to crash at the stroke of midnight. Examples of the international havoc that might have resulted include: planes falling out of the air, elevators stopping,

Figure 7.4 Although no disasters occurred, the fear surrounding the Y2K bug was proof of the world's dependence on computers.

automated bank machines spewing money, electricity systems failing, and nuclear power plants melting down. Concerned Canadians stocked up on survival supplies such as bottled water, food, batteries, and electrical generators. As it turned out, most of the problems were fixed in time for the new millennium to begin without major incident. The scare demonstrated how much the computer has become a part of modern post-industrial society.

A Global Economy

Besides changing what jobs we hold and how we view the world, the technological advances of the Information Revolution have also created a **global economy**, in which both goods and information cross national borders with few restrictions.

One of the buzzwords of the global economy is **convergence**. This term refers to the merging of a variety of communications technologies, including newspapers, television, radio, and the Internet, into one medium. For example, increasing numbers of people are using a converged version of the Internet medium to listen to radio newscasts, download new music CDs, scan online editions of newspapers, and exchange e-mail messages with friends and colleagues. This trend has triggered changes in company ownership, as the following case study shows.

Case Study: The Case for Convergence

"Over the past year, Jean Monty has been buying up properties and piling them on top of one another much like a winner at a blackjack table stacks his chips in multi-coloured towers. In February, the chairman and chief executive of BCE Inc. dished out $6.8 billion for control of Teleglobe Inc. Then later that month, came his suprising cash offer of $2.3 billion for CTV Inc. His latest deal will create a new media company that gives BCE, at one time just a phone company, control of Thomson Corp.'s *The Globe and Mail.*

"What's going on? Why is a phone company buying TV stations and a newspaper? Why is Quebecor, a newspaper company, buying a cable company? Why is Ted Rogers, the cable guy, buying a baseball team? And why is television broadcaster CanWest Global Communications Corp. buying newspapers? In a buzzword, it's all about convergence. The idea is that as all forms of media converge into one system, based on the Internet, the various pieces of these increasingly massive conglomerates will, like an army of ants, fare much better together than if each were on its own. 'There's almost a new secular religion that's emerging around the question of convergence,' says David Spencer, a media professor at the University of Western Ontario in London.

"Monty's media colossus will hold CTV, the *Globe*, a series of specialty TV channels (such as The Sports Network and Discovery Channel Canada), BCE's Sympatico-Lycos Web portal and the *Globe*'s Internet properties.

"Rumours—published most notably in the *Globe* itself—had it that BCE and Thomson also tried to take a run at the holding company of the Toronto Maple Leafs hockey team.

"If BCE does go for a sports team, it will not surprise Charles Sirois. As the entrepreneur who built up and then sold long-distance carrier Teleglobe to BCE and who now heads privately

BCE Inc.
Market value:
$23.6 billion

Bell Canada
Telephone and Internet services

Bell Mobility
Mobile phones

Bell ExpressVu
Satellite TV

BCE Emergis
E-commerce software and services

Teleglobe (23%; 100% pending)
Long-distance carrier

Chairman: **Jean Monty**

BCE-Thompson
New company to contain:

CTV Inc. (pending)
18 CTV stations, seven others, plus:

- CTV Newsnet
- The Sports Network
- Comedy Network
- Sportsnet (40%)
- Outdoor Life Network
- Discovery Channel Canada
- Talk TV

Sympatico-Lycos
Web portal

The Globe and Mail
National newspaper

ROBTv
Business TV channel (50%)

Globe Interactive
Nine Web sites, including *Globeandmail.com, Globeinvestor.com, Workopolis.com* (jobs)

Figure 7.5
With convergence, BCE's media company is a giant.

held Telesystem Ltd., he is both a keen observer of the convergence mania, and a sometime player.

"Traditionally, Sirois notes, the players that control the physical bottleneck on information—television networks, cable companies, newspaper publishers—are the ones who get rich. But he predicts that in 10 years, 70 per cent of Canadian homes will have high-speed Internet access via several competing systems, be it wireless or high-speed phone lines or cable. That means the method of delivery will become much less important and far less lucrative than the product. And that's why the telecommunications companies are buying the so-called content providers—and sure-fire draws such as sports franchises. Content is becoming king. The plan to control such sources, though, is not necessarily going to work, Sirois adds. 'If I am a content producer, why should I limit myself to one pipe?' he says. 'If I'm a pipe producer, do you really believe society will allow you to block content?'

"Monty admits his plan is not foolproof, but he says intuitively he believes convergence is the way to go. 'There's been much debate about what the ideal media company of the Internet economy should look like,' he says. 'I believe we have the right recipe. What is not known is whether with these pieces together, will the sum be greater than the parts? At the end of the day, we'll prove it by doing it.'"

Abridged from: Macklem, Katherine. 2000. "A Media Colossus." *Maclean's*. 25 September 2000.

1. Jean Monty states, "I believe we have the right recipe [for the ideal media company of the Internet economy]." Describe this recipe and Monty's goals in creating it.
2. Speculate on how convergence might affect the employees working in communications and media companies.
3. Examine the variety of enterprises owned by BCE Inc., shown in Figure 7.5. Choose two or more of them, and describe how they could converge to deliver an entirely new media experience with integrated and enhanced content.

A Different Perspective

Not everyone views the economy in the same way. Dr. Marilyn Waring of Massey University in New Zealand has been in the forefront of those who question the assumptions of traditional economic theory. She is profiled below.

REMARKABLE PEOPLE

Marilyn Waring

The ideas of Marilyn Waring have inspired many people throughout the world. She has gained a wide audience for these ideas through her film *Who's Counting? Marilyn Waring on Sex, Lies and Global Economics* (1995).

Waring's public life began at an early age. In 1975, when she was just twenty-two years old, she was elected to the New Zealand parliament. At the age of twenty-four, she became chairperson of the Public Expenditures Committee. In this office, she travelled to thirty-five countries to learn about the rules countries use to manage their national accounts. During her three terms in parliament, she was also a key player in the movement to make New Zealand a nuclear-free zone.

In 1995, the National Film Board of Canada production *Who's Counting?* was released. In this award-winning film, Waring humorously and cleverly analyzes the study of economics. She points out that modern-day economies value goods and activities only in terms of dollars, or "market value." Unpaid work, usually done by women, is not recognized as part of the global economy. In addition, the negative effects of "productive" activities are not included in economic accounting. If a factory's products are valued by a market, it does not matter if the factory pollutes the environment or makes potentially destructive nuclear bombs.

The film was based on Waring's first book, *If Women Counted* (1988). She has since published *Three Masquerades* (1996), a study of equality, work, and human rights.

1. Summarize the message of the film *Who's Counting?*
2. Why do you think the goods and services related to household activities have not been traditionally recognized as part of a country's economy?
3. Do you think it is possible to "change the rules" of economics to take unpaid work into account? Explain.

RECAP

1. Explain why some sociologists suggest that the economy is our most important social institution.
2. Outline the differences between pre-industrial, industrial, and post-industrial economies.
3. Identify the major economic and technological factors that brought about the modern Canadian economy. How have humans have been affected by these factors?

Section 7.2

The Nature of Work

Focus Questions

- What features of a job are most important for job satisfaction?
- How have people's attitudes toward work changed over time?
- How does work need to change to better ensure personal fulfillment for workers?

Why Work?

For centuries, philosophers and social scientists have pondered the nature of work and why we do it. In the post-industrial era, some specific questions they ask include: Why do some people love their jobs, while others hate them? Why do some people choose to be self-employed? Why do some people accept work at "dead-end" jobs, while others ambitiously pursue top positions at up-and-coming companies? Perhaps you have asked these same questions. What are your answers?

Personal Fulfillment

In 1997, the Angus Reid Group conducted the *Workplace 2000* survey with the sponsorship of the Royal Bank. Figure 7.6 on page 206 shows how workers rated their jobs and workplaces. Notice the categories showing what can be expected from work: economic return, career development, opportunities to contribute and be involved, and fair treatment by superiors/bosses/management. Which of these is most important to workers? Graham Lowe, in his book *The Quality of Work* (2000), writes that *personal fulfillment* in work has been a top priority for Canadian workers for over a generation. In addition to the Angus Reid survey, he cites three other Canada-wide studies in support of his claim: Burstein et al., *Canadian Work Values: Findings of a Work Ethic Survey and Job Satisfaction Survey* (surveys conducted in 1973 and 1974); Maynard's article "How Do You Like Your Job?" in *Report on Business Magazine*, November 1987, which interpreted a 1987 Environics job satisfaction survey; and Ekos Research Associates, Inc., *Rethinking Government III: Final Report* (poll conducted in 1997). The Angus Reid survey also determined that *one in four* respondents worked in their current job just to make money. Almost half reported that it was getting harder to make ends meet.

There has been an awareness, even among the earliest social scientists, that

Key Concepts

alienation
job satisfaction
job
career
vocation
profession

personal fulfillment in work is important. For example, Karl Marx's theory of **alienation** can be paraphrased as: "To be happy and fulfilled, people need to be creative in their work, appreciate the products of their labour, and take pride in the final product." But throughout the industrial era, employers were never expected to take responsibility for their workers' **job satisfaction**. Matthew Fox points out in his book *The Reinvention of Work* (1994) that studying work in the industrial era meant studying its "outer" aspects—mainly, the workplace (field, factory, or office) and the paycheque. In contrast, today's social scientists have a greater voice in identifying both the "outer" and "inner" needs of workers.

Figure 7.6 Workers' ratings of jobs and workplaces, Canada, 1997

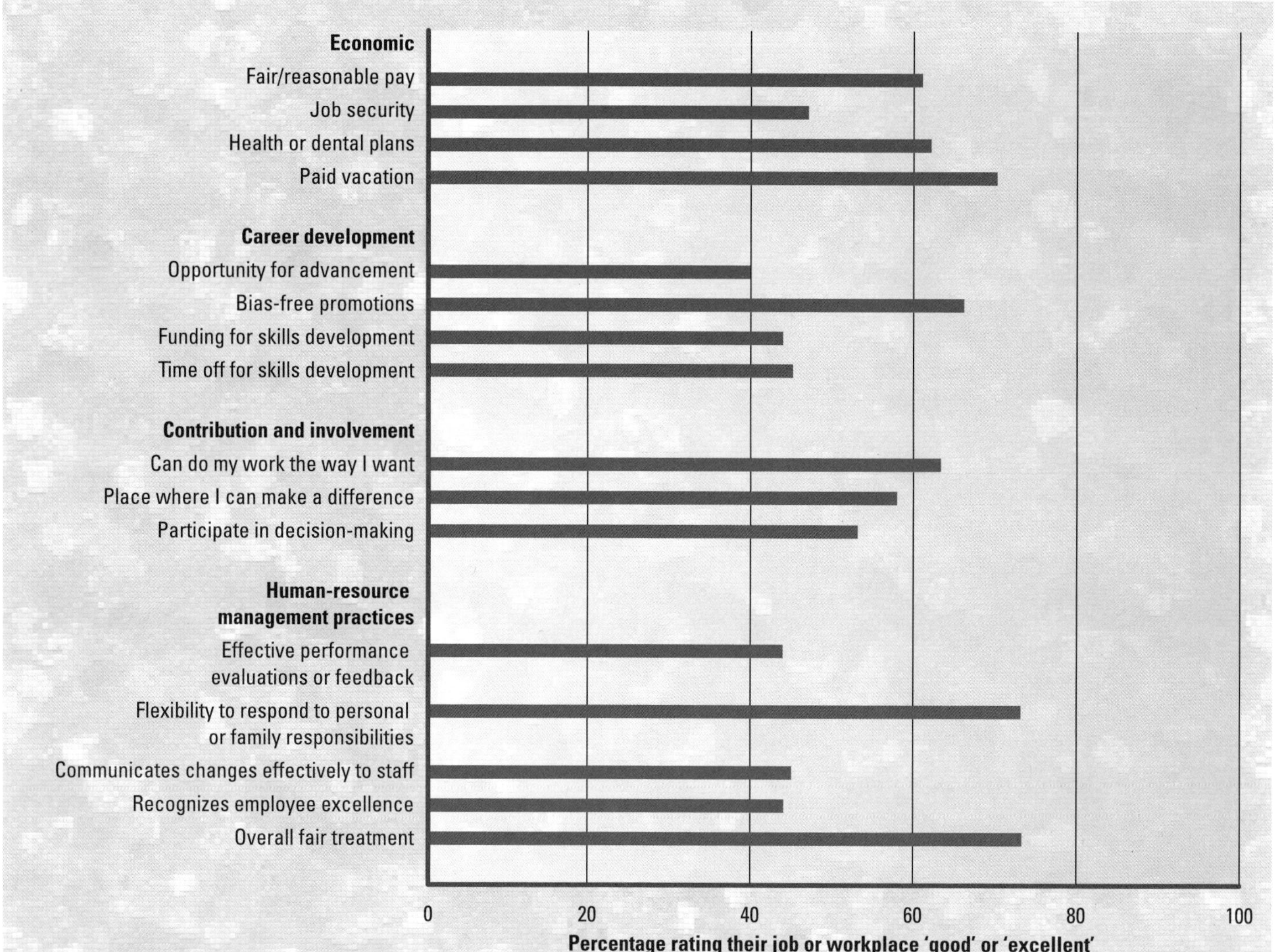

Note: Sample = 1000 employed.

Source: Based on Angus Reid Group, 1997. *Workplace 2000: Working Toward the Millennium. A Portrait of Working Canadians.*

Skill Development: Interpreting Survey Results

Job Satisfaction Survey (Burstein et al.) was designed to probe whether people actually experience in their jobs what they want from work. Just over 1000 members of the working population were surveyed. Questions focused on both which job characteristics the respondents desired and how satisfied the respondents were with these features in their jobs. After the responses were collected, they had to be interpreted. Interpreting survey results requires organizing them into useful categories, calculating averages within each category, and applying the calculations to the hypothesis to verify or falsify it.

Let's return to the sample hypothesis from page 175:

- Students who work more than sixteen hours a week have lower academic performance than those who work less than sixteen hours a week.

Suppose we administered the survey on page 177 to twenty-two students. To keep the results anonymous, we have identified each respondent in the table at the right by a letter from A to V.

Student	Hours worked	Average percentage
A	0	73
B	0	84
C	18	72
D	6	68
E	0	77
F	8	86
G	4	72
H	0	58
J	20	60
K	16	72
L	18	72
M	24	68
N	12	84
P	0	73
Q	22	78
R	14	81
S	0	88
T	14	78
U	23	72
V	28	70

Step 1

First, organize the results into categories or groups that make the data useful. In this case, three tables are called for:

a) results for students who do not have a part-time job
b) results for students who work sixteen hours or less a week
c) results for students who work more than sixteen hours a week

Step 2

Calculate a single, average set of results for each group. This will make it easier to assess the truth of the hypothesis in Step 3. In this case, fill in a table such as the one shown on the following page.

Group	Average hours worked	Average percentage
No job		
16 hours or less		
More than 16 hours		

Step 3
Evaluate the hypothesis. Apply your results from Step 2 to see whether or not the hypothesis is true.

Follow-Up

1. Do Steps 1 and 2 using the survey results.
2. Analyze your results. Write a paragraph in which you state
   a) whether the hypothesis is correct
   b) the evidence on which your conclusion is based
   c) any tentative reasons you may have to explain the results that have been obtained

Job, Career, or Vocation?

Words for work and the history of those words can tell us much about our values now and in the past. For example, many traditional cultures have no word for "work" (Kimbrell, 1999, 2). Work is so integrated into family and community life that there is no need to refer to it separately as a concept. This echoes conditions in pre-industrial economies of the past throughout the world.

Figure 7.7 In many pre-industrial cultures, work cannot be referred to separately from family life.

The word **job** has a straightforward dictionary definition: "a piece of work done for hire or profit" (*Canadian Oxford Dictionary*). The Economic Council of Canada has characterized a "good job" as one that is well-paying, secure, and skilled (Economic Council of Canada, 1990). But the word "job" has had a checkered past. It originally described a criminal or demeaning action (retained in present-day phrases such as a "bank job"). When the Industrial Revolution began, the concept of working for wages was not only new—it was contemptible. Many resented being forced away from traditional farming or handicraft activity into factory work. Expressing how demeaned they felt, they were the first to use the word "job" in relation to factory wage labour.

How can we proclaim through our vocabulary the sense of dignity and fulfillment that we hope to find in work? This sense is not to be found in the original use of **career**—"rapid and unrestrained activity," as in moving around a "racing course." In an *Utne Reader* article (1999), Andrew Kimbrell suggests a revival of the term **vocation** (from the Latin *vocatio*, "calling"). Today, the term tends to be restricted to the pursuit of a religious life. Those who have a religious vocation or answer a religious calling eventually make a **profession** (a public declaration of their beliefs and their commitment to them). Kimbrell proposes we extend these terms to transform our jobs—that is, our work should be viewed as the "profession of deeply felt values."

Kimbrell ventures predictions of what would happen if this shift in thinking were to take hold in the post-industrial workplace. First of all, the value of "empathy for the physical and mental needs of workers" would supercede the value of efficiency. Second, labour unions would widen their focus from raising worker wages to improving the quality of life in the workplace. This would mean fighting for such job characteristics as listed under "Contribution and involvement" and "Human-resource management practices" in Figure 7.6 (page 206). Third, more people would opt for self-employment. Fourth, companies would face greater negative pressure when they attempt to force transfers and relocations on employees (and thus break up families and communities). Fifth, legislation would be passed to protect and/or establish national health care, more paid vacation, better part-time working conditions, a higher minimum wage, and paid leave to fulfill family responsibilities. These measures would not only improve the quality of workplaces, but would also give certain workers the freedom to leave their current jobs and find their true vocations. Finally, formal and informal programs to mentor young people into pursuing professions would be put in place.

In Section 7.3, you will have an opportunity to assess and evaluate how far the Canadian employment scene is from this ideal. You will be able to identify the trends and patterns that create obstacles to fulfilling work. To conclude this section, we return to the *Workplace 2000* survey. Figure 7.8 on page 210 shows in what ways and to what extent Canadian workers in 1997 felt negatively toward their jobs. How have our feelings changed from those of the first workers at "jobs" in eighteenth-century England?

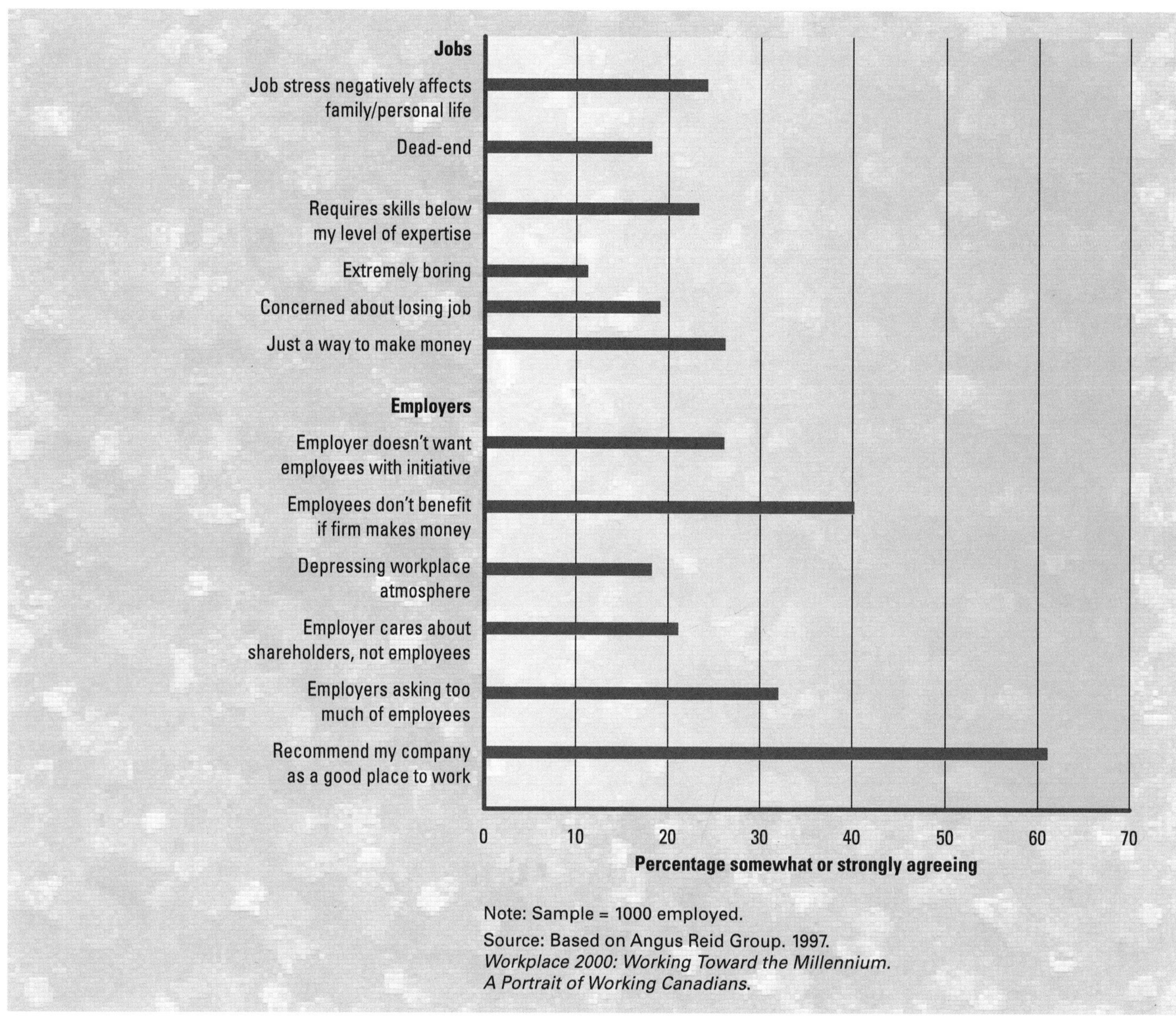

Figure 7.8 Selected evaluations by workers of their jobs and employers, Canada, 1997

RECAP

1. Summarize the findings of the workplace surveys referred to from pages 205 to 210.
2. What do the original meanings of words like "job" and "career" reveal about the feelings of past generations toward work?
3. What changes does Kimbrell suggest would result from a vision of jobs as "professions"?

Section 7.3

Post-Industrial Employment Patterns

Focus Questions

- In which economic sectors do Canadians work?
- How have demographic, economic, and technological trends affected employment patterns?
- What future trends in Canadian employment are likely to occur?

Canada's Economic Sectors

Social scientists divide a nation's economic activity into three **sectors**, or parts. In the **primary sector**, workers extract natural resources from the environment. This sector, the most prominent one in pre-industrial societies, has also been strongly associated with the Canadian economy.

Traditionally, Canadians have been depicted as "hewers of wood and drawers of water." This archaic expression refers to the fact that a majority of Canadians once made their living by trapping, fishing, mining, cutting down trees, or farming. This pattern held through the seventeenth and eighteenth centuries, and was reinforced during the **wheat boom**. This lengthy period of economic expansion was propelled by the completion of the transcontinental railway in 1885. The railway opened up the Canadian West to 2.9 million immigrants eager to work. Foreign demand for Canadian wheat rose, and the mining industry flourished. As a result, Canada entered the twentieth century with a modern resource-based economy. Our strong resource base has perpetuated an economic stereotype that is no longer true—by the early 1990s, less than 5 per cent of the labour force was employed in the primary sector.

As nations industrialize, the importance of the primary sector declines. The **secondary sector**—the part of the economy that turns raw materials into manufactured goods—increases. Manufacturing flourished as Canada industrialized during the first half of the twentieth century. It drew many Canadians from the countryside to the new urban factories. This industrial expansion was stimulated by the First and Second World Wars, when Canadian factories churned out the weapons and other *matériel* of war. The economic boom was particularly strong following the Second World War, bringing a decade of prosperity. The growth, brought on by rapidly rising consumer demands and increased exports (contributing to the rebuilding of Europe), made Canada the developed world's fourth largest industrial and trading power. In 1961, about 25 per cent of the Canadian workforce was employed in the secondary sector.

Key Concepts

- economic sectors
- primary sector
- wheat boom
- secondary sector
- tertiary sector
- demography
- new economy
- re-engineering
- telecommuting
- downsizing
- rightsizing
- self-employment
- career paths
- transferable skills
- flexible workforce
- unemployment rate

Today, about 74 per cent of all jobs (about 10.7 million) are in the **tertiary sector**. This is the part of the economy that provides services rather than goods. As we saw earlier in this chapter, the growth of this sector coincided with an Information Revolution to create a post-industrial global economy.

The Post-Industrial Labour Force

The study of population numbers, distribution, trends, and issues falls within the domain of **demography**. In their book *Boom, Bust & Echo 2000* (1999), authors David Foot and Daniel Stoffman argue that demography can help us understand past and present social and economic trends and forecast future ones. Here is an example from Canada's past.

Between the years 1946 and 1966, Canada experienced a baby boom—a marked increase in the birth rate. The people born in that generation entered the labour force between the mid-1960s and the mid-1980s. Since the country had such a large labour force during that time, there was little incentive to invest in new technology. Canada's economy relied more on people than on machinery.

Japan, in contrast, did not experience a baby boom after World War II. This meant the country was labour-poor through the 1960s, 1970s, and 1980s. In order to grow economically, Japan was forced to adopt technology. As a result, productivity rose dramatically. The country soon led the world in automotive and consumer electronic products.

Japan's economic success threatened more labour-rich countries such as Canada and the United States. In order to compete, these countries had no choice but to automate their industries. Despite large workforces, North American factories needed technology to keep up with the pace set by Japan.

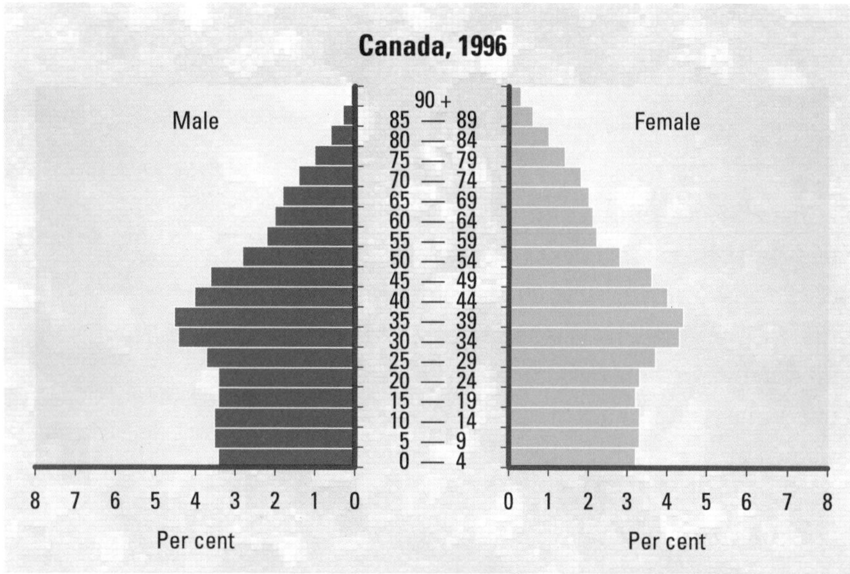

Figure 7.9 In this 1996 population pyramid, the bulge from ages thirty to forty-nine represents the baby boom (people born between 1946 and 1966).

RECAP

1. What are the three sectors of the economy?
2. Examine the population pyramid in Figure 7.9.
   a) What observations can you draw about Canada's population and labour force?
   b) Locate your peer group on the pyramid. How does your group compare in size to the others?
3. Why did Canada trail countries such as Japan in adopting new technologies?

 The "New Economy"

We have just read how birth rates and the availability of capital delayed the adoption of technology in post-industrial Canada. In the twenty-first century, however, those delays are history. Canada is a full participant in the **new economy**, which is radically changing how and where Canadians work.

There are conflicting points of view on the technological and economic trends driving the new economy. On the one hand, technological optimists predict that, in tomorrow's "wired," borderless, global economy, productivity and employment levels will be high, and prices and unemployment low. On the other hand, more doubtful theorists predict the emergence of a cut-throat competitive global economy controlled by a few large, profit-driven multinational corporations. These corporations, accountable only to their shareholders, will contribute to an ever-widening gap between "have" and "have-not" nations. A third point of view holds that it is far too early to make long-term forecasts, optimistic or otherwise.

Keep these conflicting points of view in mind as we analyze how the new economy is affecting Canadian workers.

Technological Trends

Advances in automated technologies such as computers and robotics in the 1980s forced many Canadian industries to **re-engineer,** or retool, their plants.This resulted in the dismissal of thousands of minimally skilled clerical and assembly-line workers. The long-term impact of this re-engineering and dislocation of workers has been a mixed blessing, according to Foot and Stoffman (1999). On the one hand, productivity has soared. Computers and other machines, at only half the cost of human labour by the 1990s, double their power to store information and speed operations every eighteen months. Furthermore, their cost is cut in half every three years. On the other hand, unemployment has increased. It is becoming ever more doubtful that technology will create as many jobs as it takes away.

Another trend resulting from technologies such as mobile telephones, faxes, and the Internet is **telecommuting**. As the following case study shows, a select brand of employer and employee is suited to this new work option.

Case Study: Telecommuting Finds Its Place

"Hillary Bressler wasn't looking to have her employees telecommute. On the contrary, Bressler, a new business owner, would have preferred her six-member staff work in the office of her marketing company.

"But in 1997, the supply of Internet-savvy employees was thin and Bressler needed people who understood the Web. Two of her best candidates wanted to work at home because of physical disabilities.

"Bressler said OK—and she has had no regrets. She hasn't seen either employee more than a few times in three years, but the quality of their works shows they don't need supervision.

'They are spending all their time on the computer and there are no borders to that,' said Bressler, owner of .Com Marketing, a Winter Park, Florida, company that markets Web sites. 'They could work from midnight until six in the morning so long as the work gets done.'

"Telecommuting can be great for business owners, allowing them to hire staff without the expense of adding more office space or equipment. It's clearly something that interests workers. One of every three employees in the U.S. telecommuted at some point [in 1999]—plugging into the office from their home computer and earning a pay-cheque without ever backing out of the driveway. [Statistics Canada reported that, as early as 1992, about one in four employees worked at home for at least part of the week.]

In the coming years, more workers are expected to create virtual offices at home as technological advances and personal needs—such as child care—make telecommuting a viable, even necessary option.

"There's also a whole generation of younger workers who are demanding flexibility in the workplace.

"As a result, business owners who have not considered telecommuting should do so, determining how they will respond before an employee asks, 'Mind if I work from the house?'

"Said Bressler: 'You need to find the right people for this. I was lucky I was able to.'

"Indeed, key to any business owner's decision will be the type of person involved. If someone is a slug in the office, he or she will be no more productive at home, where the TV, refrigerator and La-Z-Boy will be powerful distractions.

"The ideal telecommuter shares the traits of any good employee. He or she is a motivated self-starter capable of working on a long leash.

"There is another side to telecommuting. Certainly, the employee needs to be solid. But the employer also must consider his or her own personality and comfort level with working in an unconventional environment.

"It involves a certain level of trust. Owners who track how often their workers visit the restroom probably are too controlling to supervise telecommuters.

"Owners must measure telecommuters' performance differently from other employees. Telecommuters should be judged on completing projects within deadlines, rather than held to the equivalent of a remote time clock.

"Bressler doesn't care if her telecommuters work odd hours—in fact she knows one of them is a night owl who fires up the computer at 8 p.m. Bressler recommends supervisors help telecommuters make a list of things that need to be accomplished—that way, there's no question about what must be done."

Abridged from: Strother, Susan. 2000. "Telecommuting Finding Its Place." *The Orlando Sentinel*. 8 August 2000.

1. To be successful, what does telecommuting require on the part of business owners and employees?
2. List at least three advantages and disadvantages of telecommuting.
3. Do you think you would be a good telecommuter? Why or why not?

Economic Trends

The technological trends just described are closely linked to several global economic trends. These include increased international trade; sharper competition; and the unrestricted movement of capital, management, and labour around the world. These trends are maintained by international trade organizations and agreements, such as the World Trade Organization (WTO), the Canada-US Free Trade Agreement (1989), and the North American Free Trade Agreement (1994). They have resulted not only in a loosening of trade barriers between nations, but also in a loosening of ties between employers and workers. Since the 1980s, many businesses have been **downsizing**—permanently eliminating jobs—in order to be more competitive. Others have closed up shop and relocated to other countries where labour costs are lower. Some workers found their once promising corporate careers stalled or "plateaued." Others received layoff notices and severance packages or offers to relocate with the company elsewhere. To add insult to injury, an economic recession in the early 1990s helped drive up the unemployment rate to 11.4 per cent in 1993. This meant that over 1.6 million Canadians were looking for work that year, according to Statistics Canada. As the Canadian economy recovered in the mid-1990s, the phenomenon known as **rightsizing** emerged. Businesses continued to restructure as necessary, occasionally re-establishing the jobs they dropped—but only if those jobs contributed to the company's competitiveness.

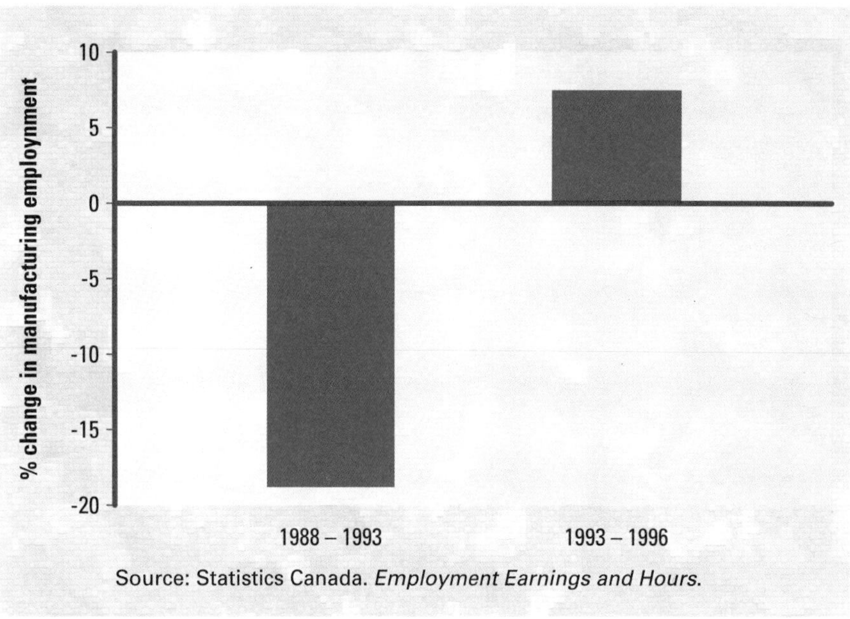

Figure 7.10 A wave of corporate restructuring and plant closures from 1989 to 1993 resulted in an 18.8 per cent decrease in manufacturing employment. Despite improvement after 1993, the overall decrease from 1988 to 1996 was 12.8 per cent.

Employment Trends

"The biggest unknown for the individual in a knowledge-based economy is how to have a career in a system where there are no careers." This statement by American economist Lester C. Thurow (1999, 66) goes to the heart of the major employment trend resulting from the new economy's technological and economic changes. According to Statistics Canada, most job creation since the 1980s has occurred in the service sector. Many of these jobs are part-time, temporary, or on a short-term contract basis and generally are lower-paying than jobs in the manufacturing sector. With full-time, high-paying jobs on the wane, **self-employment**—individuals working on their own—has grown remarkably. During the 1990s, more than three out of four workers in new jobs were self-employed. In 1997, over 2.5 million Canadians—16 per cent of the labour force—worked on their own.

INTERNET RESOURCES

Click on the "Site Map" in the Human Resources Development Canada—Ontario Region Web site at

http://www.ont.hrdc-dhrc.gc.ca/

Summarize the information available at each of the following pages under "Labour Market Information":

- "Economic and Social Trends"
- "Labour Market Analysis"
- "Local Labour Market Information"
- "Occupations and Careers"

This trend is causing a shift in the **career paths** Canadians pursue. Foot and Stoffman (1998) identify the following four basic career paths available to Canadians in the new economy:

1. **Linear.** The linear career path is the most familiar to people who entered the labour force in the twentieth century. In this path, a person gets as much education as possible, and then seeks out an entry-level job with a good company. People following this path expect to climb up a linear "job ladder." Each rung on the ladder represents a promotion with more responsibility and a higher salary. The ultimate goal in this career path is usually a senior management position. Typically, this requires you to stay with the same company throughout your working life.
2. **Steady-state.** The individual who pursues this path usually holds one occupation for life. Examples of steady-state careers are medical doctor, university professor, and member of the clergy. The goals of people pursuing this path include job autonomy, fringe benefits, social status, and tenure. We often think of these jobs as "callings."
3. **Spiral.** In this career path, an employee spirals up the corporate structure through a combination of four or five lateral moves, changes of occupation and/or job description, and linear promotions. For example, a spiral path might involve a move from sales to marketing to computer programming. A teacher might move spirally from classroom teaching to educational administration to human resources. Some moves are within the same organization, while others are from one organization to another.
4. **Transitory.** Traditionally, transitory workers have pursued whatever occupation is necessary to get a job. Transitory workers range from minimally skilled personal service providers (for example, bicycle couriers, personal shoppers, and pet walkers) to highly skilled specialists (for example, marketing consultants, recording engineers, and computer programmers). More highly skilled transitory workers are self-employed "freelancers." They work under several different arrangements. For example, they might be hired by a company to work on a short-term contract basis. Or they may be part of a temporary team brought together to work on a particular

project or problem. They may even be members of a telecommuting "virtual organization," consisting of various specialists operating under a coordinator. The coordinator calls on particular members whenever their special skills or expertise are needed.

According to Foot and Stoffman (1999), the two fastest-growing career paths are the spiral and transitory. These are the paths that best fit the needs of the new economy. Spiral workers will be employed by restructured companies that have "flattened" their previous linear structures. Freelance transitory workers will be employed by companies and individuals as necessity dictates.

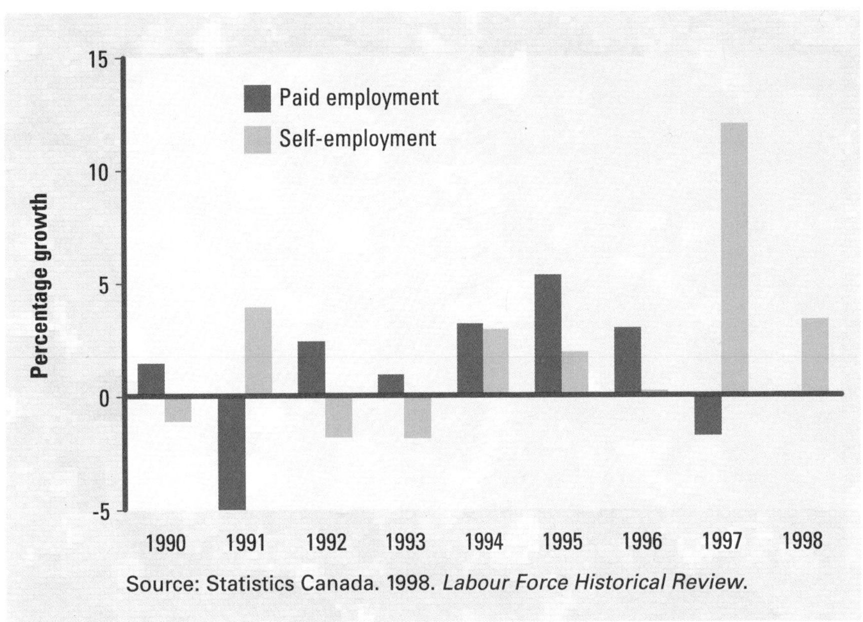

Figure 7.11 More than 75 per cent of job growth in Canada since 1989 has been in self-employment. The average annual growth rate of self-employment from 1989 to 1997 was 3.3 per cent, as compared to 0.2 per cent for paid employment.

Figure 7.12 Calgarian Cheryl Douglass was downsized from a $66 000 a year office job. At fifty, she enjoys her new career as a bicycle courier, earning $30 000 a year. Why do you think she chose this career path?

Case Study: New Economy Winners and Losers

In the following two case studies, we track one "winner" and one "loser" in the new economy. Both women profiled lost their jobs in 1992 when the companies they worked for went bankrupt. But, as you will read, the paths they have followed since have been very different.

Consulting on Contract

Marketing consultant Catherine Renaud of Mississauga is a classic example of a self-employed transitory worker in the new economy. Like most self-employed Canadians, she came by this path through a combination of necessity and personal choice.

In mid-1992, the advertising/marketing agency where Renaud had worked for about one year went bankrupt. Although she had nine years of experience, Renaud knew she would have difficulty finding another job in advertising/marketing. Many agencies had merged, downsized, or closed since the mid-1980s. After interviewing at several firms, Renaud became frustrated.

"I think some of these firms took advantage of the recession of the early 1990s. They knew that jobs were scarce and offered very poor wages," says Renaud. She also found it difficult to match her wide-ranging skills—in telemarketing, radio and television advertising, client management, and strategic planning—with the jobs she was offered.

In the fall of 1992, Renaud decided to strike out on her own as a self-employed marketing consultant. She would specialize in direct marketing and mass advertising. Eight years later in 2000, she had no regrets about her decision.

Renaud has worked on short-term contracts for several large financial institutions and numerous direct marketing/advertising agencies. She has serviced fund-raising, fashion, trade show, health services, auto industry, and insurance accounts. Her contracts have lasted anywhere from three months to two years.

Among the advantages of being self-employed, Renaud includes

- having more control over her working life (for example, being able to pick and choose contracts based on their length, hours, pay, and working conditions)
- usually being able to oversee a marketing program from start to finish and enjoy the rewards of a successful campaign
- being treated with more respect as a contract consultant than she was as a full-time employee
- not having to get involved in "office politics" and power struggles
- having more flexibility in her personal life to arrange travel/family/personal downtime and to take courses

As for disadvantages, Renaud says that having no paid employee benefits is a concern. Also, the time between contracts can sometimes be worrisome—although in recent years this has not been as big an issue as it was in the beginning.

"During my first two years, there was a wider gap between contracts than I wished, but I remained positive and took advantage of my downtime to research, network, and upgrade my skills. After a while, the work was coming back to back and I have had to turn down some interesting jobs," says Renaud.

Renaud thinks that the perception of self-employed consultants/contract people has changed since the early 1990s. "At first we often were viewed as non-conformists and outsiders. Now we are seen as hard-working, responsible 'roll-up-your-sleeves' specialists who get the job done quickly and efficiently," she says. Renaud has noticed a large increase of consultant/contract workers in her business since the mid-1990s. She attributes it to

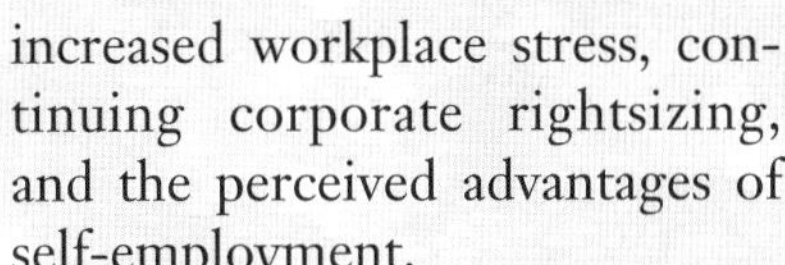

increased workplace stress, continuing corporate rightsizing, and the perceived advantages of self-employment.

Figure 7.13 In 2001, occupations requiring post-secondary education account for 60 per cent of total employment. By 2004, this figure is expected to rise to 72 per cent. How do these statistics affect workers like Caroll Herron?

Renaud says that she is asked by at least five employees a year how they can get started on their own. Her advice is simple: "I tell them to start by doing the necessary research and then plan for it by having at least five months of expense money in the bank. I warn them that it is hard work and that you must continually prove yourself, gain respect and trust, and constantly network for new clients. It isn't any gift on a silver platter." She is quick to add that people with bad attitudes and poor work ethics should not consider going out on their own.

Renaud is pleased that she took this career path. "I have met so many great people and made a lot of contacts. The work is hard, but the rewards are great. There can be a lot of stress and details to take care of, but I take one day at a time."

Disappointment and Descent

Like Catherine Renaud, Caroll Herron of Montreal is a good example of a certain class of workers. Herron represents those workers who found a place in the less high-tech economy of the 1980s, but are struggling mightily to fit into the new economy of the twenty-first century. Mary Janigan reported on her experience in a 28 August 2000 article in *Maclean's* entitled "The Wealth Gap."

Herron was working as a secretary at a shipping firm in 1992 when the company went bankrupt. A high-school graduate, Herron spent eighteen months looking for another office position. Though she is bilingual and an experienced secretary, she had no computer skills. Herron eventually took a job as a cleaner with a company that restores offices and buildings damaged by fire. Her salary fell from $25 000 a year at the shipping company to $20 300 at the cleaning company. The chemicals she came in contact with at her new workplace caused an asthma problem, and in March 2000 she was forced to quit.

Herron is desperate for computer training, and has beseeched employers and the government to provide it. In the meantime, she and her ten-year-old daughter subsist on Employment Insurance (EI) and other government payments, totalling about $15 000 per year. Her monthly expenses include $300 for rent, $250 for heat and utilities, and $400 for food. Her EI was to end in mid-December 2000.

Segment	Average 1989 pre-tax earnings*	Average 1998 pre-tax earnings*	% change
Poorest	$10 388	$8 627	- 17
Lower-middle	$31 427	$27 486	- 13
Middle	$48 776	$46 835	- 4
Upper-middle	$67 790	$68 505	+ 1
Richest	$114 178	$124 681	+ 9

*Excluding welfare, Canada Pension, and other government payments
Source: Janigan, 2000, 43.

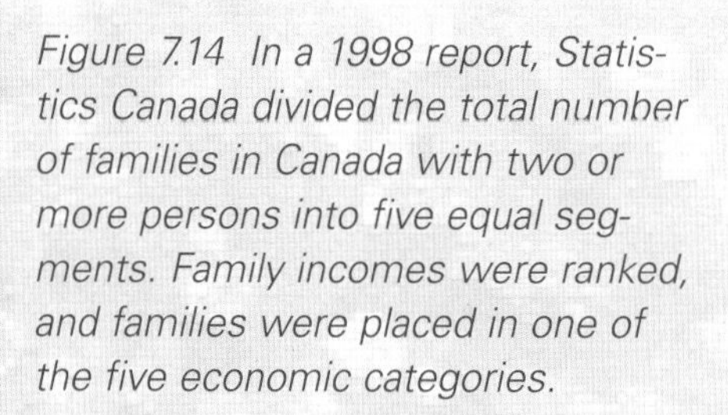

Figure 7.14 In a 1998 report, Statistics Canada divided the total number of families in Canada with two or more persons into five equal segments. Family incomes were ranked, and families were placed in one of the five economic categories.

Social scientists such as Charles Beach of Queen's University see Herron's case as part of a disturbing trend. A 1998 Statistics Canada report bears them out. The poorest fifth of Canada's income-receiving population became startlingly poorer between 1989 and 1998. Their share of total income fell from 3.8 to 3.1 per cent. Over the same period, government assistance, in the form of child tax benefits, old-age pensions, and tax relief for low-income earners, also decreased.

As Figure 7.14 shows, the average income of even the middle earning segment has decreased. Furthermore, the percentage increase in income of the upper-middle segment is far less than the percentage decrease of the poorer segments. The reason may be related to the labour/capital phenomenon discussed on page 212. Once again, Canada's labour resources are outstripping its capital resources. In this case, the labour resource consists of technologically skilled workers. In order to make use of their skills, producers have switched over to more advanced machinery. But because the Canadian economy does not have enough capital to fully fund the investment into high technology, skilled workers' salaries are hardly rising. As for unskilled workers, they have no place in more mechanized companies, so their average incomes are falling sharply.

According to Janigan and the economists she cites, the most effective response to the inequality problem is increased education. Educational programs should be regarded as absolute necessities. Government assistance should be targeted toward the initial and continuing education of every age group to ensure lifelong learning. Caroll Herron would agree. "Now that I am older and wiser, I see that I should have gone further in school. I am not envious of those who make more; they did things to make their life better. I just want a chance."

Source: Young, Rick. 2000. "An Interview with Catherine Renaud." Unpublished. Janigan, Mary. 2000. "The Wealth Gap." *Maclean's*. 28 August 2000.

1. Discuss the advantages and disadvantages of being self-employed identified in this case study. What conclusions do you reach?
2. Caroll Herron says, "I just want a chance." What do you think are her chances of economic improvement? Explain.
3. Explain the patterns you see in the income changes of the middle and upper-middle segments in Figure 7.14. How do you think a self-employed consultant such as Catherine Renaud might fit into these patterns? Explain.

The Future

Predicting the future is a risky business. Not long ago, Canadians were debating what they were going to do with their increased leisure time after automation reduced working hours. Today, there is talk of raising the maximum hours of work in Ontario from forty-eight a week to sixty (Corleone, 2000, A24). Clearly, the workplace has changed in ways many people never anticipated. In spite of these unexpected developments, it is possible to make some tentative predictions about work in the decades to come.

Information technologies will almost certainly continue to displace minimally skilled manufacturing and lower-level clerical jobs. Highly skilled computer-literate employees will continue to be in demand. Corporate rightsizing and restructuring, driven by the pursuit of global competitiveness, will most probably persist. As a result of these continuing patterns, some social scientists have suggested that jobs as we know them—with fixed tasks and hours and a permanent workplace—may even cease to exist at some point in this century. Work in such a "de-jobbed" society may be far different than it is today, as described in the rest of this section.

Career Changes

First, future workers will likely experience several career changes during their

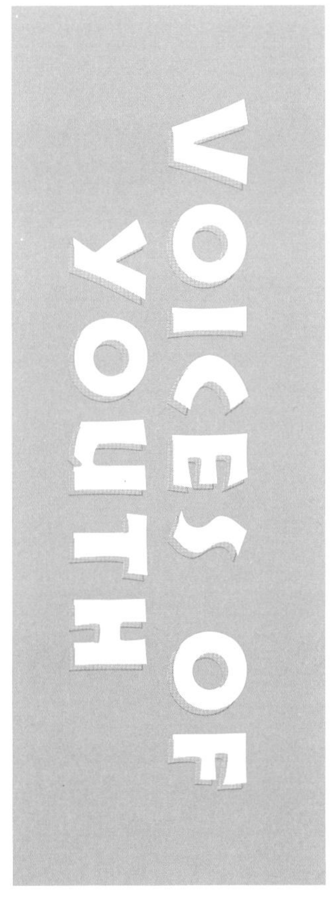

QUESTION:

Should the government limit students' part-time working hours?

Yes, I feel the government should place a limit on the number of hours a student may work. I know from my own experience it was hard to balance full-time hours and school work. I was forced to quit my job and focus on school.

—Kerri Strothard, 16

I don't believe it should because students need to be given the opportunity to be responsible. Work gives them a new element to balance. If work becomes more important to them than school, then so be it. Besides, employers are often mindful that student employees have school. They often won't even ask a student to work during school or during late hours when sleep is needed.

—Norm Wood, 18

I think that government should limit working hours to an extent. If a job takes thirty to forty hours a week, a student isn't going to be able to do well academically. S/he'll be tired and won't be able to concentrate as well. But if the limit is too strict, some students will drop out so they can take on more hours.

—Sarah Johnston, 18

working lives. The notion of working at one occupation for one employer for life will probably become the exception.

Upgrading

Second, future workers will likely be expected to upgrade their skills regularly. This will especially be true of self-employed consultants and entrepreneurs keeping up with the demands of short-term contracts and project-based workplaces. Knowledge-based **transferable skills**, such as communication, time-management, information gathering, and problem-solving, will be in demand, as will proficiency in the most current versions of technology tools and programs. This may mean a professional life in which work and study are combined at the outset, with periods for retraining recurring when necessary.

Service Sector Employment

Third, most future workers will likely have jobs in information technology and the service sectors. Minimally skilled manufacturing and clerical jobs will continue their decline as the range of employment opportunities in high-tech areas increases. Jobs in areas that were new at the turn of the century, such as biotechnology and e-commerce, will be commonplace. As the baby boom generation enters old age, more work in health care, particularly geriatric care, will be available. Adult education will also be a burgeoning field, as twenty-first-century workers retrain and upgrade their skills.

Flexible Working Conditions

Fourth, working conditions will likely be extremely flexible in the future. Telecommuting from a virtual home office will be more widespread. Along with it will come flexible working hours. A "nine-to-five" work schedule, with predictable routines and expectations, will not suit the information-based service work of the future. Rather, workers will likely put in as many hours as necessary to get the job done. There might not be a strictly defined workweek, but rather a varying week that averages out to sixty hours over the long term. In *Boom, Bust & Echo 2000* (1999), Foot and Stoffman suggest that this flexibility will continue into the last phases of people's working lives. Toward the end of their careers, workers would gradually ease out of the workforce by cutting down

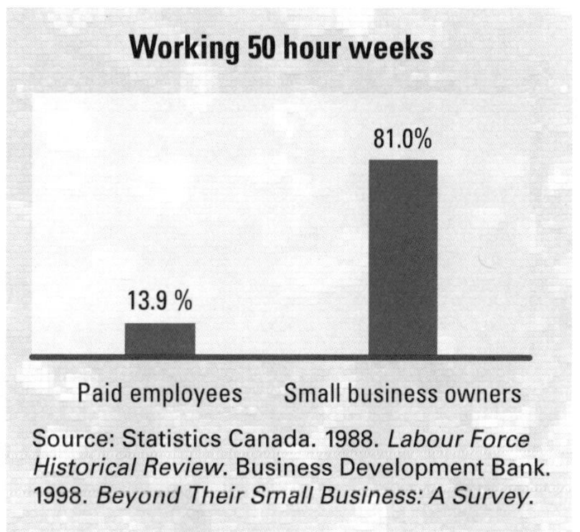

Figure 7.15 Some studies (Laver, 1999, 21; Krohe, 1999, 36–37) have linked long working hours to stress, depression, burnout, and a variety of other illnesses. Do you think the advantages of self-employment in the future will outweigh the disadvantages? Explain.

to fours days a week, then three, and so on, down to zero when in their seventies. The authors argue that a **flexible workforce** based on gradual employment and partial retirement would be psychologically beneficial and economically advantageous. All Canadians would be making their optimal contributions to the country's economy and productivity.

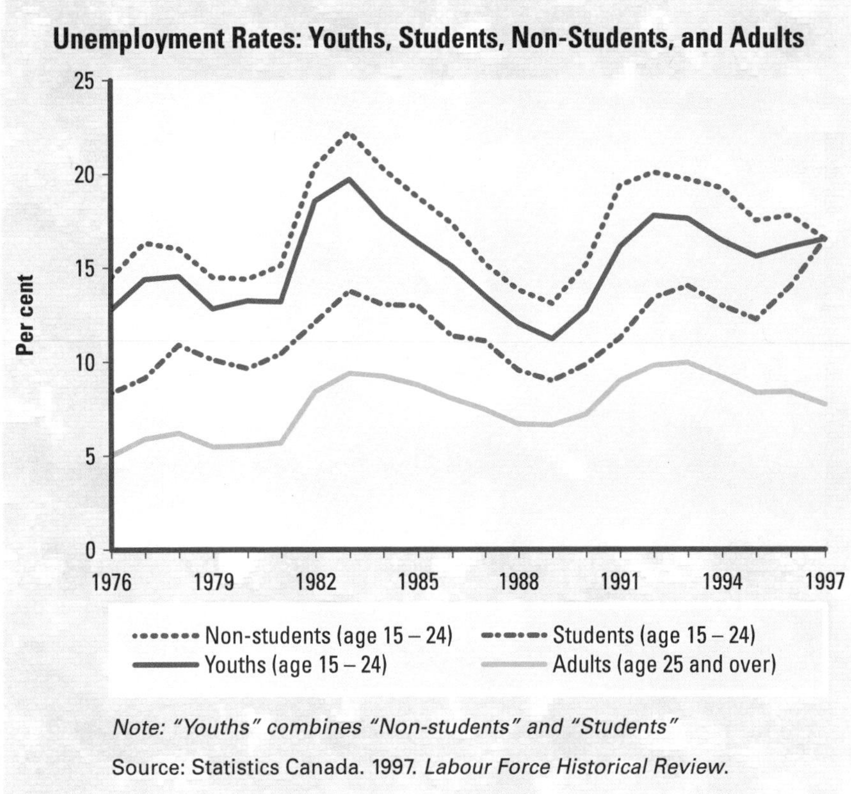

Figure 7.16 Past unemployment rates have mirrored the upturns and downturns in the Canadian economy.

Unemployment Rate

What does the future hold for Canada's **unemployment rate** (the percentage of people in the labour force who are without work but are looking and available for work)? From a high of 11.4 per cent in 1993, the rate remained around 6.8 per cent from 1995 to 2000. This trend prompted Statistics Canada to conclude in the summer of 2000 that "the economy is providing a sufficient number of jobs for the country's growing population" (Crompton and Vickers, 2000, 12–13). A less optimistic view is presented by Canadian philosopher John Ralston Saul. In his book *The Doubter's Companion* (1994), Saul notes that corporations have no motivation to create jobs or invest in long-term training. As long as corporations are free to adopt as much technology as they can, and to offer the least costly employment to workers (that is, part-time work with no benefits), they will do so. In fact, he says the economy encourages them to do so.

Only time will tell whether or not the new economy will provide sufficient employment for Canada's labour force in the twenty-first century. All that is certain is that the nature of work and patterns of Canadian employment will continue to evolve in challenging ways.

RECAP

1. Summarize the technological and economic trends that are driving Canada's new economy.
2. Explain how employment in Canada has been affected by the transition to the new economy.
3. Which of the trends described will have the most influence on the employment decisions you make? Explain.

Section 7.4

Workplace Conflict

Focus Questions

- How does our childhood have an influence on workplace conflict?
- What steps can be taken to reduce workplace conflict?
- How do different conflict-management styles affect conflict resolution?

Key Concepts

family baggage
sibling rivalry
ambiguity
overload
professionalizing
integrator
obliger
dominator
avoider
compromiser

Why Conflict Matters

Conflict—an inevitable part of human interaction—occurs in all jobs and organizations. It is inevitable because of the different personality types, attitudes toward work, problem-solving skills, and goals for the future that co-workers have. How we handle conflict determines whether or not workplace problems are successfully resolved. If workers cannot successfully resolve their conflicts, physical and mental health problems can result. In addition, productivity declines, morale is lowered, and the workplace environment is "poisoned." Eventually, people will look for jobs elsewhere.

Why Conflict Occurs

Many psychologists believe that family dynamics and our early upbringing play a major role in our workplace interactions. Clinical psychologist Amy Stark develops this viewpoint in her book *Because I Said So: Recognizing the Influence of Childhood Dynamics on Office Politics* (1992). One of the specific influences she explores is **family baggage**—memories and experiences related to family that we have accumulated. She divides this "baggage" into three components: how our parents demonstrated authority, how we related to our siblings, and the general dynamics of our primary family.

Parental Authority Issues

Stark believes that there is a strong link between how our parents corrected us in childhood and our self-esteem in adulthood. For example, your parent or guardian may have become extremely frustrated at your mistakes as a child. Comments such as "You're stupid" and "I'm sick of you" would have been permanently recorded in your "self-esteem memory bank." If your present-day boss or supervisor corrects you in a way similar to how your parents did, negative feelings will resurface. Such feelings can cause you to overreact to criticism or correction.

The following quiz from Stark's book can help you assess how you respond to discipline. On a separate piece of paper, record "true" or "false" for each statement.

1. My parents set realistic limits.

2. I constantly find myself in power struggles with my supervisors.
3. When my parents corrected me as a child, I found it difficult to accept that correction without becoming defensive.
4. I respond to limits by pretending to go along with them, but sometimes I don't like being told what to do.
5. I feel angry when someone imposes limits on me that I think are arbitrary.
6. When a supervisor verbally criticizes me, I end up feeling bad about myself.
7. I hate being told what to do.
8. I listened to what my parents said as a child, but often went off and did what I wanted when they were not looking.
9. I often feel that I know more than my supervisors do. As a result, it is difficult to hear what they have to say.
10. I hate it when supervisors put me down and are negative with me—it makes me feel inadequate.

Answering "true" to seven or more of these statements indicates some difficulty dealing with authority. People with this problem have a good chance of experiencing workplace conflicts (Stark, 1992, 42).

Figure 7.17 When employees develop disloyal and negative attitudes, it may be because they associate their supervisors' demands with memories of a harsh parent.

Sibling-Rivalry Issues

Sibling rivalry is another aspect of our childhood that can affect workplace interactions. It includes

- what you and your siblings had to do to get attention from your parents
- whether or not you learned to share properly
- whether or not you were blamed for problems your siblings caused
- how much of the housework each sibling had to deal with
- how achievement was handled among your siblings

Our behaviour with co-workers tends to reflect the patterns we established with our siblings.

The following quiz will help you to determine if you are replaying sibling-rivalry roles at work. On a separate piece of paper, record "true" or "false" for each statement.

1. I handle co-worker conflicts by ignoring them.
2. I constantly have trouble with co-workers.
3. I am not able to gain the recognition for work that other co-workers do.
4. I am annoyed about office favouritism.
5. My co-workers are cutthroat.
6. My co-workers don't respect privacy and take things without asking.
7. My co-workers aren't helpful in a crisis.
8. Conflicts at my workplace are rarely openly discussed and resolved.
9. Work is not equally assigned at my workplace.
10. The role I play in office conflict is similar to the role I play at home.

Figure 7.18 When employees develop hostile attitudes toward co-workers, it may be because they associate their co-workers with rival siblings.

If you responded "true" to five or more statements, chances are you have sibling-rivalry issues. These issues are likely to interfere with your work behaviour (Stark, 1992, 61).

General Dynamics

The general dynamics in our primary family also shape our later work relationships. Growing up in a family in which members both cared for each other and allowed each other to be individuals is a definite asset. This dynamic will have laid the foundation needed to successfully negotiate most conflicts at work. The opposite is true in families in which parents divorced and then attempted to get back at each other through their children. Dr. Stark believes this dynamic can lead to uncertainty and anxiety years later in the workplace. A child who learned to expect different rules from different sources can become easily confused and flustered as an adult. Alternatively, this childhood experience can result in a tendency in adulthood to take on the role of mediator. Instability may have pushed the role of "peacemaker" onto the child, who later feels responsible for resolving difficulties at work.

Families who move frequently can also affect the overall functioning of a future worker. Children often do not learn how to resolve conflicts with friends if they move frequently. If a problem develops, the child is moved from his or her home without getting a chance to work out the problem successfully. Many children avoid making any friends at all to avoid the pain of leaving friends behind in a move. This has a serious impact on these children's ability to understand social relationships. When they later enter the workforce as adults, they often have trouble maintaining commitments. They rarely stay with a job long enough to learn that conflicts can be resolved successfully.

Sexual Harassment

The *Canada Labour Code* defines sexual harassment as "any conduct, comment, gesture, or contact of a sexual nature that is likely to cause offence or humiliation to any employee or that might, on reasonable grounds, be perceived by that employee as placing a condition of a sexual nature on employment or any opportunity for training or promotion" (Human Resources Development Canada, 2000). The *Canada Labour Code* requires every employer to issue a policy on sexual harassment that follows specific guidelines. In addition to obvious conduct such as unwanted physical contact, sexual harassment can include more subtle behaviours. For example, implying that a person is unattractive or making comments about appropriate roles for women both constitute sexual harassment. The conduct does not need to be intentional and it does not need to involve members of opposite sexes. The key factor is that the conduct is unwelcome.

In a 1993 Statistics Canada survey, 6 per cent of working women claimed to have experienced some sort of sexual harassment during the previous year. Sexual harassment complaints to the Ontario

ASK THE EXPERT

Why should we be concerned about sexual harassment in the workplace?

There are two basic reasons why workplace sexual harassment should be an issue for all Canadians. First, as a society we have embraced egalitarian beliefs and values. In a variety of contexts, we assert that all Canadians, regardless of gender, race, ethnicity, age, disability, and other circumstances of life, should have an equal opportunity to succeed in the labour market. Any social acceptance of sexual harassment would mean allowing men (or women) to use their position and power in the workplace to oppress and humiliate other employees. Creating such an unpleasant, and even dangerous, work environment clearly undermines any equality of opportunity. Secondly, since women have been the traditional targets of sexual harassment, Canadian society has been denied the benefits of having all of its workers, female and male, working to the extent of their abilities and dreams. When workers are harassed, they often have to direct much of their energy to simply managing the work environment. Frequently, they are encouraged to withdraw to safer (all-female) workplaces. Such patterns of employment segregation are clearly not in the best interests of our economy. In order to compete, Canada needs the best from all its employees.

Dr. Ann Duffy, professor of sociology at Brock University

Human Rights Commission doubled from 1990 to 2000. A total of 1300 complaints were filed between 1995 and 2000 (Roper and West, 2000, 3).

Reducing Workplace Conflict

Many steps can be taken to understand conflicts as they develop and to reduce their impact. Organization development and training consultant Bob Wall reviews these steps in his 1999 book. In *Working Relationships: The Simple Truth About Getting Along with Friends and Foes at Work*, he argues that conflict can be reduced by following a three-part formula. You first diagnose what has gone wrong, then identify new goals, and define roles and expectations.

Wall looks for a number of factors in diagnosing what has gone wrong in a workplace. Two of these factors are ambiguity and overload. **Ambiguity** occurs when bosses fail to ensure that everyone in the workplace shares the same understanding of goals, roles, and procedures. When ambiguity occurs, conflicts increase, and these conflicts are then taken personally. **Overload** occurs when highly motivated people simply take on too much work. They feel committed to keeping their agreements and work longer and longer hours to meet those commitments. This strategy works in the short term, but has a negative effect on long-term personal relationships. Physical and mental health also suffer, leading to increased conflict because workers are tired and frustrated.

Figure 7.19 What role do you think listening plays in avoiding ambiguity?

Once the problem has been diagnosed, workers and bosses must redefine the goals of the workplace. For these goals to be achieved, the roles of each worker must be clearly defined. Disagreements over roles result in particularly intense emotional conflicts because individuals do not like to feel that someone else is doing "their" job. The conflict is made worse if employees are working hard to keep up with their workload. They might also feel like their job is being "taken over" and that the boss no longer has faith in their abilities. Thus, making sure goals and roles are clearly defined is crucial to controlling workplace conflict.

Wall points out that a professional attitude is an important part of ensuring you are satisfied and free of conflict at work. This attitude extends to **professionalizing**, rather than personalizing, conflicts. To personalize a conflict is to assume the workplace problem is a result of the personality or incompetence of another person. Once a conflict between two workers is personalized, progress can be impossible because of the anger, hurt feelings, resentment, and fear that are created. To professionalize a conflict, on the other hand, is to see the conflict as a breakdown in teamwork. Workers trained to professionalize conflicts will stop judging their co-workers' personalities and capabilities. Their discussions become more productive, focusing on how to avoid the problem in future.

How Do You Manage Conflict?

The way in which a boss manages conflict can really affect the overall health of a workplace. As you review the following conflict-management styles, think about how *you* manage conflict. Which of the following categories most applies to you? What are the strengths and weaknesses of your conflict-management style?

1. **The integrator.** An **integrator** seeks to hear a variety of opinions and have an exchange of information before making a decision. This style encourages creative thinking and is effective at problem-solving when issues are complex. It is not the most efficient style, however, because integration takes time.
2. **The obliger.** An **obliger** tends to play down the differences between people while looking for common ground. The obliging strategy is used to make another person feel better about an issue and can preserve a relationship. Unfortunately, this conflict-management style can also result in the person being taken advantage of.
3. **The dominator.** A **dominator** acts in a unilateral manner, overlooking the ideas and needs of others. Others can be alienated and hurt by this strategy, but it is effective when a quick decision is needed. It is also viable when co-workers lack knowledge or expertise on an issue.
4. **The avoider.** An **avoider** will withdraw from difficult situations, leaving others to struggle with the problems. When issues are not important, avoiding the situation can help things to cool off. But avoidance can leave others frustrated and angry—workers begin to question the competence of an avoider boss.
5. **The compromiser.** A **compromiser** has a "middle-of-the-road" conflict-management style. Compromising means taking something from all parties involved and giving up something in return. When all parties to a decision are knowledgeable and have good suggestions, this style results in good decisions. But when some parties contributing to the discussion are not fully informed, the final decision can be weak. Compromise is often useful when other methods have failed, and all parties are looking for middle ground,

Source: Career Press. 1993. *How to Manage Conflict: A Quick and Handy Guide for Any Manager or Business Owner*. Hawthorne, NJ. Career Press.

RECAP

1. How do ambiguity and overload lead to workplace conflict?
2. Outline the steps Bob Wall suggests need to be taken to reduce conflict.
3. What are the advantages and disadvantages of each of the different conflict-management styles?

Activities

Show your knowledge

1. Create a New Vocabulary glossary of the terms and phrases you learned in this chapter.
   a) Record the definition of each term.
   b) Use these terms to create four questions to ask a classmate. Make each question more difficult than the last. Follow the model used for these activities ("Show your knowledge," "Practise your thinking skills," "Communicate your ideas," "Apply your knowledge").
2. Create a historical timeline that illustrates the major social, economic, and technological changes the economy has undergone from pre-industrial to post-industrial times.
3. Describe how our concepts of work and jobs have changed since the earliest hunting and gathering human societies.
4. Explain why the economic stereotype of Canadians as "hewers of wood and drawers of water" is inaccurate in the twenty-first century.
5. Outline the relationship of each of the following to Canada's post-industrial new economy:
   a) advanced information-based/communications technologies
   b) labour-saving technologies
   c) globalization
   d) demographics
6. Describe how Canada's workforce has been affected by continuous re-engineering, restructuring, downsizing, and rightsizing.
7. Explain why some futurists predict the end of the nine-to-five job as we know it.
8. Explain how parenting style can affect self-esteem. Explain how self-esteem can affect workplace interactions.

Practise your thinking skills

9. What do you think makes work worth doing? Give examples based on the type of work/job you foresee yourself doing in the future.
10. What are the advantages and disadvantages of our dependence on the computer and other advanced communications technologies?
11. As recently as the 1970s, some futurists envisioned a post-industrial society of much less work and much more leisure time. Yet, by the

opening decade of the twenty-first century, many Canadians find themselves working harder and longer than ever. Account for this trend and comment on its desirability.

12. Since the 1990s, a widening gap between the incomes of wealthy and poor Canadians has become a major issue of concern in government and academic circles.
    a) To what extent do you think Canada's transition from an industrial resource-based manufacturing economy to a post-industrial information-based economy has contributed to this trend?
    b) What can Canadians do to combat and/or reverse this trend?
13. Describe what you learned about your own family dynamics and the impact these dynamics may have on you as a future worker.

Communicate your ideas

14. Create and interpret the results of a class survey on the jobs and career paths of students' parents or guardians.
15. Using the case study of Catherine Renaud as a guide, interview self-employed workers from your community about their experiences. Share your findings in a print or an audiovisual format with your classmates.
16. Invite a representative from the federal ministry of Human Resources Development Canada to talk to your class about the "Jobs of Tomorrow." Prepare some questions to ask beforehand.
17. Locate a recent article on sexual or racial harassment in the workplace, and present a summary of it to the class. In your summary, identify
    a) the major issue(s) in the case
    b) the arguments for the plaintiff and the respondent
    c) the outcome (if applicable), or your prediction regarding what the outcome should be

    Also prepare two to three questions to stimulate discussion of the case after your presentation.

Apply your knowledge

18. Research the transition period when the English economy was being transformed from a handicraft agricultural-based system to an

Activities

Activities

industrial one. Compare that period to today's transition into a global information-based economy.

19. Develop your own predictions about the future of the new global economy. Include your forecasts and explanations regarding
    a) the productivity of the global economy
    b) employment rates and patterns
    c) income inequalities in Canada and worldwide
    d) the types of convergence we can expect to see
20. Explain how the suggestions for reducing workplace conflict in this chapter can be applied to other conflict situations.
21. Human rights legislation generally divides sexual harassment into two categories.
    a) An example of quid pro quo ("something for something") harassment is trading a promotion for a sexual favour. Think of another example of conduct in this category.
    b) "Chilly or hostile environment" harassment is making someone feel uncomfortable. Describe two examples of conduct that would fall into this category.
22. In each of the following situations, apply two different conflict-management styles. Describe any differences in how the problem is solved, and try to give reasons for the differences.
    a) Two employees have a loud argument over who is responsible for a number of tasks.
    b) Two employees are let go. Their responsiblities are added to the regular workload of two other employees, who become resentful.
    c) In a work team of three, two employees give the third one "the silent treatment." The third employee is known to have a difficult personality and refuses to expend the extra effort that is sometimes needed for the team project. Several other people remark on the lack of harmony on the team.

Chapter 8

Education Structures

Overview of Chapter

Learning Expectations

By the end of this chapter, you will be able to

- explain the structural changes that are occurring in education in Canada
- analyze the psychological and sociological impact of changes in education on individuals, groups, and communities
- analyze how different decision-making models in education systems affect the provision of education in a society

OPEN FOR DEBATE

SCHOOL CODE A STEP FORWARD

The peculiar alchemy that makes for a productive classroom or a successful school is a prized blend of several important ingredients: students who have seen their self-image and confidence validated and boosted by adults, parents who show an interest and take an active role in the education of their sons and daughters, teachers who exude enthusiasm for learning and new methods of instruction, administrators to whom both teachers and students can look for fairness and consistency, and school boards that effectively mobilize available resources to allow others to teach and learn at optimal levels.

Within these complex relationships, none are more critical than those between teachers and students. When the chemistry is right, teaching and learning are unparalleled joys. When it's wrong, schools and classrooms become jungles of misbehaviour and resentment. The best classrooms are those in which conduct simply isn't an issue because of positive reinforcements from students' homes and the creativity of teachers in handling classroom disruptions. Legalism, on its own, is doomed to fail; positivity stands a better chance of winning the day.

Ontario's educators and students turn that idealism into reality on a regular basis. When it slips from grasp, however, the code of conduct proposed by Education Minister Janet Ecker will provide good protections for students and those who instruct them. Suspensions for certain offences, such as swearing at teachers or possessing alcohol, will be automatic; suspended students will be required to take part in alternate programs. Immediate suspensions will occur and expulsion hearings convened in more serious cases. A formal appeal process will be available for expulsions. Police will be involved if warranted.

In reality, the proposed code isn't far from the standards of conduct many schools already enforce. But its clear language, no-nonsense approach, enhancements for the disciplinary powers of school staff and provincewide application represent a step forward for Ontario' s education system for the most troublesome cases. For times when our best efforts fail.

Source: "School Code Step Forward." 2000. *The London Free Press*. 27 April 2000.

Think About It

1. What ingredients does the author believe are necessary for a successful school? What additional points would you add to the list?
2. The government's "code of conduct" (slated to come into effect in January 2001) gives teachers the power to hand out one-day suspensions. What do you think about this provision? In what ways might it improve the classroom environment? How might it lead to additional problems?
3. Identify one or two teachers who have had a significant impact on your life. Explain why each stands out as particularly important to you.

Section 8.1

Issues in Education

Focus Questions

- What changes have been implemented to improve school discipline?
- How is dropping out of school linked to a cycle of poverty?
- What are schools doing to reduce violence?

Key Concepts

code of conduct
expulsion
culture of violence
alienation
bullying

School Discipline

In April 2000, a new **code of conduct** for Ontario schools was unveiled. The code is intended to improve the school climate by making the school a more positive learning environment. While it is similar to the codes of behaviour that exist in many schools already, the new code does introduce some new elements. For example, students are now required to sing, rather than just stand for, the national anthem. The code originally mandated the recital of the pledge of citizenship in classrooms, but parents' complaints led to an amendment. It is now up to individual schools to decide if the pledge will be recited.

Several of the provisions were written to improve school discipline. They include dress codes and suspension/expulsion policies, described below.

Dress Code

In the new code, parents can require any school to impose a dress code or uniform for students. The only condition is that the majority of parents of students at the school request the uniform. A former Minister of Education said about the dress code: "What we're trying to do is create an environment that is most conducive to learning...Not just the uniform itself, but the atmosphere that's engendered with the uniform—the discipline, the general air that it brings to the school...Obviously there are views that if students are dressed in a totally unsuitable manner, in a sloppy manner, [it] makes it difficult to conduct proper teaching in the school" (MacLeod, 1999, 37). It will be interesting to see over the next few years how many parents will opt to introduce uniforms into high schools.

Suspension and Expulsion

As of January 2001, teachers were given the power to suspend students. Previously, suspensions could only be handed out by vice-principals or principals. In addition, principals will have the power to expel students, a power previously held by school boards alone. Students who are suspended or **expelled**—permanently kicked out of school—must attend "strict-discipline schools." These schools were expected to be fully operational by the fall of 2001.

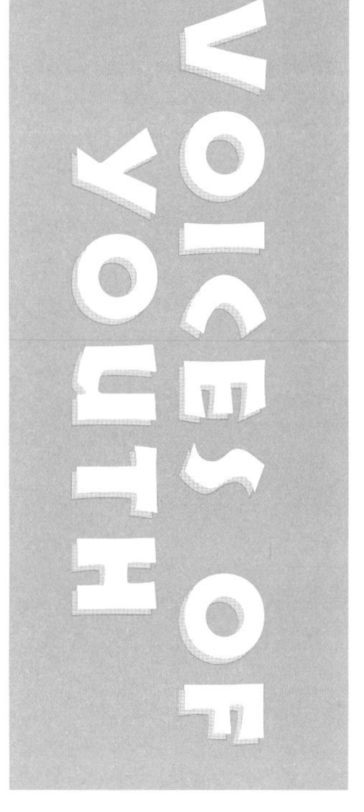

QUESTION:
What is the greatest source of pressure at school?

The pressure to be popular, have nice clothes (brand names), and to find friends that you trust.

—Elizabeth Mullen, 16

Pressure to succeed in what you do at school. Nobody wants to be a failure or to let down themselves and those who are close to them.

—Heather Ambos, 16

Juggling priorities. School, friends, family, a job—all are important to me. Focusing on just one, even if it's the most important, would disrupt my life considerably.

—Ann Cassidy, 18

The growing class sizes and teachers with less time are some of the greatest sources of pressure.

—Nathan Sullivan, 19

Some observers want the new expulsion schools to be modelled after the Toronto District School Board's program for expelled students. Begun in 1994, the Toronto program uses self-discipline rather than strict discipline as a method of control. The program teaches teens anger management and works to improve their self-esteem while giving them a chance to keep up their school work. The teens are given the power to decide when they come to school, for how long, and even what they study. In this way, the whole responsibility for learning is placed on them. By all accounts, the program seems to work, even though strict discipline is not the focus. Of the over eighty students who went through the program from 1994 to May 2000, about half were admitted back into school. One-third went on to find jobs.

Dropping Out

The 1991 Canadian School Leavers Survey gathered a wide range of data on students who dropped out of high school.

- Approximately 184 000, or 16 per cent, of all eighteen- to twenty-year-olds left school before graduating.
- By 1995, the vast majority of these dropouts—160 000—had not returned to school.
- Almost 40 per cent of dropouts were under seventeen years of age when they left.
- Thirty-two per cent had no more than a Grade nine education.
- The rate of leaving school was considerably higher for men (18 per cent) than for women (10 per cent).

Before the recession of the 1980s, those who dropped out were often able to find employment in the manufacturing sector. These jobs provided stable, decently paid work, with good benefits. Young people who drop out of school today, however, do not have the option of landing a well-paid job in a factory. Instead, they are most likely to find a job in the low-paid service sector. And no matter how dedicated young workers are to their jobs, it is almost impossible to earn promotions and move into higher-paid management without a high-school diploma.

Many dropouts are unable to find any work at all. In 1997, unemployment rates for youths without a high-school diploma were almost two times higher than the rate for high-school graduates, and three times higher than those of university students. Therefore, there is a direct link between dropping out of school and poverty. This cycle of poverty continues to the next generation, as the children of dropouts are more likely to have trouble in school and drop out themselves.

The Characteristics of Dropouts

In their book *Class Warfare: The Assault on Canada's Schools* (1994), Maude Barlow and Heather Jane Robertson report that high-school dropouts tend to share the following traits:

- Their fathers never completed high school.
- They change schools a number of times.
- They live alone or with friends rather than with family.
- They work while attending school.
- They have friends or family who do not consider completing high school to be important.
- They had been pregnant or had dependent children.
- They are disabled.

Other studies have focused on the link between dropping out and crime. Dropouts who later became involved in crime report that they were bored in school. They found school rules too strict, and they had friends who placed little value on education. In the case of many teenage girls, they became pregnant.

Research indicates that there is an interesting relationship between school, work, and dropping out. Students who work a moderate number of hours per week have a reduced risk of dropping out. Working many hours per week increases the likelihood of dropping out for *males*, whereas *lack of employment* increases the risk of dropping out for *females*. Various explanations have been offered to account for these patterns. In the case of students who work moderate hours and stay in school, it may be that work skills such as punctuality and initiative increase behaviours associated with success. This in turn increases self-esteem. Working in low-skill, low-paying jobs may convince students with raised self-esteem to stay in school longer. This gives them the option of better employment and higher earnings in the future.

What can be done to reduce the dropout rate? Jock Simpson, an Ottawa teacher who specializes in working with dropouts, and Peter Howe, a social worker with the Ottawa Board of Education, have addressed this question. They have compiled a list of tips for parents to help their kids stay in school. The recommendations include the following:

- Keep an eye on absenteeism—frequent absences indicate lack of interest in school or other problems.
- Watch for warning signs such as changes in sleep patterns, a drop in marks, uncompleted homework, defiance of authority, withdrawal, and an extremely negative attitude.
- If a student receives a suspension, make sure the time is spent doing school work, not sleeping late and watching television.
- Encourage teens to become involved in extracurricular activities, as these can increase a student's overall interest in school.
- Show interest in your teen's school performance, and make it part of the family routine to talk about favorite and least favorite subjects and teachers.

Figure 8.1 Working a moderate number of hours at a part-time job may increase some students' self-esteem.

RECAP

1. Create a list of school discipline issues you feel pose a problem in your classes and your school hallways. Do you believe the new code of conduct in Ontario will help to eliminate those problems? Explain.
2. Explain the link between working part-time and academic performance.
3. Rewrite the list of tips for parents to make it a list of tips for students.

Violence in Schools

The headlines in Figure 8.2 were compiled over a two-month period (April and May of 2000). They reveal what appears to be a major problem in our schools—violence.

How violent and unsafe are our schools? What percentage of students ever witness or participate in a violent episode involving weapons? Is the media reporting on isolated events, or is school violence on the rise? Whatever the answers to these questions are, there is no doubt that anxiety and concern over school violence have increased. In this section, we assess the extent of the problem, offer explanations for it, and suggest ways to improve the situation.

Figure 8.2 Headlines from April and May 2000

Sources: *The Calgary Sun*, 9 May 2000; *The Toronto Sun*, 21 April 2000; *The Ottawa Sun*, 11 May 2000; *The London Free Press*, 21 April 2000; *The Toronto Star*, 11 May 2000.

The Extent of Violence

On 20 April 1999, two students entered Columbine High School in Littleton, Colorado and opened fire. Twelve students and one teacher were killed, and dozens of students were injured. The shooters finally turned their guns on themselves and took their own lives.

The Columbine shootings received intense media coverage. For weeks afterwards, the public was exposed on a daily basis to images of the massacre and the grieving students and parents. Students in schools throughout North America talked constantly about the emerging details. Two of the most frequently asked questions were: "Why did the boys do it?" and "Could it happen here in Canada?"

The latter question was answered in the affirmative just a week after the Columbine shootings. A fourteen-year-old walked into his former high school in Taber, Alberta, and started shooting. He killed one student and injured another. Incidents the next year included the following:

- Three students were shot outside Toronto's Emery Collegiate.
- A "hit list" of fourteen potential murder victims was confiscated from a teenager at East York Collegiate.
- Five people were stabbed at an Ottawa high school.

In addition, there were numerous bomb threats and reports of students plotting to show up at their schools with guns.

It is difficult to generalize from incidents such as these about school safety in Canada. Statistics may bring us closer to a more accurate picture. For example, a

1998 study reported that about 17 per cent of girls and 25 per cent of boys are routinely picked on by their classmates. Such harassment can quickly escalate into serious violence. Other statistics tell us that students in inner city schools in major urban centres carry weapons in greater numbers than their rural counterparts. A 1993 survey by the Calgary Board of Education found that one in five students carried some sort of weapon to class, feeling a need to protect themselves. But perhaps the most important measure is that the vast majority of Canadian students are never involved in a violent incident during their school years.

While limited violence is preferable to widespread, no level of violence is acceptable. As a society, we need to learn why it occurs and what we can do to reduce it.

Explanations for Violence

Some analysts from other countries could not understand why North Americans were shocked by the Columbine killings. One reporter for the British magazine *The Economist* said that North Americans live in a **culture of violence**. They therefore should not be surprised when citizens act in a violent manner. What accounts for this culture?

Anthropologists would explain the culture on the basis of widespread imagery that condones or excuses violence. For example, fashion magazines feature female models with bruises around their eyes, or sprawling on the floor at the feet of men in mock-rape images. Highly rated "shock TV" programs like the *Jerry Springer Show* feature daily fist fights and public humiliation of vulnerable people. Many media critics believe that so-called reality-based police shows exist mainly to feed the audience's appetite for conflict. Hollywood realized long ago that violent action films make far more money than thoughtful, socially relevant dramas and comedies.

Psychologists would argue that alienation and bullying play a role in the violence. Individuals experiencing feelings of **alienation** sense they do not fit in with others around them or with society as a whole. They may feel that no one likes them or understands them, and they may not share the interests and values of those around them. Feelings of anger, bitterness, and alienation characterized both shooters at Columbine High School, as well as the shooter at W.R. Myers High School in Taber, Alberta.

Unfortunately, youths who are alienated by their peers are also often bullied by their peers. **Bullying** frequently involves not only name-calling and

Figure 8.3 Students at Centennial Academy and College in Montreal get checked with a metal detector prior to entering the school in May 1999.

Figure 8.4 Eric Harris (left) *and Dylan Klebold* (right) *as they appeared in the 1999 Columbine High School yearbook*

rejection, but also physical intimidation and assault. The shooters at Columbine and W.R. Myers had endured years of bullying at the hands of other students. Columbine student Brooks Brown said that athletes at the high school routinely cursed and shoved Eric Harris and Dylan Klebold, the two shooters. The police investigation revealed that the two boys were repeatedly slammed into lockers and had rocks and bottles thrown at them.

Student Garrett Holstine stated that the fourteen-year-old shooter at W.R. Myers High School in Taber was often bullied by his peers. Holstine feels guilty that he did not do more when others were calling the boy an "outcast, a psycho, or anti-social." Holstine concludes that the shooter "suffered from severe physical and mental abuse from the people around him and did not know how to fight back or to express his feelings to anyone but his closest friends" (CBC, 1999, 10).

Psychologist Kim Zarzour addressed these issues in her book *Battling the Schoolyard Bully* (1994). She notes that if bullying is not addressed in early elementary school, it can develop into very dangerous behaviour. If bullying is not stopped, Zarzour argues, children learn three basic things: that might means right; that there is strength in numbers; and that the adult world will not, or cannot, help. She also notes that there is a statistical correlation between bullying behaviour in young children, the carrying of weapons in high school, and other criminal behaviour. On the other side of the problem, victims of bullies often suffer from transient or permanent anxiety and depression, sleeping disorders, and school avoidance.

Reducing School Violence

In many schools across Canada, students, parents, teachers, and other professionals are mobilizing to "reclaim" schools from violence. Their initiatives range from fundraising and peer mediation to violence intervention programs.

At Northview Heights Secondary School in Toronto, Grade 12 student Tom de Larzac became involved in this movement after a disturbing incident. In November 1999, fifteen-year-old Dmitri (Matti) Baranovski, a student at Tom's school, was kicked and beaten to death in a North York park. Tom had backpack crests created that said, "This can never happen again." He and other students raised over $6000 selling the crests, which they donated to the Kids Help Phone and CAVEAT, an organization that promotes violence-prevention education programs.

Dr. Chuck Cunningham of the Children's Hospital at the Hamilton Health Sciences Corporation develops peer mediation programs. In these programs, students are trained to patrol the playground and lunchroom and mediate disputes. Surprisingly, bullies frequently volunteer to become peer mediators. Training is usually about twelve hours long and involves developing skills and practising mediation strategies. When the program goes into effect, there is usually a morning announcement stating who is "on duty." A duty roster is posted in the school, and there are weekly team meetings and workshop retreats. Dr. Cunningham has worked with forty-six schools. In schools where peer mediation is properly introduced and sufficiently supported, Cunningham says playground incidents can be cut in half.

Another approach to making schools safer is sending young people to talk to their peers about violence prevention. One program that does this is described in the article "Safety First" by Catherine Patch of the *Toronto Star* (17 August 2000). The Violence Intervention Program (VIP) runs out of East Metro Youth Services in Scarborough, Ontario. The program employs about a dozen students who are at high risk for violence. These students present workshops and seminars throughout Toronto on violence prevention and anger management. The high-risk youths receive help and counselling, and by sharing their stories with others, they regain a sense of control and power. Students in the audience seem very receptive to the information because they know the VIP students have really experienced the issues under discussion.

INTERNET RESOURCES

The *Healthy Relationships Curriculum* promotes non-violence in Grades 7, 8, and 9. The developers of the curriculum are "Men For Change," a Halifax-based group. They believe that helping students analyze our culture of violence is the first step in empowering them to create a violence-free culture. The curriculum includes lessons on exploring and expressing emotions, dealing with rejection and disappointment, exposing gender stereotypes, and exploring the roots of homophobia. Visit the Men For Change Web site at

http://www.m4c.ns.ca

What steps could you take to see that this program was instituted at your board's senior public schools?

RECAP

1. How do anthropologists explain the existence of school violence?
2. Explain the psychological impact of bullying.
3. What programs are in place in your school to reduce violence? What additional steps could be taken?

Section 8.2

The Purpose of Education

Focus Questions

- Why do we have a formal system of education?
- How do functionalists view the purpose of education?
- In what ways does the functionalist position contrast with the conflict perspective?

Key Concepts

functionalism
social integration
conflict theory
hidden curriculum

The Functionalist Approach

Functionalism is a school of thought that analyzes how the parts of a society should work to achieve stability and well-being for all. Functionalists see education as a social institution that performs functions for the benefit of society. Schools do this by fulfilling four main functions: teaching knowledge and skills, facilitating the cultural transmission of values, facilitating social integration, and replacing functions that are no longer being provided by the family. These are all categorized as manifest functions, meaning they are intentional consequences of education (see Chapter 5, page 125, where this term is introduced).

Knowledge, Skills, and Cultural Values

The most obvious manifest function is the first one—teaching knowledge and skills. In contemporary society, knowledge and skills consist of reading, writing, arithmetic, and computer skills.

The second manifest function of education is the transmission of cultural values. This is a process in which schools pass on a society's core values from one generation to the next. One way that this is done is by controlling the language of instruction. As sociologists James Henslin and Adie Nelson note, "It has long been recognized that language of instruction is closely tied to cultural preservation" (Henslin and Nelson, 1996, 480). That is why the government of Quebec has fought so hard for French to be the exclusive language of instruction in the province. Speakers of other languages also promote non-English instruction. Heritage language programs now provide education in the traditional language of ethnic groups where the numbers warrant.

The term "latent function" (that is, unintended function) was introduced in Chapter 5 (see page 125). Functionalists argue that one of education's latent functions is to further the dominance of Western culture. These sociologists argue that the Canadian education system promotes Western values of individualism, competition, and patriotism. Individualism is promoted by focusing on individual assignments rather than group work.

Report cards often print the student's individual mark as well as the class median, indicating whether the student has performed "above" or "below" others. The absence of a dress code or uniform also allows each student to identify her- or himself as unique, rather than as part of a larger, similar community.

The value of competition is stressed both in the classroom and in the schoolyard. Teachers routinely divide the class into teams to compete for "first place" in spelling bees or review games. As well, the school's formal sports program focuses on competitive games such as baseball, football, basketball, soccer, hockey, and volleyball. Although these sports involve teamwork, individuals who excel are routinely singled out for special privileges. They may be designated team captains or awarded "most valuable player" status.

Many Canadians tend not to think of themselves as belonging to a very patriotic nation. Witnessing the high levels of

Figure 8.5 What hidden values are associated with success in today's schools?

Case Study: An Alternative "Afrocentric" Program

If functionalists are correct and schools transmit cultural values, the question arises as to *which* group's cultural values should be transmitted?

Black parents have long argued that black students are not well served within the traditional school system. While black students account for between 7 and 12 per cent of the Ontario school population, the vast majority of their teachers are white and middle-class. These parents feel that white teachers have lower expectations of black students. As proof of this claim, they point to the overrepresentation of black students in non-university-track high-school courses.

In response to these concerns, an alternative program for black students—called the Nighana program—operates out of Toronto's Eastdale Collegiate Institute. The program includes courses in black African history, and allows students to learn with other black students and teachers. The Nighana program is believed to increase students' academic confidence. In doing so, it re-integrates them into a system that has alienated, neglected, or rejected them.

1. In what ways do schools promote white, mainstream cultural values?
2. Explain how this could have a negative effect on non-white students.
3. Describe the Nighana program. Could your school benefit from this program or a program for (an)other cultural/ethnic group(s)? (Specify the group(s)).

patriotism in the United States, they consider that Canadians pale in comparison. Nevertheless, patriotism is another value promoted in Canadian schools. Canadian students are taught that Canada is the best country in the world in which to live. This is often done by highlighting problems that exist elsewhere (for example, high levels of crime in the United States). Other features of the country that are lauded are its historic political and social leaders, its enlightened social institutions, and its respect for multiculturalism.

Figure 8.6 How do you think the members of this diverse group of children will change as a result of their schooling?

Social Integration

Functionalists believe that another purpose of education is **social integration**—that is, helping to socialize students into mainstream culture. When children first come to school, they bring with them the speech patterns, ways of dressing, behaviours, and attitudes of their family and social class. Exposure to peers and the school promotion of Canadian culture integrate or mould this diverse collection of students into a more or less cohesive unit.

According to functionalists, if people believe their society's social institutions are the basis of their welfare, they will have little reason to rebel. In fact, they will help to maintain the system as it is.

Replacing Family Functions

The fourth purpose of education, according to functionalists, is replacing some of the functions formerly provided by the family. For example, now that most families have two wage earners, child care has become a manifest function of schools. Schools now provide sex education, a responsibility that used to rest solely on parents. In some cases, the roles of confidant and adviser, once fulfilled by family members, have been taken over by guidance counsellors and teachers.

RECAP

1. How do schools transmit cultural values?
2. In what ways are students socially integrated by schools?
3. Make a list of all the ways that your school performs family functions. Do you think any of the points on your list would be better handled by the family? Explain.

The Conflict Perspective

In contrast to functionalists, **conflict theorists** view society as composed of groups fiercely competing for scarce resources. Conflict theorists see the educational system as a tool used by those in power to control society and maintain dominance. To these sociologists, the real purpose of education is to teach a **hidden curriculum** of unwritten goals (for example, promoting obedience to authority and conformity to cultural norms). The purpose of this hidden curriculum is to teach students the work habits and values needed to work for the elite. In this way, school ultimately perpetuates social inequalities. One conflict theorist who has researched these ideas and claims to have found evidence for them is Harry Gracey.

Kindergarten as Boot Camp

After a 1991 participant-observation study, Harry Gracey has concluded that kindergarten is a "boot camp". He argues that impressionable young children are drilled in the behaviours and attitudes deemed necessary for their student role. Among the required behaviours and attitudes are talking only when asked to speak, requesting permission to speak, and obeying authority figures. Gracey observed kindergarten teachers quietly scolding non-conforming students while giving approval for conforming behaviours. The goal of kindergarten, in Gracey's view, is to mould individuals from many diverse backgrounds into a compliant group. The members of this group will, on command, unthinkingly follow classroom routines.

Classic Study

RESEARCHER:
Harry Gracey, Sociologist

TIME:
1991

SUBJECT:
Hidden Curriculum of Kindergarten

ASK THE EXPERT

What are some important "hidden cultural values" transmitted through the Canadian education system?

The Canadian education system values the production of an educated pool of workers who are tailored to the needs of the job market. The hidden values the system transmits to this pool of graduates include individuality, competitiveness, achievement, excellence, and hard work.

This set of values and outlook are primarily Western European. They reflect Canadian history, in which European immigrants gained power over Canada's Aboriginal peoples by asserting their individuality and competing for the country's land and resources. The hidden message is that Aboriginal and non-European cultural values are not as good or as worthwhile as the Western European value system. As a result, the contributions of other peoples to world civilization can be devalued.

A problem with this particular set of values is that they are detached, or exist apart, from social justice issues and the needs of local communities. In other words, the values of community, social responsibility, and openness to a diversity of cultures are not the "hidden values" of the Canadian educational system.

Dr. George J. Sefa Dei, professor of sociology at the Ontario Institute for Studies in Education at the University of Toronto

Maintaining Class Structure

For conflict theorists, the bottom line is that education reproduces the social-class structure. Forces behind the curriculum and classroom procedures promote the interests of society's elite and perpetuate social-class divisions. Regardless of abilities, children from wealthy families are more likely to be placed on university-bound tracks. Children from poor families, on the other hand, are overly represented in vocational programs. Support for these arguments was supplied as far back as 1982, in the book *Stations and Callings*, by John Porter, Marion Porter, and Bernard Blishen. The authors found that students from a higher social class were four times more likely to pursue academic streams of education than were those from a lower social class. Sociologists James Henslin and Adie Nelson report that the same general relationships hold today (Henslin and Nelson, 1996, 490). And because people with higher educations in turn earn more money, patterns of inequality tend to reproduce themselves.

Figure 8.7 Imagine you are a conflict theorist researching scholarship programs for high-school graduates. What aspects of these programs would you investigate? How do you think a functionalist would view these programs?

Scholarship Sampler

Award	Value	Criteria	Awarded annually	Applicants (1999)
TD Canada Trust Scholarships for Outstanding Community Leadership	$14 000, plus four years of tuition and summer employment	a record of leadership and community service	20 (maximum)	2700
Canadian Merit Scholarship Foundation Awards	$20 000, plus four years of tuition and an opportunity to participate in a mentor or internship program	a record of leadership and community service	30 (maximum)	3200
Imperial Tobacco Canada Ltd. Scholarship Fund for Disabled Students	$5000	must be an undergraduate living with a disability	10 (maximum)	271

Source: Schofield, 2000, 98.

RECAP

1. What do conflict theorists mean by a "hidden curriculum"? Does one exist in your school? Explain.
2. How might schools perpetuate social-class divisions? What purpose would this serve in society?
3. Reflect on what you learned about the functionalist and conflict perspectives. Which do you believe does a better job explaining the purpose of education in society? Include at least three supporting points in your answer.

Section 8.3

Past Challenges in Education

Focus Questions

- What differences are there between traditional and progressive philosophies of education?
- What changes have taken place in the structure of the Ontario curriculum since 1945?
- What is the structure and philosophy behind the *Ontario Curriculum* (1999)?

Key Concepts

traditional philosophy
conservative philosophy
progressive philosophy

Two Competing Philosophies

Major changes have been made to the Ontario school system, particularly the high-school system, since 1945. For example, in 1945 only 41 per cent of students entering high school graduated. In 1999, by contrast, this figure had risen to 92 per cent. But behind the graduation numbers a host of related changes took place. This chapter will concentrate on a few of these to show how the Ontario education system has evolved.

Two competing philosophies have fought for dominance within the world of educational reforms. One philosophy is the **traditional**, or **conservative**, **philosophy**. It holds that schools have a primary duty to teach students skills for fitting into society and finding employment. This should be done in a disciplined manner, with a clearly laid-out curriculum that is rigidly followed. Students must be trained not only to learn curriculum content but also to accept the curriculum's underlying philosophy.

Former Education Minister William Dunlop expressed the traditional philosophy in a 1951 talk with Toronto teachers:

> Too many fads are creeping into education these days, to the exclusion of down-to-earth fundamentals. [They encourage] self-expression and day-dreaming and are slowly giving the taxpayer the impression that he is contributing to psychological laboratories rather than schools. The prime purpose of schooling is to produce loyal, intelligent, right-thinking, religious, and freedom-loving citizens. But this cannot be accomplished until the last shreds of the so-called progressive education are gone (Stamp, 1982, 193).

Dunlop alluded to the **progressive philosophy** of education, which holds that the curriculum should not be fixed and inflexible. Rather than forcing students to adapt to the curriculum, the curriculum should adapt to the student. This philosophy was outlined in the 1968 Ontario Royal Commission on Education report entitled *Living and Learning* (commonly called the Hall-Dennis Report). The document criticized the province's schools for holding students as a "captive audience" whose learning experiences were "imposed, involuntary, and structured." It was far better, the report concluded, to put "the needs of the child at the heart of the educational function." Students should be allowed to select what they wanted to learn and be involved in deciding the best way to learn it. A member of the Royal Commission later stated:

> What we meant is that the child is primarily a human being and he is primarily a learner, and it is to these roles that attention should be paid...We were for a humane educational system...We were for permissiveness—responsible permissiveness (Stamp, 1982, 217).

1945 Education Figures

For every 100 students who entered Grade 1:

- 58 entered secondary school
- 21 graduated from Grade 12
- 13 graduated from Grade 13

The struggle between the traditional and progressive philosophies dominated the educational debate throughout the last half of the twentieth century. As the remainder of this chapter shows, the debate between them is still very much with us.

The 1950s: Traditional Curriculum

During the Second World War (1939–1945), the war effort took precedence over

REMARKABLE PEOPLE

Hilda Neatby (1904–1975)

Hilda Neatby was born in Surrey, England, in 1904. She earned her B.A. and M.A. at the University of Saskatchewan and her Ph.D. at the University of Minnesota (1934). From 1949 to 1951, Neatby served as the only female member of the Royal Commission on the Arts and Letters. This experience, combined with her work as a history professor at the University of Saskatchewan, led Neatby to call for higher standards in education. Her book *So Little for the Mind* (1953) strongly criticized the public education system in Canada. In it, she claimed that progressive learning techniques failed to exercise, train, and discipline the mind. She called for greater substance with a stronger appreciation for the values and achievements of the past. She equated education with intellectual and moral development. Neatby is featured on Canada Post's Millennium Collection of stamps with the inscription "In love with learning."

1. What did Neatby consider to be the purpose of education?
2. Which philosophy of education did Neatby promote? Explain your answer.

all other concerns in Canada. As military victory became the national goal, funding for education and other social programs remained severely limited. As the war drew to a close, the need for educational reform became apparent. In 1945, the Ontario government appointed a Royal Commission on Education, chaired by Justice John A. Hope. The Commission's hearings became a battleground between progressivism and traditionalism. A thirty-page document from the Department of Education supported progressive ideas. They included learning by doing, co-operative group work, and using social sciences to examine problems in society. Traditionalists struck back with tales of horror from the United States, where progressive ideas were at their height. Among the traditionalists were the province's Latin teachers, who believed that their subject should be compulsory for all students in all years. Many at the time believed that an understanding of Latin was the basis of civilized life.

Traditionalist Reforms

When the Hope Commission finally published its report in 1950, it was clear that the traditionalists had won. Selected quotations give an overview of the report's conclusions:

- "Two virtues about which there can be no question—honesty and Christian love—should be at the centre of the curriculum."
- "Mastery of subject-matter is the best present measure of effort and the most promising source of satisfaction and achievement."

REMARKABLE PEOPLE

Betty Murray (1917–1996)

Educational leader Dr. Elizabeth (Betty) Murray began her teaching career in the 1940s. Finding herself in a one-room rural school in Colchester County, Nova Scotia, she began an extended series of school and community projects. These ranged from building a library to beautifying the school and its grounds. Murray quickly got her students involved in community life—visiting elderly people, presenting concerts, and performing in music festivals. Murray's program of "learning by doing" caught the attention of other educators. She was invited to lecture at Acadia University on how to teach in ways that reflect the community's social, economic, and cultural needs. Murray's responsibilities grew as she became the first regional representative of the Halifax Adult Education Division. In all her activities, she brought together children, parents, and community members from a wide range of social backgrounds to improve the quality of both education and community life.

1. Which philosophy of education did Murray demonstrate? Explain.
2. Paraphrase what Murray considered to be the purpose of education.

- "Efforts should be made to impress on pupils that all who work hard and honestly...are partners in the good society and warrant social recognition."
- "School tasks should be challenging because much of life is equally so."

Although the Ontario government did not accept all of the report's recommendations, it did share the Commission's traditionalist views. This was evidenced by the reforms introduced in the 1950s. They included

- an increase in the number of compulsory subjects and a reduction in the number of options
- the teaching of History and Geography as separate subjects (replacing experiments in the teaching of Social Sciences)
- a cutback in the powers of local groups of teachers developing their own course materials
- abolition of financial grants for gyms and auditoriums (to focus more money on academic learning)

The Results

Education Minister Dunlop told the Ontario legislature in 1959: "We do not need to copy the educational systems of any other country. Ontario's educational system is the best in the world." Was he right?

One positive result of the reforms was an enormous expansion in enrolment. But academic subjects were being emphasized at the expense of other legitimate aspects of education. The major function of schools seemed to be selecting the most academically able students and preparing them for Grade 13 and university. Technical and business subjects received little attention.

Figure 8.8 How was high school education in the 1950s different from high school education today?

Ontario School Enrolment, 1945 and 1960

	1945	1960
Elementary	545 000	1 126 000
Secondary	120 000	262 000
Total	665 000	1 388 000

The 1960s: Progressive Reforms

One of the greatest weaknesses of education in the 1950s was the downplaying of technical and vocational programs. As manufacturing industries became more important during the 1960s, industries complained that there were not enough trained technical personnel. The federal government responded in 1962 with its Technical and Vocational Training Assistance Act. This act provided, via federal funding, 75 per cent of the cost of installing vocational facilities in high schools. This program allowed Ontario to build 335 new schools and make additions to 83 others, at a total cost of $806 million. The program's funding ran out in 1967.

A new curriculum came into effect in September 1962. It was officially called the "Reorganized Programme," but was commonly referred to as the "Robarts Plan" (John Robarts was the newly appointed Education Minister). The plan divided students into three streams at the end of Grade 9. One stream put students through an Arts and Science program, leading to graduation at the end of Grade 13. The Business and Commerce stream led to graduation at the end of Grade 12. The Science, Trades, and Technology stream gave students the option of graduation at the end of Grade 12 or a diploma at the end of Grade 10.

The new plan stated: "A principal purpose of the reorganization is to retain in school, until at least the end of Grade 12, a much higher proportion of the pupils who enroll in Grade 9." In this, it succeeded. In 1960, 67 per cent of fifteen- to nineteen year-olds were in secondary school; by 1968, the figure had risen to 77 per cent.

Another positive feature of the plan was the importance placed on technical education. From this point on, technical education became a permanent part of the high-school curriculum.

The major failing of the new system was that it was extremely rigid. For example, students could not easily transfer from one stream to the other—they were "locked in" from Grade 10 onward. Another example of the plan's rigidity was that university acceptance was wholly determined by performance in province-wide final exams. Students wrote "departmental exams," which were created in Toronto and returned there for marking. Hundreds of teachers were gathered together in a hockey arena to work on the exams through July. Term work was not counted in determining final marks.

In response to criticisms of the plan's rigidity, the credit system for student course selection was adopted. This reform was among the many progressive changes recommended by the 1968 Hall-Dennis Report, which also urged the following:

- Students should have maximum freedom in choosing the types of courses they want to study. Compulsory courses should be kept to a minimum.
- Learning should focus on the students' own interests and strengths (as opposed to the rigid requirements of the curriculum).
- Students should be challenged to think and analyze, rather than just memorize facts.
- Rigid streaming of students should end, and no distinctions should be made between

students on the basis of the program they take.

- Students should not be punished for bad behaviour, but encouraged to reform. "Punishment is demoralizing because it negates moral responsibility. It fosters cynicism and a belief that the thing to do is simply to avoid being caught by those who have authority to punish" (Stamp, 1982, 217–218).

In response to the 1968 report, the province of Ontario phased in a new program over the period from 1969 to 1972. It was known as High School 1 (HS 1), and it abolished province-wide exams at the end of Grade 13. To graduate, students needed any twenty-seven credits, provided they completed three credits in each of four broad areas. A further six credits at year 5 (Grade 13) were required for university admission. In many school boards, all exams were abolished, and students were graded entirely on the basis of term work. Experimental courses were encouraged, as was regular consultation between students and teachers on what and how to learn.

HS 1 was replaced in 1985 by the somewhat more rigid *Ontario Schools: Intermediate and Senior*. Commonly known as OSIS, the program required thirty credits for graduation and abolished the distinction between Grade 12 and Grade 13 graduation. Individual courses had to be offered at one of three levels—Basic, General, or Advanced. Students planning to attend university would have to focus on Advanced courses in academic subjects. Otherwise, many of the progressive reforms brought in by the Hall-Dennis Report remained in place.

Ontario School Enrolment, 1969

Elementary	1 416 000
Secondary	530 000
Total	1 846 000

The 1970s and '80s: Multicultural Education

The Hall-Dennis Report and the reforms that followed it created a progressive climate that led to still more changes. A good example of this is the adoption of a multicultural education program.

The federal government officially recognized multiculturalism as a key feature of Canadian life in 1971. The Charter of Rights and Freedoms acknowledged, in 1982, Canada's multicultural nature. Materials were developed showing the cultural features of different racial and ethnic groups. An attempt was made to encourage classroom celebration of the diversity of the nation. Special multicultural fairs were held in many high schools, while guest speakers and performers from different groups made class presentations. There was some criticism that the approach was superficial, concentrating on "foods and festivals." Parading the external, stereotypical aspects of cultures emphasized differences, failing to teach how diversity can make everyone stronger.

Later developments tried to take multiculturalism into the mainstream of the curriculum. Teachers tried to incorporate a multicultural element in regular classroom activities. So, for example, when studying the Second World War, students would see examples of volunteers who fought for Canada from a variety of ethnic backgrounds. When studying folk songs in music class, they would learn songs from a variety of cultures. The intent of such studies was to show that there is nothing different about racial or ethnic groups. Canadians of all backgrounds have contributed to and continue to play a role in the nation's growth.

In recent years, multicultural studies have broadened into anti-racist education, examining the roots of inequality and power imbalances in society. Examples of racial injustice are used to demonstrate the evils that can come from intolerance. These examples include the Jewish Holocaust in Nazi Germany, the treatment of ethnic groups in Canada during the Second World War, and the expulsion of the Acadians from New Brunswick in the 1750s.

Aboriginal Education

Responsibility for Aboriginal peoples belongs to the federal government, while responsibility for education lies with the provinces. As a result, both levels of government are involved in this area.

By 2000, the *Ontario Curriculum* allowed all high schools to offer credit courses in Native Languages and Native Studies. The language courses focus mainly on the Algonquian and Iroquoian families of languages. As with any language course, studies are broken down into strands such as Oral Communication, Reading, Writing, and Grammar. In Contemporary Aboriginal Voices, a Grade 11 college preparation course, students study Identity, Relationships, Sovereignty, Challenges,

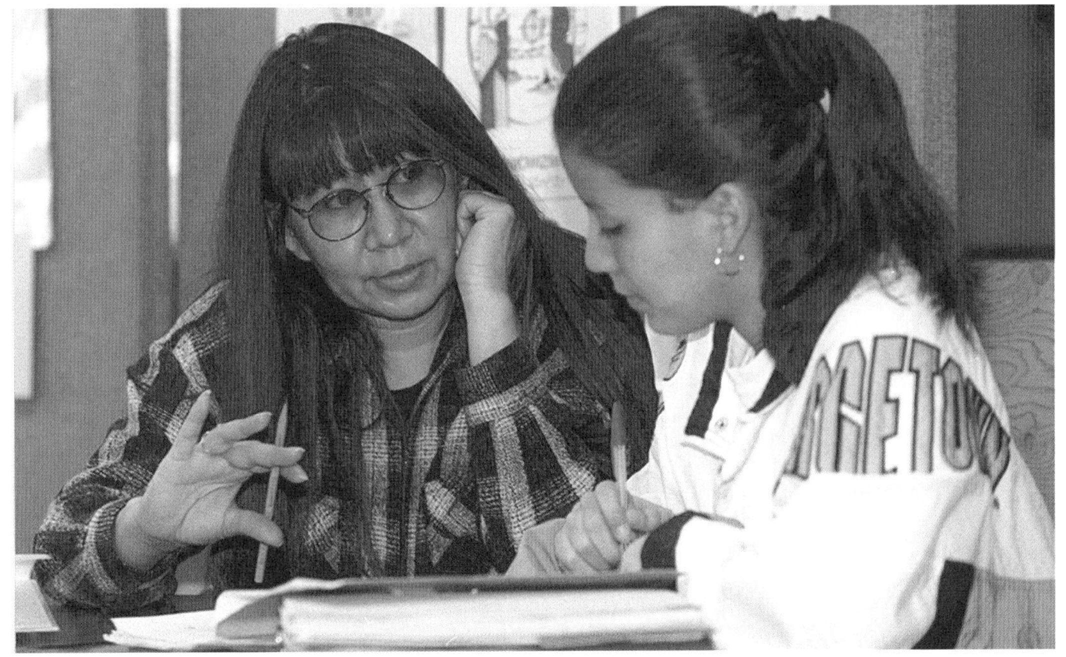

Figure 8.9 Aboriginal language teacher Annie Boulanger gives a lesson to Grade 12 student Amanda Thompson.

and Writing. In courses such as these, it is possible to teach an Aboriginal languge to classes consisting of both Aboriginal and non-Aboriginal students.

In some cities, Aboriginal leaders have worked to create separate schools for Aboriginal students. Plains Indians Cultural Survival School (PICSS), in Calgary, is a good example. Founded in 1979 as a joint project of the Calgary Board of Education and PICSS, it offers courses from Grades 7 to 12. Here is what PICSS says about its program.

Figure 8.10 Student Whiley Eagle Speaker sits in front of a mural at the Plains Indians Cultural Survival Shool (PICSS).

While following the established Alberta Curriculum, English and Social Studies courses emphasize Aboriginal issues, history, politics, and literature. Cultural courses include Native languages, beading, bustle-making, Native crafts, drumming, singing, and Native traditions. Additional enrichment is provided through sweetgrass ceremonies, traditional feasts and pow-wows, pipe ceremonies, and wilderness survival camps.

The linking of Aboriginal culture, history, and language with academic, social, and community programs in a supportive school setting leads to greater understanding by students of their own identity. It increases their personal, social, vocational, and educational potential. The main objectives of PICSS are to:

- encourage and develop a feeling of worthiness, increased self-esteem, and a stronger Aboriginal identity
- focus on Aboriginal cultures and languages from a historical and contemporary perspective
- explore Aboriginal and non-Native community values and needs and examine the decision making process involved in political, social, economic, and cultural matters
- develop and encourage personal decision-making and life-skills which will expand the individual's capacity to function effectively within the community
- strengthen and improve academic skills
- provide adult students with an opportunity to upgrade their educational credentials leading to greater career choices or post-secondary opportunities

Source: Plains Indians Cultural Survival School. [Online]. Available http://www.cbe.ab.ca/b864/default.htm#school
4 December 2000

The students who attend Leo Ussak School in Rankin Inlet, Nunavut, are mainly Inuit. Situated on the coast of Hudson Bay, at one time the school was quite isolated. But now, with the Internet, the students are plugged in to the world just like students at the biggest school in a large city. The box at the bottom is an extract from a conference held between a Grade 6 class at the school and a similar class in Hawaii.

The Internet makes it possible for both sets of users to learn about each other and the wider world around them. At the same time, both are retaining their cultural heritage.

The result of advances in multicultural and Aboriginal education has been a much more varied educational system.

INTERNET RESOURCES

Do you want to learn more about PICSS and Leo Ussak School? Go to

http://cbe.ab.ca/b864/default.htm#school

http://www.arctic.ca/LUS

At the first site, click on "About PICSS" to find out about the history of the school. Click on "Calgary Board of Education" to find out what advantages it perceives the PICSS project to have.

At the second site, click on "Much sought after NUNAVUT FACTS" to find out interesting details about life in the Arctic.

Q: What do you eat for lunch?

A: Many of the same things as you; pizza, hamburgers, fries, etc. But we also eat fish, caribou, and seal meat. A special treat is called *muktuq* (whale blubber).

Q: What games do you play? Do you play hockey?

A: Indoor soccer is very popular at our school. So is hockey, basketball, volleyball, and curling. Baseball and Inuit games are also very popular.

Q: How cold is it?

A: In mid-winter, -40 to -30 degrees Celsius with strong winds is normal. Our kids often play out at recess in this weather. In mid-July it can be warmer here than in southern Canada!

Q: Have you seen an igloo?

A: Igloos are still used today by hunters when they need to overnight on the land in winter. Igloo-building competitions are often held during holiday celebrations in our community. Our students learn igloo-building skills from their parents and our land skills instructor Jack Kabvitok. Many of our grade six students sleep overnight in igloos during their annual spring camping trip.

Q: What do you do in your classroom?

A: Many of the same things that you do in your classroom, but we also learn things like Inuktitut [the Inuit language].

Q: Have you ever seen a polar bear?

A: Yes! Check this out! At certain times of the year, we see them regularly.

Q: Is it hard sleeping when it is light all of the time?

A: On June 21st, it is light almost all of the time. People sometimes put cardboard, plastic garbage bags or aluminum foil on their windows to help make it dark enough to sleep. It is darkest on December 21st, when the sun rises at 9:45 a.m. and goes down at 2:45 approximately. Sleeping is no problem then!

Source: Leo Ussak School Home Page. [Online]. Available http://www.arctic.ca/LUS/FAQ.html 4 December 2000

POINT AND COUNTERPOINT

Is School Structure More Difficult for Girls or Boys?

The points below are taken from two different articles. One argues that girls face greater challenges at school. The other considers school to be more difficult for boys.

Girls:

- Girls' self-esteem tends to fall after puberty. This causes many girls to experience more emotional turmoil during their high-school years.
- Girls feel pressured to look a certain way to be accepted. For example, an increase in smoking among girls has been linked to the pressure girls feel to lose weight. Some girls report trying to get out of school when their skin breaks out badly.
- Girls tend to value long-lasting relationships among their friends. This may cause them to put their own needs second to keep a particular relationship going. As a result, they may not feel good about themselves in certain ways.
- Signs of depression based on low self-confidence are significant in young women aged fifteen to nineteen.
- Some health experts link low self-esteem to the early onset of sexual activity. Teenage girls in this situation may have to deal with pregnancy.

Source: Morris, Chris. 1999. "Self-esteem Fleeting, Fragile for Canadian Kids." Canadian Press. 28 October 1999. [Online]. Available http://www.canoe.ca/Health9910/28_esteem.html

Boys:

- In Saskatchewan, surveys reveal that high-school girls have higher career ambitions than boys.
- In Ontario, only 38 per cent of Grade 6 boys are at or above the provincial standard (compared to 59 per cent of girls).
- Nationwide, only 33 per cent of thirteen-year-old boys are at an advanced reading level (compared to 55 per cent of girls).
- Nationwide, only 70 per cent of males have graduated by age eighteen (compared to 81 per cent of females).
- Boys make up 65 per cent of those needing special education for learning disabilities, 83 per cent of those needing special classes for emotional or behaviour problems, and 76 per cent of those needing help because of problems at home.
- According to a nationally representative survey of their teachers, 40 per cent of elementary school girls are expected to obtain a university degree compared to 37 percent of boys.

Source: Fine, Sean. 2000. "Are the Schools Failing Boys?" *The Globe and Mail.* 5 September 2000.

1. What is the main argument for why girls have greater difficulty in school than boys?
2. What is the main argument for why boys have greater difficulty in school than girls?
3. Based on your own observations, which group, if either, has the greater difficulty in (*a*) the early grades, (*b*) the middle grades, and (*c*) the senior grades? Be sure to give evidence and reasons for your opinion.
4. Do you think that all-boy and all-girl classes in specific subjects would help to address some of the problems identified? Explain your reasoning.

The 1990s: The Ontario Curriculum

By the late 1990s, change was on its way again. Concerned that a significant number of students found the jump from elementary to secondary school too great, the Ontario government introduced a "destreamed" Grade 9 program in 1993. In Grade 9, there were no Basic, General, or Advanced courses. Students with a variety of abilities were placed in the same classes, similar to the method used in elementary school. Based on their teachers' recommendations in Grade 9, students proceeded to Basic, General, or Advanced courses in Grade 10.

These changes were short-lived. In 1995, a new government was elected to power, and it embarked on another wave of reforms. As government downsizing and budget-cutting took place, attention became focused on educational costs and student performance. With respect to costs, in 1993, Canada was spending 6.9 per cent of its gross domestic product (the total value of all the goods and services it produced) on education. Only Norway and Sweden spent a higher proportion, and the average among eighteen leading industrial countries was 5.8 per cent. With respect to performance, some groups expressed concern that graduation standards were not high enough.

Over $1 billion was removed from the budgets of school boards between 1996 and 1999. Believing that these budget cuts would compromise the quality of education, teachers conducted a province-wide walkout in the fall of 1997, shutting down almost all publicly funded schools for two weeks.

The *Ontario Curriculum* began its phase-in with Grade 9, in September 1999. Grade 13, or the Ontario Academic Course system, was to be abolished in 2002, when students in the new program reached Grade 12. High school would become a four-year program in Ontario, as it was in other provinces. The number of courses required for graduation would remain unchanged at thirty, but compulsory courses were increased from fourteen to eighteen, and optional courses were reduced from sixteen to twelve. In addition, there was a graduation requirement that students complete a minimum of forty hours of volunteer work during high school.

The way teachers evaluate their students became more uniform across schools. In high schools, 70 per cent of the final mark for any course was to come

Figure 8.11 Over 7000 Ontario teachers filled Ottawa's Civic Centre on the first day of their province-wide strike in 1997. The strike was the largest illegal teachers' strike in Canadian history.

INTERNET RESOURCES

The following two organizations approach current educational issues from different perspectives. What different concerns can you find?

Go to Ontario's Education Improvement Commission Web site at

http://eic.edu.gov.on.ca/eicroot/english/home/default.asp .

Visit the Canadian Teachers' Federation Web site at

http://ctf-fce.ca/main_eng.htm

from evaluations throughout the term; 30 per cent was to come from final evaluation. "Learning expectations"—what students are supposed to learn in a course—were made more rigid, and individual school flexibility in tailoring courses for their students was reduced. Grades 11 and 12 courses, previously designated by type (Basic, General, Advanced), became designated by student destination (Workplace, College, University, Open). In Grades 9 and 10, there would be two levels (Applied and Academic), with transfer courses allowing students to move from one to the other.

The new program placed greater emphasis on province-wide testing of students, particularly in reading, writing, and mathematics. Elementary school students began to be tested in Grade 3 and Grade 6. In order to graduate, secondary school students had to pass a literacy test at the beginning of Grade 10. The test focuses on language and communication, particularly reading and writing.

Supporters of the new program claim that it provides a clearer, more consistent picture of student achievement. Students pick the type of courses to get them to their desired destination. Province-wide testing alerts parents and teachers to potential problems, they say, and guarantees the quality of a graduation diploma. Standardized evaluation makes it easier for parents and employers to compare performance among students from different parts of the province.

Opponents of the new program believe that it is too rigid. They believe that it allows little room for local variation based on the needs of students in different communities. They say that the emphasis on testing encourages teachers to "teach to the test." Efforts are directed toward the cramming of facts into students rather than toward creative classroom learning experiences. Finally, opponents point out that the new curriculum moulds students instead of responding to their needs.

The debate over the new curriculum once again revolves around the traditional and progressive philosophies. As the debate continues, more reforms are bound to come along.

Ontario School Enrolment, 1997–1998

Elementary	1 394 000
Secondary	701 000
Total	2 095 000

Different Educational Models

The educational debate that has taken place in Ontario since 1950 has revolved around different perspectives or models of what the effective school is. Looking at the following three models can help you understand your own views on education.

The Traditional School

Supporters of the traditional school believe that the curriculum should be clearly outlined and that all students should be moulded as far as possible to fit it. Curriculum decisions are centralized, so that the educational bureaucracy makes all important decisions regarding what is taught.

Standards of behaviour are developed externally, with little input from people who spend their daily lives in schools—the students and teachers. Codes of conduct and rules are clear, and the expectation is that there will be swift punishment for breaking the rules. Negative reinforcement is often a strong element in the traditional school.

In order to meet the curricular expectations, there are regular class drills. Students are rewarded publicly (for example, by getting gold stars or extra privileges) for meeting the expectations. There is little classroom discussion about what students would like to learn or how they should learn it. There is regular testing to ensure that students are meeting learning expectations, and both quality and quantity of work are emphasized in a competitive atmosphere (Brent, 183, 4–7).

The Behaviourist School

The behaviourist model of education is the result of the research done by Ivan Pavlov (see pages 28–29) and B.F. Skinner. Behaviourists believe that positive reinforcement is much more effective than negative reinforcement in stimulating learning. So in a behaviourist school, the teacher's role is not so much forcing students to achieve externally developed expectations as it is consulting with them on methods of achieving desired goals. Since repeated negative reinforcement is generally ineffective, great emphasis is placed on praising and encouraging students to produce their best work.

Behaviourists follow the stimulus-response model developed by Pavlov and Skinner. They believe that the role of

Figure 8.12 How would a behaviourist explain the importance of consultation between teacher and student?

testing is not so much to measure how well students have met externally developed expectations as it is to measure how much each student has learned from a starting point. Students are given a pretest, provided with teaching and learning opportunities, and tested again. The difference between the student's pre- and post-test scores represents the amount of learning. Students should be encouraged to increase their learning as much as possible and perform to their individual abilities.

The behaviourist school, with its emphasis on the consultative approach to learning, is based on the assumption that students and teachers should work together to determine what should be learned and how it should be learned. The most important measure of student success should be how much the student has learned, not where the student ranks in relation to others (Brent, 1983, 7–11).

The Marxist Free School

Marxist free schools, such as the Islington White Lion Free School in London, England, are entirely collaborative in their approach to learning. This means that teachers and students work together to develop individual learning programs. Each student decides what he or she would like to learn, and the teacher's role becomes one of guiding him or her in the learning process.

In these schools, students are not graded against each other. Marxists believe that competition leads to alienation among those who "fail."

RECAP

1. What was the main philosophy behind each of the following?
   a) the curriculum of the 1950s
   b) the reforms of the 1960s
   c) the development of multicultural education in the 1970s and 1980s
   d) Aboriginal education
   e) the claim that girls have greater difficulty in coping with school structure and culture
   f) the claim that boys have greater difficulty in coping with school structure and culture
   g) the *Ontario Curriculum* of the 1990s
2. How has the focus of multicultural education changed since it was first introduced?
3. What are the main features of the following?
   a) the Traditional School
   b) the Behaviourist School
   c) the Marxist Free School

Section 8.4

The Future of Education

Focus Questions

- What are some of the changes and issues going on in education at present?
- How are such changes likely to improve the delivery of education?
- What problems are there with some of these changes?

Key Concepts

distance learning
charter school
corporatization

Distance Learning

Distance Learning (DL) allows students to take a course without being physically present in the school, college, or university offering it. It is not a new idea. London University in England first offered external programs for overseas students in 1858. Students could receive study material by mail, complete and return assignments, and take examinations locally. They were supervised by a responsible person who returned student work to London for marking. In this way, students could obtain degrees without leaving their home area.

Total students served: 24 000

	%		%
Females:	59	Males:	41
Under 15:	1	Eastern:	11
16–20:	30	Central:	29
21–30:	41	Toronto:	37
31–40:	17	Western:	20
41–64:	10.5	North:	11
65+:	0.5	Outside Ontario:	2

Source: Independent Learning Centre. [Online]. Available http://ilc.edu.gov.on.ca/01/02.htm 4 December 2000

Figure 8.13 Student profile of Ontario's ILC, 1999–2000.

Ontario opened its Independent Learning Centre (ILC) in 1926. In its early years, elementary school-age children in remote areas would complete correspondence courses. These courses would prepare them for a residential secondary school. In the 1950s, a complete secondary school program became available, resulting in increased adult enrolment. Adults are now the principal student group at the ILC.

Although DL is not a new idea, technological developments have changed the way in which it can operate. Electronic mail (e-mail) delivery makes instant communication between students and school possible. Much of the delay in mailing assignments and tests from one to the other has been eliminated.

The Alberta Distance Learning Centre (ADLC), similar to Ontario's ILC, was founded in 1925. Since 1995, students have had the option of submitting and receiving information electronically. The ADLC is one of the most developed electronic DL schools in Canada, offering a complete Online School. Here is how it describes itself:

What Is an Online School?

Under Alberta legislation, an online school is considered to be a school like any other school. It receives the same funding and has the same responsibilities. Although their students study at home, online schools do not come under the umbrella of "home education programs."

If an online school is not technically "home education," what is it? It is a "school" in cyberspace. The students and teachers are not physically present in the same space; instead, they communicate by such means as email, Internet conferences, telephone, and fax machine. 2000-2001 is our fifth year of offering online schooling, and it is an exciting field. Things are constantly changing. What is impossible one year becomes possible the next, and commonplace the year after that!

Our students work from a combination of online and ADLC prepared materials, and generally complete their answers and submit them electronically. Assignments completed online are corrected and are then available for student review.

Backup copies of course assignments should be kept until you receive your final grade in that course.

A fulltime student should study a minimum of 30 hours per week and send in assignments daily. In most cases, about half that time will be spent on the computer. Alberta Learning mandates two face-to-face meetings in the school year.

Parents'/Guardians' Responsibilities

- See that your child submits assignments daily and keeps up to date. (**This will be your primary responsibility as an online school parent/guardian.**)
- See that your child spends a minimum of 30 hours per week doing schoolwork. This will include reading, writing practice exercises, doing assignments on the computer, and may include viewing videos provided with a course, and listening to required audio cassettes.
- See that your child gets help if he or she runs into any roadblocks while doing the course. If the teacher is unable to help, contact the Vista-Virtual school coordinator.
- Provide supervision of your child's use of Netscape or Internet Explorer to help them avoid offensive material on the Internet…

Truancy Policy

According to the Alberta School Act, all students under 16 years of age are legally required to attend school. In the case of an online school student, this means submitting assignments on a regular basis.

Students Under 16 Years of Age:

- Expectations are outlined in the Registration Guide.
- The teacher in consultation with the student and/or parents will determine a schedule for submission of assignments.
- ADLC will attempt to contact students when assignments are not received on a regular basis.
- Parents will be informed of the lack of progress.
- If in the opinion of the school the quantity and quality of assignments submitted by the student do not meet the minimum standards, the student will be referred to the Attendance Review Board of Alberta Learning.

Source: Alberta Distance Learning Centre. [Online]. Available http://www.adlc.ab.ca 4 December 2000

INTERNET RESOURCES

Electronic universities are becoming more common. For more information, go to

http://distancelearn.about.com/education/distancelearn/library/blpages/blnews01170.htm

Click on "Athabasca University" to find out how Alberta's electronic DL university works. Click on "LearnSoft" to find out about Unexus, a private electronic university in Ottawa, offering degrees in business.

To find out what courses are offered electronically at all of Ontario's universities, go to

http://node.on.ca

Use "search the courses database" to find out what is available.

As electronic communication technology becomes even cheaper and more reliable, DL may become more popular. Students and families may be drawn to designing their own study schedules without being limited by a fixed school day. For governments, there is the attraction that if more students learn at home, fewer expensive schools are needed. But critics wonder who will take over the schools' important socialization role if increasing numbers of students "attend" cyberschools.

Figure 8.14 What are the advantages of learning online?

Home-Schooling

Another development in the structure of education is the growth of home-schooling. In this model, parents teach their own children at home, or sometimes families co-operate to run inter-family schools. It is perfectly legal in all provinces and territories not to send your children to school and to home-school them instead. In Ontario, for example, there are no special forms to fill in, and you need ask no one's permission. Furthermore, there is no obligation to allow educational officials into your home to test your children or inspect your home school.

Some home-schooling families consider the attitudes in public education to be overly permissive. Some believe that they can tailor their children's education to their own value system and protect them from values that they consider harmful. Other families believe that when families share home-schooling, it enriches community life. A home-schooling parent from Nova Scotia wrote:

> The important issues in regards to home schooling are not the numbers, the statistics, the grades, the finances, the qualifications. The important issues are character, morals, motivation, self-reliance, self-esteem, service, and wisdom...The family is the foundation of our society. Parents are responsible to...build such attributes into their children and to demonstrate them to the community. Institutions [like schools] cannot and do not take the place of the family (Smith, 1996).

With such an emphasis on values, home-school associations urge families to consider carefully whether they have the necessary skills and attitudes to do the job.

> No one should undertake to home school without coming to terms with this fundamental truth: It is the fabric of your own life you are deciding about, not just your child's education. When I talk about home schooling I am talking about less affluence in the name of more education (Smith, 1996).

The number of students being home-schooled is hard to establish accurately, since home schools usually do not need to be registered. The Canadian Home School Association believes that the number is around 30 000, or about 0.02 per cent of all school-age children in Canada. Analysts believe that home-schooling is unlikely to become a major part of the educational structure in the foreseeable future. It does, however, represent an opportunity for interested families.

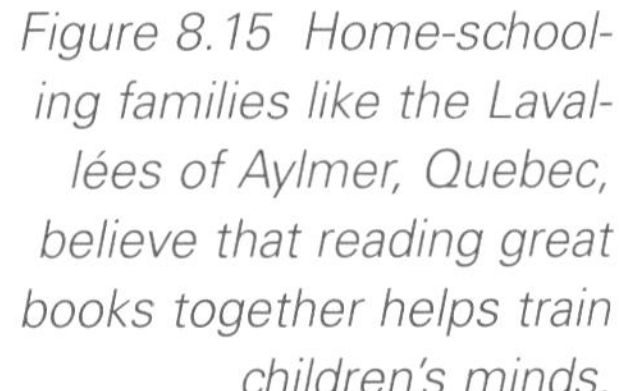

Figure 8.15 Home-schooling families like the Lavallées of Aylmer, Quebec, believe that reading great books together helps train children's minds.

 Charter Schools

Charter schools are independent schools supported by public funds. They are normally formed when the parents at an existing public school vote to take the school out of the control of the local school board. The parents then hire a management team to run the school independently. Students normally attend the school for free, as the school is paid for by the funds the government would have allotted for each student were she or he at a public school. Families receive a voucher that is submitted to the government, which then issues funds to the school for each student.

Each school has its own charter (something like a constitution) that outlines the purpose and philosophy of the school. The charter also outlines the way in which the school will be accountable to the parents for its performance. Control of the school is held not by a school board, but by the management team and students' parents.

Great Britain changed its education law in 1988 to permit chartering, leading to the establishment of 1166 schools by 1996. New Zealand made all of its existing 2600 schools available for chartering in 1989. In Canada, only Alberta currently permits charter schools, but has restricted them to a total number of fifteen. It also prohibits charter schools from being based on a religion. Some of the present schools use a traditional "back-to-basics" approach. Others use student-centred, individualized, progressive methods. Still others are designed as alternative schools for "at risk" students in danger of dropping out.

Supporters claim that charter schools are less bureaucratic than public schools and more answerable to parents. Opponents believe that the bureaucracy of the public school model provides necessary checks and balances. In that model, the school board is made up of trustees elected by all voters in the community. The trustees can ensure that all school board employees—superintendents, principals, teachers, and support staff—are working effectively. Opponents point out that one of Alberta's first charter schools was forced to close because of suggested financial irregularities.

The debate continues. In the following "Point and Counterpoint," arguments for and against charter schools are presented.

Figure 8.16 At Alberta's Boyle Street charter school, alternative courses such as cosmetology (makeup and hairstyling) are offered.

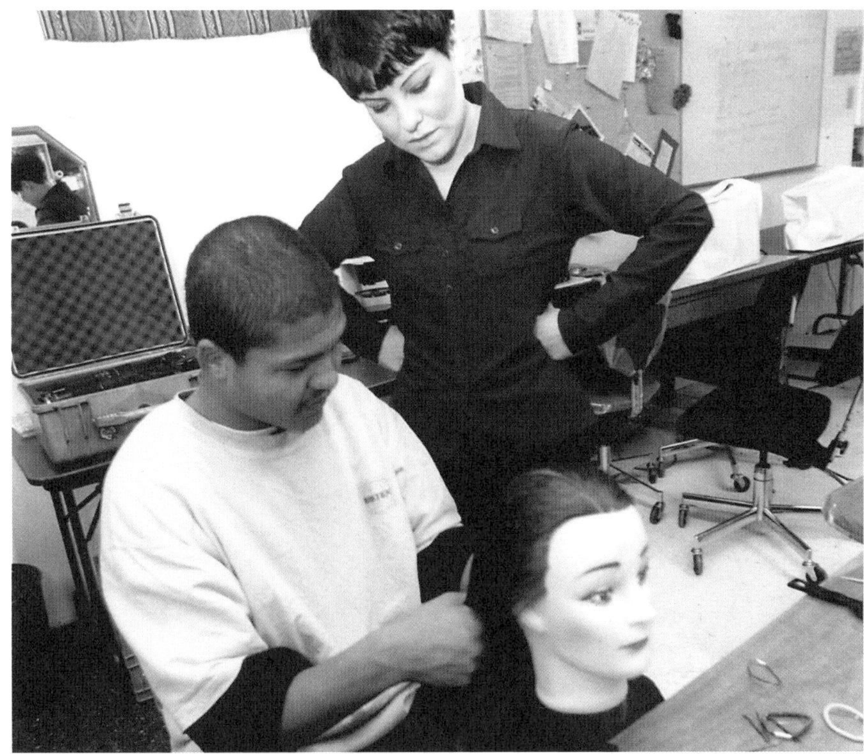

POINT AND COUNTERPOINT

What Are the "Pros" and "Cons" of Charter Schools?

The following points are taken from two articles with different viewpoints on charter schools. One sees charter schools as improved public schools. The other views them as schools for the elite that threaten the principles of public education.

Arguments in Defence of Charter Schools:

- School-site management of funds reduces expenditures.
- Layers of expensive and meddlesome bureaucracy are eliminated. For example, there is no need for collective bargaining between teachers' unions and school boards. A school's charter authorizes the school to conduct its business independently of both teachers' unions and school boards.
- Charter schools can respond more effectively and accountably to the concerns of parents and taxpayers. If a school does not achieve the goals specified in its charter, it will be forced out of business.
- Charters must be reviewed every three to five years. This term limit allows parents and teachers to evaluate and improve the charter on a regular basis. Schools can opt to make their standards higher than those of other schools in the local district.
- Charter schools use pooled public funds and spend the same per pupil as regular public schools.
- Charter schools may not discriminate on the basis of race, religion, or ability.

Source: Freedman, Joe. 1997. *Charter Schools in Atlantic Canada.* Atlantic Institute for Market Studies. [Online]. Available http://www.aims.ca/Publications/charterschool/charterpg1.html#top March 1997
Reprinted by permission of Atlantic Institute for Market Studies, a public policy think tank based in Halifax, N.S.

Arguments Against Charter Schools:

- A school's charter can result in the exclusion of certain students and parents. Such exclusion goes against the objectives of modern public education.
- The traditional curriculum most popular among charter school supporters has a hidden agenda that can be linked to racism, homophobia, and sexism.
- The authoritarian classroom model many charter schools adopt does not inspire higher levels of thinking and learning among students.
- By forsaking school boards and teachers' unions, charter schools resist and reverse much of the educational and social progress made since the 1970s.
- In a study conducted by the New Zealand Council for Educational Research, teacher workload at charter schools had risen while teacher morale had fallen.
- The study also found inequities between schools in high- and low-income areas. Many schools had raised "voluntary" school fees and relied on fundraising that widened the gap between rich and poor schools.

Source: Robertson, Heather-Jane. 1997. "Charter Schools Take Us Backward, Not Forward." *Education Monitor.* Ottawa. The Canadian Centre for Policy Alternatives. Summer 1997.

1 What are the major arguments in favour of charter schools? What are the arguments against them?
2 To whom do you think the education system has its greatest responsibility—students as individuals, or all students as a group? Explain.
3 Which structure for education—school boards running several schools, or individually chartered schools—do you think serves students best? Explain your answer.

Corporatization

One of the major issues schools today must deal with is funding. In the era of downsizing and budget restraints, many schools have found themselves with insufficient money. They cannot pay for all the computers, library resources, and extra-curricular programs they would like. Anxious to raise revenues, many school districts have signed agreements with soft drink manufacturers. The school allows the company to be the exclusive supplier to the schools in return for a fee. Others allow advertising in their gyms and cafeterias. This trend, in which school districts get money from commercial businesses in return for product exposure, is called **corporatization.**

Some of the most intense arguments about this topic relate to Youth News Network (YNN). YNN belongs to Athena Education Partners, a Canadian company based in Montreal. It produces daily twelve-and-a-half-minute news broadcasts, containing two-and-a-half minutes of advertising, tailored for people aged thirteen to nineteen. Athena is trying to reach agreements with Canadian high schools about the use of YNN. The schools sign a contract that makes YNN available to classrooms (teachers decide whether or not they wish to show YNN to students). In return, participating

Figure 8.17 How might schools benefit or suffer as a result of signing a contract with Athena Education Partners?

schools are given free of charge the following items:

- a satellite dish and VCR to receive and play the daily broadcasts
- one 27-inch monitor for about every twenty-one students in the school
- one camcorder
- a state-of-the-art computer lab

A large school could receive equipment and infrastructure valued at up to $200 000. When the contract is complete, the school gets to keep all the video equipment. In an era of tight budgets, there is tremendous appeal in such arrangements.

Discussion over YNN has revolved around the commercial nature of the project. Should schools offer their students as viewers of commercial broadcasts in return for electronic equipment?

Advantages of YNN

In the 1999–2000 school year, the Peel District School Board undertook a pilot project to decide on the future use of YNN. One of the participating schools was Meadowvale Secondary in Mississauga, Ontario. In a letter to parents, Laurie Pedwell, the school's principal, outlined the benefits of watching the daily programs (Pedwell, 1999):

- Students can become more aware of news stories and have the opportunity to discuss and understand issues that affect all Canadians.
- Teachers can incorporate news stories into their regular curriculum in a way that makes them come alive and be relevant, thus enhancing learning for students.
- Students can become more interested in the news and look for other sources—newspapers, television, and radio—to add to their knowledge.
- Students can develop a lifelong interest in the news and make a habit of staying informed.

YNN itself points out several features of its programs that would benefit students. One is that students have an opportunity to produce regular segments for news programs. In doing so, they can learn television production and present their work to a national audience of peers. Both student and regular news segments are produced by qualified and award-winning professionals experienced in both print and broadcast jounalism.

YNN stresses that care has been taken to ensure that YNN program content, as well as the commercials, are suitable for high-school students. An independent self-governing body called the Educational Advisory Council (EAC), consisting of educators, parents, and students, evaluates the commercials and sets standards for news content. YNN claims that these standards exceed those of the Canadian Broadcasting Code. YNN also claims that the ads, which are generally the same ones shown on TV, cannot be proven to have a negative impact on students (YNN, 2000).

Disadvantages of YNN

It is the last point above that is in contention by opponents of YNN. Advertisers in a school setting have a more captive audience than they do in any other environment. Many teachers strongly disapprove of forcing this commercial influence on students in a classroom. The negative effects cannot be measured physically, but many believe them to include increased materialism. The idea behind all product advertising—that people need more things—is reinforced whenever a commercial is viewed. To allow the reinforcement of this idea at school rankles certain teachers and parents alike.

A second obvious disadvantage of YNN is that is uses up valuable instructional time. Some teachers object to trading in time for other kinds of learning in order to view the YNN programs.

Another disadvantage is less obvious, but potentially more disturbing. Once schools sign agreements with YNN, they are giving a certain amount of control to the corporation. How will the corporation and the school interpret the rights of the corporation in situations of conflict? Will criticism of YNN and its editorial slant be allowed? According to the Adbusters organization, Meadowvale Secondary disqualified a student band from a school competition when a band member appeared on stage with a T-shirt criticizing YNN with the words "YNN Stinks" (Brand, 2000).

A fourth potential disadvantage is that government funding may diminish if schools are funded by corporate sponsors. The Canadian Teachers' Federation (CTF) sees corporate sponsorship as a dangerous temptation that will encourage governments to shirk their responsibilities with regard to funding.

In December 1999 and January 2000, an Environics Focus Canada poll on advertising in schools was conducted on behalf of the CTF. Of the over 2000 Canadians interviewed, about 70 per cent were opposed to advertising of any kind in the classroom. Ninety per cent opposed advertising in schools if obligating students to watch advertisements is tied to the promise of money and equipment (Canadian Teachers' Federation, 2000). More information on the results of this survey can be found in the "Skill Development" section below.

Skill Development: Presenting Survey Results

Survey results are presented in a format that shows the overall patterns in the survey answers. The Canadian Teachers' Federatiion (CTF) chose two formats to make their survey results meaningful to their audience. Both formats were visual, or graphic, since this type of presentation can show the patterns in the results most strikingly. In this section, you will learn about these two formats—bar graphs and circle graphs—and a third—scatter graphs.

The Advertising Survey

The following two questions were asked in the survey. Only people who chose (*1b*) were asked Question 2.

1. There has been some debate about the issue of allowing companies to advertise in public schools in Canada. Which one of these two statements most closely represents your point of view?

a) Advertising has no place in schools, since school is a place where children should learn without having products and services provided.
b) Advertising in schools is perfectly acceptable if it allows the school to receive cash, services, or equipment in exchange.

2. Would you agree or disagree with allowing advertising in schools if it meant requiring students to watch video or computerized commercial advertising on TV or computers as part of their instructional day?

Figure 8.18 This table shows the results of the CTF survey.

a) Responses (in %) to Question 1

Opinion	Canada	Atlantic	Que.	Ont.	Man.	Sask.	Alta.	BC
Advertising has no place in schools	70	75	61	75	71	79	74	67
Advertising in schools is perfectly acceptable	29	23	38	24	28	20	25	32
Don't know	1	2	1	2	1	1	1	1
Total	100	100	100	100	100	100	100	100

b) Responses (in %) to Question 2
[Sub-sample: Respondents who think advertising in schools is perfectly acceptable]

Opinion	Canada	Atlantic	Que.	Ont.	Man.	Sask.	Alta.	BC
Disagree	71	62	80	64	58	66	63	78
Agree	28	38	19	35	42	34	35	22
Don't know	1	-	*	1	-	-	2	-
Total	100	100	100	100	100	100	100	100

- Nil; *Less than 1%
Note: Totals may not equal 100% due to rounding.
Source: Environics Research Group. 1999. *Canadians Say No to Advertising in Schools.* Canadian Teachers' Federation.

Format 1: Bar Graph

The two bar graphs in Figure 8.19 are a simple representation of the results from Figure 8.18.

The data in both Table *b* (Figure 8.18) and Graph *b* (Figure 8.19) are hard to interpret. This is because they represent a sub-sample of respondents. For example, in Ontario, only 24 per cent of respondents (see Table *a*) are represented in Table *b*. Thus, the 64 per cent of people in the "Disagree" row in Table *b* represent 64 per cent of 24 per cent—that is, about 15 per cent of the *total sample*. Added to the 75 per cent of Ontarians totally opposed to advertising (see Graph *a*), the result is 90 per cent opposed to advertising, at least under certain conditions.

The CTF decided it would be more meaningful to do these calculations for each province. That is, the percentage of the *total sample* is worked out for each "Disagree" percentage of the sub-sample. Then this number is added to the percentages of those totally opposed to advertising (Question 1). This combination of two kinds of opponents to advertising is shown in the taller bars in Figure 8.20. Note that the "Immediate Opposition" results in Figure 8.20 have been ranked left to right from highest to lowest.

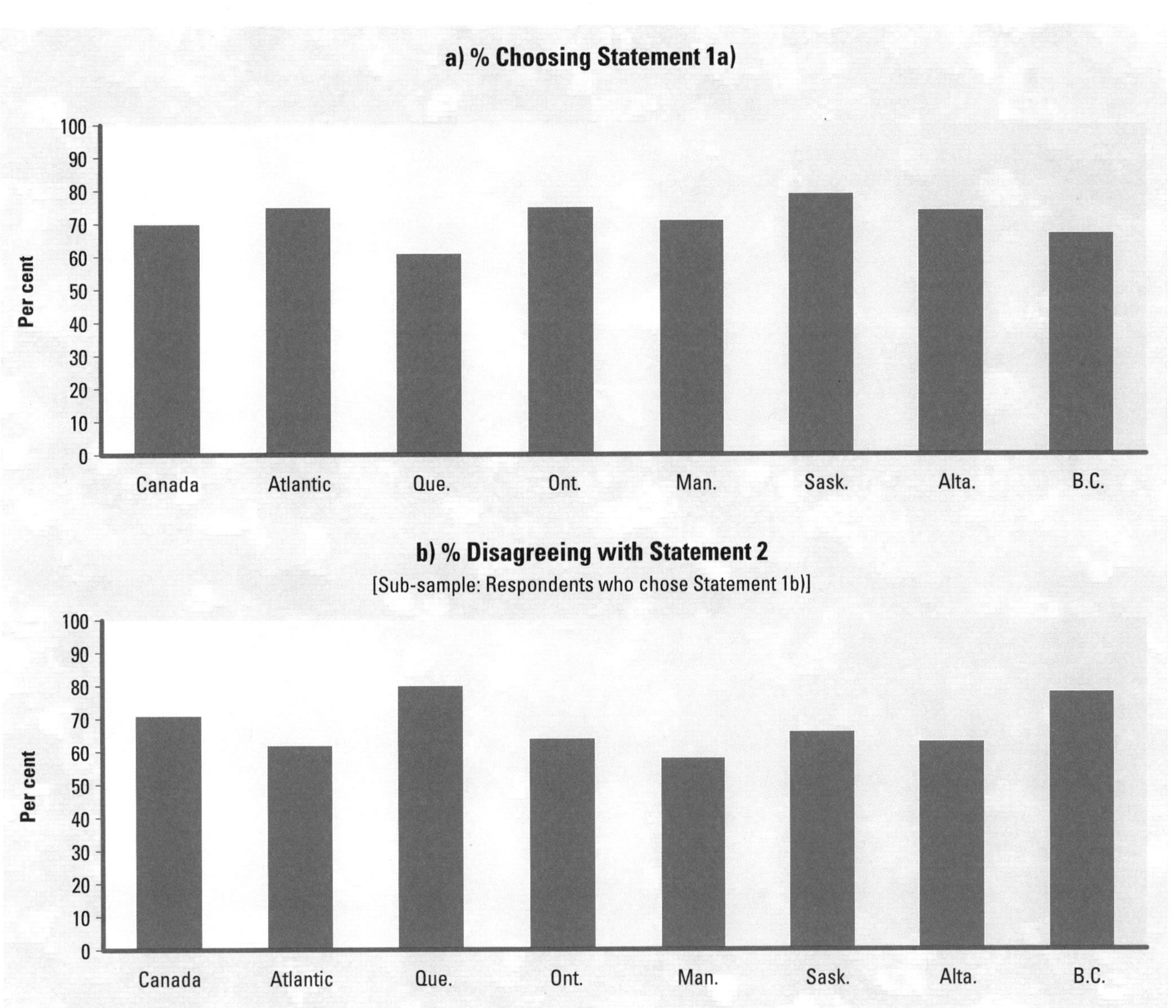

Figure 8.19 Bar graph representation of results

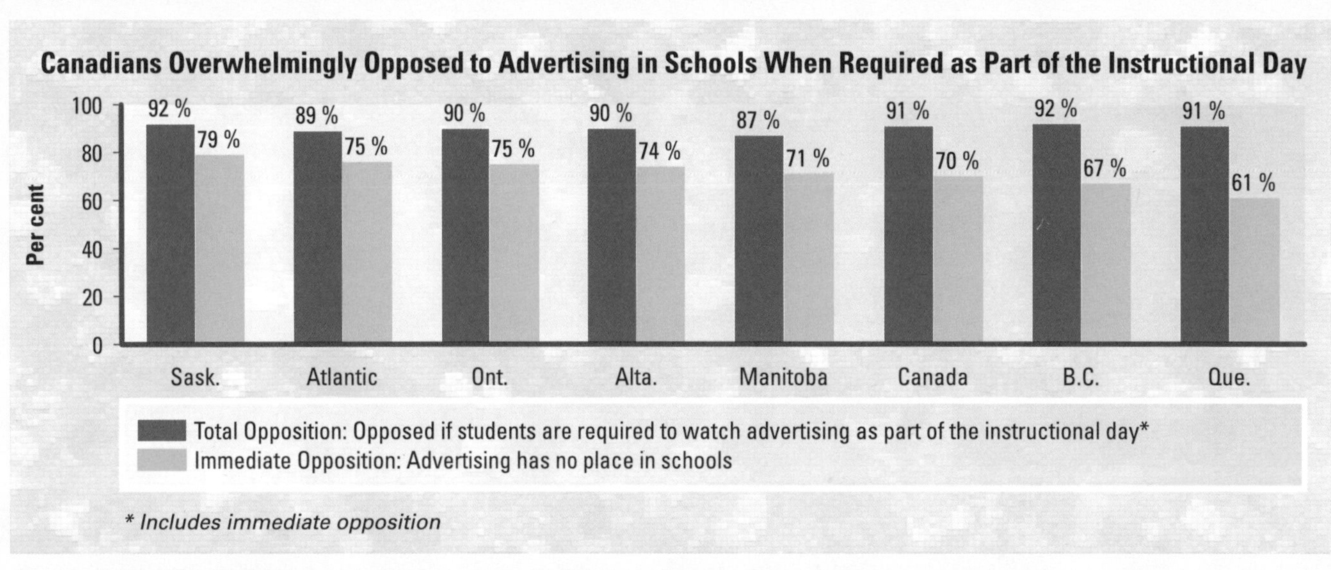

Figure 8.20 Why is this bar graph more meaningful than the two bar graphs in Figure 8.19?

Format 2: Circle Graph

Circle graphs, like bar graphs, are good at displaying absolute information. This means that they effectively represent simple, measurable numbers (for example, number of respondents in a category, percentage of respondents in a category). Some people prefer the circle graph format because it gives a better idea of how large a proportion of the whole each percentage represents. For example, we have determined that in Ontario 75 per cent say advertising has no place in schools; 15 per cent say advertising is not acceptable if students *must* watch commercial advertising in school; most of the remaining 10 per cent truly support advertising in schools (with a small remainder answering that they don't know). A circle graph visually shows how large a proportion of the total each of these opinions represents—it gives an immediate graphic sense of how heavy the majority opinion is.

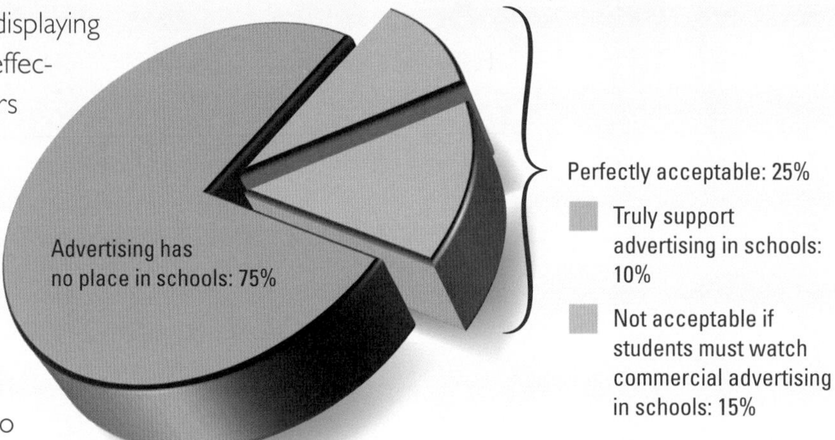

Figure 8.21 The Ontario results in a circle graph format

The disadvantage of this format, in this case, is that a separate circle graph needs to be drawn for each column in Tables *a* and *b*.

Format 3: Scatter Graph

Scatter graphs show how two sets of results relate to each other. They are used when the hypothesis the survey was designed to test states how one variable correlates with a second variable. For example, look back at the sample hypothesis on page 207. The hypothesis to be tested is that "hours worked" correlates negatively with "academic performance (average percentage)." (In a negative correlation, an increase in one variable coincides with a decrease in the other variable. In a positive correlation, an increase in one variable coincides with an increase in the other variable.) In Figure 8.22, the results for the table on page 207 are plotted. The *x*-axis represents the hours worked, and the *y*-axis represents the average percentage. A single dot is plotted on the graph for each student, showing both variables.

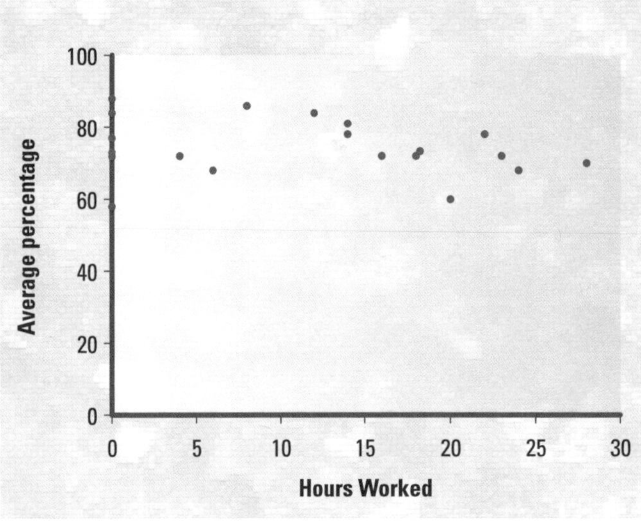

Figure 8.22 Scatter graph results for the table on page 207.

Follow-Up

1. Look at the tables you constructed for Question 1, Step 1, on page 208. For each table, create a bar graph. What are the advantages of using a bar graph for this type of information?

2. Using the information in Tables *a* and *b*, create three circle graphs to show the results for Quebec, Manitoba, and BC. Use Figure 8.22 as a model.

3. Explain why a scatter graph would not be an effective format to present the CTF survey results.

4. Formulate a hypothesis for which survey results would be most effectively presented using a scatter graph.

RECAP

1. What arguments are used in favour of each of the following educational changes?
   a) distance learning
   b) home-schooling
   c) charter schools
   d) corporatization
2. What problems or difficulties can you see with each change?
3. Will education be better or worse if changes such as these become widespread?

Activities

Show your knowledge

1. Create a New Vocabulary glossary of the terms and phrases you learned in this chapter.
   a) Record the definition of each term.
   b) Use these terms to create four questions to ask a classmate. Make each question more difficult than the last. Follow the model used for these activities ("Show your knowledge," "Practise your thinking skills," "Communicate your ideas," "Apply your knowledge").
2. In what ways do we live in a culture of violence?
3. What are the manifest functions of education?
4. What are the main differences between those people who believe in progressive education and those who believe in traditional education?
5. What are the main goals of multicultural education? In what ways has multicultural education changed over the years?
6. What are the main features of the *Ontario Curriculum*, introduced in 1999?
7. Which countries have established charter schools? Where in Canada are they permitted? How are they different from other publicly funded schools?
8. What are some examples of corporatization in our schools?

Practise your thinking skills

9. Debate whether or not teachers in your school should have to follow a dress code. Write down at least three arguments for each side of the debate.
10. Would you consider yourself to be a bully? Regardless of your answer, record at least two situations where you were mean to another person, or where you stood by and allowed others to be mean.
11. Why do you think bullies frequently volunteer to become peer mediators?
12. Make an organizer summarizing the major developments in education through each of the following periods. Label each development as traditional (T) or progressive (P).
    a) the 1950s
    b) the 1960s

Activities

c) the 1970s and '80s
d) the 1990s

13. Which developments—traditional or progressive—do you think have benefited students more? Give reasons for your answer.
14. Debate whether or not your school should become a charter school. Which side of the argument do you take? What are the major points you would present to support your side?
15. What do you think are the strongest advantages of the YNN program? What do you think are the most disturbing disadvantages? What is your position? Explain.

Communicate your ideas

16. Write a letter to the Ministry of Education discussing some of the reasons that students drop out. In your letter, outline a plan of action you would like the Ministry to take to address the dropout issue.
17. Create a diary entry where you describe a really bad day at school when you were picked on by others. Describe how you felt, why you didn't ask someone for help, and the impact the incident will have on your future behaviour.
18. Reflect on ways in which schools promote competition. Write a short opinion piece where you argue that this value needs to be abandoned in favour of a school system based on co-operation.
19. This section has focused mainly on Ontario.
    a) Research educational changes that have taken place in another province or territory. Report your findings to the class.
    b) Compare the changes in Ontario to those in the region you researched. Which changes have led to a better educational system? Explain.
20. Put yourself in the place of a parent with a child about to enter high school. In which decade between 1950 and 2000 do you think your child would have the best educational experience? Explain.
21. Imagine that your charter school has been approved. You have been asked to draw up a code of conduct for submission to the parents' council.
    a) Work with a partner to design a code covering students and teachers. Include a rationale outlining the purposes of your code

Activities

and the sanctions that the school will apply to those who violate the code.

b) Compare your code with those of other students. What similarities and differences do you note?

c) How effective do you think such codes would be? Explain.

22. Research other corporatization and sponsorship programs between businesses and schools, particularly any that you can find in your own school district. Report to the class about whether or not you think these programs will result in long-term benefits for your school and its students.

Apply your knowledge

23. Learn more about heritage language programs offered in your community. How many language programs are offered? For what ages? What are the benefits of these programs?
24. Imagine that you are going to create your own private high school. (You might want to look at the Web site of the Canadian Association of Independent Schools for some ideas. Go to http://www.cais.ca)
    a) Make a list of personal and educational values that your school believes in.
    b) Identify the type of student your school is designed to serve.
    c) Describe the way your school will operate, and how this will help to serve your target group of students. (For example: What type of behaviour do you expect? How will decisions be made? How will students learn? What qualities will you look for in the teachers you hire? What will you do when students misbehave?)
    d) Is your school progressive or traditional? Explain.
25. Imagine you are on a committee to draw up rules governing corporatization and sponsorship programs between your school and business interests. What rules would you put in place? Explain why you think these rules are needed.

Unit 4

Social Organization

Canadian society is held together by the bonds people form with each other to meet their needs. The bonds they form create many different types of groups—marriages, families, circles of friends, clubs, sports teams, gangs, cults, business companies, political parties, social movements, and more. How do these groups manage to coexist in society? What causes conflict between them? What are the consequences of conflict?

This unit will help you understand the characteristics and influence of groups. It will also help you develop a perspective on conflict and discrimination in society.

U N I T S T U

Unit Contents

Overall Expectations

In this unit, you will

- demonstrate an understanding of the characteristics of groups in Canadian society as identified by anthropology, psychology, and sociology
- analyze the psychological impact of group cohesion and group conflict on individuals, groups, and communities
- describe the characteristics of bureaucratic organizations

Topics by Discipline

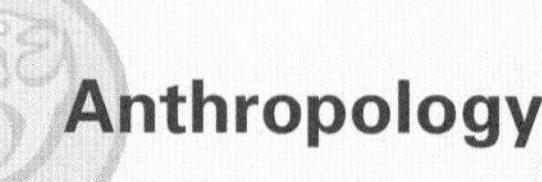

Anthropology

Chapter 9

- Dyads and larger groups in different cultures
- An anthropological perspective on why a teenager joins a sports team
- An anthropological perspective on bureaucra
- Parallels between bureaucracies and stratified cultures
- The effect of primary kinship groups on individual behaviour
- The evolution of groups and communities

Chapter 10

- An anthropological analysis of aggression and violence
- The exclusion of Aboriginal cultures
- The disenfranchisement of Aboriginal wome

Psychology

Chapter 9

- A psychological perspective on why a teenag joins a sports team
- A psychological perspective on burcaucracy
- Reasons why people join groups
- A psychological perspective on the effect of group membership on individual behaviour
- The Milgram conformity experiment

Chapter 10

- The causes and outcomes of conflict
- A psychological analysis of aggression and

violence: modelling theory and frustration-aggression theory
A psychological analysis of prejudice and discrimination: authoritarian personality
Accounting for altruism and heroism
Gender and altruism/heroism
Making Canadian society more cohesive

Sociology

apter 9

Dyads and larger groups in Canadian society
A sociological perspective on why a teenager joins a sports team
Formal organizations
A sociological perspective on bureaucracy
The functions performed by Canadian groups and organizations
A sociological perspective on the effect of group membership on individual behaviour
The Stockholm and Battered Spouse Syndromes
The evolution of groups and communities

apter 10

The causes and outcomes of conflict
A sociological analysis of aggression and violence: the Genovese syndrome, dehumanization, and competitive sports
A sociological analysis of prejudice and discrimination: functionalism, conflict theory, and symbolic interactionism
The exclusion of Aboriginal cultures in Canadian society
Public opinions on Aboriginal rights
Accounting for altruism and heroism
Making Canadian society more cohesive

Skill Guide

One of the methods social scientists use to understand group behaviour is **field observation**.

In this unit you can develop the skills needed to do a field observation. These skills are

- Designing a Field Observation (pages 315 to 317)
- Interpreting and Reporting Field Observation Results (pages 353 to 356)

Research and Inquiry Skills Learning Expectations

The skill development in this unit will enable you to

- describe the steps involved in social science research and inquiry, including developing and testing a hypothesis
- demonstrate an understanding of various research methodologies for conducting primary research (for example, observation)
- demonstrate an understanding of the ethical guidelines of social science research
- evaluate the relevance and validity of information gathered through research
- demonstrate an ability to organize, interpret, and analyze information gathered from a variety of sources
- record information and key ideas from your research
- effectively communicate the results of your inquiries

Chapter 9

Groups and Organizations

Overview of Chapter

Learning Expectations

By the end of this chapter, you will be able to

- identify and compare different social science perspectives on groups
- categorize various types of groups in Canadian society
- demonstrate an understanding of reasons and ways people form groups
- describe different types of groups that form to serve collective needs
- explain, from a social science perspective, how membership in different groups influences individuals, the family, and the community
- identify examples of bureaucratic organizations
- compare bureaucratic and non-bureaucratic organizations from a social science perspective

Open for Debate

France Adopts Tough Anti-Sect Law

The French National Assembly adopted Europe's toughest anti-sect legislation [on 22 June 2000], creating a controversial new crime of "mental manipulation" punishable by a maximum fine of $75 000 and five years' imprisonment.

The new law allows judges to order the dissolution of any sect whose members are convicted of a criminal offence. It also bans sects from advertising and prohibits them from opening missions or touting for new members near schools, hospitals, or retirement homes.

But the law's key weapon is the new crime of "mental manipulation," defined as "exercising, within a group whose activities are aimed at creating or exploiting psychological dependence, heavy and repeated pressure on a person, or using techniques likely to alter his judgement, so as to induce him to behave in a way prejudicial to his interests."

A Justice Ministry spokeswoman said the legal definition had been prepared carefully to ensure that it could not be applied to legitimate churches.

But some Catholic leaders have expressed reservations about the law, saying that it may lead to "over-zealousness and judicial excess" as well as discrimination against genuine religions.

"This is a steep and slippery slope for democracy," said Danièle Gounord, a spokeswoman for Scientology, which is not recognized as a religion in France. "In Western Europe, the only regime so far to pass a law on mental manipulation was the fascist government of Mussolini in an attempt to get rid of the communists."

Abridged from: Henley, Jon. 2000. "France Adopts Tough Anti-Sect Law." *The Guardian*. 22 June 2000.

Think About It

1. Do you think using extreme pressure to make a person dependent on a group should be made a crime? Explain.
2. The proposed law bans sects from advertising and recruiting new members near schools or retirement homes. What is your viewpoint on this part of the law?
3. Do you think the proposed law is a challenge to religious freedom? Is this good or bad? Explain.

Section 9.1

Why Join a Group?

Focus Questions

- According to anthropologists, why might people join groups?
- According to psychologists, why might people join groups?
- According to sociologists, why might people join groups?

Small and Large Groups

One of the earliest lessons that children must learn is how to get along with others. They must learn to play co-operatively both one-on-one and in larger groups.

Social scientists call a two-member social group a **dyad**. We participate in dyads when we have lunch with a close friend, go to the movies with a significant other, or plan for the future with a spouse. A dyad can be difficult to maintain over a lifetime, because both members must be committed to preserve and actively sustain it. This is why society tries to reinforce the marital dyad with legal, economic, and religious ties.

We become members of larger groups for reasons different from those that cause us to form dyads. Larger groups can accomplish far-reaching goals. For example, if a community wants constant protection from fire, it will create a volunteer fire department. The department must be a larger group because not every member will be available every time there is a fire. The task of putting out fires in itself requires a number of people. One of the advantages of larger groups is their stability. As members leave, they can be replaced by others, enabling the group to exist forever. Cultures that allow people to take more than one spouse benefit from this feature of larger groups. Theoretically, households in these cultures are stable, but the ties among the spouses may be weaker than they are in dyads.

Different social science disciplines have different perspectives on why we join groups. In the following section, we describe a hypothetical situation that we can then analyze from different social scientific points of view.

Joining a Group: An Example

Elaine Spira is a Grade 11 student in an Ottawa high school. She is an excellent student and has some good friends. Her mother is disabled, and she has a brother who is in Grade 3. Her father works long hours, and the family has come to rely on her to look after her brother and do a number of household chores on a regular basis. Elaine felt that she needed to do some sort of extracurricular activity after school because she was having problems with academic and family stress. Her

Key Concepts

dyad
primary group
secondary group
norm
culture
material culture

mother's brother has just moved back to the area and is living with the family. He has offered to take over some of Elaine's responsibilities in exchange for free rent.

Elaine is not at all artistic, but has always been strong and well-coordinated. She decided to try out for the Junior Girls' soccer team, as she liked the sport. She just made the team and, although she is not a starter, she has had regular playing time. Her skills have improved as the season has progressed. Elaine's stress problems have been reduced with the regular exercise she is getting. She is considering trying out for one of the indoor teams (volleyball or basketball) next year.

The Sociologist's Explanation

In the sociologist's view, Elaine needed to join a group that was very different from her family. Her family is a **primary group**. In such a group, the members have close personal relationships with one another. They display a sincere emotional concern for the welfare of all the members. Although there are great benefits in belonging to a primary group, it is important for a person to learn to relate to others in a more structured way.

In a **secondary group**, such as the soccer team, members relate less personally and more formally with each other. A variety of official roles are taken on by group members, such as "coach" and "team captain." The group's structure and rules enable the group to meet specific goals, such as winning games.

People join secondary groups partly because they enjoy or approve of the group's rules and **norms** (accepted standards of behaviour). For example, Elaine enjoys the way each team member has a role to play in helping the team perform on the field. She also likes the discipline that group membership imposes on everyone. Although she hates getting up early, she understands the demands on gym time and willingly makes one 7:00 a.m. practice a week. Although she was an occasional smoker in Grade 10, she has stopped smoking entirely in obedience to team rules.

The Psychologist's Explanation

A psychologist would look at Elaine's personality to explain why she joined the soccer team. Elaine is a logical problem-solver. She became aware that her many responsibilities at home were causing her to suffer. She had personal needs for recreation and relationships with people outside her family that were not being met.

As she pondered over what kind of group might help her, she again used her logical approach. Both of her parents were born in Europe and liked to watch European professional soccer games on television. Whenever possible, Elaine had sat and watched the game with her family. She understood the rules of the game so, even though she had never before been involved in school sports, she chose the soccer team as the solution to her stress. She believed such a group activity would satisfy her personal needs. When she found that it did, she committed herself to the team.

The Anthropologist's Explanation

Social anthropologists find that different **cultures** or subcultures coexist in a community. When Elaine joined the soccer team, she gravitated toward the specific culture of team sports. It is a culture she can identify with, in which players encourage each other, reassuring a player when she makes a mistake. Making strategic decisions for the benefit of the group is an important feature of the culture—if the team is winning, the best players are pulled off the field to give inexperienced players more practice. If the team is losing, the best players are expected to give an extra effort. The rituals of the game also appeal to Elaine. They include sharing water bottles at halftime, hugging a teammate after a goal is scored, and making faces if the referee makes a mistake.

In addition to all these elements, Elaine is attracted by the game's **material culture**—for example, the team's stylish uniform with the school crest on the shirt.

Figure 9.1 What are some of the appealing features of the culture of team sports?

RECAP

1. What is the sociologist's explanation for why Elaine joined the soccer team?
2. What is the psychologist's explanation for why Elaine joined the soccer team?
3. What is the anthropologist's explanation for why Elaine joined the soccer team?
4. Write three paragraphs identifying which aspects of each explanation you find the most convincing. Explain why.

Section 9.2

Formal Organizations and Bureaucracies

Focus Questions

- What are formal organizations?
- What are some important features of bureaucracies?
- What influence do formal organizations have on communities?

Key Concepts

formal organizations
bureaucracies
utilitarian bureaucracies
normative bureaucracies
coercive bureaucracies
stratified

Formal Organizations

Formal organizations are structured groups with comprehensive and elaborate rules. These rules stipulate who is eligible to join, who is responsible for what activities, and how the rules themselves are to be made and enforced. Formal organizations are frequently voluntary associations that one can choose to join or not. Examples include political parties or Neighbourhood Watch groups. But there also are formal organizations with compulsory membership. For example, to practise as a family doctor in Ontario, you must be a member of, and pay annual dues to, the Ontario College of Physicians and Surgeons. As a student at a university or college, you will probably be compelled to belong to, and pay dues to, the campus students' organization. Whether membership is voluntary or compulsory, however, formal organizations tend to function in similar ways.

One similarity shared by formal organizations is their hierarchical structure. If the organization is international, it usually has both an international office and national offices. The national offices report to the international centre from various major cities. In addition, regional offices or "chapters" may coordinate national initiatives at a more local level.

The national organization and regional chapters are generally headed by elected governors. The role of these governors is to ensure that the organization is meeting its stated goals. Governors usually hold some other job outside the organization, since the office of governor tends to be an unpaid position. Salaried employees are appointed to carry out the day-to-day operations of the group. This pyramid structure of international, national, and regional associations, as well as the mix of unpaid volunteers and salaried employees, are typical of many formal organizations.

Bureaucracies

Many large formal organizations are **bureaucracies.** To understand the nature of a bureaucracy, we can contrast a family-run doughnut shop (non-bureaucracy) with the accounting department of a large doughnut chain with outlets across the country (bureaucracy). Note the following three differences between the shop and the accounting department.

First, a bureaucracy has a rigid operational style, in contrast with flexible working conditions at the shop. For example, workers at the shop can spell off for each other. If you cannot work tonight because you want to go to a friend's birthday party, maybe your brother or sister will take over for you. But if you work in the accounting department, getting time off probably requires making an appointment with your manager. Your manager may have to check company procedures, and you may have to fill out a standardized request form.

Second, a bureaucracy has a clearly defined management structure, while the shop has only one or two levels of rank. For example, your parents at the shop might have the final say on all decisions. If they go on vacation, you or a sibling will take over with very little discussion needed. In the accounting department, you may spend years slowly climbing the management ladder. The higher up ladder you go, your salary, prestige, and responsibilities also grow.

Third, a bureaucracy tends to be impersonal, in contrast with the open, personal relationships at the shop. Since your family runs the shop, you are in constant contact with one another, and work issues are intermingled with family issues. But you can work your whole life for the large doughnut company and never come into contact with a member of the top management team.

Examples and Categories of Bureaucracies

Bureaucracies are everywhere in our society. Government departments, such as the federal Department of Foreign Affairs and International Trade, or Ontario's Ministry of Education, are run as bureaucracies. The same is true of virtually all large business corporations, churches, hospitals, factories, political parties, labour unions, police services, and military forces. While they are large and impersonal, they tend to get the job done, and in this lies their major advantage.

Social scientists divide bureaucracies into three major categories. **Utilitarian bureaucracies** are those that operate as business enterprises to make a profit for their owners. Most large companies, such as Canadian Tire or Tim Horton's, fall into this category. **Normative bureaucracies** are those based on norms such as

Figure 9.2 Which characteristics of a bureaucracy are represented in this scene of a formal meeting of employee and manager?

helping others or making society a better place. Examples of this category include community service organizations, such as the Canadian Cancer Society, most religious organizations, such as the Roman Catholic Church, and multicultural foundations, such as the Canadian Jewish Congress. **Coercive bureaucracies** are those that force involuntary residence on their clients. These include prisons and psychiatric hospitals.

Regardless of which category a particular bureaucracy belongs to, it will tend to share all the major characteristics of bureaucracies.

Classic Study

RESEARCHER:
Max Weber, Sociologist

TIME:
1920

SUBJECT:
The Characteristics of Bureaucracies

Max Weber on Bureaucracy

In Chapter 2, we introduced the work of Max Weber (see pages 21 to 22). Among his many famous studies is his essay on bureaucracy. He identified six characteristics of bureaucratic organizations.

1. Areas of responsibility are fixed and official, and are enforced by rules.
2. There are multiple levels of authority; lower levels are supervised by higher ones.
3. Management is based on official documents called "files."
4. Managers are systematically trained for their jobs.
5. Managers must work full time, often putting in extended hours.
6. There are rules for all aspects of the bureaucracy's operations.

Although these principles seem fairly obvious to people today, they were regarded as revolutionary in Weber's day. Bureaucracies were just being established throughout Europe and North America, replacing the social organization of the previous 500 years, in which officials pledged their loyalty to a king or queen, rather than to the nation. The characteristics Weber observed have become considerably more entrenched since Weber's time.

Bureaucracy and Efficiency

Supporters of bureaucracy claim that one of its greatest advantages is its efficiency. The clear procedures bureaucracies follow tend to guarantee that workers know what to do, how to do it, and when to do it. They usually understand the organization's goals and are given highly structured methods to achieve those goals.

But a bureaucracy is only as efficient and flawless as the people who work within it. This point is elaborated on in the description below.

> [Bureaucracies] can screw up just as easily as any other organization because of informal actions and relationships that exist within the formal organization. When we post a letter it just has to get to its destination. The book of policies and procedures says it must and will within a specified number of days. Then someone puts a half-eaten bologna and mustard sandwich on top of it and it goes in the waste bin. Gone are one letter, one half sandwich, and one perfect system (Mansfield, 1982, 106).

The varied features of bureaucracy have made it an intriguing topic for social scientists to study. As you might expect, their perspectives on why bureaucracies develop and how they affect people vary considerably.

The Anthropologist's Perspective

Anthropologists see bureaucracies as a natural and necessary part of the culture of countries such as Canada and the United States. With their large populations and complex economies, such countries have what anthropologists call **stratified** cultures. This means that the population is divided into different layers, such as rich and poor, educated and non-educated, or skilled and unskilled. Each layer or level within the culture is given a certain status. For example, the rich and educated are generally seen as making a greater contribution and having a higher status than the poor and uneducated. Even though these statuses may have no basis in reality, they are still believed to be valid by most members of the culture.

INTERNET RESOURCES

To find out more about Max Weber's perspectives on bureaucracies, visit the following two sites. Search them to answer the questions below.

http://www.utoledo.edu/~ddavis/weber.htm

http://www.humanities.mq.edu.au/politics/y64109.html

Why did Weber study bureaucracy in the first place? Why, according to him, were bureaucrats prepared to take on highly responsible jobs for relatively low pay? What does this tell us about some people's motivations in today's workplaces?

Figure 9.3 How would an anthropologist characterize the status of these individuals? How does this analysis relate to the existence of bureaucracies in this society?

To an anthropologist, a bureaucracy is a stratified and organized set of formal statuses. As such, it is a miniaturized reflection of the culture in which it operates. A bureaucracy's managing director, just like the rich in society, has more status, power, and income than the bureaucracy's caretaking staff (paralleling the poor in society). In a bureaucracy, the rights and responsibilities of every person holding a particular status are spelled out in detail.

Patterns in Bureaucracies

The fact that each level in a bureaucracy has a distinct role and status might lead us to expect certain patterns in how bureaucracies work. In this section, we identify these patterns. As you will read, some patterns do not occur as expected in the actual practice of bureaucracies.

First, in an ideal bureaucracy, each employee will perform her or his role to specifications, with the result that the bureaucracy functions smoothly. In practice, however, higher management in a large bureaucracy may feel that the lowest status workers are uncommitted to the bureaucracy's goals. Similarly, the lowest status workers sometimes feel that senior management neither understands nor cares about the difficulties they face in their jobs. It is a huge challenge for a large bureaucracy to meet the needs of all its employees regardless of their status.

Another common pattern resulting from stratification is that low-status workers have more rules to follow. For example, members of the caretaking staff are likely to have their starting and finishing times clearly set out. In contrast, the vice-president may be free to come and go as she or he pleases. This pattern, in which the rules made by powerful people have the greatest effect on those with the least status, is common to many cultures. There is another side to the above example comparing caretakers and the vice-president. If the caretakers are asked to work beyond their normal hours, they will probably be paid overtime. The vice-president, however, is unlikely to be paid extra for staying late to fulfill a responsibility.

Finally, with all of its clearly spelled-out relationships and procedures between levels, a bureaucracy can become entangled in its own complexity. Sometimes only insiders with long-standing experience really understand how things work. As a result, those who are served by the bureaucracy may become extremely frustrated. For example, imagine you are an outsider being served by a bureaucratic university or college. How do you figure out whom to talk to in order to have your academic transcript reconsidered? How many people must you question before you get an answer? Or, if you are being served by an airline, whom do you talk to about getting a last-minute compassionate fare to visit a dying parent? Some people lack the patience to wade through the "red tape" and end up paying the high-priced full fare.

Cultures Without Bureaucracy

As anthropologists have studied cultures from around the world, they have noted many examples of non-bureaucratic organizations. In many indigenous cultures, for example, bands and chiefdoms are not

Figure 9.4 How are children educated in non-bureaucratic societies?

bureaucratically organized. What are the features of a non-bureaucratic social structure?

First, many tasks are done without having formal procedures in place. For example, children may be educated through informal dealings with family and non-family members. Justice matters may be resolved in gatherings where all participants are free to speak directly.

Second, in many cases, kinship structures, rather than written-down rules, determine who performs which job in the community.

Third, rules of appropriate behaviour are more likely to be enforced by social pressure and example than by formal trial and punishment.

One of the most important functions a bureaucracy can have is providing essential social or public services. In stratified cultures, people take academic courses that lead to specific professions in the social or public service. In non-bureaucratic cultures, these services are often provided by elite classes whose members have been trained from birth for specific purposes. For example, an individual may be selected and groomed to assist in childbirth or to perform a specific religious function.

The Psychologist's Perspective

The area of psychology that is concerned with bureaucracy is called organizational psychology. One of the topics organizational psychologists study is how change is managed in bureaucracies.

Researchers in this field have discovered that humans like predictability and have a general distaste for change. Humans tend to feel comfortable with familiar methods of performing tasks and meeting goals. As they get older, they become resistant to change.

The Ministry of Correctional Services, the branch of the Ontario government in charge of running provincial prisons, can provide a good case study of how members of a bureaucracy struggle with change. Many workers in the ministry have become familiar and comfortable with its procedures. In 2002, the province's first privately run prison is due to open in Penetanguishene. A private company will operate the prison, charging the provincial government a daily fee for every inmate. Many workers currently employed in the prison service are worried that private management will eventually take over all prisons. They fear the changes this trend might bring. For example, will they have to accept lower wages? Will they have fewer colleagues to call on in an emergency situation? Will their pensions be cut back? Whether or not these changes ever come to pass, the fear that they might causes stress.

Workers in the Ministry of Correctional Services are not the only people fearing changes. Globalization and the development of information technology have significantly changed the way many people work. For example, middle-management executives at one time had secretaries to organize their time, take dictation, and type or even draft correspondence. Now many managers perform such tasks themselves. The demand for travel agents has been reduced as people have learned to book tickets online from their homes. Changes like these can be very stressful for those affected by them.

Organizational psychologists propose solutions for such stress. They develop systems for managing change and overcoming people's resistance to new methods. To arrive at solutions, they first research the relationship between employers and employees. They use their findings to develop improved methods of communication and team-building.

Besides change, one of the greatest causes of employee stress is the feeling that workers have no control over their workplace. For example, supermarket cashiers cannot work at their own pace—they must keep up with the flow of customers coming through their checkout. Airline baggage handlers must gear their workday to arrivals and departures schedules. If 11:00 a.m. to 2:00 p.m. is a peak time at a particular airport, many workers must schedule their lunch breaks around these hours.

Organizational pscyhologists also propose solutions for this type of stress. One of their success stories is described in Chapter 1 (see pages 5 to 7). The Honda assembly plant in Alliston, Ontario, agreed to changes proposed by organizational psychologists to increase employee control over working conditions. The results were reduced absenteeism, more job satisfaction, and improved quality control.

Working Without Bureaucracy

Organizational psychologists also study non-bureaucratic operations. A classic

Figure 9.5 When Abitibi-Consolidated took over Donohue Inc. in August 2000, Donohue's chief executive became chairman of the combined company. After six months on the job, he resigned. The culture clash between the two organizations was so intense, one analyst called the senior executive situation "very dysfunctional."

example is the entrepreneur who is trying to bring a new product to market. To win investor approval, the entrepreneur must operate non-bureaucratically. That is, she or he must be flexible in scheduling meetings and quick to respond innovatively to changing circumstances. Entrepreneurs who get tied down by procedures and set ways of doing things are rarely successful. Those types of people who are comfortable in routines and who maintain clear boundaries between work and recreation time should not even attempt to find entrepreneurial work.

The Sociologist's Perspective

Sociologists focus on why people choose to group together in such a way that a bureaucracy is formed. They believe that people create bureaucracies in order to achieve specific complex goals they could not otherwise attain. These people have learned that formalizing their relationships with one another and defining each person's responsibilities and rewards are necessary steps to pursuing ambitious aims.

Outside of this common general origin, bureaucracies differ widely in their overall cultures. These differences make up another topic of study for sociologists. Rarely are these differences more dramatically displayed than when one company takes over another. In August 2000, Abitibi-Consolidated Inc., a pulp-and-paper company headquartered in Montreal, took over its smaller rival Donohue Inc. There was an immediate clash of cultures between the two organizations. Abitibi appeared to be more eager to spend money on executive perks. The culture of Donohue, in contrast, was leaner, more cost-conscious, and more formal. Within three months, three senior managers from the Donohue side of the new organization resigned. The culture clash was so severe that investors lowered the value of the company. If you had $100 worth of Abitibi shares in August, they would have been worth $78 in November. Clearly, conflict between cultures can have a great effect on how a bureaucracy is perceived by both insiders and outsiders.

Departments within a single bureaucracy may also vary in culture or rigidity. Consider the example of a college or university bureaucracy. Employees in the finance department follow rigid procedures, making their work fairly routine and predictable. Professors belonging to the faculty experience much different working conditions. Rather than submitting to formal rules and regulations, they value above all the principle of academic freedom. Their activities vary from year to year as they teach different courses or go on research leaves. Bureaucratic procedures play a minor, if not non-existent, role in their work life, in contrast to their colleagues in the finance department.

Explaining Non-Bureaucracy

Since bureaucracies are viewed as a means to accomplishing complex goals, they are not necessary when an organization's goals are straightforward. The goals of a shoe repair business, for example, are simple enough for one or two people to accomplish. The tasks to be performed are fairly limited—buying supplies, cataloguing shoes as they come in and go out, repairing the shoes, collecting money, and paying the bills. If one worker in the business needs ten minutes to go to the bank, the other workers can probably cover for her or him. Since non-bureaucratic operations are comparatively straightforward, they are not a major topic of study for sociologists.

RECAP

1. What are the major categories used by social scientists to classify formal organizations?
2. What are the major structural features of formal organizations?
3. How is a bureaucracy different from a family-run business?
4. What does the story of the half-eaten bologna and mustard sandwich reveal about formal organizations?
5. Construct an organizer that compares the strengths and weaknesses of bureaucracies. Which do you find more significant—the strengths or the weaknesses? Explain your answer.

Section 9.3

Types of Groups

Focus Questions

- What are some of the reasons why people join organized groups?
- What are some different ways in which organized groups are formed and operate?
- What effects can organized groups have on communities and society as a whole?

Meeting Needs Through Groups

Our study of Elaine Spira (see pages 281 to 283) introduced some reasons why a teenager would join an organized sports team. In this section, we look at examples of groups in Canada that perform the following functions:

- improve the quality of members' lives
- help members gain control over their lives
- improve members' position or status in society
- relieve the suffering of others
- achieve specific social goals
- achieve specific environmental goals

The groups we examine in this section are varied in size and purpose. One feature they share is that group members know each other either personally or as a result of group structure. This feature distinguishes groups from **categories**, which are collections of people who have something in common but do not know each other. For example, teenagers are a category but not a group. In contrast, the members of a local youth club are a group—many of them know each other personally, and the group structure or membership gives them a formal link to each other.

Improving Quality of Life

A very early discovery in human history was that people can make their lives better when they work together. Two examples of how people put this principle to work in more recent history can be found in the late nineteenth century.

In this period, many women in Canada had no choice but to spend their adult lives working in the home. They were either married and raising children or working as servants and nannies in the homes of the rich. Only a small percentage worked outside the home as elementary schoolteachers. In such a social atmosphere, single women, especially those who had immigrated and/or lived in cities, were hard pressed to achieve a place for themselves. Some wives and mothers also faced hardships if their husbands had difficulties providing for them or were

Key Concepts

category
feminist
self-government
First Nation
advocacy groups
non-profit organizations
non-governmental organizations (NGOs)
progressive
militant

abusive. These conditions sparked the rise of the first **feminist** organizations—groups that pursued goals of specific importance to women's lives. The Girls' Friendly Society, formed in 1882, provided support and education for single immigrant women. The Dominion Order of the King's Daughters, formed in 1886, worked to support single women in Canadian cities. The Women's Christian Temperance Union (WCTU) was formed in 1874 in Owen Sound, Ontario. It tried to ban the sale of alcohol, which was having highly destructive effects on family life.

A group does not have to be committed to a humanitarian goal to improve the quality of its members' lives. As we saw in the example of Elaine Spira, even joining a soccer team can make a person's life better. The team provides an opportunity for recreation and an outlet for stress. A feeling of well-being results from sharing experiences with people with similar outlooks and goals.

Figure 9.6 What goals did the Women's Christian Temperance Union pursue? How would this goal improve the quality of women's lives?

VOICES OF YOUTH

QUESTION:

What is a feminist?

A feminist is a male or female who believes and/or fights for women's rights. I don't consider myself a feminist. I've always experienced gender equality. Active feminism often seems to be a waste of time, where activists try to force something on people.

—Blair Hatch, 16

A feminist is someone who fights for the rights of women. Sadly, feminists still get stereotyped as angry man-haters. A feminist can be male or female, gay or straight. The main thing is that person stands for the rights of women. We still have a long way to go for women's right. In many places around the world, women get paid less than men for doing the same work.

—Sandra Cordova, 19

To me, feminism is an excuse for women to ask for special treatment just for being women. I find it pathetic. The goal of feminism is to eliminate giving men any power in the workforce or in relationships and to hand that power over to women. Women take the idea of equality to much greater extremes than men would.

—Krys Cappelman, 17

Empowerment

Closely related to the function of improving quality of life is the function of empowerment. A group that empowers its members helps them to gain control over their lives and affairs.

We have already seen how women have formed groups to make themselves stronger in the face of difficult life conditions. The same process has occurred in Aboriginal communities in Canada.

In the nineteenth century, virtually all decision-making powers had been taken away from Aboriginal communities by Canadian governments. In the twentieth century, the Department of Indian and Northern Affairs had ultimate control over Aboriginal peoples. The negative effects of disempowerment have been particularly dramatic in the Innu community of Davis Inlet, Newfoundland. Suicide rates have reached 178 per 100 000 people, compared with the Canadian average of 12 per 100 000. In some reserves in northern Ontario and Quebec, substance abuse among teenagers is ten to twenty times the rate among teenagers in towns and cities.

Psychiatrist Derryck Smith of the British Columbia Children's and Women's Health Centre in Vancouver sees these problems as part of the empowerment issue. He states: " I believe that the major interventions that need to be done are more at a societal level than sending squads of doctors into [Aboriginal] communities.

The answer lies in the economic empowerment of individuals" (Ferry, 2000, 906).

For Aboriginal communities, the ultimate mark of empowerment is **self-government**. A self-governing community has the power to make its own laws in areas such as policing, taxation, logging, fishing and hunting regulations, and welfare payments. According to a University of British Columbia study conducted by Michael Chandler, Aboriginal communities with a high degree of self-government had a mean youth suicide rate of 18.2 per 100 000 people. Those communities without any self-government had a rate of 121.0 per 100 000 (Ferry, 2000, 906).

The most celebrated self-government agreement to date was signed in 1999 and became effective in May 2000. By the agreement, the Nisga'a people of the Nass Valley in northwestern British Columbia obtained the right to govern almost 2000 km^2 of land. They also received \$26.3 million in immediate funding from the federal government and the promise of an eventual total of \$200 million. On the first day of self-government, the Nisga'a governing council passed eleven laws that restored Aboriginal customs. The agreement also imposes new obligations on the Nisga'a. Currently, they do not pay taxes on goods purchased for personal use. Starting in 2008, they will have to pay provincial sales tax on all purchases. Starting in 2011, they will also have to pay the federal goods and services tax (GST).

In Chapter 10, we look in more detail at the social and institutional practices that disempowered Aboriginal peoples. In the following case study, the successful efforts of one specific Aboriginal group to gain greater control of their affairs is presented.

Figure 9.7 BC Premier Glen Clark and Nisga'a Tribal Council President Joe Gosnell shook hands after signing the Nisga'a Final Agreement in April 1999.

Case Study: Walpole Island First Nation

Walpole Island First Nation is situated at the north end of Lake St. Clair in Ontario. The label **First Nation** means that the community's members live and work together but do not have official status as a band. The people of this First Nation are descended from the Ottawa, Ojibwa, and Potawatomi Nations who lived in the area at various times in the past. Research shows that they had established an economy based on hunting, fishing, trapping, and planting corn as early as 1300 years ago.

Walpole Island is known as *Bkejwanong* ("where the waters divide") in the Algonquian language of its inhabitants. Because it is situated close to the cities of Sarnia, Windsor, and Detroit, it receives the sewage outflows from these cities. It also receives highly toxic chemical discharges from Sarnia's petrochemical industry. By the 1970s, raw and semi-treated discharges from the cities were having a devastating effect on the wildlife and agriculture of the island. Particularly hazardous was the heavy metal buildup in the silt of the river and lake beds. The beds were dredged every three years or so to keep the shipping channels open, stirring up a toxic sludge that washed onto the island.

Walpole Island's residents realized that it would be up to them to create a safe and sustainable environment for their people. In 1973, they began a project to research land claims and Aboriginal and treaty rights. In 1983, the project's work was expanded to include environmental research and resource management. In 1989, the Walpole Island Heritage Centre was formed as the foundation for continued research. The centre relies on traditional and scientific sources for information that can be used to serve the community.

Aboriginal land claims were first recognized in Canadian law by the Royal Proclamation of 1763. By this act, the British Crown acknowledged the Aboriginal claim to a vast area of territory in present-day Canada and the USA. Five treaties between 1764 and 1796 specifically recognized Walpole Island First Nation. With this historical precedent as a basis, Walpole Island residents began to negotiate directly with Canadian and American governments in the 1980s. Their aim was to reduce the pollution problems they faced.

In 1989, the governments of Canada, Ontario, and Walpole Island signed a "Framework Agreement" to negotiate a solution to outstanding problems. Surprisingly, the limits of the First Nation's territory had never been officially recognized in Canadian law. The Heritage Centre also began to meet with large industrial producers, such as Dow Chemical and Petro-Canada, in order to promote better management of hazardous chemical by-products. In another initiative, 10 ha of prime land were planted with corn to provide a wildlife and bird sanctuary for migrating waterfowl.

The efforts of the Walpole Island Heritage Centre were eventually recognized by many organizations. One such organization was the International Joint Commission, a Canadian-American body that supervises matters relating to the boundary between the two nations. In June 1997, the commission held a hearing at Walpole Island on the continuing concerns of the Heritage Centre. The commission praised the efforts of the inhabitants to solve serious problems in a constructive manner.

Problems still remain. It is not clear when Walpole Island and other First Nations in Ontario will reach agreements with the federal government over self-government and land claims. In 1997, ICI, a Sarnia petrochemical company, received permission from the Ontario government to release several billion litres of treated water that could negatively affect downstream environments. The Heritage Centre has been challenging this decision in the courts.

Despite ongoing challenges, the Walpole Island experience attests to the positive results that can be achieved by a group that is determined to empower itself.

1. Which key concepts of this chapter apply to Walpole Island First Nation (for example, dyad, category, primary group, secondary group, formal organization, bureaucracy)? Explain why certain terms apply while others do not.
2. What problems have threatened the quality of life of Walpole Island First Nation?
3. Which other groups did Walpole Island First Nation work with in order to find solutions for these problems?

Improving Social Status

The desire of Aboriginal peoples for self-government is unique. Instead of fighting for a better position in mainstream society, self-governing communities have fought to run their own society alongside the mainstream one. This is not a situation Canadians are likely to see in any other sector of the population. What they are likely to see is some people joining groups to improve their status in the mainstream. Groups with this purpose are called **advocacy** groups. "To advocate" means to work on behalf of a cause of principle. A number of feminist groups formed after the Second World War were organized specifically to improve the status of women.

The first major improvement in women's status in the twentieth century came about not because of a group, but because of a remarkable individual. In 1928, Emily Murphy (1868–1933), a journalist and magistrate from Alberta, challenged the Canadian government's refusal to appoint women to the Senate. The government's position was that women were not "persons" as defined in the British North America Act (now the Canada Act) of 1867. That is, since women did not have the right to vote in 1867 when the Senate was created, they had not been persons in the political sense and remained ineligible for Senate participation. Murphy took her challenge to the Supreme Court where, surprisingly, she lost. The Privy Council in London, England, overturned the decision in 1929, and the first Canadian woman was appointed to the Senate. In a show of spite, the government gave the appointment to Cairine Wilson, not Emily Murphy.

The experiences of the First World War (1914–1918) and the Second World War (1939–1945) showed that women were capable of doing jobs previously thought of as "men's jobs." They built guns and bombs and flew planes from the factories to the airfields. But they were required by law to give up these jobs to men who returned from the war in 1918 and 1945. Despite women's contributions during wartime, society still held on to the idea that a woman's place was in the home.

A woman's main concern was considered to be the care of her husband and children.

A second wave of feminism produced its first specifically female organization in 1960. The Voice of Women pressed for a number of reforms to improve the status of women. In 1967, the federal government responded to pressure from this group and others by creating a Royal Commission on the Status of Women. The commission made a number of important recommendations for reforming employment, family, and divorce law.

The government was slow to make the changes recommended by the Royal Commission. Frustrated by these delays, a number of women's organizations came together to form the National Action Committee on the Status of Women (NAC) in 1972. One of NAC's most important successes was making guarantees of sexual equality stronger when the Canadian constitution was changed in 1982. Concerned that guarantees of equality were weak in the early drafts of the Canadian Charter of Rights and Freedoms, NAC spearheaded the creation of the Ad Hoc Committee on the Constitution. Under pressure from the committee, the federal government ultimately adopted the strong equality language now in section 15 of the Charter. It reads:

> [E]very individual is equal before and under the law and has the right to equal protection and equal benefit of the law without discrimination based on race, national or ethnic origin, colour, religion, sex, age or mental or physical disability.

Through advocacy, NAC had made a major accomplishment. Women, who had not legally been considered "persons" until 1929, were from 1982 onward guaranteed complete equality with men under the law.

INTERNET RESOURCES

To find out more about NAC, go to

http://www.geocities.com/CapitolHill/9740/PINKPAPR.html

Summarize the work of NAC in the following areas:

- violence
- Aboriginal women
- jobs

Figure 9.8 Laura Sabia was active in pressuring the government to call a Royal Commission. She was the first president of the National Action Committee on the Status of Women.

POINT AND COUNTERPOINT

What Should Be the Focus of Women's Advocacy Groups Today?

All advocacy movements struggle with disagreements over certain aspects of their goals. In the women's movement, two organizations with differing goals are The Women's Legal Education and Action Fund (LEAF) and REAL (Realistic, Equal, Active, for Life) Women of Canada. Which group's vision do you agree with most?

LEAF:

- Intervenes in equality rights cases...covering a wide range of issues including sexual harassment, pregnancy discrimination, unfair hiring practices, violence against women, sex bias in welfare regulations and employment standards, pension inequities and reproductive freedom.
- Participates in government consultations, public inquiries and legislative reform.
- Undertakes research and public education on equality rights for women.

Legal. LEAF uses the law to protect the equal rights of women and girls in Canada.

Education. LEAF knows it is impossible to create change using only the law so LEAF's public education materials are used to raise awareness about its work and significance.

Action is absolutely necessary for any of LEAF's work to have meaning. LEAF puts the theory of the Charter into practice by actively participating in new cases that affect women's rights.

Fundraising is another important part of LEAF's work....Much of LEAF's work is financed mainly by private donations and fundraising efforts.

Source: Women's Legal Education and Action Fund. "About LEAF." *LEAF.* [Online]. Available http://www.leaf.ca/ 8 January 2001.

REAL:

Our view is that the family, which is now undergoing serious strain, is the most important unit in Canadian society. We believe that the fragmentation of the Canadian family is one of the major causes of disorder in society today.

Our objectives are as follows:

1. To reaffirm that the family is society's most important unit...
2. To promote the equality, advancement and well being of women, recognizing them as interdependent members of society, whether in the family, workplace or community.
3. To promote, secure and defend legislation which upholds the Judeo-Christian understanding of marriage and family life.
4. To support government and social policies that make homemaking possible for women who, out of necessity, would otherwise have to take employment outside the home.
5. To support the life of all innocent individuals from conception to natural death.

Source: REAL Women of Canada. "Who We Are." *REAL Women of Canada.* [Online]. Available http://www.realwomenca.com/ 8 January 2001.

1. What similarities can you observe between the statements of LEAF and REAL Women?
2. What differences can you observe between the two positions?
3. Which organization's statement could you more easily support? Why?

REMARKABLE PEOPLE

Hedy Fry

Dr. Hedy Fry was first elected as a Member of Parliament for Vancouver Centre in 1993 and re-elected in 1997 and 2000. In 1996, Dr. Fry was appointed Secretary of State for Multiculturalism and the Status of Women, and reappointed after the 1997 and 2000 federal elections. Dr. Fry was appointed parliamentary secretary to the Minister of Health from 1993 to 1996. She was also a member of the Task Force on Reform of the Social Security System in 1994. Dr. Fry sat as a member on the Standing Committee on Health, the SubCommittee on AIDS, and the SubCommittee on the Plain Packaging of Tobacco.

Although now known for her work as a politician, Dr. Fry has also been a medical practitioner for over twenty years in British Columbia. Her concern for the welfare of the community has been reflected by her involvement in various areas of the medical profession. She was president of the British Columbia Medical Association, president of the Vancouver Medical Association, president of the BC Federation of Medical Women, and editor of the Canadian Federation of Medical Women's national newsletter. She was chair of the Canadian Medical Association's (CMA) Multicultural Committee and was a member of the CMA committee responsible for preparing a brief on the Royal Commission on Reproductive Technologies.

Dr. Fry was born in Trinidad and obtained her medical degree from the Royal College of Surgeons in Dublin, Ireland. She is a resident of Vancouver, BC, and is the mother of three children: Peter, Jeremy, and Doug.

1. How has Dr. Fry's work with groups and organizations had an impact on people's lives?
2. What accomplishments has Dr. Fry achieved that would qualify her as a remarkable person?
3. Do you think her work as a politician or as a doctor is more significant? Why?

Relieving Others' Suffering

The advocacy groups previously described are formed to work for benefits to their own membership. Other advocacy groups are created to work for improvements to the conditions of disadvantaged groups in society. These groups are normally registered as charities or **non-profit organizations**. This title enables financial contributors to qualify for income tax relief on their donations. In 2000, individuals giving $100 would receive an income tax rebate of $17 from the federal government. Provincial or territorial governments provide a further rebate of about $8. These income tax rebates are designed to encourage donations to qualifying associations.

At a national level, the goals of such groups might include reducing child poverty in Canada. When such groups have an international focus, they take on

INTERNET RESOURCES

To find out more about MSF Canada, go to its Web site at

http://www.msf.ca/canada/html

In which countries has MSF Canada worked to relieve suffering?

tasks such as helping refugees escape war environments or raising health and educational standards in developing nations.

Most such groups are **non-governmental organizations (NGOs)**. This term refers to the fact that, as they perform their national or international charitable work, they scrupulously maintain their independence from government bodies. Members of NGOs believe that having too close a relationship with governments will introduce politics into their operations. They fear that political entanglements could stand in the way of delivering aid directly to those in need.

An example of a successful NGO is Médecins Sans Frontières. Abbreviated as MSF, the name of this organization means "Doctors Without Borders." MSF was originally founded in France in 1971. MSF Canada was founded in 1991 to provide humanitarian assistance to people in need. It sees its purpose as relieving suffering among populations harmed by war, epidemics, famine, flood, or civil unrest. Its national office is in Toronto, with branches in Ottawa, Montreal, Halifax, and Vancouver. Between 1991 and 1999, MSF Canada sent over 500 volunteers to Rwanda, Bosnia, Afghanistan, Cambodia, Liberia, Angola, Sudan, and Sri Lanka. Since 90 per cent of all death and suffering from infectious diseases occurs in developing countries, this is naturally where MSF is busiest.

Many of MSF's volunteers are qualified medical personnel who leave safe homes and successful practices in Canada to face dangerous and disease-ridden conditions. Their contributions are so valuable that MSF Canada was awarded the Nobel Peace Prize in 1999. In accepting the award, Dr. James Orbinski of MSF Canada said:

> More than offering material assistance, we aim to enable individuals to regain their rights and dignity as human beings. As an independent volunteer association, we are committed to bringing direct medical aid to people in need. But we act not in a vacuum, and we speak not into the wind, but with a clear intent to assist, to provoke change, or to reveal injustice. Our action and our voice [constitute] an act of indignation, a refusal to accept an active or passive assault on the other (Orbinski, 1999).

Many young people are inspired by the prospect of experiencing other parts of the world as volunteers. Non-governmental organizations (NGOs) and governmental organizations have programs that send youth on volunteer placements, both within Canada and overseas. One such organization, Canada World Youth (CWY), places young people in communities in Canada and in developing countries, where they learn about other cultures and assist in community development programs. CWY is supported by the

Canadian International Development Agency, a federal government agency, and by thousands of donors across Canada.

Founded in 1971, CWY has placed more than 26 000 young people, between the ages of seventeen and twenty-four, in more than sixty countries around the globe and in more than 600 communities in Canada. CWY programs last between six and eight months, with participants spending half of this time in Canada and the other half overseas. Participants are paired with a counterpart from their exchange country and live with host families. They participate in community programs that focus on issues such as health care, environmental protection, and rural development. The participants are expected to fundraise $1500 from their communities and pay a $250 participation fee.

Another organization aimed specifically to help young people is an NGO called the United Nations International Children's Education Fund (UNICEF). Many readers of this textbook may have raised money for this organization as children by filling up UNICEF boxes on Halloween night. The case study on the following page shows how another NGO directs its recruiting and fundraising toward children and teenagers.

INTERNET RESOURCES

Find out how to join CWY by visiting the organization's Web site at

http://www.cwy-jcm.org/

Click on "About Us" to find out more about what CWY does. Click on "Apply" to find out how you can participate.

Figure 9.9 Canada World Youth participant Adam Sherrard assists with a community garden project during his exchange in Burkina Faso.

Case Study: Free the Children

The success of the Free the Children movement is a source of pride to many young people in Canada. Started in 1995 by twelve-year-old Canadian Craig Kielburger, Free the Children tries to persuade governments and industry to stamp out child labour in developing countries.

The organization is very youth-oriented in its operation. Only members under eighteen are allowed to vote on policy decisions, with people over eighteen acting as mentors or chaperones. An adult board of directors, including a lawyer and an accountant, handle legal and financial matters.

Young members raise money through such events as walkathons, bake sales, and raffles. Free the Children is also supported by corporate sponsors and has begun to apply for government grants to help fund its work. In 2000, it was a registered not-for-profit organization in twenty countries.

Free the Children has helped bring the issue of child labour to the attention of many Canadians who would otherwise be unaware that it exists. After all, in Canada, laws require children to go to school until they are sixteen and prohibit their employment before the age of fourteen. But in many parts of the world, children are forced by poverty to do full-time work from the age of about eight onward. Many of them are forced to work in filthy and unsafe sweatshops. People in the developed world, often without knowing it, support this state of affairs by buying the goods produced in these shops.

Free the Children challenges all Canadians by asking such questions as: Who cut the material that went into your favourite shirt? Who ran the machine that stitched together the panels on your team's soccer ball? Was it an adult or a child? Do you care?

To encourage teenagers to get involved in its goals, Free the Children has identified a

Seven Steps To Sweatfree Status

1. **CREATE A GROUP**—One person can bring a "sweat-free" resolution to the decision-makers (board of education, etc.) but it is much more effective (and energizing) to have a group (of teachers, students, parents, principals, etc.) who will take the lead in moving a school/district/college toward a sweatfree status....
2. **ASK DECISION-MAKERS TO ENDORSE THE CAMPAIGN**...[Send letters asking people to support the campaign. Adapt [the campaign] to your specific situation...and send [letters]...to your superintendent or board of education or college president. The cover letter will ask that the decision-makers join a statewide effort to eliminate child labor and sweatshop apparel from the educational institution....
3. **TAKE INVENTORY**—of all apparel purchased by the school/district/college. It is the responsibility of the administration to do this, since they have access to records and they know their personnel. It is almost impossible for students or parents to do a complete inventory in a timely manner.
4. **IDENTIFY AND PLAN FOR TEACHING**—Identify any teacher or any materials (curriculum, videos, etc.) presently used in the school/district/college which promote awareness of the pervasive reality of child labor and sweatshops. Evaluate what is being done and devise a plan to increase educational opportunities on this issue.
5. **CONTACT ALL BUSINESSES AND VENDORS**—Following inventory, each business from which apparel is purchased is sent the Campaign's Code of Conduct. Each business must respond to each part of the Code of Conduct Compliance Form. Each business must be informed that failure to respond to the Compliance Form will mean that they do NOT meet the Code's standards and that alternative businesses which do meet the standards will be sought.
6. **IMPLEMENT CODE OF CONDUCT AS POLICY**—The group should again write to or meet with the decision-makers, asking them to adopt the Code of Conduct as policy for the school/district/college. This means that any business wishing to enter into contract with the school/district/college must meet the standards of the Code.
7. **CLAIM THE TITLE "SWEATFREE"!**

Source: Free the Children. *Child Labour: What Can Be Done: Seven Steps to Sweatfree Status*. [Online]. Available http://freethechildren.com 15 January 2001.

Case Study: Free the Children

seven-point program for high schools, districts, and colleges. The program encourages schools and other institutions to be "sweatfree"—that is, to stop purchasing the products of child labour.

The members of Free the Children believe that developed countries should provide grants and assistance to poorer countries so that they can build schools for all children. It also believes that countries like Canada should refuse to trade with nations that refuse to outlaw child labour.

1. Why do you think Free the Children has been one of the most successful of all youth-oriented NGOs?
2. How might Free the Children be different if only adults made the policy decisions? Explain.
3. Even though Free the Children is an NGO, it has sought help from government bodies. Describe the nature of this help, and explain why you think the organization chose to seek this help.

Figure 9.10 Craig Kielburger speaks to children working in a garbage dump in Manila, Philippines.

Achieving Social Goals

Rather than target specific people in need, some advocacy groups work to achieve social goals that more broadly affect a wider community. Examples of the goals of such groups include strengthening gun control laws, decriminalizing marijuana possession, and protecting Canada's social programs. Many of these social movements are non-profit organizations that, at the same time, receive direct grants of money from various levels of government.

The Council of Canadians is a good example of an advocacy group with broad social goals. Founded in 1985, it consists of over 100 000 members organized into fifty chapters across the nation. According to its founding principles, the council's role is to lobby politicians and business leaders to protect Canada's social programs, promote economic fairness, and preserve Canadian independence. The chair of the council writes in the introduction to the council's Web site:

> The dominant development model of our time is economic globalization, a system fuelled by the belief that a single global economy with universal rules set by global corporations and financial markets is inevitable. Everything is for sale, even those areas of life once considered sacred. Increasingly,

INTERNET RESOURCES

Do you want to find out more about the views and work of the Council of Canadians? Visit

http://www.canadians.org

Click on "About Us" or "Campaigns" to find out what projects the council has underway.

> these services and resources are controlled by a handful of transnational corporations who shape national and international law to suit their interests. At the heart of this transformation is an all-out assault on virtually every public sphere of life, including the democratic underpinning of our legal systems (Barlow, 1999).

The Council of Canadians has organized protests against what it sees as the growing Americanization of Canada's economy and social programs. It believes that this process will hurt Canadians in the long run.

The Canadian Centre for Policy Alternatives (CCPA) is a social movement with similar goals to the Council of Canadians. Founded in 1980, it promotes research on economic and social issues from a **progressive** point of view. Such a point of view seeks to protect the interests of ordinary people against the harmful influence of big business. The CCPA criticizes any economic policies it believes can result in poverty, inequality, and insecurity. Following are two of CCPA's key positions regarding the corporate community:

- Businesses pay too little income tax on their profits, in contrast to poorer private citizens who pay unfairly high taxes.
- Businesses have too much influence on government policies; this influence must be claimed back by private citizens.

To use CCPA's own words:

> There has been no increase for more than twenty years in the real annual earnings of Canadian men working full time. Average weekly earnings, adjusted for inflation grew just 2.8 per cent from 1989 to 1998....The average after-tax...income of Canadians fell by 5.6 per cent over the 1990s, with poorer families experiencing a decline of 12 per cent (Robinson, 2000).

In short, the membership of CCPA believes that Canada's economic policies are unfair. Unless they are reversed, people's incomes will continue to decline and social problems will increase.

Bread Not Circuses (BNC) is a Toronto-based social movement. Members of this group believe that too much money is spent on glamorous projects in big cities ("circuses") and not enough on social programs to help the most needy ("bread"). BNC points to Toronto's Skydome stadium/arena, opened in 1989, as a classic example of "circus-based" decision-making. Skydome was supposed to receive $30 million in public money from the province of Ontario. The rest of the money needed for its construction was to come from the private sector. After various operating fiascoes and financial restructurings, the final bill for the province came in at over $350 million. A short time later, in 1996, Ontario stopped funding all public housing. BNC questions how Ontario can justify spending hundreds of millions of dollars on an arena for highly paid professional athletes while refusing to spend a dime on low-rental housing for poor people.

More recently, BNC members have expressed anger at Toronto's bid to host the summer Olympic games in 2008. BNC sees the bid as another example of what it calls the "Skydome syndrome." Winning the bid means that a few select people become very rich, while less money is available for needed social programs. In 2000, BNC organized a series of public marches in support of the city withdrawing its bid. But the municipal government remained unconvinced and hoped to be

INTERNET RESOURCES

What specific policies does the CCPA promote? Find out by looking up

http://www.policyalternatives.ca

Clicking on "Commentary" or "Educational Project" provides specific information on CCPA's initiatives.

What other situations in Toronto does Bread Not Circuses confront? What methods does it propose to improve life in the city? Find out by looking up

http://breadnotcircuses.org

Clicking on "What did TO-Bid promise the IOC?" provides specific information on BNC's reasons for opposing the bid.

Figure 9.11 Why did Bread Not Circuses oppose the construction of Toronto's Skydome?

INTERNET RESOURCES

Do you want to find out what kind of work OCAP is doing now? Visit

http://www.tao.ca/~ocap

Visit the following site to explain what OCAP means when it says it seeks "the co-operation and organization of a local radical politics via communication and agitation":

http://www.toronto.tao.ca

the winning city when the announcement was made in 2001.

The Ontario Coalition Against Poverty (OCAP) takes a no-compromise approach in support of Ontario's poor. As such, it can be described as a **militant**, or aggressively active, social movement.

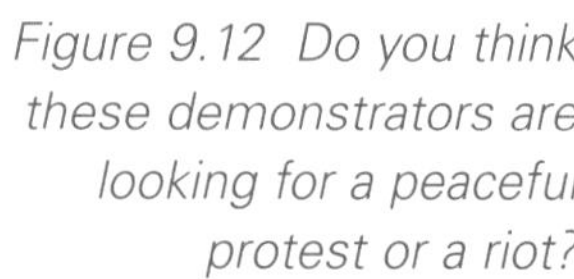

Figure 9.12 Do you think these demonstrators are looking for a peaceful protest or a riot?

In 2000, OCAP identified several Ontario government policies as threats to poor people's ability to survive by legal means. As a result of some of these policies, OCAP claimed, nineteen homeless people died in the streets of Toronto between January and June of 2000.

The militant nature of OCAP's beliefs is evident in the following extract from an open letter it sent to the premier of Ontario.

> On June 15 [2000], we will [organize] a march on your Legislature. This time, however, you will not be able to ignore us or guffaw with your cronies while we make speeches outside. This is because we are demanding of you, as Premier, the right to address the Legislature in session so those whose lives you have so profoundly damaged can bring just call for redress before the entire Assembly of the provincial Parliament (Ontario Coalition Against Poverty, 2000).

In June 2000, about 1000 OCAP members staged a demonstration in front of the Ontario legislature. It turned into a riot, with fights breaking out between some demonstrators and armed, mounted police equipped with riot gear. Twenty-five demonstrators, twenty-eight police officers, and ten police horses were treated for injuries.

Is violence a legitimate tactic for militant social movements to use? Opinion on this subject is divided, as shown by the following quotations (Van Rijn et al., 2000, A1).

> This is a group that wanted to get a message, presumably to me and to our

government. I've heard that message. You don't need to engage in violence to give me that message.

—Premier Mike Harris of Ontario

You can go by the rules of democracy...but eventually when people, and I mean ordinary people, feel the game is fixed, they are going to start going over the edge.

—A supporter of the demonstrators

Achieving Environmental Goals

Like social groups, environmental groups usually offer their members a variety of ways to contribute. For example, some members simply make financial donations. Others involve themselves more actively—for example, by handing out leaflets, writing letters, or marching in demonstrations.

Another distinctive feature of such groups is a high level of intellectual stimulation. More committed members are eager to share their vision with newer members, leading to an exciting mix of ideas.

Greenpeace Canada, based in Vancouver, is an example of a group working for the environment. It states as one of its principles the need "to ensure the ability of the earth to nurture life in all its diversity." Its specific goals include

- ending the clear-cutting of old-growth forests by British Columbia forestry companies
- ending the dumping of waste from ships at sea

Similarly, the Sierra Club has lobbied against offshore oil drilling in fragile environments. It was also a part of OntAIRio, a coalition of groups that worked to put solving air pollution high on the political agenda during the 1999 Ontario election.

INTERNET RESOURCES

What other issues are being tackled by environmental groups in Canada? Find out by going to the following sites:

http://www.greenpeacecanada.org

Click on
- "Take Action"
- "Get Involved"

http://www.sierraclub.ca

Click on
- "About Us"
- "About Sierra Club of Canada"
- "Recent Postings"

RECAP

1. For what reasons do people join the types of groups described in this section?
2. Using specific examples, describe different ways the groups in this section organize their members and structure their operations.
3. Using specific examples, describe different ways the groups in this section affect their members' lives and the life of the wider community.

Section 9.4

Group Membership

Focus Questions

- How do social scientists explain the effects of group membership on behaviour?
- What are the main characteristics of Stockholm Syndrome?
- How do virtual communities compare to more traditional groups?

Key Concepts

informal group
collectivist
conformity
Stockholm Syndrome
field observation
virtual community

Belonging and Behaviour

To varying degrees, groups expect their members to think and act in certain ways. Think of some of the groups that you belong to—they might be based on academics, athletics, social life, or family life. What unique behaviours do you feel a particular school club might expect of you? How do those behaviours compare with your role on a sports team? If you join a community or church youth group, what new expectations might you face? How is your life as a family member distinct from your experience in these other groups?

Social scientists have recognized that belonging to a group affects behaviour. Their explanations for why this occurs differ according to whether their focus is anthropological, psychological, or sociological. We examine these different perspectives in this section.

The Anthropologist's Perspective

As we have seen throughout this book, many anthropological studies focus on pre-industrial cultures. This was especially true in the early years of the discipline. Groups in such cultures are **informal groups** rather than formal, secondary organizations (see Chapter 6, pages 159–161, for a description of informal justice systems in non-European cultures). Kinship relations usually determine how such a group is organized. The group's main function is to take care of the material needs of its individual members.

Since the group is so important for every individual's survival and well-being, it is not surprising that its members co-operate with it. This is especially true if the culture is isolated and does not have opportunities to trade with other cultures. Group members depend on each other and must work together to maintain the food supply and meet other needs. Individuals tend to have a **collectivist** outlook, placing the welfare of the community above their own interests. The analysis of these cultures highlights an important point. Our commitment to a group, and our level of co-operation with its demands, relates to how well and thoroughly the group meets our needs. This explains why primary groups (see page 282) affect our behaviour more strongly than secondary groups.

The Psychologist's Perspective

While the anthropological focus is often on primary kinship groups, many psychologists have studied the power of non-family groups on individual behaviour. In particular, they have studied **conformity**, which occurs when a person adjusts her or his thoughts, feelings, and behaviour to match the behaviour or standards of a group. How can we explain the power of a peer group or a cult to steer someone to new ways of thinking and acting? How does an individual manage the pressure and conflicts that a group can create?

In the twentieth century, we saw numerous examples of extreme conformity. They include war criminals who claimed no reponsibility for their actions because they were following the orders of their group leaders. Over 900 members of the People's Temple cult in Jonestown, Guyana, committed mass suicide in 1978 under orders from their leader Reverend Jim Jones. In 1993, eighty members of the Branch Davidian cult in Waco, Texas, chose to be burned alive rather than leave their compound. In 1994 and 1995, Solar Temple cult members in Canada, Switzerland, and France committed both murder and suicide. On a smaller scale, numerous psychological experiments have successfully triggered conformity in subjects. These studies have reached what may be a disturbing conclusion. It is possible to convince people in a group situation to commit acts that they know, or should know, are wrong.

The Milgram Conformity Experiment

Stanley Milgram wanted to create experimental conditions under which a subject would experience the pressure to conform. He thought up an ingenious but, some scientists claim, unethical experimental design.

In each trial, he misled an individual subject into thinking the experiment was to study the impact of punishment on learning. He asked the subject to play the role of "teacher." The two other participants were called the "learner" and the "experimenter." Both were actually colleagues planted to play their parts.

The learner was hooked up to what looked like an electrical box with wires coming out of it. Acting their parts, the learner expressed concern over his slight heart condition and the experimenter said that there was nothing to worry about. The experimenter took the teacher into another room and sat him or her at a desk with a series of switches. The switches were labelled with different levels of voltage, from 15 to 450 volts. The teacher was told to read a series of word pairs to the learner, and then to read back the first word of a pair. Each time the learner got the second word wrong, the teacher was told to activate one of the voltage switches to give the learner an electrical shock. The voltage switches were not electrically hooked up so no shock was actually given, but the teacher did not know this.

Classic Study

RESEARCHER:
Stanley Milgram, Psychologist

TIME:
1963

SUBJECT:
Individual Conformity to Group Behaviour

Each time the learner got a word wrong, the teacher was told to increase the level of shock. After a time, the learner began to scream in pain and ask for the experiment to be stopped. The learner claimed to be worried about the effect the shocks were having on his heart. The experimenter told the teacher to ignore these outbursts.

The switch labelled "450 volts" also had a notice alongside it saying "Danger. Extreme Shock." The experiment ended when the teacher either refused to continue or pressed the 450-volt switch. When the experiment ended, the teacher-subjects were told that they had not given any shocks at all.

How many of the subjects went all the way? That is, how many administered what they believed to be an extreme shock that only increased the apparent agony of the already screaming learner? Milgram's disturbing finding was that 63 per cent of the subjects were persuaded to go to this level.

Studies such as Milgram's show that humans can be persuaded to harm others (or themselves) in group situations. In the Milgram case, the key factor in persuading the subjects was that the subjects were not personally responsible for what happened. The subjects deferred to the authority of another member of the group (the experimenter).

A slightly different factor seems to operate in the case of mass suicide in cults. Psychologists suggest that the people involved are persuaded that their membership in the group takes priority over their personal safety.

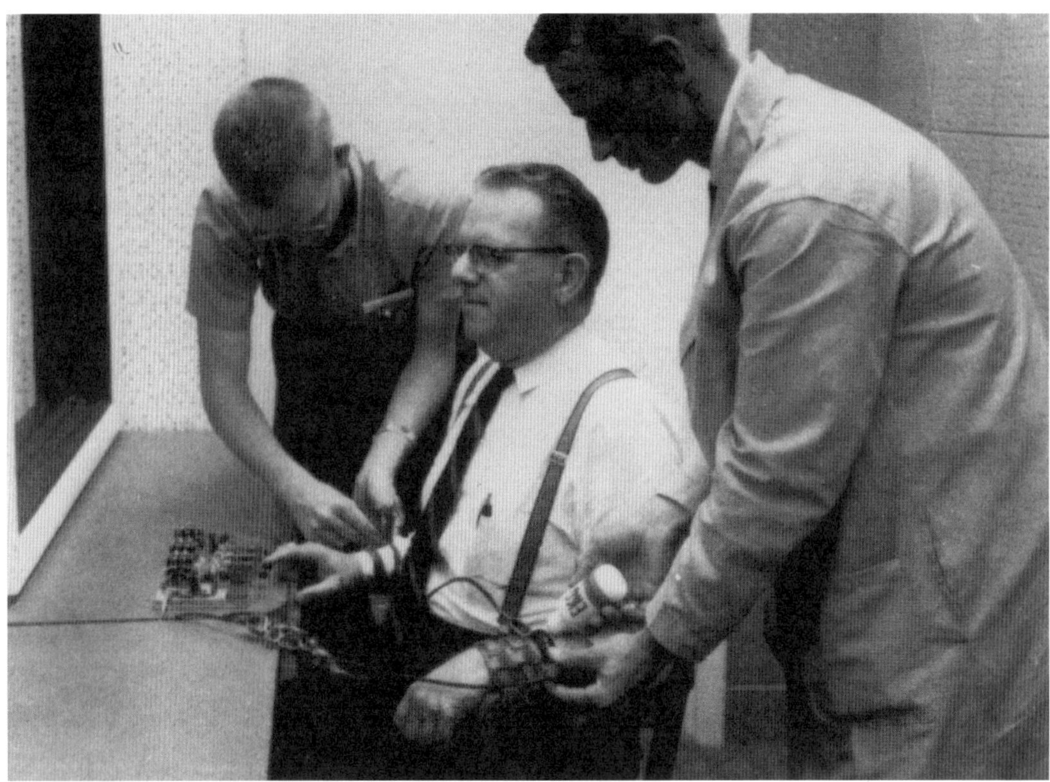

Figure 9.13 What did the Milgram experiment reveal about conformity in group situations? How might the results be explained?

The Sociologist's Perspective

One aspect of group membership studied by sociologists is how groups help form an individual's identity. This topic is very closely related to the topic of socialization. In other words, how does a group such as a family, a marriage, a friendship, a club, or a set of co-workers influence a person's sense of self?

Sociologists see primary social groups as behaviour models. Individuals pattern themselves after the members of their primary social groups in order to gain security and acceptance in society.

Secondary formal organizations do not play as integral a role in shaping identity as primary groups do. This is because secondary groups tend to be goal-oriented and therefore downplay personal relationships. But such organizations do tend to have established rules of acceptable behaviour that an individual member will follow. Examples of such rules were given in our analysis of Elaine Spira (see pages 277 to 279). In that analysis, we saw that a person looks to join organizations with rules that match aspects of the person's identity and personality. As a result, most people find security and work productively while conforming to group expectations.

When a person identifies too strongly with a group, there can be negative results. Members of "in-groups" can easily construct overly positive views of themselves and their group. When this happens, they see all others as outsiders, lacking in skills or personal worth. In some cases, this viewpoint becomes an excuse for provoking or humiliating those not part of the in-group. In extreme cases, it can lead to racist or sexist attitudes and behaviour.

The following case study on page 310 deals with this topic of identifying too strongly with a group. It highlights the great degree to which humans feel the need to belong, especially in stressful situations.

Figure 9.14 Racist organizations have had some success recruiting skinheads, a subculture of mostly young people with shaven or close-cropped hair worn as a symbol of anarchy, nonconformity, or racism.

Case Study: The Stockholm Syndrome

In 1973, a group of bank robbers in Stockholm, Sweden, held four hostages captive for six days after the robbery attempt failed. The hostages actively resisted rescue by police. In the aftermath, they refused to testify against their captors and raised money for the defence. One of the hostages, Kristin Enmark, even broke off her engagement and became romantically involved with (some reports claim engaged to) the captor Clark Olofsson during his jail term.

Social scientists sought to explain this bizarre behaviour. They concluded that the victims of these criminal actions identified with the perpetrators and therefore could not act against them. The phenomenon has since become known as the **Stockholm Syndrome**.

One of the most famous cases of the syndrome occurred in California in 1975. A group calling itself the Symbionese Liberation Army (SLA) kidnapped and tortured a young woman named Patty Hearst. Hearst was the heir to a vast fortune made in the newspaper business. After a few weeks in captivity, Hearst adopted the revolutionary name of Tania and joined the SLA. She even participated in armed bank robberies to obtain funds for its activities.

Figure 9.15 Two months after she was kidnapped by the SLA in 1974, Patty Hearst was photographed carrying a gun during an SLA holdup of a San Francisco bank.

How does this feeling of identification with an essentially hostile and deadly group come about? Social scientists say the process begins after about three or four days in captivity. The victim has become convinced that escape is impossible and has been threatened with death. Crucially, the victim has also been shown acts of kindness by the captor. As a result of this mix of factors, the victim becomes committed to trying to keep the captor happy. Identification with the captor is the final outcome.

Many victims of domestic violence undergo a similar set of experiences and may also end up identifying with their abusers. In this case, the phenomenon is called Battered Spouse Syndrome. Observers know that the syndrome has taken hold when victims resist the attempts of police and social workers to help them.

Social scientists stress that four conditions must exist in order for Stockholm Syndrome to occur:

- The captor must threaten to kill the victim and must be seen by the victim as having the ability to do so.
- The victim must not have any hope of escape.
- The victim must be isolated from outsiders, so that only the viewpoint of the captor is available to the victim.

- The victim must believe that the captor has shown, and will continue to show, occasional kindness toward the victim.

The powerful bond between victim and perpetrator created by the Stockholm Syndrome is evidence of how strongly humans are motivated to belong to groups, especially when feeling threatened.

---

1. The Stockholm victim Kristin Enmark eventually felt romantic love toward her captor Clark Olofsson. Earlier in this book, romantic love was analyzed as made up of passion and intimacy (see page 169). How do you think the Stockholm Syndrome might produce what seem to be feelings of passion and intimacy?
2. In what ways are the Stockholm and Battered Spouse Syndromes similar?
3. Patty Hearst was sentenced to seven years in prison for her participation in a bank robbery. (After serving two years, her sentence was commuted.) Devise a list of questions you would have asked Hearst at her trial to determine if she was truly a victim of Stockholm Syndrome.

Skill Development: Designing a Field Observation

Field observation is one of the methods sociologists use to gather data about people's behaviour in groups. In field observation, the investigator observes one or more subjects in their own environment. Like surveys (see pages 175–177), field observations are done to prove or disprove specific hypotheses about people's behaviour. It is critical that field observations respect their subjects' right to privacy. Therefore, they are conducted in public places where subjects do not engage in private actions.

Let's take an example. Suppose you wanted to find out the following as it applies to high-school students:

- How does gender influence how comfortable students are with each other in group interactions?

Step 1

First, formulate a hypothesis based on the question you want answered. As with surveys, the hypothesis must be specific. It should identify the key target groups you need to observe at the same time that it identifies the prediction you need to prove or disprove. In this case, you might formulate a hypothesis like the one below.

- Three or four all-female teenagers in a group are more comfortable with each other than the same number of all-male or mixed-sex teenagers.

Step 2

Identify the specific, measurable behaviours that you will record as you observe. In this case, what specific, measurable behaviours will you cite as evidence of how "comfortable" students are?

- Examples of "comfort" indicators:
  1. Subjects sit or stand close to each other.
  2. Subjects' facial expressions are mostly friendly.
  3. Subjects' physical contact is mostly friendly.
  4. Subjects' speak in mostly low voices instead of shouting.

Once you have identified the specific factors you want to record, you should decide on a time limit for your observation. Within this time limit, you will observe and record relevant aspects of your subjects' distance from each other, facial expressions, physical contact, and voices.

Step 3

Design a record sheet that will allow you to measure by check marks or simple numbers exactly how often the specific behaviour occurs during the time limit. The sample pages on page 313 show a possible design for such a record sheet. Note that you are to circle one option whenever options are listed in a row separated by slashes. The "Distance" section is designed for you to first put a check mark in the box corresponding to the targets' position at the beginning of the observation. Each time the distance changes during the observation because a subject moves, add an additional check mark. The "Observable Behaviours" section is designed for you to check each time an option is observed. In the "Other observations" section, record any additional information that might affect behaviour. For example, if the observation occurs outside, weather conditions might be a factor and should be recorded.

Step 4

Conduct your observations. Follow these three guidelines:

1. Choose locations that allow you to observe *discreetly* (without being too obvious).
2. Do not discuss your observations.
3. Try to make the same number of observations for each target group. For example, if you observe twenty-five all-female groups, observe twenty-five all-male and twenty-five mixed-sex groups.

Follow-Up

1. a) Formulate a hypothesis that you think could be proved by field observation within a high-school setting.
   b) Write out your hypothesis, making sure that it is measurable. Also make sure that your hypothesis identifies the key target group(s) you need to observe.
2. a) Identify when, where, and how you would conduct your observation.
   b) Identify the measurable behaviours you would focus on.
   c) How would you ensure that your observation was both discreet yet close enough to record behaviours?
3. a) Design a Field Observation Sheet similar to the one in the sample pages.
   b) Ask a partner to evaluate whether or not your design is likely to give you measurable results. Make modifications as necessary.

Field Observation Sheet

Observer(s): ______________ **Timer:** ______________

____

Location: ______________________________

Time: ______________ a.m./p.m.

Length of observation: ________ min

Group details: All-female/All-male /Mixed-sex

(Note: Each group must consist of 3 or 4 teenagers.)

Distance of group members from one another:

Less than 30 cm	30–60 cm	60cm–1m	More than 1m

Observable Behaviours:

Facial expression	Friendly	Passive	Aggressive
Touch	Friendly	Warning	Aggressive
Voice	Whisper	Talk	Shout

Other observations: ______________________________

____

Groups and Communities

In early human history, the concept of "group" was virtually identical to the concept of "community." That is, a kinship group served as its own community, moving from place to place hunting and gathering food for all. Society became more complex with the introduction of agriculture and the creation of food surpluses (see Chapter 7, page 198 for more detail). "Group" became distinct from "community" as permanent settlements were established and grew. Secondary organizations also became distinct from primary groups. For example, guilds of workers specializing in particular handicrafts formed.

Prior to the Information Age (see pages 201–202), secondary groups and organizations existed only in the context of their local community. For example, early feminist groups such as the Girls' Friendly Society formed as chapters to help single immigrant women in the immediate area. As such, they could potentially have a very positive impact on the community. This potential continues today with groups such as Walpole Island First Nation. Its initiatives have made the community safer and more environmentally sound.

Advances in communication technology allow advocacy groups and humanitarian organizations to have international impact. For example, Free the Children, originating in Toronto, has improved and even saved the lives of children in countries such as Pakistan and India. But whether an organization focuses its efforts on the local community or a distant place of need, its members have traditionally been organized in local groups or chapters. The local chapter has functioned through face-to-face meetings of its members.

The Internet revolutionized the concept of group by promoting the creation of **virtual communities**. A virtual community is a group of people with a particular shared interest linked to each other via their keyboards and modems. There is no physical contact between members. This aspect of virtual communities makes them dramatically different from traditional groups, which could not exist without a physical meeting space in a specific community.

People form virtual communities for all the same reasons that they join traditional groups. As a result, there is as wide a variety of virtual communities as there are types of traditional groups. By logging on to the Internet, you can join a feminist group, a computer group, an abuse recovery group, a singles group, and any kind of hobby group.

Figure 9.16 The heroine of the movie The Net *(1995) is a lonely telecommuter who never leaves her house. She orders pizza by modem and socializes only via computer chat rooms. How realistic do you find this portrayal of people who shun the outside world in favour of their computers? Explain.*

ASK THE EXPERT

Dr. Robert J. Brym, professor of sociology at the University of Toronto

Does the Internet isolate people socially or can it promote intimacy?

Some people believe that if you use the Internet intensively, you become isolated from people in the real world. However, recent research dispels this myth. A few years ago, a major telephone company created an experimental community near Toronto in which all houses had free, high-speed Internet access. Sociologists found that Internet use strengthened social relations and community involvement (Hampton and Wellman, 2000, 194–208). Recently, sociologists investigated nearly 6600 Canadians who use online dating services. They found that people who meet and select dates online are about as socially active as anyone else, often visiting friends and family, belonging to many clubs, and frequently going out socially. They also found that 4 per cent of online daters met someone online whom they eventually married, 27 per cent met at least one person they regarded as a "partner," and 60 per cent formed at least one long-term friendship. So the Internet does not necessarily make people socially isolated, and it can promote intimacy (Brym and Lenton, 2001).

Virtual communities have their critics. Concerned observers charge that some people become so obsessed with their Internet interest or "chat" group that they have broken away from meaningful, face-to-face contact with other humans. Others are critical of the anonymity that virtual communities allow their members. If you never meet the other members of your support group, can any truly intimate bonds form? Observers will be watching carefully over the next several years to evaluate whether virtual communities are a positive development in the history of groups and communities.

RECAP

1. What different aspects of group membership are focused on by anthropologists, psychologists, and sociologists?
2. What conclusions about human behaviour can be drawn from the Milgram experiment?
3. What are the advantages and disadvantages of membership in virtual communities?

Activities

Show your knowledge

1. Create a New Vocabulary glossary of the terms and phrases you learned in this chapter.
   a) Record the definition of each term.
   b) Use these terms to create four questions to ask a classmate. Make each question more difficult than the last. Follow the model used for these activities ("Show your knowledge," "Practise your thinking skills," "Communicate your ideas," "Apply your knowledge").
2. Why is large group membership important if we want to accomplish larger goals?
3. What are *(a)* the major features of and *(b)* the differences between non-bureaucratic organizations and bureaucracies?
4. Summarize the effects of women's organizations of both the nineteenth and twentieth centuries on their local communities and on Canada as a whole.
5. Why did the International Joint Commission praise Walpole Island First Nation? Include specific examples in your answer.
6. What rights and obligations do Aboriginal self-government agreements confer?
7. What are the goals and methods of
   a) Médecins Sans Frontières
   b) Canada World Youth
   c) Free the Children?
8. What are the goals and methods of
   a) the Council of Canadians
   b) the Canadian Centre for Policy Alternatives
   c) Bread Not Circuses
   d) the Ontario Coalition Against Poverty
   e) Greenpeace Canada?

Practise your thinking skills

9. Think of a group that you have joined in the past. Read the three explanations of why Elaine Spira joined her school's soccer team. Which of the explanations most closely resembles your reasons for joining the group? Why?

10. Review the "Point and Counterpoint" feature about LEAF and REAL Women (page 296). Which group's position do you think is closer to that of
    a) the majority of students in your school
    b) the majority of people in your community?

    Explain your answers.
11. Examine the operations of your school.
    a) From your viewpoint, which of of Weber's characteristics of bureaucracy apply? Give examples.
    b) Ask five teachers for their viewpoints on the question in *(a)*. How do their viewpoints compare to yours? What conclusions can you draw from this comparison?
12. With regard to poverty issues, do you think the militant approach of the Ontario Coalition Against Poverty or the more moderate approach of Bread Not Circuses is more likely to succeed? Why?

Communicate your ideas

13. Imagine your class is organizing a one-day conference on women's issues in Canada. Assume you have a large budget to fund the conference and its speakers.
    a) Design a brochure for the conference. It should include
       - the titles of two large-session speeches for all delegates
       - a list of five smaller workshop titles from which delegates choose two to attend
    b) Research and present your findings on the people who might be qualified to deliver these sessions.
14. Visit the Web sites of one of the following organizations:
    - Assembly of First Nations http://afn.ca/AboutAFN/about_afn.htm
    - Council of Canadians http://www.canadians.org
    - Canadian Centre for Policy Alternatives http://www.policyalternatives.ca
    - Bread Not Circuses http://breadnotcircuses.org
    - Ontario Coalition Against Poverty http://www.tao.ca/~ocap.

    Find and present information on the organization's
    a) work
    b) goals
    c) membership
    d) structure

Activities

Activities

15. With a partner, create a "Point and Counterpoint" discussion on whether a militant or moderate approach is most effective in winning support for a cause. Compare your "Point and Counterpoint" with that of another pair of students. What similarities and differences do you note?
16. Create a poster in support of achieving "Sweatfree Status" for your school. Be sure to include a catchy slogan and visuals. Present your poster to the class. How effective do you think your poster would be? Why?
17. As a class, search the Internet for groups and organizations in Canada similar to the ones described in this chapter. Find and present information about the organizations. Which organizations appear to be most successful? Why?

Apply your knowledge

18. Find information on a formal organization that operates in your community.
    a) Is it bureaucratic or non-bureaucratic? Provide evidence.
    b) What are its goals?
    c) What types of people join it?
    d) Is it militant or moderate? Explain.
    e) How successful has it been? How successful will it continue to be? Why?
19. Select one of the advocacy groups profiled in this chapter.
    a) Has it been successful in your community or region?
    b) Why or why not?
20. Research one of the following examples of a virtual community:
    a) a feminist group
    b) a computer group
    c) a recovery group
    d) a self-help group
    e) a hobby group

    How would this community compare to its traditional counterpart (that is, a group with face-to-face meetings)? (Caution: Some virtual community sites have pornographic, racist, and/or violent content. If you accidentally come across such a site in your research, quickly move on to another.)

Chapter 10

Conflict and Cohesion

Overview of Chapter

10.1 Aggression and Violence in Society
10.2 Prejudice, Discrimination, and Exclusion
10.3 Discrimination Against Aboriginal Peoples
10.4 Building Cohesion in Society

Learning Expectations

By the end of this chapter, you will be able to

- identify, compare, and analyze different social science perspectives on conflict and cohesion
- demonstrate an understanding of discrimination and exclusion in social relationships
- analyze examples of social or institutional discrimination and exclusion that existed in earlier historical periods

Open for Debate

Gender Wars

The folks at Wilfrid Laurier University have decided it's time to snag a woman, and no one's going to stop them. When *University Affairs* rolls off the presses this week, the new issue will publish the first public ad for what is already the most infamous unfilled spot in Canadian academia: a tenure-stream position in the psychology department open only to women. The folks at the school are certain they are doing the right thing. At the moment, there are only four female faculty members in a department of 22, teaching an undergraduate group that is 76 per cent female. "Other institutions have handled this dilemma in a covert fashion," says Angelo Santi, chair of the department. "We decided not to be covert."

Clive Seligman disagrees with Laurier's action. Last month, Seligman, a 52-year-old professor of psychology at the University of Western Ontario, filed a complaint with the Ontario Human Rights Commission, challenging what he calls Laurier's exclusionary hiring. "It's not a human right to have a teacher of the same sex," argues Seligman. "But why this persistent belief that men like to hire men? Why are we so obsessed?"

Nancy Hopkins, a prominent molecular biologist at the Massachusetts Insititute of Technology, is also no fan of the Laurier approach. "It's an insult to excellence," says Hopkins. "There are great women out there." Of course there are—and more than ever before. In the past 15 years, women have accounted for 80 per cent of the enrolment growth in Canadian universities. When it comes to earning doctorates in psychology—the degree Laurier is looking for—Canadian women have outstripped men since 1986. But if women earn almost twice as many doctorates in psychology on an annual basis, why is it that of the 26 new appointments in psychology in Canada in 1996, only nine went to women? "Systems," says Hopkins, "tend to reinforce themselves."

Adapted from: Dowsett Johnston, Ann. 1999. "Welcome to the Gender Wars." *Maclean's*. 27 September 1999.

Think About It

- Why do you think so few women are appointed to positions as professors in Canada?
- If women truly are under-represented in faculty positions across the country, why did the Laurier employment ad stir up so much controversy?
- When steps are taken to rectify past or present discrimination, is this "reverse discrimination"? Provide a detailed explanation.

Section 10.1

Aggression and Violence in Society

Focus Questions

- According to social scientists, what are the root causes of aggression and violence?
- What are the costs to our society of this type of conflict?
- How can social scientific studies help us reduce aggression and violence?

Key Concepts

conflict
cohesion
alienation
dehumanization
anonymity
diffusion of responsibility
ghetto
sanctioned violence
modelling theory
frustration-aggression theory

Conflict: Causes and Outcomes

Living with others in a complex society presents a great many challenges. Every day you come into contact with people who have different opinions, interests, and values than you do. You also interact with people of different races, ethnic backgrounds, social classes, and genders. While these differences are what make life so interesting and fascinating, they can become a source of **conflict**. Whether or not they do depends on your personality and your communication skills. Although the word "conflict" is often used to describe a verbal or physical fight, it also applies to situations that create negative feelings. When conflicts are unresolved, they can result in aggression and violence against others, or discrimination toward and exclusion of others. The costs of these unresolved conflicts to us as individuals, and to our society, are considerable. The good news is that while we will never be free of conflict in society, there are certain factors that can help our society to have more **cohesion**. In other words, there are ways to work more closely together and to solve most of the problems that arise.

High Costs

Once a person has become the victim of violence, her or his life is changed forever. The physical and emotional scars may result in a victim being unable to complete school or function effectively at work. As well, the victim may have trouble trusting people. Some victims find it hard to leave their home after the incident.

Family members and friends of victims and offenders are also impacted by violent crime. Many family members blame themselves for not being able to protect the person who was victimized. They have to deal with grief and depression after the violent episode. Sometimes feelings of anger and rage simply do not go away, leading some to take the law into their own hands and commit an act of violence themselves. The impact on the family of the offender includes feelings of guilt, humiliation, and anger.

ASK THE EXPERT

Paul McKenna, president of Public Innovation, Inc. (a consulting service to police organizations)

In what ways does our society encourage conflict over cohesion?

Our society encourages conflict over cohesion, first of all, in an adversarial criminal justice system that pits the prosecution against the defendant. Within that system, the accused person is essentially "attacked" by the state and must mount a defence that will allow the accused to "win" against the prosecution.

Secondly, amateur and professional sporting events celebrate direct struggle between individuals and teams as they engage in formalized conflict with one another for victory.

Thirdly, our capitalist economy is grounded in conflict, with people competing with one another to sell products, services, and labour in a global marketplace.

Fourthly, our democratic form of government encourages conflict over cohesion. The physical layout of the Canadian Parliament in Ottawa is designed so that the government party faces its "opposition." "Question Period" is often aggressive, pitting politicians against one another. The political party system is similarly rooted in conflict. During elections, candidates compete by running against one another for votes.

It is only very slowly that a spirit of cohesion is beginning to be valued in human affairs.

In addition to these personal costs, aggressive and violent acts result in huge costs to our society. From a financial perspective, victims of violence require medical and counselling services. They miss time from work and sometimes are not able to return to their former level of productivity for a long period of time, if at all. Arresting, prosecuting, and incarcerating offenders are also very expensive. Figure 10.1 summarizes estimates of some of the economic costs of violence against women in just one Canadian province.

Estimates of Some Costs of Violence Against Women in British Columbia, 1996

	$ millions
Policing	47
Corrections	39
Criminal injury compensation	17
Victim assistance program	3
Counselling for women	5
Aboriginal programs	3
Mental health care (partial)	18
Alcohol and drug treatment	7
Income assistance	161
Transition houses	25
Sexual and woman assault centres	2
Women's loss of work time	54
Children who witness violence	2
Treatment programs for assaultive men	2
Total identified costs	**385**
Emergency medical care costs	unknown but large
Intergenerational costs (e.g., behavioural problems of victims' children at home and school)	unknown but large

Source: Kerr and McLean, 1996.

Figure 10.1 Which costs would you label as directly associated with a violent act? Which costs would you label as indirectly associated? Do you think certain costs take priority over others? Explain.

Even beyond these financial costs is the emotional drain that aggression and violence create throughout society. Crime reports in the newspapers make us fearful for our own safety, even if crime is not on the rise. If we are afraid to go out at night, or are uncomfortable being home alone, then we, too, have been affected by violence and aggression.

An Anthropological Analysis

Anthropologists believe that aggression and violence are behaviors that are created by the culture in which an individual lives. Aggression and violence exist in Canada, therefore, because our culture teaches people to act aggressively and violently. By living among people with cultures quite different from our own, anthropologists observe how other cultures encourage people to relate to one another. In the process, they have discovered some cultures that are free from aggression and violence.

Classic Study

RESEARCHER: **Robert Levy, Anthropologist**

TIME: **1969, 1973**

SUBJECT: **Non-Violence in Tahitian Culture**

The Non-Violent Tahitians

For two years in the early 1960s, anthropologist Robert Levy, of the University of North Carolina, lived among the Tahitians in the South Pacific. Levy found Tahitian culture to literally be free from violence. He identified three main factors that contributed to this non-violence. First, Tahitians co-operated and shared with one another, rather than competing with one another. Land ownership was shared, and food and material goods were distributed freely so that the basic needs of all members were met. As a result, Tahitians did not experience many of the economic frustrations found in other societies, including our own.

Another factor he identified was the fact that child-rearing responsibilities were shared by the entire community, rather than falling to individual parents alone. In fact, mothers who were not ready or able to care for their babies were encouraged to have them adopted by another family who had greater resources to raise the child. The acceptance of adoption meant that parents would not become unduly burdened with having large families. They would, therefore, be able to do a better job of raising the children they keep.

An important factor that contributed to this non-violent culture was the fact that children were socialized to be non-aggressive. Children were taught that hostile or aggressive behaviour was shameful. Hostile or aggressive behaviour received little sympathy from adults. If a child acted in a hostile manner, the parents would not intervene until the child's behaviour backfired. For example, adults would not intervene if they saw a child taunting an animal. If the animal bit the child, then the adult would step in and explain to the child that it was his or her behaviour that caused the animal to bite. In this way, children learned not to express hostility. They grew up wanting to be accepted by the important adults around them. In order to be considered mature and competent by the adults in their family and community, they avoided aggressive and violent behaviour.

REMARKABLE PEOPLE

Elliot Leyton

Canadian anthropologist Elliot Leyton rocked the law enforcement and criminology communities when his book *Hunting Humans: The Rise of the Modern Multiple Murderer* appeared (revised edition, 1995). In this book, he asserted that mass murderers and serial killers are not freaks. Rather, they are the natural outcome of a culture that portrays violence as both exciting and "manly." Violence is further portrayed as a legitimate response to frustration. For police and academics struggling to understand these human predators, Leyton's thesis represented a breakthrough in thinking. As a result, Leyton became an acknowledged expert in the field. "He gave us a whole new way of identifying and interpreting criminal behaviour," explains Sergeant John House, head of the Royal Newfoundland Constabulary's newly formed criminal behaviour analysis unit. Up to this point, most research was aimed at discovering what was wrong with the brains of serial killers. Leyton has pushed investigators to focus instead on why and how society promotes feelings of **alienation** that can result in desperate acts of violence.

Born in Leader, Saskatchewan, Leyton has taught at Queen's University in Belfast, the University of Toronto, and now is a tenured professor at Memorial University in Newfoundland. Not surprisingly, his third-year anthropology course, War and Aggression, is very popular. In addition to *Hunting Humans* he is the author of *Sole Survivor: Children Who Murder Their Families*, now in its fourth printing in Europe, and *Men of Blood: Homicide in Modern England.* The walls of his study display covers from the various editions of his books, which have been published in Canada, the United States and Britain and will soon come out in Japan. They also display plaques from the South Yorkshire (UK) police and the Royal Newfoundland Constabulary, thanking him for assistance he has provided. Leyton is a member of an informal, international working group on serial sexual assaults and homicides that includes members of the FBI, Scotland Yard and Interpol. The group meets yearly to develop new techniques for profiling criminals. However, Leyton prefers not to become directly involved in investigations himself.

Leyton spends a great deal of time doing media interviews—about 150 a year, by his count. "There is a natural human fascination in acts that are regarded as appallingly evil," he explained. "I think that is very healthy in that it allows people to redefine for themselves the difference between good and evil." Leyton is horrified by what he sees as our culture's portrayal of these "monsters" as celebrities. He walked out of *The Silence of the Lambs* and refused to see Oliver Stone's bloodsoaked satire *Natural Born Killers*. In describing the killers he studies, Leyton says, "These are not supermen. These are losers and goons—recreational killers—who are so socially incompetent that the only way they can relate to other human beings is to humiliate or destroy them."

Adapted from: DeMont, John. 1994. "Murder, He Wrote: A Newfoundland Anthropologist Has Become an Expert on Serial Killers." *Maclean's*. 31 November 1994.

---

1. According to Professor Layton, what cultural factors are associated with the creation of serial killers?
2. How does this viewpoint differ from traditional approaches to this issue?
3. Why is he "horrified" by the way our culture views serial killers?

A Sociological Analysis

Sociologists believe that aggression and violence are the result of the interaction between individuals and certain factors in society. Sociologists examine the effect that variables such as living conditions, class, and power have on the behaviour of individuals.

Classic Study

RESEARCHERS:
Several

TIME:
1964

SUBJECT:
Apathy/The Genovese Syndrome

The Murder of Kitty Genovese

It was just after 3:00 a.m. on 13 March 1964 when twenty-eight-year-old Kitty Genovese returned from her job as a manager at a bar. She parked her car on the road about a block away from her apartment building. She got out of the car, locked it, and began the 30-m walk toward her apartment. She spotted a man standing along her route, and, presumably afraid, she changed her course and headed in the opposite direction where there was a police call box. The man overtook her and grabbed her, and she began screaming. Residents of nearby apartment houses turned on their lights and threw open their windows. Witnesses reported that Kitty screamed, "Oh, my God, he stabbed me! Please help me!" A man in a window shouted, "Let that girl alone," and the attacker walked away. The apartment lights went out and the witnesses slammed their windows shut. Kitty staggered toward her apartment, but the attacker returned and stabbed her again. Again Kitty screamed loudly, this time shouting, "I'm dying!" The apartment windows facing the street opened again, and the attacker got into a car and drove away. Kitty dragged herself inside the front door of an apartment house at 8262 Austin Street. Her attacker returned once again and followed the trail of her blood into the apartment lobby. He found her sprawled on the floor, still breathing, and stabbed her again. This time he killed her.

It was not until 3:50 that morning, approximately forty-five minutes after Kitty's first screams were heard, that a neighbour called police. Officers arrived two minutes later and found the body. They identified the victim as Catherine Genovese, known to her friends and neighbours as Kitty. Detectives investigating Genovese's murder discovered that no fewer than thirty-eight of her neighbours had witnessed at least one of her killer's three attacks but had neither come to her aid nor called the police. The one call made to the police came after Genovese was already dead. Assistant Chief Inspector Frederick Lussen, commander of Queens detectives, said that nothing in his twenty-five years of police work had shocked him so much as the apathy encountered on the Genovese murder. "As we have reconstructed the crime, the assailant had three chances to kill this woman during a thirty-five minute period," Lussen said. "If we had been called when he first attacked, this woman might not be dead now."

The fact that no one responded to Kitty's cries for help outraged the police and the public. The case became symbolic of the fact that many Americans had become too indifferent, too frightened, too alienated, or too self-absorbed to get involved in helping another human being in dire trouble. The term "Genovese syndrome" was coined to describe the apathy that had settled on America.

The Process of Dehumanization

Following Kitty Genovese's murder, a number of sociologists began studying the conditions in urban centres that contribute to aggression and violence in society. A large body of research on the process of **dehumanization** developed. According to sociologists, dehumanization is a process in which people come to see each other no longer as human beings but as simple objects. Once we no longer see someone as human, it is easier to act cruelly toward him or her. Part of the reason dehumanization occurs in cities is because they are large and overpopulated. In a large, crowded city, people lose their sense of identity and begin to feel like one of the crowd. This feeling of **anonymity**, a sense that one is faceless and nameless, tends to make people more likely to engage in violence, or at least to tolerate it. As well, we are less likely to help someone we do not know and identify with, so if we are surrounded by strangers in cities, we are less likely to take action on their behalf.

The other major finding that came out of the sociological research following Kitty Genovese's murder was the concept of **diffusion of responsibility**. Researchers found that if several people are present at an emergency, individuals tend not to feel that it is their responsibility to take any action to help. That is, if a number of people witness a crime, individuals are *less likely* to take action to stop the crime, apparently because they believe that someone else will do it. Each individual feels less responsible for taking action. Conversely, if you know you are the only one who is witnessing an assault at school, for example, you are more likely to take action to either protect the victim or make sure that the proper person is punished.

Does Dehumanization Occur in Canada?

As Canadians, we pride ourselves on the fact that our country is relatively safe. In particular, the lack of violent crime in Canada is one of the qualities many Canadians believe make their country better than the United States. Would Canadians have intervened to help Kitty Genovese? Or are the same dehumanization factors at play in our large cities? Sociologist Marc Ouimet, from Concordia University, conducted a comparative analysis of crime rates in Canadian and American cities. Ouimet was able to confirm that there definitely is more crime per capita in large

Figure 10.2 What conditions in urban centres contribute to aggression and violence in society?

cities than in small ones and that, therefore, crime rates are positively correlated with city size. Ouimet was also able to demonstrate that Canada has fewer murders than the United States and that large Canadian cities are less dangerous than American ones. The study concluded that many factors contribute to Canada's safer cities.

One main factor involves the administration of social services. Compared to Canada, the United States has passed on more responsibility to local districts and communities for the administration of services. When day care, mental health, nutrition, and other programs are delegated to local governments, poor people are pressured to group together within the limits of a central city to get access to these services. This leads to the formation of **ghettos**, which in turn leads to higher levels of violence in central cities. In contrast, in Canada, the responsibility for administration of services traditionally remained more exclusively with the federal and provincial governments. As a result, ghettos and ghetto-related violence have not been widespread in Canadian cities.

Figure 10.3 How do some sociologists explain high levels of violence in some US cities?

There is another closely related factors that helps explain Canada's safer cities. Many American cities have traditionally grouped welfare recipients in specific areas of housing projects. These projects have often been made up of high-rise buildings in which crime can run rampant. This practice has proven so disastrous that many of the housing projects built in the 1970s have been closed. In contrast, welfare apartments in Canadian jurisdictions are generally dispersed across a wider range of the city's territory.

These contrasts reveal that Canadian cities are in good shape—for now. Dr. Ouimet points out, however, that despite the relative safety of cities, Canadians' fear of crime is on the increase. This fear may actually lead to an increase in crime if wealthier Canadians choose to leave central cities for the perceived greater safety of the suburbs. Such a migration pattern could transform Canadian central cities into ghettos. As well, if fear keeps people from walking the streets of central cities, there will be more opportunities for criminals to isolate victims. At the same time, there will be fewer potential witnesses of crime. The end result of fewer people on the street is thus a greater crime rate—making Canadian cities almost identical to their American counterparts.

POINT AND COUNTERPOINT

Do Gun Control Laws Decrease Violence?

Many Canadians link a higher American crime rate to the role that guns play in American culture. For example, the US Constitution guarantees the "right to bear arms"; Canada, on the other hand, has very strict gun-control laws. In the United States, there are 230 million guns in a population of 270 million; these guns kill 13.7 out of every 100 000 people each year. In contrast, in Canada, there are 7 million guns in a population of 30 million. These guns kill 3.8 out of every 100 000 people each year. The interpretation of these statistics is hotly debated. Is the availability of guns a key factor in crime rates? Does restricting access to guns decrease crime rates? Where do you stand?

Those who oppose gun control commonly make statements such as:

- "Guns do not kill people; people kill people."
- "Restricting access to guns will not prevent criminals from getting the weapons they want."
- "Violent movies and video games have far more influence on criminal behaviour than guns do. We should restrict access to these influences rather than to guns."
- "Guns are needed for protection. It is a fact of life that violent criminals exist. It is also a fact of life that police cannot protect all people at all times. If you are a law-abiding citizen, being allowed a gun is only fair."
- "By arming themselves, homeowners make criminals think twice before breaking into homes. This automatically leads to a decrease in crimes."

Those in favour of gun control commonly make statements such as:

- "You cannot shoot people without a gun."
- "Guns give the holder an enhanced sense of power and a false sense of security. This can make potentially violent people violent."
- "Our culture's violent movies and video games are not weapons and do not kill. Guns, on the other hand, are weapons and make it possible to kill on a large scale."
- "A person in a murderous rage can kill instantly with a gun. Without a gun, killing someone is much more time-consuming and difficult. In the time it takes, an outraged person has a chance to cool off, and there is a chance for others to intervene."
- "Laws restricting guns make it harder for people to locate and purchase guns. This automatically reduces the rate of gun-related violent acts."

1. Do you think a cultural difference between the United States and Canada is the reason for different death rates from firearms? Explain.
2. Rank the ten statements above from most to least valid, in your opinion. Explain your choice of most valid.
3. Add at least one argument (in the form of a statement) to both the "Point" and "Counterpoint" lists.

Do Competitive Sports Promote Violence?

Hockey fans and critics alike were horrified on 21 February 2000. During an NHL game, Boston Bruins defenceman Marty McSorley swung his stick like a baseball bat at the head of Vancouver Canucks forward Donald Brashear. For hockey critics, the deliberate attack, which occurred when Brashear's back was turned, epitomized everything that is wrong with hockey. The attack even had fans shaking their heads in wonder. Kevin Allen, a writer with *USA Today*, said that when McSorley swung his stick, he wounded the National Hockey League as severely as he did Brashear.

It seems that Kevin Allen's prediction was correct. A CTV poll conducted on 4 April 2000 showed that 68 per cent of Canadians agreed that criminal charges should be laid against McSorley. Seventy-one per cent said that they felt the game has become too violent and that new rules are necessary to get the game under control. Furthermore, fully three out of four Canadians—75 per cent—said that that there is more unnecessary violence in the game than ever before. How did this happen to Canada's national sport?

A growing number of people are starting to speak out about the high cost of competitive sports. Such sports pit players against each other and promote the value of winning at any cost. The result is a high level of **sanctioned violence**—in other words, violence that is encouraged and goes unpunished, even though it would not be permitted outside the playing field or arena. Is such violence damaging to our society?

Bruce Kidd is a professor at the University of Toronto, a former gold medalist at the 1962 Commonwealth Games, and a former member of Canada's Olympic team. He believes that sports in Canadian society are viewed in the same way as military battles. He notes that military metaphors are often used in sports; for example, quarterbacks "throw the long bomb," and coaches encourage their teams to "whip," "punish," and "savage" their opponents. Kidd recalls being encouraged by his softball coach to "take out" members of the opposing team while rounding the bases. In fact, this team of nine-year-olds were offered ten dollars for every bag they "took." Kidd believes that such attitudes can have a harmful effect on young minds. When sports are viewed as battles, the opponents become the enemy. Victory can come only at the expense of others.

Figure 10.4 After being convicted of assault with a weapon, Marty McSorley was given a conditional discharge. Do you think McSorley should have served time in jail? Explain.

This harmful effect is not limited to young players and fans. Professional athletes can also be negatively affected by the culture of competitive sports. Michael Farber of *Sports Illustrated* feels that today's professional hockey culture puts players in an impossible position. If a player is taunted by an opponent or has suffered an injury, it is almost impossible to back down from the situation and ask for assistance. Montreal Canadiens assistant coach Dave King says, "Playing hurt is a status thing. It's the simplest way of getting the respect of teammates, opponents, and coaches. As coaches, we're always judging players. After a hard check or a big-time slash, is he the kind of guy who gives up on the play and heads to the bench, or does he stay with the play? After a guy blocks a shot, does he lie on the ice or get back up? Pain is one of hockey's measuring sticks."

Those players that fail the "toughness test" are frowned on by others. Members of the Montreal Canadiens questioned the decision of Vladimir Malakhov to miss a playoff game because of neck pain. Fans and teammates alike questioned Buffalo Sabres goalie Dominik Hasek when he took himself out of a playoff game after suffering a knee injury. And some coaches put considerable pressure on players they believe are not acting tough enough. For example, in a 1989 playoff game, Montreal Canadiens coach Pat Burns refused to let trainer Gaetan Lefebvre onto the ice to attend to a downed player. Burns believed the player was exaggerating his injuries.

Fans make up yet another group negatively affected by aggression and violence in sports. Fans "turned on" by aggression will idolize certain players, not because of how many points they earn in a season, but because of how many penalty minutes they get. Some critics believe that certain fans who see aggression and violence sanctioned are more likely to repeat the behaviour themselves.

The environment in which competitive sports are played can make an aggressive atmosphere worse. Excited fans packed into a noisy arena become physiologically aroused. Heart rate increases, blood pressure rises, and adrenalin pumps through the body. This adrenalin boost makes people more emotional. Combine this with a competitive spirit, a feeling of anonymity, and, in some cases, consumption of alcohol, and a dangerous breeding ground for violence is created.

RECAP

1. In what ways do the living conditions in large cities contribute to aggression and violence in society?
2. According to Marc Ouimet, how might Canadians' fear of violence lead to degradation or decline in Canadian cities?
3. In what ways do competitive sports encourage conflict between individuals?

 A Psychological Analysis

Psychologists generally believe that aggression and violence are rooted within the individual. This means that everyone has the potential for violence, although not everyone will act on it. What psychologists do not agree on is what makes some people act violently while others do not.

Dr. Jane Sprott and Dr. Anthony Doob studied 3434 Canadian children to determine the personality characteristics associated with very aggressive behaviour (Sprott and Doob, 2000, 123–133). The study focused on ten- and eleven-year-old children. The authors isolated 10 per cent of the children who were the most aggressive and examined how members of this group saw themselves. Regardless of gender, the children in the "most aggressive" category described themselves in "unhappy" terms when compared to children in the "other" category. That is, they reported feeling less happy than other children and feeling left out of school. They also had trouble enjoying themselves and had a negative self-image.

The authors presented similar findings on the children's social relationships. Almost 50 per cent of the girls in the "very aggressive" category reported having negative relations with family—only 25 per cent of girls in the "other" category reported the same feelings. The same trend held for boys. The "very aggressive" children were more likely than the "other" children to report having negative relations with friends, and to perceive their parents as rejecting them and their teachers as being unfair. The "very aggressive" children were also more likely to report that children say mean things to them and bully them. The authors concluded the study by stating that aggressive children are definitely less happy with their lives than are other children. Aggressive behaviour, at least in these children, does not stem from a feeling of superiority over others.

 Two Theories

Aggression and violence have long been concerns of psychologists. The following two classic studies present theories that help explain aggressive behaviour.

Classic Study

RESEARCHERS:
Albert Bandura, Psychologist

TIME:
late 1970s

SUBJECT:
The Learning of Aggression

Modelling Theory

An important psychological theory that attempts to explain the roots of violence was developed by psychologist Albert Bandura. Bandura's **modelling theory** states that humans learn aggression by observing others who behave in an aggressive manner. In other words, aggression is learned—it is not *innate* (something we are born with).

Bandura's theory developed out of the following experiment. A child was given an art activity to work on. In another part of the room, an adult was playing with a "Bobo doll"—an inflatable doll that bounces back up after someone knocks it down. In some cases, the adult was an aggressive role model. In other cases the adult was a non-aggressive role model. In the experiments with aggressive role models, the adult hit the Bobo doll with a mallet and yelled things like "sock it in the nose" and "hit it." After observing the role model, the child was taken into a playroom containing a variety of toys, both aggressive and non-aggressive.

The children who had witnessed the aggressive role model were more likely to choose aggressive toys, such as plastic weapons, and imitate the aggressive behaviour. The children who had witnessed a non-aggressive role model played calmly with non-aggressive toys. This led Bandura to conclude that observing aggressive behaviour teaches aggressive behaviour.

Modelling Theory Today

Is Bandura's theory valid today? Professor Daniel Lai of Okanagan University College in Kelowna, British Columbia, recently conducted a study to determine the impact of exposure to violence on the mental health of adolescents in small towns (Lai, 1999, 181–187). After studying 346 adolescents, Lai found that adolescents who witnessed violence reported higher levels of psychiatric problems, higher levels of depression, and more self-esteem problems. And like Bandura's study, Lai's study found that violence committed by adolescents is explained significantly by the level of violence they *witness* rather than the violence they *experience*. Lai's study also demonstrated that living in a rural or urban setting has no effect on the impact of exposure to violence.

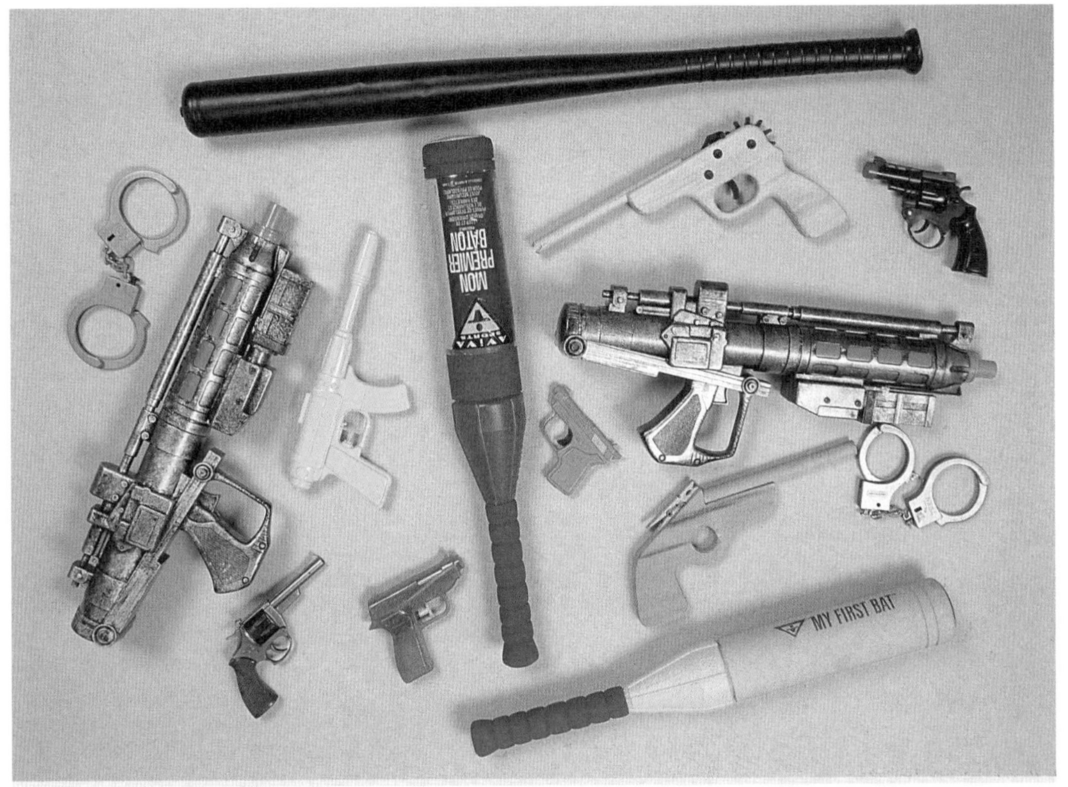

Figure 10.5 Children use aggressive toys to act out aggression symbolically and explore issues of power and control. If such toys are not combined with nurturing, expressive, and imaginative fantasy toys, what might be the psychological result?

QUESTION:

Why do you think males commit more violent crimes than females?

A lot of the time the male is mentally inferior to the female but wants to feel superior. So the male uses the one thing he usually has more of than the female: his strength.

—Warren Hipel, 19

I think males commit more criminal offences than females because males are taught to suppress their emotions. It's acceptable for females to talk about what's wrong and cry, but males are usually expected to be tough. Crimes may be the way men's negative emotions eventually surface.

—Elise Arnold-Levene, 16

I think males commit more crimes because they have a "macho" image to fulfill. They have to prove to their buddies that they are "bad" and "cool." I think men are also less sensitive than females, so the thought of doing something wrong does not frighten them. Also, some men do not care about the future and just act in the present.

—Kaitlin Laidlaw, 15

Classic Study

RESEARCHERS:
John Dollard, Psychologist

TIME:
1939

SUBJECT:
Frustration As a Trigger of Aggression

The Frustration-Aggression Theory

In 1939, psychologist John Dollard of Yale University theorized that an experience of frustration is necessary for aggression to occur. Dollard believed that if a person is motivated to achieve a certain goal, and is then prevented from achieving it, the aggressive drive builds up. Eventually, he argued, this aggression has to be released. The level of aggression a person releases depends on how much satisfaction the person anticipated from achieving the goal.

According to Dollard, the only factors that would prevent aggression would be social inhibitions and fear of repercussions. In some cases, this fear leads a person to displace aggression onto a person who is less likely to retaliate.

RECAP

1. According to Sprott and Doob, what personality characteristics do aggressive children have?
2. How does Albert Bandura explain aggression and violence? Is this theory valid today? Explain your answer.
3. What does John Dollard's work teach us about aggression and violence?

Section 10.2

Prejudice, Discrimination, and Exclusion

Focus Questions

- What types of prejudice and discrimination exist in society?
- How do psychologists explain prejudice and discrimination?
- How do sociologists explain prejudice and discrimination?

Key Concepts

prejudice
discrimination
stereotypes
ignorance
authoritarian personality
ambiguity
anti-Semitism
scapegoat
capitalism
selective perception

A Major Cause of Conflict

In the last topic, we viewed aggression and violence as the *results* of unresolved conflict. A major *cause* of conflict in our society lies in prejudice and discrimination. We are all prejudiced. We hold both positive and negative prejudices. A teacher might have a positive prejudice toward students who arrive in class on time and attend classes regularly. The teacher may assume that those students are the most interested in, and committed to, their studies. This is a **prejudice** because the teacher has prejudged the students without having all the facts. The teacher made an assumption about certain students' motives based on just one aspect of their behaviour. If the teacher then *acted* on the prejudice, he or she would be practising **discrimination**.

Discrimination, because it is a matter of action and not just thoughts, is easier to control than prejudice. Laws can be passed to prohibit people from discriminatory acts—but laws cannot control how people think. As long as a person does not act to offend or infringe on the rights and freedoms of others, she or he is free to hold any opinion. This right is made explicit in the Charter of Rights and Freedoms, which preserves freedom of conscience, thought, belief, opinion, and expression for all people.

A Psychologist's Perspective

Psychologists believe that prejudice and discrimination are not innate—rather, they are the result of socialization.

Children learn by observing their parents and other family members, their neighbours, and their friends. If children hear these people expressing prejudices, they are likely to adopt the same beliefs. And if they see these people discriminating against others, they are likely to imitate that behaviour.

Children are also socialized by books, television, and the language of their culture. Unfortunately, books and other reading materials have perpetuated **stereotypes** (oversimplified generalizations that assign certain characteristics to particular groups). In both words and pictures, they often present men and women in traditional roles—for example, men as doctors and women as nurses. In addition, white people are featured much more frequently than visible minorities. Advertising has also tended to depict white people in the key roles, with minorities included only as tokens. Finally, the language of our culture is laden with biased terminology. To refer to a fireman rather than a firefighter teaches children to make certain assumptions about gender roles and career choices. Terms such as "Black Monday" associate the colour black with something negative. Can you think of other phrases or words in our culture that are "value-laden"?

Two other causes of prejudice and discrimination noted by psychologists are **ignorance** and fear. Ignorance simply refers to a lack of information. When we lack information about something, we are more likely to believe in stereotypes. Imagine, for example, that someone told you the following: "Inuit are unable to do basic math functions because they are exposed to fewer hours of daylight in the far North." You would be more likely to believe this statement if you had never personally known an Inuit, or had never read anything about Inuit culture. It is therefore not surprising that psychological studies have repeatedly shown less educated people to be more prejudiced than more highly educated people.

Fear tends to result when you are in a situation you don't understand because it is different from what you are used to. Fear can make feelings of prejudice even stronger. This increases the likelihood of someone acting in a manner that is discriminatory.

Figure 10.6 Fear of immigrants often leads to discrimination. In 1999, Austria's Freedom Party, led by Jorge Haider, was elected to a new coalition government. Its platform included a halt to all immigration. In February 2000, over 300 000 people demonstrated against the country's far-right, anti-immigrant government.

Personality and Prejudice

Psychologist Theodor Adorno wanted to discover if personality could be the dominant cause of prejudice. Based on studies of over 2000 people, he identified a type he called the **authoritarian personality**. He concluded that people with this personality type are more highly prejudiced than others. These people shared the following characteristics:

- high levels of intolerance
- great insecurity
- respect for authority
- submissiveness to superiors
- relatively high levels of conformity (that is, they would change their personal beliefs and behaviour to fit in with the larger group)
- low tolerance for **ambiguity** (Ambiguity means that something can be understood or interpreted in more than one way; authoritarian personalities, with their low tolerance, believe that things are either *right* or *wrong*—particularly in matters of religion or sex.)

Based on his studies, Adorno concluded that the authoritarian personality type was formed during childhood. It was the result of bigoted, cold, and aloof parents who disciplined their children too harshly.

Adorno's research was considered to be very controversial within the social scientific community. Many followed up on Adorno's theory, conducting more than 1000 research studies. The majority concluded that people who are older, less educated, less intelligent, and from a lower social class are more likely to be authoritarian. Critics of the authoritarian personality theory argue that the studies simply show that the less educated are more prejudiced than those with higher levels of education—something that we already know.

A Sociologist's Perspective

Sociologists believe that the key to understanding prejudice is not the *internal* state of individuals. Rather, prejudice is the result of factors *outside* individuals. The following three sociological theories of prejudice were adapted from James Henslin and Adie Nelson's 1996 book *Sociology: A Down-to-Earth Approach.*

1. A functionalist would argue that prejudice and discrimination occur when they are functional; that is, when they serve a purpose for a particular group. For example, the Nazis promoted **anti-Semitism** (high levels of prejudice and discrimination against Jewish people) because it was functional for them—it served a purpose. By providing Jewish people as a **scapegoat**—a group they could unfairly blame for their troubles—the Nazis could unite the German people behind a common "enemy."
2. Conflict theorists believe that prejudice and discrimination are the result of competition inherent in capitalism. **Capitalism** is the economic system we have in Canada. It allows for unrestricted accumulation of wealth. Conflict theorists argue that capitalism pits group against group in a no-win situation. For

Classic Study

RESEARCHER:
Theodor Adorno, Psychologist

TIME:
1950

SUBJECT:
The Authoritarian Personality

example, a group of workers in one company puts all its energy into doing better than the workers in a competing company. Fearing unemployment if they fail, group members experience rising frustration, anger, and hostility. Eventually they turn on each other.

3. Symbolic interactionists study how labels and stereotypes produce prejudice. These sociologists believe that the way we label others creates prejudice because it causes **selective perception**. In other words, labels lead people to see certain things and blind them to other things. Once a label or stereotype has been assigned to a group, people filter their experiences with the group, processing only those observations that fit with the existing stereotype. Figure 10.7 shows the vicious cycle that can result.

Discrimination Against Categories of People

In Chapter 9, the term "category" was introduced to describe a collection of people who have something in common, but do not know each other (see page 289). When we speak of discrimination against "groups," we usually are referring to categories of people (for example, Aboriginal peoples, black people, physically disabled people, and so on). The following three case studies examine discrimination against three broad categories: women, boys, and young adults. The study on women focuses on specific cases in cultures outside of North America. The other two studies, on boys and young adults, are very much rooted in mainstream North American culture.

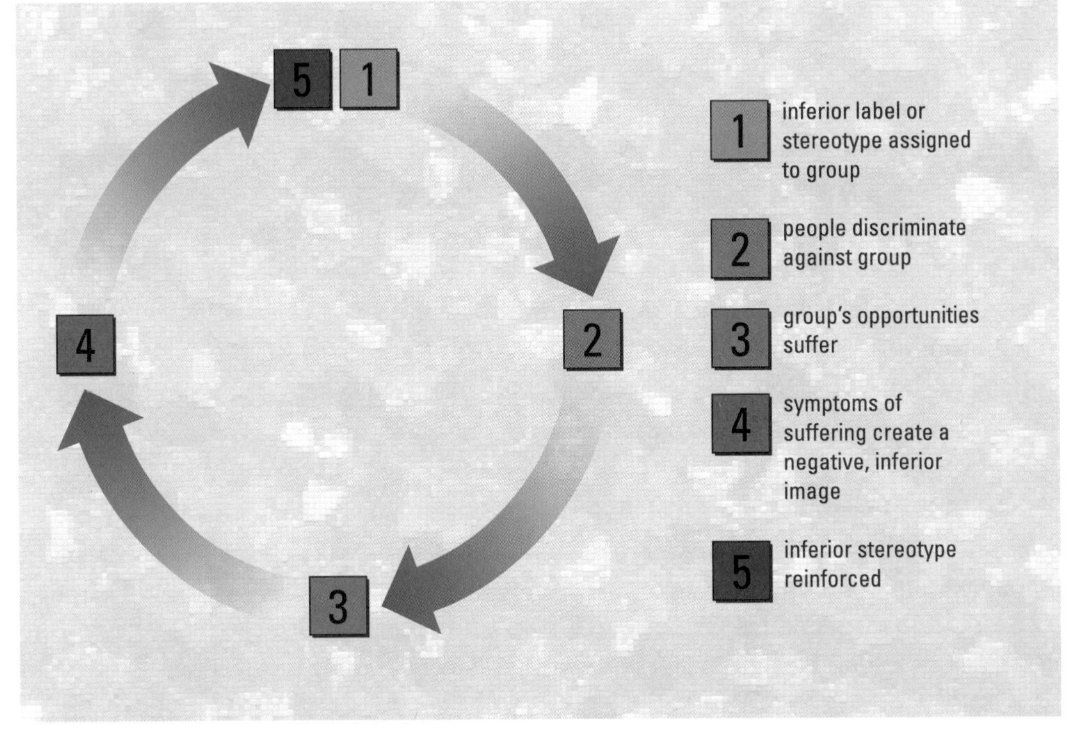

Figure 10.7 Choose a group in society that experiences prejudice or discrimination. Does this group fit into the vicious cycle shown here? Explain, giving specific examples of the stereotypes, limited opportunities, and negative images that apply to the group.

Case Study: Discrimination Against Women

In 1980, the United Nations reported that women, while making up one-half of the world's population,

- did two-thirds of the world's work
- earned one-tenth of the world's income
- owned one-hundredth of the world's property

Although women living in North America have made great strides in achieving equality, the level of equality in any particular case varies with the age, social class, race, and ethnicity of the woman. In 1996, the United Nations Human Development Report stated that in no country in the world were women treated as well as men. Read and respond to the following three cases, which were reported in 1996 and 1997.

"Lee Un Kee lives in a tiny farming village in South Korea named Punsooilri, thirty miles [48 km] from Seoul, the capital city. He has been married for twenty-four years. When asked if he has beaten his wife, he indignantly replies, 'How could I have been married all these years and not beaten my wife? Of course, you have to apologize afterward,' he adds. 'Otherwise, you can have bad feelings in your relationship with your wife.' Chong Chin Suk, a fifty-six-year-old woman who runs Punsooilri's village store, admits that, 'Of course my husband beats me. But it was my fault because I scolded him.' She explains, 'Maybe there are some cases where it's just the man's fault. But ultimately the woman is to blame, because if she won't argue with her husband, he probably won't beat her.' (Kristof, 1996, A4)."

"In 1996, a reactionary Islamic movement called the Taliban gained power in Afghanistan. Imposing what it interpreted as strict Islamic principles, the Taliban placed women into a state of virtual imprisonment. In Kabul, the country's major city, women were forbidden to work or to go to school. If they left their homes, they were ordered to wear garments that completely covered their bodies and concealed their eyes behind cloth mesh. If they did leave their homes, they ran the risk of being assaulted by militiamen who might deem their attire not sufficiently modest. 'I'm very afraid to go out on the street,' said a female surgeon. 'It's terrible for a woman to be hit by a strange man.' (Cooper, 1996, A01)."

"Late one night in Lima, Peru, a group of drunken men in their twenties raped Maria Elena, a seventeen-year-old girl who was on her way home from work. In Peru, however, the law exonerates a rapist if he offers to marry the victim and she accepts. This creates a situation in which relatives of rape victims, particularly in poor and rural areas, put pressure on the girl to accept the rapist's offer. This course, they believe, will restore honor to the victim and her family. Maria Elena's family, though incensed by the attack, encouraged her to accept when one of the rapists offered to marry her. In some cases, the rapist threatens the victim if she refuses the offer. When Maria Elena first declined to marry one of her attackers, his two accomplices threatened to slash her face. Yielding to the threat and pressure by her family, she finally relented. 'What choice did I have?' she asked. 'Everyone insisted that the way to solve the problem was for me to get married.' Three months after the wedding, her husband abandoned her. (There are similar laws pertaining to rape in fourteen other countries.) (Sims, 1997, 41)"

1. Record the specific example of discrimination and exclusion experienced by the women in each case study.
2. What do all of these case studies have in common?
3. Analyze the three cases using the perspectives presented in this chapter. Which perspective—psychological or sociological—do you think is most helpful in understanding the discrimination?

Case Study: Discrimination Against Boys

"Christina Hoff Sommers is a philosopher by training and a fellow at the American Enterprise Institute in Washington, DC. She disagrees with traditional feminists who believe that girls in North America are disadvantaged. In her book *The War Against Boys: How Misguided Feminism is Harming Our Young Men* (2000), Hoff Sommers argues that boys, not girls, are the ones who need the most help in school. She claims that they are unlikely to get it because resources are now heavily weighted in favour of girls. She disagrees that girls are silenced in adolescence and that boys are favoured by teachers in classrooms. She cites statistics from the U.S. Department of Education to show that American girls get better grades, have higher aspirations, and follow more rigorous academic programs than boys. According to data from the American Association for University Women, 81 per cent of girls and 69 per cent of boys believe that girls are smarter than boys. Substantial majorities also said that teachers pay more attention to girls and call on them more often in class [see Chapter 8, page 256, for some equivalent Canadian statistics].

Figure 10.8 What kinds of evidence would you look for to prove that boys suffer discrimination?

"Hoff Sommers is critical of recent school reforms that encourage boys to be more sensitive, empathetic, and nurturing. She argues that it is bad for boys to be taught to be more sensitive. 'A boy's biology determines much of what he prefers and is attracted to, and they learn best in a single-sex environment where they are taught by men, permitted to rough-house, and encouraged to compete. Aggression and violence are biologically determined male attributes: Try to suppress them and boys suffer.'"

Source: Martin, Sandra. 2000. "Boys' Own Feminist Crusader." *The Globe and Mail*. 17 June 2000.

1. Do you agree that boys and men are discriminated against in our culture? Provide examples to support your answer.
2. a) Why does the author criticize the school system for teaching boys to be more sensitive?
   b) How do you feel about this argument?
3. Which side of the nature-nurture debate (see pages 82 to 87) does Hoff Sommers support? Explain your answer.

Case Study: Age Discrimination

Many people assume that the term "age discrimination" applies exclusively to elderly people. The following case brings a less expected aspect of the term to light. It reports on a legal challenge made by a twenty-five-year-old after he was dismissed from his job.

"It began in 1993, when Michael Sisler was an employee at New Era, a local bank his grandfather had founded. As Sisler tells the story in court papers, chairman Anthony Bruno of Bergen Commercial, a larger financial institution in the same area, began phoning him at New Era. Bruno said he had heard good things about Sisler. He eventually asked the young man to become Bergen's vice president of credit-card operations—a swank job for anyone, let alone a 25-year-old college dropout. He would make $70 000 a year and have use of a company car. Sisler said yes.

"A few days before Sisler started, Bruno took him to lunch. He then asked a question that had somehow not occurred to him before: How old are you, anyway? Bruno was floored by the answer. Don't tell anyone, the bank chief warned. Sisler's youth could embarrass coworkers and worse, anger Bergen's board. Days after Sisler started the job in September 1993, he got a call from Bruno. It wasn't working out, Bruno said. Sisler asked for a chance to prove himself but says he never got one. Sisler was told to report to a fellow vice president (instead of the chairman) and was assigned to a forlorn branch. In January 1994, Sisler was fired-without-cause, he claims.

"Sisler cried age discrimination. The bank brushed him off at first, saying that even if it had fired him solely because of his age—which it denied—only older people could sue on such grounds. New Jersey's highest court disagreed, ruling in February of 1999 that the state's Law Against Discrimination prohibits bias on any consideration of age. The New Jersey decision was unusual. The bank would have won in most states, where anti-discrimination laws—like the federal one—set a minimum age of 40 for those claiming age bias."

Source: Cloud, John. 1999. "Can a Man of 25 Claim Age Bias?" *Time*. 16 August 1999.

1. a) What labels or stereotypes are often associated with young people?
   b) To what extent do you think these labels and stereotypes explain the concerns of Sisler's co-workers and the board members?
2. What other explanation might psychologists and sociologists apply to this case? (Choose one from the psychology and another from the sociology discipline.)
3. a) Why do you think most American anti-discrimination laws only apply to people over forty?
   b) Should there be an age limit on these anti-discrimination laws? Explain.

RECAP

1. What is the primary difference between prejudice and discrimination?
2. What is the primary difference in the way that psychologists and sociologists view prejudice and discrimination?
3. Make point-form notes summarizing the various psychological and sociological perspectives presented.

Section 10.3

Discrimination Against Aboriginal Peoples

Focus Questions

- What specific government policies have excluded Aboriginal peoples from mainstream society?
- In what ways have Aboriginal women been doubly discriminated against?
- How are public attitudes toward Aboriginal peoples contradictory?

Key Concepts

assimilate
heathen
Indian Act
ethnocentrism
disenfranchisement
residential schools
special status
self-government

The Exclusion of Cultures

Sometimes government policies actually *create* discrimination and exclusion. They do this by withholding certain rights and privileges from a particular group of people in society. Or they do this by creating legal and social conditions that make it impossible for certain individuals or groups to fully participate in society.

This is exactly what happened to Aboriginal peoples in Canadian history: specific government policies and institutional practices excluded Aboriginal peoples in Canada from mainstream society. These policies, beyond taking away the rights and privileges of Aboriginal peoples, have been very costly for Canadian society as a whole. We are paying for these costs as a society today.

The Indian Act

The first government policy to exclude Aboriginal peoples from mainstream society was the **Indian Act** of 1876. The act made Aboriginal peoples "wards of the state" by placing them on reserves and under the direct control of the federal government. The act denied Aboriginal peoples the right to vote, restricted their travel and property rights, and forbade the practice of traditional ceremonies and rituals. The Indian Act even stipulated that Aboriginal peoples needed government permission to wear traditional costumes off their reserves. In some cases, Aboriginal languages were outlawed.

The purpose of the Indian Act was to help **assimilate** Aboriginal peoples into non-Aboriginal society. To assimilate a group means to cause it to resemble or be like a larger group. The act reflected the dominant bias held by English and French settlers at this period in Canadian history—namely, that Aboriginal peoples were "uncivilized barbarians" and "savages."

One of the reasons for this attitude was that Aboriginal peoples were not Christian. To the early settlers, this meant that Aboriginal peoples were **heathens**, or godless. Of course, Aboriginal peoples were very spiritual and worshipped numerous gods in their culture. But to the

European settlers, Aboriginal peoples did not worship the "correct" god.

In addition to exhibiting different religious practices, Aboriginal cultures in general were very foreign to Europeans. Aboriginal peoples ate different food from the settlers, had different kinship patterns and family arrangements, and held different values and beliefs. This was another reason why Europeans wanted to see Aboriginal peoples assimilated.

Anthropologist Franz Boas noted that human beings have a tendency to judge people who are different as *inferior*. Instead of viewing the contrast between cultures as interesting, and indeed fascinating, our tendency is to look down at the other culture. Boas noted that even anthropologists were not immune from this type of bias, which he labeled **ethnocentrism**. He therefore encouraged social scientists to keep highly accurate records of their observations when they studied other cultures. Their conclusions would be valid only if they were supported by large amounts of data.

The Disenfranchisement of Women

Under section 12(1)(b) of the Indian Act, Aboriginal women lost their "status" when they married non-Aboriginal men. This **disenfranchisement**, or loss of status as an Aboriginal person, did not happen to Aboriginal men who married non-Aboriginal women. In the 1970s and 1980s, women like Mary Two-Axe Early, Jeanette Lavell, and Sandra Lovelace worked

Figure 10.9 Anthropologist Franz Boas (left) set up the scene in this photograph of a Kwakwaka'wakw woman spinning cedar bark. A "cropped" version of the photograph would appear in a museum exhibit, showing only the woman. But the full image would be available to researchers, showing the photograph to be a staged event. How do his efforts show a concern for accurate record-keeping?

tirelessly to have this discriminatory section of the act repealed. In 1985, their hard work paid off, and Bill C-31 was passed, which amended the Indian Act. Bill C-31 originally looked like it would be a success, as thousands of women and children who had lost their status were reinstated. The amendment has, however, ushered in a whole new set of circumstances that still work against women and children.

Fay Blaney of the Aboriginal Women's Action Network presents some examples of these problems (Blaney, 1998, 32). Blaney reports that the registration process is "so convoluted and uncoordinated that people going through it often either give up before they have attained the status which is rightfully theirs or accept a lesser degree of status than they are entitled to." As a result, the Native Women's Association of Canada has predicted that many First Nations communities are actually headed for extinction. It won't be because membership in these bands will die off, but rather because eventually all members will lose their status and all rights associated with it.

The greatest problem with Bill C-31 is that women are the ones responsible for registering their children for status, and part of this procedure involves proving paternity and providing evidence of the status of the father. If a father is unwilling to sign a sworn affidavit stating that he is the father, then the Department of Indian Affairs automatically registers the child as having one non-status parent. This puts the child in the section 6(2) category, which gives the child "status Indian" identity but does *not* allow the child to pass on that status to his or her offspring.

Residential Schools

Another example of institutional discrimination and exclusion was the placement of Aboriginal children in **residential schools.** Residential schools were institutions, jointly run by the federal government and four Canadian churches, whose aim was to teach Aboriginal children "white" culture and strip them of their own. First established in 1879 by Sir John A. Macdonald's government, over 100 000 Aboriginal children attended the schools over the period of about a century. Often, the children were from the poorest families or from families that were in crisis. Documents dating back to the nineteenth century claimed the children would be kept "within the circle of civilized conditions" where they would get the "care of a mother." Tragically, many of these children received drastically different care, exposed to emotional, physical, and sexual abuse.

Residential schools have left a bitter legacy. Adults who were students at the schools are haunted by negative memories. For Lorne Pratt, who attended Gordon Residential School in Saskatchewan, they include the day he tried to commit suicide. Only twelve years old, he wrapped an elastic belt around his neck and hung himself from the metal frame of his bunk bed. It was the only way he could think of to escape the sexual abuse he had suffered over a five-year period. Fortunately, Pratt was discovered and cut down by school employees. After spending five days in a coma in hospital, he recovered and was returned to his mother in Saskatchewan. Other children were not as lucky, some spending over ten years in these institutions. Adult survivors of childhood abuse often have trouble trusting others and dealing with anger. They may suffer from anxiety attacks and other psychological problems, and often become substance abusers as a way to deal with their pain.

In 1998, the federal government officially apologized to Aboriginal peoples for placing their children in residential schools. The government also announced a $350-million "healing fund" to help victims receive the counselling and treatment they require. Many of the survivors of the schools, however, feel that more needs to be done. There is evidence that churches and government knew of the abuse going on in the schools, but did nothing to protect the children or close down the schools. The churches involved, as well as the government, are being named in lawsuits. The Anglican Church of Canada recently announced that the cost of defending the cases alone will bankrupt the church's national head office by the year 2001.

Figure 10.10 The legacy of shame.

1879 Residential schools are first established.
1894 Ottawa passes an amendment to the Indian Act, making it mandatory for Aboriginal children to attend the schools.
1947 The United Church wants to shut down residential schools in favour of non-denominational day schools, citing harm to children in being separated from their families. Over the next two decades, many schools close.
1969 Ottawa takes over full management of the 60 remaining schools from the churches.
1973 A new federal policy gives control of Aboriginal education to bands and tribal councils.
1986 The United Church becomes the first church to apologize to its Aboriginal congregations.
1989 The first residential school lawsuit is filed in British Columbia.
1990 Phil Fontaine, grand chief of the Assembly of First Nations, states publicly that he was sexually and physically abused at a residential school in Manitoba in the 1950s.
1996 The $58-million Royal Commission on Aboriginal Peoples releases its report denouncing the treatment of children at residential schools.
1996 The last residential school in Canada, on the Gordon reserve in Saskatchewan, closes.
1998 Indian Affairs Minister Jane Stewart apologizes to Aboriginal peoples for residential schools and announces the establishment of a $350-million healing fund.
2000 The number of plaintiffs who have filed individual lawsuits against residential schools surpasses 6300. Churches publicly voice concerns that the lawsuits will bankrupt them.

Source: O'Hara, Jane. 2000. "Abuse of Trust." *Maclean's*. 26 June 2000.

RECAP

1. In what ways have Aboriginal peoples had to deal with double discrimination as a result of the Indian Act?
2. Explain how the Indian Act and residential schools were examples of systemic, or institutionalized, discrimination and exclusion.

REMARKABLE PEOPLE

Phil Fontaine

"In November 1997, Phil Fontaine became the new national chief of the Assembly of First Nations. In his acceptance speech on the night of the election, Fontaine, the former grand chief of Manitoba said: 'The need is to restore and reorganize and revive the AFN (Assembly of First Nations). There is a need to open doors and build bridges.' There was every reason to believe that Fontaine may be just the man to build those bridges.

"The 52-year-old divorced father of two grew up on the Fort Alexander reserve, 128 km north of Winnipeg. He attended a Catholic residential school, where he suffered sexual and physical abuse, before going to the University of Manitoba to study political science. Several stints in the Federal Department of Indian Affairs gave him experience with government bureaucracy. Fontaine is known as a consensusseeker and dealmaker. In his victory speech, he announced he would not fight the agreements that Ottawa has been reaching with regional bands without AFN involvement—deals like the one Fontaine himself made in Manitoba to dismantle the Department of Indian Affairs in that province. 'I am prepared to be conciliatory,' he told reporters [one week] after his [election] victory. 'I am prepared to negotiate. I am prepared to do what is necessary to protect the people I represent.'"

Source: DeMont, John. 1997. "Fontaine's Vision: The New Grand Chief Aims for Unity." *Maclean's*. 11 August 1997.

1. Identify three ways in which Fontaine is "remarkable."
2. What specific government policy caused Fontaine to suffer discrimination and/or exclusion?

Public Opinion on Aboriginal Rights

In 1994, sociologists J. Rick Ponting and Jerilynn Kiely of the University of Calgary explored public opinion on Aboriginal rights (Ponting and Kiely, 1999, 142–150). The study was based on a sample of over 1800 telephone interviews. Their findings indicated that Canadians have a contradictory attitude toward Aboriginal peoples. On the one hand, most Canadians are sympathetic to Aboriginal peoples in the abstract. But they know very little about them.

Aboriginal peoples have fared worse than any other ethnic or racial group in the country. Their traditional way of life was targeted for destruction by European colonization. Not only do a number of Canadians fail to recognize the historical and social context in which Aboriginal peoples became victims, but they also put the blame for their plight on Aboriginal peoples themselves. Fully 31 per cent of Canadians believe that "most of the problems of Aboriginal peoples are brought on by themselves."

There are other contradictions in Canadian attitudes toward Aboriginal peoples. Although approximately 65 per cent of respondents were against special status for Aboriginal peoples, 56 per cent of respondents did believe that Aboriginal peoples should be given the right to self-govern. (In this study, **special status** meant that Aboriginal peoples would be treated differently than non-Aboriginal Canadians in some areas of the law. For example, for crimes committed by Aboriginal persons on reserves, there would be special courts with Aboriginal judges only. **Self-government**, on the other hand, relates to Aboriginal peoples having the right to develop and implement their own policies in regard to health, education, and child welfare.)

As well, while most Canadians reported that they want to see action to solve Aboriginal problems, they wanted that action limited to royal commissions. Royal commissions only study the issues. Respondents were generally opposed to boycotts, demonstrations, and other assertive actions on the part of Aboriginal peoples to help themselves.

Ponting and Kiely concluded that, although Canadians are sympathetic to Aboriginal peoples in principle, concrete public support for Aboriginal peoples is actually slipping. The authors believe this is because Canadians have a low tolerance for the kinds of protest strategies and tactics that create leverage for disempowered people. When Aboriginal peoples resort to those strategies, feeling they have no other choice, they come into conflict with private and commercial interests in the larger society.

Figure 10.11 In September 2000, First Nations in British Columbia demonstrated their support for Mi'kmaq fishers in Burnt Church, New Brunswick. The Mi'kmaq asserted their treaty rights to fish year-round and without federal licences, but the federal government claimed the fishery was illegal.

Advocating for Aboriginal Rights

In Chapter 9, we saw how Aboriginal groups have achieved victories in advocating for their rights (see pages 296 to 298). In addition, various non-Aboriginal organizations have spoken out on behalf of Aboriginal peoples. The perspective of such organizations is described in the article excerpt below.

> Canada has a lot of work to do at home before it can boast about being a world leader in upholding basic human rights. That's what the country's church leaders and rights lobbyists said in 1988 during 40th anniversary

celebrations of the United Nations' Universal Declaration of Human Rights. Some say that is as true now as it was a decade ago.

Canada has earned a reputation as an international champion of human rights. And, while violations of human rights at home pale compared to some of the horrors taking place in other parts of the world, there still are a few areas that need work. Aboriginal rights is one of them. Back in 1990 Max Yalden, head of the Canadian Human Rights Commission (CHRC) said: "If there is any single issue on which Canada cannot hold its head high in the international community, any single area in which we can be accused of falling down on our obligations, it is in this area of Aboriginal relations. Respecting differences means, very simply, that we do not hurt, cheapen, or humiliate other human beings, on any grounds whatsoever—period. And that is not simply because the Charter of Rights or the Human Rights Act tell us so; it is surely the central belief on which this country is founded."

As recently as March 1997, the Canadian Human Rights Commission warned the Canadian government that it cannot afford to ignore the 1996 Royal Commission Report on Aboriginal Peoples. After five years of studying Aboriginal life, the commission produced a six-volume, 3537-page report. Its recommendations include an independent tribunal to monitor land claims, parliamentary acts to address broken treaty promises, and an Aboriginal parliament. It also recommends that Aboriginal communities be provided with adequate land and funding to help them to become self-reliant.

The CHRC's annual report criticizes the government for its lack of action on Aboriginal rights. It also points to discrimination against people with disabilities, and calls on Canadians to stop denying that racial and ethnic discrimination are quite common features of life in Canada. Canadians have to "confront the evidence of their little hypocrisies when it comes to treating all human colours, creeds, and cultures as equally deserving of respect and fairness," the report says. Patterns of employment continue to show Aboriginal people and members of racial and ethnic minorities with limited opportunities, according to the report.

Abridged from: "Human Rights—Canada: Keeping Our Own House in Order." *Canada and the World Backgrounder*. 1 May 1997.

RECAP

1. In what ways do Canadians hold contradictory attitudes toward Aboriginal peoples?
2. Write a five-point response to the 31 per cent of Canadians who believe that "most of the problems of Aboriginal peoples are brought on by themselves."
3. What groups or institutions have criticized Canada's treatment of Aboriginal peoples? Do you believe these criticisms are justified or not? Explain your answer.

Section 10.4

Building Cohesion in Society

Focus Questions

- What factors are linked to altruism and other helping behaviours?
- Can animals act in an altruistic manner?
- What can we do to improve cohesion in our society?

Key Concepts

altruism
heroism
rescuers
kin selection
conflict resolution

The Other Side of Conflict

With so much attention paid to conflict in our society, it is easy to lose sight of the fact that, every day, the vast majority of people choose to abide by the law, do nice things for one another, and work for social change and justice. One reason we forget this is that more negative than positive news events are covered by the media. Furthermore, mainstream movies and television usually explore the dark side of human nature and contain a great deal of violence. In fact, an American Psychological Association study found that children watch an average of 8000 murders and 100 000 acts of violence on television before they finish elementary school. But the fact remains that **altruism**—behaviour in which a person voluntarily gives more time or money to another person or to a cause than they can possibly expect in return—is all around us.

Factors Linked to Helping Behaviours

Both altruism and **heroism** (when someone faces danger while helping another) are behaviours that involve helping others for no personal reward. Even if a reward does come later, it is not the motive for the behaviour. Numerous social science studies have tried to determine why some people are willing to help others when there is no benefit to themselves.

Although the Holocaust was one of the darkest periods in human history, it was also a period where some people chose to help others, often at significant risk to themselves. Interviews with these **rescuers** revealed that those who helped shared a number of characteristics in common:

- They had a strong sense of what was right and wrong and felt a real moral responsibility to help others.
- They spoke of at least one parent, with high moral values, who had a great influence on their lives.
- They identified strongly with the victims—either because they knew the person(s) they were helping, or because they too had been bullied or persecuted at some point in their lives.
- They frequently had a strong sense of adventure and reported that they never really feared for

their lives when involved in rescuing others.

Two psychology professors who have studied altruism over a twenty-year period are John Dovidio of Colgate University in New York and Samuel Gaertner of the University of Delaware. They found that people are more likely to help in an emergency if they are the only witness to the emergency. According to their studies, in an emergency where there was only one witness, the witness helped between 83 and 95 per cent of the time, regardless of the race of the person in need. Race, however, did become a factor once the number of bystanders increased. When white subjects believed that there were two other witnesses to the emergency, they were much less likely to help, particularly when the victim was African American. Dovidio and Gaertner found that the white subjects helped the black victim half as often as they helped the white victim (38 per cent versus 75 per cent). Therefore, the number of people present at an emergency, and the race of the victim, affect helping behaviour. The more similar the victim is to the helper, the more likely the witness is to help.

Other studies have also identified factors that affect the likelihood of someone helping another. It seems that if people feel guilty about something, they are more likely to help someone else. Psychologists believe that people may choose to help another when they have the opportunity to appease their conscience over an earlier transgression or error in judgment. As well, people are more likely to help if they are in a good mood and if they are not rushed for time. This information helps us to understand incidents of road rage. People are in a rush, they are in a bad mood, and therefore they overreact to a driving error made by another.

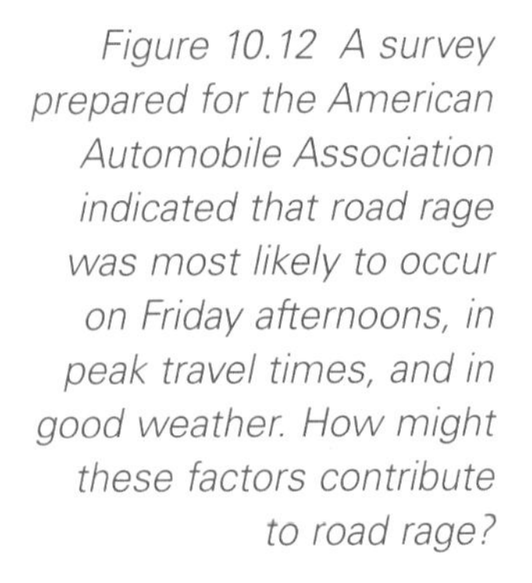

Figure 10.12 A survey prepared for the American Automobile Association indicated that road rage was most likely to occur on Friday afternoons, in peak travel times, and in good weather. How might these factors contribute to road rage?

Skill Development: Interpreting and Reporting Field Observation Results

To study altruism, a social scientist may undertake a field observation. After the observation is designed and conducted, the results must be interpreted and reported. Interpreting involves examining the data from observation sheets for completeness and consistency. Reporting involves organizing data into categories, scoring data, and drawing conclusions.

Let us return to the sample field observation from Chapter 9 (pages 311 to 313). Recall that the observation was of teenagers and their comfort levels with each other. Let us assume the observation is now complete.

Step 1

Inform your subjects of what you have done. This step is taken for ethical reasons. Obtaining the informed consent of subjects before including them in any findings is a strict requirement of social science research. In this case, you must tell each person observed when, where, and how the observation took place. You must tell them the purpose of the observation. You must guarantee that you will not identify them to anyone other than your partners in the observation. If any individual does not consent, the entire observation for that subject group must be discarded.

Step 2

Your next task is to examine all Field Observation Sheets for completeness. Discard any sheets that lack important information. If some sheets are almost, but not completely, filled in, use your own judgment about whether to keep or discard them. Let us return to the sample sheets from Chapter 9 for an example.

Suppose you have twenty-five fully complete sheets of all-female and all-male group observations, but only twenty fully complete sheets of mixed-sex group observations. In addition, you have five mixed-sex group sheets in which you missed some facial expressions in a group because one of the subjects was facing away from you. You may choose to use the other data from the five sheets so that you have an equal number of mixed-sex, all-female, and all-male sheets for most of your results. However, when you report the results for facial expression, you must make clear that you are using different totals for mixed-sex groups than for the other groups.

Step 3

Compare all the completed Field Observation Sheets. Check that the data are consistent with each other. When you find inconsistencies, you should either discard the inconsistent data or identify the cause of the inconsistencies as an intervening variable. Here are two examples of inconsistencies and how to deal with them:

- You observed students on a Tuesday and a Thursday. A tragic road accident killed three students on Wednesday afternoon. On Thursday, the students were dealing with their grief. Thursday's data are very different from Tuesday's data.
  - Discard all observations from that week and begin again the following week.
- You observed students outside in a smoking area, and the weather conditions on two observation days were different. The data from the second day, which was rainy, differ greatly from the data from the first day, which was sunny.
  - Note the weather conditions as an intervening variable. In Step 5, you will deal with this variable in detail.

Step 4

Add up the total number of observations. Use a tally sheet like the one in Figure 10.13. You may want to discard sheets to make your totals in each subgroup match.

	Total number of groups observed
Subgroup 1: All-female	28
Subgroup 2: All-male	25
Subgroup 3: Mixed-sex	25

Figure 10.13 Tally sheet

Step 5

a) Score the complete results from the sheets. An example is shown in Figure 10.14.

b) Write as many preliminary summary statements of the results as you can. Here are some examples of statements that could be made from Figure 10.14.
   - All-female groups had the highest number of check marks for standing or sitting extremely close to one another (less than 30 cm).
   - All-male groups had the highest number of check marks for standing 60 cm or more from one another.
   - All-female groups had the highest number of friendly facial expressions.
   - All-female groups had the highest number of friendly touches.
   - All-female groups had the highest number of whispered conversations.

c) Look back at any intervening variables you noted in Step 3. If you suspected in Step 3 that an intervening variable affected the data, you may wish to score the data a second time. For example, suppose that you identified weather conditions in Step 3 as an intervening variable. To check, divide each set of sheets into two piles. One pile is observations taken on the sunny day and the other is for observations taken on the rainy day. Figure 10.15 shows the top of your scoring sheet in this case. After completing this scoring sheet, revise or add to your summary statements if necessary.

Step 6

Examine all the scoring sheets and decide whether your original hypothesis is correct or incorrect.

- If you conclude that your hypothesis is *correct*, explain how the numbers support the hypothesis.
- If you conclude that your hypothesis is *incorrect*, come up with another statement that accurately reflects the data.
- If you conclude that your hypothesis is *partially correct*, explain which part of the hypothesis is correct and which part is incorrect.
- If you have difficulties coming to any conclusion at all, describe what further research you would need to do to reach a conclusion. If your problem is that you have too much information to process, revise the hypothesis into a more specific or limited statement. Use only the information relevant to the revised hypothesis to draw conclusions.

	All-female groups of 3 or 4 # of √	**All-male groups of 3 or 4** # of √	**Mixed-sex groups of 3 or 4** # of √
Distance			
- less than 30 cm	31	21	26
- 30-60 cm	45	45	26
- 60 cm-1 m	8	45	27
- more than 1 m	9	19	14
Facial Expression			
- friendly	15	6	10
- passive	13	25	19
- aggressive	6	6	0
Touch			
- friendly	12	1	8
- warning	0	0	1
- aggressive	0	8	4
Voice			
- whisper	14	2	1
- talk	15	15	20
- shout	9	15	4

Figure 10.14 Scoring sheet

	All-female		**All-male**		**Mixed-sex**	
	sunny day # of √	**rainy day** # of √	**sunny day** # of √	**rainy day** # of √	**sunny day** # of √	**rainy day** # of √

Figure 10.15 Headings for weather as an intervening variable

Step 7

Present your findings in a written report or a visual display. Include your completed Field Observation Sheets with your report. Ensure that there are absolutely no marks, numbers, or descriptions on the sheets that could identify any of the subjects. Also make and include graphs to represent your findings. Decide whether bar graphs, circle graphs, or scattergraphs (see pages 269 to 273) are the best methods of representation.

Follow-Up

1. Devise a method for obtaining the informed consent of all the subjects of an observation.
2. Make thirty copies of the Field Observation Sheet that you created for Activity 3 on page 313. Exchange your sheets with another student. Fill in each other's sheets with random check marks as if you had conducted an observation. Return the thirty sheets to their designer.
3. Using your returned sheets, complete Steps 2 to 6. For Step 6, use your hypothesis from Activity 1 on page 313. Which kind(s) of graph would you use to represent your results? Explain your choice.

Taking Gender into Account

Altruism and heroism are moral attributes. When and how do people acquire these attributes? In Chapter 5, we discussed the work of two psychologists who proposed different theories of how moral development proceeds throughout a lifetime (see pages 138 to 139). We review that work here. As you read, think about how gender differences can lead to different "styles" of altruistic or heroic behaviour.

In the 1960s, Lawrence Kohlberg conducted research that led to his moral development theory. He concluded that young children are at the "preconventional" level of moral development. At this stage, young children's sense of "rightness" simply amounts to "what serves my needs" or "what feels good to me." Teenagers have moved to the second stage, the "conventional" level of moral development. Teens begin to acknowledge their own selfishness and begin to define right and wrong in terms of what pleases parents and what is consistent with broader cultural norms. In making moral decisions, teens try to assess intention in addition to simply observing what others do. Individuals at the final stage of development, the "postconventional" level, ponder the more abstract principles of ethics. Individuals at this level are able to criticize their own society and argue, for instance, that what is traditional or legal still may not be right. In Kohlberg's theory, it is rare for a person to reach the highest level of moral reasoning.

There is some question as to whether Kohlberg's model applies to people in all societies. A greater concern with

Kohlberg's findings is that his research was based only on male subjects. He generalized the results of his male subjects to all of humanity. It was this fact that prompted Carol Gilligan to conduct her own research on moral reasoning.

Carol Gilligan, a psychologist at Harvard University, compared the moral development of boys and girls. She found that boys tend to have a "justice" perspective when making moral judgments. That means that boys, in general, tend to rely on formal rules and abstract principles to define right and wrong. Girls, on the other hand, have a "care and responsibility" perspective when making moral judgments. They tend to judge a situation by considering personal relationships and loyalties. In Gilligan's research, when boys and girls evaluated a situation where a man stole medicine for his dying wife, the boys tended to see the action as wrong because it broke the law. Girls tended to consider why the man chose to steal, and looked less severely on the man because he did so with the intention of helping another person. Gilligan concluded her research by pointing out that while the two sexes make moral judgments in different ways, it is important not to consider one method of reasoning superior to the other. Both methods have merit.

Figure 10.16 Assuming that Gilligan's ideas are valid, what effect do you think changing gender expectations will have on the moral development of males and females? Explain.

Case Study: Animal Altruism?

Scientists have long believed that animals act on instinct, not as the result of conscious thought. But every now and then a case comes along that confounds the experts and gives us all food for thought. The following article was written by Frans B.M. de Waal, a psychology professor and director of the Living Links Center at Emory University. His recent books include *Good Natured: The Origins of Right and Wrong in Humans and Other Animals* (1996) and *Bonobo: The Forgotten Ape* (1997).

"The most absurd animal exhibit I have ever seen was at a small zoo in Lop Buri, Thailand, where two medium-sized dogs shared a cage with three full-grown tigers. While the tigers cooled their bodies in dirty water, the dogs moved freely, hopping unconcernedly over the huge striped heads that rested on the concrete rim of the pool. The dogs were walking snacks for the tigers, but the tigers evidently failed to perceive them as such. I learned that one of the dogs had raised the tiger cubs along with her own puppy, and that the whole family had lived together happily ever

Figure 10.17 Under what circumstances might tigers display altruism? What evidence can you cite in support of your answer?

since. What could explain the dog's selfless behavior?

"The incredible sacrifice of the mother dog in rearing three tigers falls under the biological definition of altruism—that is, she incurred a serious cost for the benefit of others. She didn't do it for herself, her family, or even her species, so why did she do it? What energy she must have put into raising three giant animals so totally unlike herself!

"Biologists often explain altruism by what is known as **kin selection**. Kindness toward one's kin is viewed as a genetic investment, a way of spreading genes similar to one's own. Assisting kin thus comes close to helping oneself. Sacrifices on behalf of kin are pervasive, from honeybees that die for their colony by stinging intruders, to birds—such as scrub jays—that help their parents raise a nest full of young. Humans show the same bias toward their kin, giving rise to expressions such as 'blood is thicker than water.'

"It is hard to imagine that the mother dog at the zoo in Thailand was unable to tell a tiger cub from a puppy by sight, let alone by smell. Yet she bestowed tender, loving care and nourishing milk on individuals that could not possibly be her relatives. So kin selection cannot explain her behavior. An alternative explanation can be summarized by the expression 'you scratch my back, I'll scratch yours,' which means that you are likely to help someone who is willing to repay the service.

"But does that explanation fit the dog's behavior? One could argue that the tigers repaid her by not devouring her, but such altruism-by-omission is a bit of a stretch. It certainly doesn't explain the mother's generosity. Had she simply rejected the cubs, she would not have had to contend with them as dangerous adults at all. Clearly, she got little or nothing out of the whole deal.

"Scientists are familiar with examples of animals' behaving normally under unusual circumstances. In 1996, Binti Jua, a lowland gorilla at Chicago's Brookfield Zoo, scooped up and rescued an unconscious boy who had fallen into her enclosure, an action that no one had taught her. In another incident, dolphins protected a tourist in the Gulf of Aqaba, off the Red Sea. While cavorting with the dolphins, the man was attacked by sharks. As his blood stained the water, the dolphins surrounded the screaming victim, leaping up and smacking the water with their tails and flippers and successfully keeping the sharks at bay.

"Such examples make a deep impression on us mainly because they benefit members of our own species. But in my work on the evolution of empathy and morality, I have found many instances of animals' caring for one another and responding to one another's distress—evidence so rich that I am convinced that survival depends not only on strength in combat but also at times on cooperation and kindness."

Adapted from: De Waal, Frans B.M. 1998. "Survival of the Kindest." *The Chronicle of Higher Education*. 7 August 1998.

1. What did the dog do that was so unusual?
2. How does Professor de Waal explain the dog's behaviour?
3. Why does the professor conclude by saying that he is convinced survival depends not only on strength but also on co-operation and kindness?

Making Canadian Society More Inclusive

The social scientific research conducted on altruism and helping behaviours can teach us a lot about the steps we can take to improve our society. If we understand the factors that increase the likelihood of helping behaviours, we can try to implement or influence those factors in our schools and communities.

Improving Cohesion in Schools

One way to reduce conflict and improve cohesion in our society is by becoming better at **conflict resolution**. This term means to solve problems by consensus, without violence. Some high schools have already started to teach students anger management and conflict resolution skills. Students are taught to express their feelings without blaming others, to listen to the other person's side of the story, to manage their anger, and to propose solutions. Student mediators are trained to help their peers resolve conflicts that range all the way from schoolyard teasing to potentially violent fights between high-school gangs.

Woodroffe High School in Ottawa started one of the country's first high-school peer-mediation programs in September 1988. Some students were not initially interested in mediation—they preferred more physical "solutions." Some teachers thought mediation was not tough enough—that it was simply a way for kids to avoid sanctions. But by 1993, the school reported that the process had been accepted by students and administrators.

Figure 10.18 What methods are used to provide conflict resolution in high schools?

Improving Cohesion in the Workplace

In April of 1999, Pierre Lebrun went on a fatal shooting rampage at his former place of work, OC Transpo (see pages 10 to 14). At the inquest into the shooting, Peter Collins, a forensic psychiatrist, explained to the jury how rage prompted Lebrun to gun down four OC Transpo workers. This rage was fuelled by harassment and fanned by a workplace environment that did nothing about it. In his report to the inquest, Collins stated: "Pierre Lebrun worked in a poisoned environment. He was repeatedly harassed due to his speech impediment and his (facial) tick disorder and this appeared to be common knowledge. He complained about the ridicule to a number of individuals at OC Transpo. It was severe enough to contribute to his psychological problems, which are well documented by his family practitioner. Although it would be impossible to foretell the events of April 6, 1999, there was enough known of both the personal and workplace factors that the potential for some form of workplace violence was present."

When the inquest ended in March 2000, the jury specifically targeted OC Transpo, stating: "Evidence indicated that complaints in the workplace were not taken seriously and no action was taken." The jury also made over seventy recommendations aimed at improving workplace environments.

- One recommendation was that provinces should enact a mandatory zero-tolerance harassment and violence policy in the workplace. The policy should define not only physical violence, but also psychological violence such as bullying, mobbing, teasing, ridicule, or any other act or words that could psychologically hurt or isolate a person in the workplace.
- Another recommendation was that there needs to be a broader recognition that non-physical violence can have as much impact on the victim as physical abuse.
- As well, the jury stressed that we need to acknowledge violence as a workplace safety issue and work to *prevent* it. By seeing violence otherwise, that is, as only a criminal matter, treatment will always be after the fact, which is too late.
- Finally, the jury recommended that violence and harassment policies should include
  - mandatory reporting
  - a process in which the employee can see that action has been taken.

REMARKABLE PEOPLE

Arn Chorn Pond

"In the killing fields of Cambodia, he used to help undress the children and hold their hands while the Khmer Rouge chopped their skulls open with a makeshift pickax. 'It sounded like splitting coconuts,' says Arn Chorn Pond, now a youth program coordinator for the Cambodian Mutual Assistance Association, a community outreach group in the United States. 'If you showed any emotion, they'd kill you,' says Pond. 'You had to be numb.' The Khmer Rouge killed between 1.5 million and 1.8 million Cambodian peasants during a state-sponsored massacre between 1975 and 1979. Pond was only nine years old when he lost his family in a Khmer Rouge death camp set up in the Buddhist temple where his family used to pray. He was one of 500 children forced into the Watt Aik camp. Only 60 survived.

"But today he is anything but numb. Pond preaches peace between Laotian and Cambodian gangs in Lowell, Massachussetts, and also returns each year to Cambodia to work with children. This slim, humble man is always laughing, passionate, and caring. He has won a slew of awards, including the prestigious Reebok Human Rights Award. 'He saves lives one by one, sometimes at great risk to himself,' says US District Judge Mark Wolf, a friend of Pond's. 'Arn is almost beyond heroic. He's endured horrible hardships to get to this country, and instead of being embittered, he's developed tremendous compassion and remarkable insights into solutions.'

"As a peacemaker, Pond sometimes gets grief from both sides. 'My kids say, "Arn, you agree too much with the police" and they spit on my face and say "I don't need your help." Then the police say, "Arn, you're on the gangs' side. We should throw them in jail and toss away the key." And it hurts me. But being the middle is being the bridge. It takes two hands to clap and very clearly I hold my stance.'"

Adapted from: Grossfeld, Stan. 2000. "He Saves Lives." *The Boston Globe*. 19 June 2000.

1. In what ways does Pond deserve the title "remarkable"?
2. What steps has he taken to make the world a better place?
3. What message can we take from Pond's comment that "being in the middle is being the bridge. It takes two hands to clap and very clearly I hold my stance"?

RECAP

1. What have some schools done to improve cohesion among the students and staff?
2. What is the link between workplace stress and violence?
3. Do you agree with the comment that psychological abuse is just as damaging to the victim as physical abuse? Explain your answer.

Activities

Show your knowledge

1. Create a New Vocabulary glossary of the terms and phrases you learned in this chapter.
   a) Record the definition of each term.
   b) Use these terms to create twelve questions to ask a classmate. Make each question more difficult than the last.
2. What are the major causes of conflict in society? In your view, what is the most important cause of conflict in society today? Explain fully.
3. Carefully outline three of the high costs associated with conflict in contemporary Canada. In your opinion, which of these costs has the greatest impact? Why?
4. Describe five ways conflict can be reduced. Rank order them from most effective to least effective.
5. Briefly describe three types of discrimination in Canada today. Which are most prevalent in your community?
6. What are the major factors that have contributed to the high level of exclusion experienced by Aboriginal peoples?
7. Describe five factors linked to helping behaviour.
8. Which two recommendations of the jury in the OC Transpo case do you believe were most important? Explain your reasoning.

Practise your thinking skills

9. If it were proven conclusively that competition has a number of negative effects on humans, how might each of the following be altered to make them less competitive?
   a) sports
   b) schools
   c) workplace environments
10. Record five steps that parents could take to raise their children to deal with conflict more effectively. Explain two of these steps in some detail. Which if any were practised in your home?
11. Find articles from your local newspaper that deal with violence and aggression in your community. From your analysis of the articles, which social science—anthropology, sociology, or psychology—is best able to explain this type of human behaviour? Carefully explain your position with specific arguments and evidence.

Activities

12. What could be done in your local community to reduce the conditions that cause dehumanization?
13. Why do you think most people do not reach Kohlberg's final stage of moral development? How far along on Kohlberg's scale would you rank yourself? Why?
14. Develop a list of important "peacemakers." What characteristics do they have in common? Which of these characteristics do you personally have? Which of these characteristics do you not have?
15. Does "conflict" or "cohesion" best describe the general atmosphere in your school? Use examples to support your answer. What practical steps could students and staff take to reduce conflict and increase cohesion?
16. If you had been present in New York on the night of Kitty Genovese's murder, what do you think you would have done? Why? Be as honest as possible in your answer.

Communicate your ideas

17. Write a one-page opinion piece that describes how you feel about the way Aboriginal peoples were treated in Canadian history. Be prepared to share your thoughts with your classmates.
18. Write a letter to the editor of your local newspaper arguing either for or against greater gun control restrictions in Canada. Send the letter after you have had it peer- or teacher-reviewed.
19. Research and write a short profile of a person who has worked to improve the cohesion of your school or local community. Present your profile to the class, or, if possible, invite your subject to visit the class to discuss his or her work.
20. Create a "Conflict Journal" in which you note all examples of conflict that you encounter on a daily basis. Assign each of them a rank from 1 to 5, with 1 being minor and 5 being major. At the end of one week, write a brief summary of the number, sources, and results of conflicts in your life.
21. Write a one-page description of an incident involving discrimination that you have personally encountered. Include details of how the incident affected you.

Activities

22. Debate the following proposition: "All attempts to resolve past discrimination are doomed to failure."
23. In small groups that include both male and female students, discuss the "Voices of Youth" feature on page 332. Offer your own interpretations. Record the best "voices" and be prepared to share them with the rest of the class.

Apply your knowledge

24. Record three conflict situations you recently experienced.
    a) Explain what the conflict was about.
    b) Describe how you dealt with the conflict.
    c) Analyze how you could have resolved the conflict in a more positive manner.
25. Record the names of two friends or family members who solve problems very effectively.
    a) What personality characteristics do these people have?
    b) What is their greatest "trick" in dealing with problems?
    c) How do their personality characteristics compare to yours?
    d) Which of your personality characteristics should you work at improving so that there is more cohesion and less conflict in your life?
26. Look through a newspaper and compare the number and length of stories describing conflict to those involving altruistic behaviour. Which type of story is most common? Which type of story has the most space devoted to it? Suggest reasons for your findings.
27. If Carol Gilligan is correct in her analyis that males and females employ different moral perspectives, explain how society might change if there were more women
    a) in elected political positions
    b) heading major corporations
    c) heading international organizations such as the United Nations

Bibliography

Chapter 1

Beauchesne, Eric. 1999. "Workplace Stress Hurts, Bosses Learning." *The Calgary Herald.* 10 December 1999.

Bonner, Raymond, Fessenden, Ford. 2000. "States Without Death Penalty Have Lower Homicide Rates." *New York Times.* 22 September 2000.

Canadian Centre for Justice Statistics. 1983-1999. "Homicide in Canada." Volumes 2 (1), 16 (11), 17 (9), 18 (12).

Corbett, Ron. 2000. "Two Workers Shot by Pierre Lebrun Recount Coming Face to Face With Killer." *The Ottawa Citizen.* 15 January 2000.

Morgenthau, Robert M. 1998. "The Death Penalty Hinders the Fight Against Crime." In Steve Schonebaum, ed. *Does Capital Punishment Deter Crime?* San Diego, CA. Greenhaven Press.

Pataki, George E. 1998. "The Death Penalty Is a Deterrent." In Steve Schonebaum, ed. *Does Capital Punishment Deter Crime?* San Diego, CA. Greenhaven Press.

Chapter 2

Adams, Richard A. 1988. *The Eighth Day: Social Evolution as the Self-Organization of Energy.* Austin, TX. University of Texas.

Benedict, Ruth. 1946. *The Chrysanthemum and the Sword.* Boston. Houghton Mifflin.

Benedict, Ruth. 1959. *Patterns of Culture.* New York. Houghton Mifflin.

Bodley, John H. 2000. *Cultural Anthropology: Tribes, States, and the Global System.* 3rd ed. Mountain View, CA. Mayfield Publishing Company.

Freeman, Derek. 1983. *Margaret Mead and Samoa: The Making and Unmaking of an Anthropological Myth.* Cambridge, MA. Harvard University Press.

Galdikas, Biruté. 1995. *Reflections of Eden: My Years with the Orangutans of Borneo.* Boston, MA. Little, Brown & Co.

Knutilla, Murray. 1996. *Introducing Sociology: A Critical Perspective.* Toronto. Oxford University Press.

Mead, Margaret. 1973 edition. *Coming of Age in Samoa: A Psychological Study of Primitive Youth for Western Civilization.* New York. William Morrow & Co.

Murdock, George. 1945. "The Common Denominator of Cultures." In Ralph Linton, ed. *The Science of Man in the World.* New York. Columbia University Press.

Parsons, Talcott. 1969. *Politics and Social Structure.* New York. Free Press.

Shirky, Clay. "What a Difference a Gene Makes." *FEED Magazine.* [Online]. Available http://www.feedmag.com/feature/fr335lofi.html 15 May 2000.

Chapter 3

American Anthropological Association. 1997. *Principles of Professional Responsibility.* Washington, D.C. AAA. (The principles can be also be found at http://www.ameranthassn.org/ethcode.htm)

Angle, Roderick, Niemark, Jill. 1997. "Nature's Clone." *Psychology Today.* 30 (4).

Argyle, Michael, Dean, Janet. 1965. "Eye Contact, Distance and Affiliation." *Sociometry.* 28.

Buist, Steve. 2000. "Racial Intelligence at Issue." *The Hamilton Spectator.* 15 April 2000.

Chagnon, Napoleon A. 1983. *Yanonamö: The Fierce People.* 3rd ed. New York. Holt, Rinehart & Winston.

Coleman, Simon, Watson, Helen. 1990. *An Introduction to Anthropology.* New York. Chartwell Books Inc.

Eysenck, Hans, Eysenck, Michael. 1989. *Mind Watching: Why We Behave the Way We Do.* Toronto. McGraw-Hill Ryerson Ltd.

Schultz, Emily A., Lavenda, Robert H. 2001. *Cultural Anthropology: A Perspective on the Human Condition.* Mountain View, CA. Mayfield Publishing Company.

Statistics Canada. 2000. *The Daily: 18 October 2000.* [Online]. Available http://www.statcan.ca/Daily/English/001018/d001018.htm 19 October 2000.

"The Mirror of Your Soul." 1998. *The Economist.* 346 (8049).

Tierney, Patrick. 2000. *Darkness in El Dorado: How*

Scientists and Journalists Devastated the Amazon. New York. C.H. Norton.

Urquhart M.C., Buckley, K.A.H., eds. 1971. *Historical Statistics of Canada*. Toronto. Macmillan Company of Canada.

Valentine, Charles. 1978. "Introduction." In Betty Valentine, *Hustling and Other Hard Work*. New York. Free Press.

Chapter 4

AABA. 1997. "Ads and Eating Disorders: Organizations Respond." *Newsletter of the American Anorexia Bulimia Association*. 12 January 1997.

Allen, Laura, Gorski, Roger. 1992. "Sexual Orientation and the Size of the Anterior Commissure in the Human Brain." *Proceedings of the National Academy of Sciences of the USA*. 89.

Atkinson, D.R., Morten, G., Sue, D.W. 1983. *Counselling American Minorities: A Cross-Cultural Perspective*. Dubuque, IA. William C. Brown.

Barry, Dave. 2000. "Men Have to Work at Humouring Women." *The Kitchener-Waterloo Record*. 18 March 2000.

Colapinto, John. 2000. *As Nature Made Him: The Boy Who Was Raised a Girl*. New York. Harper Collins.

Cooley, Charles. 1902. *Human Nature and the Social Order*. New York. Scribner.

DiManno, Rosie. 1999. "The Queen of Cunning." *The Toronto Star*. 4 November 1999.

Field, Sharon, Hoffman, Alan, Posch, Margaret. 1997. "Self-Determination During Adolescence: A Developmental Perspective." *Remedial and Special Education*. 18.

Follain, John. 1999. "Science Puts Love to the Test." *The Toronto Star*. 14 January 1999.

Fraser, Laura. 1997. *Losing It: America's Obsession with Weight and the Industry That Feeds On It*. New York. Dutton.

Gillespie, Kelly. 1999. "Dismantling the Wall, Brick by Brick." *The Toronto Star*. 21 February 1999.

Gillespie, Kerry, Shephard, Michelle. 1999. "Dorothy Homolka: Mother Supports Daughter's Campaign." *The Toronto Star*. 4 November 1999.

Haney, Daniel Q. "Designer Babies." *CNEWS*. [Online.] Available http://www.caldercup.com/CNEWSScience003/21babies2.html 21 March 2000.

"High Incidence of OCD in Kids Suffering Head Injury." *Medical Post*. 33.

Kidwell et al. 1995. "Adolescent Identity Exploration: A Test of Erikson's Theory of Transitional Crisis." *Adolescence*. 30.

King, Tara. 1999. "For Nez Pearce, Their Real Names Are Their Real Selves." *The Seattle Times*. 12 December 1999.

Kurman, Jenny, Eshel, Yohanan. 1998. "Self-Enhancement, Generality Level of Self-Evaluation and Emotional Adjustment." *The Journal of Social Psychology*. 138.

Mead, George Herbert. 1962. *Mind, Self and Society*. Chicago, Ill. The University of Chicago Press.

Michaels, Evelyne. 1994. "High Anxiety." *Chatelaine*. 1 January 1994.

Naylor, Cecile, Wood, F.B. 1988. "Sex Differences in Cortical Activation Patterns During an Orthographic Analysis Task Using rCBF Methodology." *Society for Neuroscience Abstracts*. 14.

Nilsen, Richard. 1999. "TV Leaves an Emptiness in the Soul." *The Arizona Republic*. 6 April 1999.

Peele, Stanton, DeGrandpre, Richard. 1995. "My Genes Made Me Do It." *Psychology Today*. July 1995.

Seaman, Debbie. 1999. "Bad to the Bone." *Time*. 27 December 1999.

Sheppard, Robert. 2000. "How We Think." *Maclean's*. 1 May 2000.

Sue, S., Sue, D.W. 1971. "Chinese-American Personality and Mental Health." *Amerasia Journal*. 1.

Tannen, Deborah. 1994. *Talking from 9 to 5: How Women's and Men's Conversational Styles Affect Who Gets Heard, Who Gets Credit, and What Gets Done at Work*. New York. W. Morrow and Company.

Yeh, Christine, Huang, Karen. 1996. "The Collectivistic Nature of Ethnic Identity Development Among Asian-American College Students." *Adolescence*. 31.

Chapter 5

Bodley, John H. 2000. *Cultural Anthropology: Tribes, States and the Global System*. 3rd ed. Mountain View, CA. Mayfield Publishing Company.

Gilligan, Carol. 1992. *In a Different Voice: Psychological Theory and Women's Development*. Cambridge, MA. Harvard University Press.

Goffman, Erving. 1961. *Asylums: Essays on the Social Situation of Mental Patients and Other Inmates*. Garden City, NY. Anchor.

Macionis, John, et. al. 1997. *Sociology*. Scarborough, ON. Prentice-Hall Canada Inc.

Mahmood, Cynthia, Brady, Stacy. 2000. *The Guru's Gift: An Ethnography Exploring Gender Equality with North American Sikh Women*. Mountain View, CA. Mayfield Publishing Co.

Orr, David. 2000. "Afghans Look to Escape Oppression." *The Globe and Mail*. 9 June 2000.

Shelley, Robert. 2000. "Starving for Acceptance." *The Globe and Mail*. 17 July 2000.

Smith, Graeme. 2000. "Parents May Hit Children: Judge." *The Toronto Star*. 6 July 2000.

"Tips on Curfews." [Online]. Available. http://parentingteens.about.com/parenting/parentingteens/library/weekly/aa111699.htm 4 December 2000.

Vollman, William T. 2000. "Across the Divide." *New Yorker*. 15 May 2000.

Chapter 6

Adams, Michael. "Canadian Attitudes Toward Crime and Justice." *FORUM on Corrections Research*. 2(1). [Online]. Available http://www.csc-scc.gc.ca/text/pblct/forum/e02/3021f.shtml 1990.

Angus Reid Group. 1996. *Alternatives to Incarceration, Final Report Submitted to Solicitor General*. Ottawa. Angus Reid Group.

Bennet, Vanora. 1998. "Russia's Social Institutions Fail to Prepare Youths for Society."*Los Angeles Times*. 22 September 1998.

Berscheid, E., Hatfield, E. 1978. *Interpersonal Attraction*. New York. Random House.

Boyd, Monica, Norris, Doug. 1999. "The Crowded Nest: Young Adults at Home." *Canadian Social Trends*. Spring 1999.

Canadian Centre for Justice Statistics. 1997. *Adult Correctional Services in Canada, 1995-1996*. Ottawa. Minister of Industry.

Faleh, Waiel. 2000. "Mass Weddings Help Couples Navigate Sanctions Against Iraq." *Kitchener-Waterloo Record*. 12 August 2000.

"Fear Imprisons Debate on Jail Issue." 1998. *The Toronto Star*. 28 November 1998.

Fisher, H.E. 1992. *Anatomy of Love: The Natural History of Monogamy, Adultery, and Divorce*. New York. W.W. Norton.

Gibbs, James L. 1963. "The Kpelle Moot." *Africa*. 33. Also in Aaron Podolefsky and Peter J. Brown, eds. 1999. *Applying Cultural Anthropology: An Introductory Reader*. 4th ed. Mountain View, CA. Mayfield Publishing Company.

Gibson, Valerie. 1999. "Never Met? Say 'Hello' and 'I Do.'" *The Toronto Star*. 11 February 1999.

Goldstein, Melvyn C. 1987. "When Brothers Share a Wife." In Aaron Podolefsky and Peter J. Brown, eds. 1999. *Applying Cultural Anthropology: An Introductory Reader*. 4th ed. Mountain View, CA. Mayfield Publishing Company.

Henslin, James, Nelson, Adie. 1996. *Sociology: A Down-to-Earth Approach*. Scarborough. Allyn & Bacon Canada.

Isaac, Jennifer. 2000. "Wed Through the Web." *The Calgary Sun*. 24 March 2000.

Kilbride, Philip L. 1996. "African Polygyny: Family Values and Contemporary Changes." In Aaron Podolefsky and Peter J. Brown, eds. 1999. *Applying Cultural Anthropology: An Introductory Reader*. 4th ed. Mountain View, CA. Mayfield Publishing Company.

Linden, Rick. 2000. *Criminology: A Canadian Perspective*. Toronto. Harcourt Canada.

Macionis, John J., Nancarrow Clarke, Juanne, Gerber, Linda M. 1997. *Sociology*. 2nd Canadian ed. Scarborough. Prentice Hall Allyn and Bacon Canada.

Monaghan, John, Just, Peter. 2000. *Social and Cultural Anthropology: A Very Short Introduction*. New York. Oxford University Press.

Murstein, Bernard. "What's Love Got to Do With It? The Changing Role of Love in Marital Choice Across the Centuries." *Connecticut College Magazine Online*. 5(1). [Online]. Available http://www.conncoll.edu/Spiff/CCMOnline/51/Features/love.html Summer 1995.

Schellenberg, Kathryn. 1996. "Taking It or Leaving It:

Instability and Turnover in a High-Tech Firm." *Work and Occupations*. 23(2).

Smith, Douglas A. 1987. "Police Response to Interpersonal Violence: Defining the Parameters of Legal Control." *Social Forces*. 65(3).

Smith, Douglas A., Visher, Christy A. 1981. "Street-Level Justice: Situational Determinants of Police Arrest Decisions." *Social Problems*. 29(2).

Solicitor General Canada. "Alternatives to Incarceration." *Solicitor General Fact Sheets*. [Online]. Available http://www.sgc.gc.ca/Efact/ealtincarceration.htm 15 February 2001.

Sternberg, Robert. 1986. "A Triangular Theory of Love." *Psychological Review*. 93.

Sudarkasa, N. 1988. "African and Afro-American Family Structure." In J. Cole, ed. 1988. *Anthropology for the Nineties*. New York: Free Press.

Chapter 7

Angus Reid Group, the Royal Bank. 1997. *Workplace 2000: Working Toward the Millenium: A Portrait of Working Canadians*.

Burstein, M., Tienharra, N., Hewson, P., Warrander, B. 1975. *Canadian Work Values: Findings of a Work Ethic Survy and a Job Satisfaction Survey*. Ottawa. Information Canada.

Career Press. 1993. *How to Manage Conflict: A Quick and Handy Guide for Any Manager or Business Owner*. Hawthorne, NJ. Career Press.

Corleone, Elvira. 2000. "Planned 60-Hour Work Week Alarms Labour." *The Toronto Star*. 25 August 2000.

Crompton, Susan, Vickers, Michael. 2000. "One Hundred Years of Labour Force." *Canadian Social Trends*. Summer 2000.

Economic Council of Canada. 1990. *Good Jobs, Bad Jobs: Employment in the Service Sector*. Ottawa. Economic Council of Canada.

Ekos Research Associates Inc. 1997. *Rethinking Government III: Final Report*. Ottawa. Ekos Research Associates Inc.

Foot, David, Stoffman, Daniel. 1999. *Boom, Bust & Echo 2000: Profiting From the Demographic Shift in the New Millennium*. Toronto. Macfarlane Walter & Ross.

Fox, Matthew. 1994. *The Reinvention of Work: A New Vision of Livelihood for Our Times*. New York. HarperCollins.

Harvey, Robin. 2000. "A Lesson in Finding Work." *The Toronto Star*. 20 June 2000.

Human Resources Development Canada. *Pamphlet 12—Sexual Harassment*. [Online]. Available http://info.load-otea.hrdc-drhc.gc.ca/labour_standards/pamphlets/harass.htm 15 December 2000.

Janigan, Mary. 2000. "The Wealth Gap." *Maclean's*. 28 August 2000.

Kimbrell, Andrew. 1999. "Breaking the Job Lock." *The Utne Reader*. January-February 1999.

Krohe, James, Jr. 1999. "Workplace Stress." *Across the Board*. 36(2).

Laver, Ross. 1999. "The Best and Worst Jobs." *Maclean's*. 31 May 1999.

Leahy, F.M. ed. 1983. *Historical Statistics of Canada*. 2nd ed. Ottawa. Statistics Canada.

Lowe, Graham S. 2000. *The Quality of Work: A People-Centred Agenda*. Toronto. Oxford University Press Canada.

Macklem, Katherine. 2000. "A Media Colossus." *Maclean's*. 25 September 2000.

Maynard, Rona. 1987. "How Do You Like Your Job?" *Report on Business Magazine*. November 1987.

Roper, Thomas A., West, John B. *Recent Developments in Employment Law: Sexual Harassment*. [Online]. Available http://www.lexpert.ca/areas/employment.html 15 December 2000.

Saul, John Ralston. 1994. *The Doubter's Companion: A Dictionary of Aggressive Common Sense*. Toronto. Penguin.

Stark, Amy. 1992. *Because I Said So: Recognizing the Influence of Childhood Dynamics on Office Politics*. New York. Pharos Books.

Statistics Canada. 1986. *Census of Canada—Population—Industry Trends*. Catalogue 93-152. Ottawa. Minister of Industry.

Statistics Canada. 1998. *Labour Force Historical Review*. Catalogue 71 F0004XCB. Ottawa. Minister of Industry.

Statistics Canada. *Employment by Detailed Industry and Sex*. [Online]. Available http://www.statcan.ca/english/Pgdb/People/Labour/labor10a.htm 22 February 2001.

Strother, Susan G. 2000. "Telecommuting Finding Its Place." *The Orlando Sentinel*. 8 August 2000.

Wall, Bob. 1999. *Working Relationships: The Simple Truth About Getting Along with Friends and Foes at Work*. Palo Alto, CA. Davies-Black.

Young, Rick. 2000. "An Interview with Catherine Renaud." Unpublished.

Chapter 8

Alberta Distance Learning Centre. *Online School Registration Guide*. [Online]. Available http://www.adlc.ab.ca 4 December 2000.

Barlow, Maude, Robertson, Heather Jane. 1994. *Class Warfare: The Assault on Canada's Schools*. Toronto. Key Porter Books.

Brand, David. "Corporate Censorship in the Classroom." [Online]. Available http://www.adbusters.org/campaigns/commercialfree/toolbox/ynnsucks.html 4 December 2000.

Brent, Allen. 1983. *Philosophy and Educational Foundations*. London. George Allen & Unwin (Publishers) Ltd.

Canadian Teachers' Federation. "Canadians Say No to Advertising in Schools." [Online]. Available http://209.121.244.130/E/PRESS/ATTACH-5.HTM 15 December 2000.

CBC. 1999. "Children In Trouble: Guns In Schools." *CBC News in Review Resource Guide*. September 1999.

Fine, Sean. 2000. "Are the Schools Failing Boys?" *The Globe and Mail*. 5 September 2000.

Freedman, Joe. "Charter Schools in Atlantic Canada." *Atlantic Institute for Market Studies*. [Online]. Available http://www.aims.ca/Publications/charterschool/charterpg1.html#top March 1997.

Henslin, James, Nelson, Adie. 1996. *Sociology: A Down-to-Earth Approach*. Scarborough. Allyn & Bacon Canada.

Independent Learning Centre. [Online]. Available http://ilc.edu.gov.on.ca/01/02.htm 4 December 2000.

Leo Ussak School Home Page. "Frequently Asked Questions." [Online]. Available http://www.arctic.ca/LUS/FAQ.html 4 December 2000.

MacLeod, Susan. 1999. "One Size Fits All." *Today's Parent*. 9 January 1999.

Morris, Chris. 1999. "Self-Esteem Fleeting, Fragile for Canadian Kids." Canadian Press. 28 October 1999.

Neatby, Hilda. 1953. *So Little for the Mind*. Toronto. Clarke, Irwin.

Patch, Catherine. 2000. "Safety First." *The Toronto Star*. 17 August 2000.

Pedwell, Laurie. 1999. "Letters to Parents on the YNN Pilot at Meadowvale." [Online]. Available http://www.peel.edu.on.ca/facts/ynnletters.htm 4 December 2000.

Plains Indians Cultural Survival School. "About PICSS." [Online]. Available http://www.cbe.ab.ca/b864/default.htm#school 4 December 2000.

Porter, John, Porter, Marian, Blishen, Bernard. 1982. *Stations and Callings*. Toronto. Methuen.

Robertson, Heather Jane. 1997. "Charter Schools Take Us Backward, Not Forward." *Education Monitor*. Summer 1997.

Schofield, John. 2000. "Shopping for Scholarships." *Maclean's*. 20 November 2000.

"School Code Step Forward." 2000. *The London Free Press*. 27 April 2000.

Smith, D.S. 1996. "Parent-Generated Home Study in Canada." *The Canadian School Executive*. 15(8). [Online] Available http://user.fundy.net./fplace/overview.htm 4 December 2000.

Stamp, Robert M. 1982. *The Schools of Ontario: 1876-1976*. Toronto. University of Toronto Press.

YNN. "Frequently Asked Questions." *Athena Educational Partners*. [Online]. Available http://ynn.ca/faqs/faqs.html 15 December 2000.

Zarzour, Kim. 1994. *Battling the Schoolyard Bully*. Toronto. Harper Perennial.

Chapter 9

Brym, Robert, Lenton, Rhonda L. 2001. *Hot Flashes in a Cold Climate: Online Dating in Canada*. Toronto. MSN.CA.

Hampton, Keith N., Wellman, Barry. 2000. "Examining Community in the Digital Neighbourhood: Early Results from Canada's Wired Suburb." In Toru Ishida and Katherine Isbister, eds. *Digital Cities: Technologies, Experiences, and Future Perspectives*. Heidelberg, Germany. Springer-Verlag.

Henley, Jon. 2000. "France Adopts Touch Anti-Sect Law." *The Guardian*. 22 June 2000.

Mansfield, Nick. 1982. *Introductory Sociology: Canadian Perspectives*. Toronto. Collier Macmillan.

Ferry, Jon. 2000. "No Easy Answer to High Native Suicide Rates." *The Lancet*. 355(9207).

Women's Legal Education and Action Fund. "About Us." *LEAF*. [Online]. Available http://www.leaf.ca 8 January 2001.

REAL Women of Canada. "Who We Are." *REAL Women of Canada*. [Online]. Available http://www.realwomenca.com 8 January 2001.

University of Michigan. "Walpole Island Study Site." [Online]. Available http://www-personal.umich.edu~ksands/Warpole.html 25 November 2000.

Chapter 10

Blaney, Fay. 1998. "Bill 31 Still Discriminates." *Kinesis*. November 1998.

Cloud, John. 1999. "Can a Man of 25 Claim Age Bias?" *Time*. 16 August 1999.

Cooper, Kenneth J. 1996. "Women Under Virtual House Arrest." *The Washington Post*. 7 October 1996.

DeMont, John. 1997. "Fontaine's Vision: The New Grand Chief Aims for Unity." *Maclean's*. 11 August 1997.

DeMont, John. 1994. "Murder, He Wrote: A Newfoundland Anthropologist Has Become an Expert on Serial Killers." *Maclean's*. 31 November 1994.

De Waal, Frans B.M. 1998. "Survival of the Kindest." *The Chronicle of Higher Education*. 7 August 1998.

Dowsett Johnston, Ann. 1999. "Welcome to the Gender Wars." *Maclean's*. 27 September 1999.

Grossfeld, Stan. 2000. "He Saves Lives." *Boston Globe*. 19 June 2000.

Henslin, James, Nelson, Adie. 1996. *Sociology: A Down-to-Earth Approach*. Scarborough. Allyn & Bacon Canada.

Hoff Sommers, Christina. 2000. *The War Against Boys: How Misguided Feminism is Harming Our Young Men*. New York. Simon & Schuster.

"Human Rights – Canada: Keeping Our Own House in Order." *Canada and the World Backgrounder*. 1 May 1997.

Kerr, Richard, McLean, Janice. *Paying for Violence: Some of the Costs of Violence Against Women in B.C.* [Online]. Available http://www.weq.gov.bc.ca/paying-for-violence/payingforviolence.stm May 1996.

Kristof, Nicholas D. 1996. "Do Korean Men Still Beat Their Wives? Definitely." *The New York Times*. 5 December 1996.

Lai, Daniel. 1999. "Violence Exposure and Mental Health of Adolescents in Small Towns: An Exploratory Study." *Canadian Journal of Public Health*. May/June 1999.

Martin, Sandra. 2000. "Boys' Own Feminist Crusader." *The Globe and Mail*. 17 June 2000.

O'Hara, Jane. 2000. "Abuse of Trust." *Maclean's*. 26 June 2000.

Ouimet, Marc. 1999. "Crime in Canada and in the United States: A Comparative Analysis." *Canadian Review of Sociology and Anthropology*. August 1999.

Ponting, J. Rick, Kiely, Jerilynn. 1999. "Public Opinion on Aboriginal Rights." In Robert J. Brym, ed. *Society in Question: Sociological Readings for the 21st Century*. Toronto. Harcourt Brace Canada.

Sims, Calvin. 1997. "Justice in Peru: Rape Victim is Pressed to Marry Attacker." *The New York Times*. 12 March 1997.

Sprott, Jane, Doob, Anthony. 2000. "Bad, Sad, and Rejected: The Lives of Aggressive Children." *Canadian Journal of Criminology*. April 2000.

Glossary

A

acculturation the process of slowly adopting the customs of the country in which you live

acculturation theory a theory that identifies different categories or labels for the different ways people integrate their attitudes toward their ethnic group with their attitudes toward the larger society

adversarial the term describing a certain type of criminal justice system. In adversarial systems, two sides compete to win a case, sometimes at the cost of the search for truth.

advocacy groups groups that operate to better the conditions of their own members or another specific group of people or cause

agoraphobia a fear of leaving the home, or a general fear of open spaces

alienation in the work of Karl Marx, a feeling of unhappiness and estrangement caused by a work situation in which workers are not allowed to be creative and do not appreciate or take pride in their work. In a wider context, a feeling of not fitting in with other people or with society as a whole.

altruism showing active concern for other people, often resulting in voluntarily giving more time or money to a person or a cause than can possibly be expected in return.

altruistic suicide the term originated by Émile Durkheim for suicide that occurs when people knowingly enter an impossible situation and sacrifice their lives for another

ambiguity in the work world, confusion that results from goals, roles, or procedures being unclear. In a wider context, a state of affairs that, in part or entirely, can be understood or interpreted in more than one way.

analytical psychology the branch of psychology founded by Carl Jung that, in opposition to psychoanalysis, regards sexuality as only one of many factors influencing human behaviour

anomic suicide the term originated by Émile Durkheim for suicide caused by an individual's being overwhelmed by sudden change in society

anonymity a state of being faceless and nameless

anthropology the scientific study of the development of the human species and of the various cultures that make up humanity

anticipatory socialization the process of learning how to think ahead and to plan appropriate behaviour in new situations

anti-Semitism hostility to or prejudice and discrimination against Jewish people

antisocial personality disorder a relatively rare psychotic disorder whose symptoms involve pathological lying, taking pleasure in causing others pain, and a lack of guilt over one's harmful actions

arranged marriage a form of marriage in which the parents of each member of the couple select who their child will marry (also known as **endogamy**)

assimilate to absorb a person or group into a larger group or culture, especially by causing them to acquire the characteristics of the larger group or culture

authoritarian personality a personality type proposed by psychologist Theodor Adorno. People with this personality type are more prejudiced than others, having high levels of intolerance, insecurity, and respect for authority.

avoider a person who manages conflict by withdrawing from difficult situations

B

baby boom the period of time following the Second World War during which family size began to increase

behavioural psychology the school of psychology originating with John Watson and others that has as its goal the prediction and control of human behaviour

blended families families formed when couples

remarry and bring with them children from their former relationships

bourgeoisie the term used by Karl Marx for the rich and powerful groups in society who own factories, land, and machinery

bride-wealth in pastoralist cultures, the value a bride brings to a marriage, in the form of cattle transferred from the bride's family to the groom's family

bullying acting in a hostile, aggressive way towards another. Specific acts of bullying include name calling, rejection, physical intimidation, and assault.

bureaucracies large, highly-structured organizations that tend to function in an impersonal manner, first studied by Max Weber

burqah head-to-foot clothing worn by females in some Islamic countries such as Afghanistan

C

capitalism an economic system that allows for the unrestricted accumulation of wealth by private parties investing in and owning capital

career in the work world, a person's profession or occupation, or a person's advancement through life in a profession

career paths the distinct job or sets of jobs that people choose to work in during a lifetime of employment

category a large collection of people who have something in common, but do not know or interact with each other, such as "teenagers" or "criminals"

caste lines a term used in Hindu culture for social classes. Each caste line is characterized by a distinct economic background and family status.

causal theories theories in which one variable is claimed to be the cause of another variable

charter school an independent school supported by public funds and overseen by representatives from the parent community

citations mentions of sources of information. Citations take different forms depending on whether they appear within text paragraphs or in bibliographies.

class conflict the concept originated by Karl Marx of struggle between powerful and powerless groups in society

claustrophobia a fear of enclosed spaces

code of conduct a set of rules introduced by the Ontario government in April 2000. The rules are intended to improve the climate of schools by increasing discipline.

coercive bureaucracies rigid structures, such as prisons, that operate to correct or change the behaviour of people

cognitive psychology the branch of psychology that studies how people perceive and deal with their environment, as well as how they learn, remember, and forget

cohesion a sense of unity that often results from working closely together with others to solve problems

collectivist, collectivistic the term describing the practice of placing the welfare of the group or community above the freedoms of the individual

common-law relationships relationships in which a couple lives together without getting legally married

communal the term describing a lifestyle in which all members of a community live and work together

compromiser a person who manages conflict by taking something from all parties involved and giving up something in return when making a decision

concrete notes detailed notes that provide a full description of an incident, including its participants, location, tone, and conclusion

conditioned response the term used by Ivan Pavlov for a response that is based on previous learning, such as feeling excited before meeting an old friend

conditioned stimulus the term used by Ivan Pavlov for a stimulus—for example, the sound of a can opener—that causes a response in a subject—for example, salivation in anticipation of food—only after the subject has learned to associate the response with the stimulus

conflict a state of opposition, hostilities, or struggle characterized by negative feelings that sometimes result in verbal or physical fights

conflict resolution the process of solving disputes, especially in ways that rely on consensus rather than violence

conflict school, conflict theory the branch of sociology, or the theory, based on the work of Karl Marx, that studies how humans compete for scarce resources. Two of the key resources examined are power and control in society.

conformity changing one's thoughts, feelings, and behaviour to meet the expectations of a group or authority figure

conscious mind the term used by Sigmund Freud for the part of our minds containing memories that we can recall

conscription the practice of forcing single men to join the military during a war or in anticipation of a war

consensus model a decision-making model that allows everyone to have input. Many sociologists have found that women tend to favour this type of decision-making model.

consequential theories theories that try to predict what will happen to a second variable if a first variable is changed

conservative philosophy the belief that the main purpose of schools is to teach students a rigid curriculum that includes skills for fitting into society and finding employment

consumption the use of goods and services

convergence in the global economy, the merging of a variety of communications technologies into one medium

corporatization the practice whereby businesses provide money, services, or facilities to schools in return for product exposure, such as free advertising

corpus callosum a thick bundle of nerves that runs between the left and right hemispheres of the brain

cultural anthropology the study of the cultures of living peoples

cultural diffusion the belief of early anthropologists, now largely discounted, that civilization developed in a single place on the earth and then spread to all others, sometimes in a deteriorated form

cultural evolutionism the now largely discounted belief of early anthropologists that all societies and cultures evolve through a series of predictable stages

culturally constructed concept an idea about the world and/or the people in it that is formed as a result of a person's cultural upbringing

culture beliefs and behaviours that are transmitted from generation to generation

culture of violence a culture that excuses the widespread use and depiction of physical acts that injure or harm others. Some anthropologists maintain that North America has such a culture.

D

dastaar a turban worn by Sikh men and increasingly by Sikh women

defence mechanisms the term used by Sigmund Freud for the techniques that the human mind uses to deal with feelings of anxiety, frustration, tension, or worry. Freud believed these techniques maintain our self-esteem by protecting our ego against negative feelings.

degradation ceremony an embarrassing ritual that some total institutions force members to take part in in order to weaken members' identities

dehumanization a process whereby people come to see each other no longer as human beings but as simple objects

delusions incorrect beliefs that a person holds even when faced with evidence to the contrary

demography the study of the statistics of births, deaths, disease and so on, as a means to understand the conditions of life in communities

dependent variable a factor that is caused or influenced by another variable

deterrence the use of fear to discourage or prevent criminal behaviour

deterrent a form of strict punishment of lawbreakers that frightens others from similarly breaking the law

diffusion of responsibility a process that may occur when several people witness a crime. In this process, individuals avoid taking action to stop the crime because they believe that someone else will do so.

discrimination action based on prejudice, especially prejudice regarding race, age, or sex

disenfranchisement Aboriginal women's loss of Aboriginal status upon marrying non-Aboriginal men. This loss of status was stipulated in Section 12(1)(b) of the Indian Act.

displacement a defence mechanism by which we lash out at someone because we have suppressed anger or frustration from an earlier situation

dissonance an experience of confusion resulting from conflict between one's own beliefs and the beliefs of others

distance learning an alternative form of education that allows students to take courses without being physically present in the learning institution

distracter questions questions added to a survey to obscure the survey's true purpose

distribution the delivery of goods and services

division of labour the specialization of workers in the process of production

dominator a person who manages conflict by acting in a unilateral manner, often overlooking the ideas and needs of others

double-blind principle an experimental practice in which neither the experimenter nor the subject knows to which group (the control or experimental group) the subject belongs

downsizing permanently laying off or firing workers

dyad a social group consisting of two members

E

economic sectors distinct parts or branches of the economy

economy a social institution that organizes the production, distribution, and consumption of goods and services within a society

ego the term used by Sigmund Freud for the part of the unconscious mind that encourages us to do good things. It is the part of the mind most closely linked to our sense of self.

egoistic suicide the term originated by Émile Durkheim for suicide that is caused by an individual's not sharing any of the major values or goals of society

Electra complex the term used by Sigmund Freud for the rare case of a daughter's sexual attraction to her father and hostility toward her mother

empathy the ability to understand or experience the thoughts or feelings of other people

enculturation the learning process whereby we begin to learn the ideas, values, and beliefs of our culture

endogamy a form of marriage in which the parents of each member of the couple select who their child will marry (also known as an **arranged** marriage)

entrenched in the state of having existed for a long period of time and being well established as a result

equilibrium as used by Auguste Comte, the belief that society has a natural tendency to find a balance between forces of change and forces of stability

estrogen the female sex hormone

ethnicity a trait resulting from an individual's relationship to a group with which the individual believes he or she shares a common ancestry

ethnocentric the term describing the incorrect attitude, belief, or stance that one's own culture is superior and/or worthier than other cultures

ethnocentrism the term originated by anthropologist Franz Boas for the evaluation of other cultures by criteria specific to one's own, resulting in a judgment that other cultures are inferior

ethnographic studies studies of the culture and traditions of distinct peoples

expulsion the permanent removal of a student from school

extrovert the term used by Carl Jung for a person who seeks a large number of close associations with others and who draws strength or energy from these associations

F

family baggage memories and experiences related to family that we have accumulated and that sometimes interfere with our adult relationships

feminist the term describing groups that pursue goals of particular importance to women's lives

ferals human children raised by wild animals such as female wolves

field observation a sociological method used to gather data about behaviour. In this method, the investigator observes and records notes on subjects in their own environment.

First Nation an Aboriginal band, or an Aboriginal community functioning as a band but not having official band status

flexible workforce a workforce whose members can switch between various states of employment (for example, employed full-time, employed part-time, employed gradually through a course of training, partially retired, and so on)

formal organizations structured groups with comprehensive and elaborate rules

fraternal polyandry a form of marriage in which two or more brothers jointly take a wife

fraternal twins twins who have half their genes in common

free association the technique originated by Sigmund Freud in which a subject matches pairs of words to enable a therapist to gain entry into the subject's unconscious mind

free-choice marriage a marriage that results from both partners seeking and developing their relationship on their own initiative, without the intervention of a third party

frustration-aggression theory the psychological theory developed by John Dollard that states that if a person is motivated to achieve a certain goal, and is then prevented from achieving it, the aggressive drive will build up until it is eventually released

functional theory the idea originated by Bronislaw Malinowski that all institutions are designed and modified to meet the needs of the majority

functionalism, functionalist school the branch of sociology that studies society as a whole and analyzes how the parts of a society should work to achieve stability and well-being for all members

fundamentalist the term describing people who believe that religious laws must be strictly interpreted and that no compromise should be made with modern society

G

gallows humour humour that tends to focus on gory and sick situations

gender differences the physical differences that exist between males and females

gender roles the roles that society expects people to play based on their gender. Aggressive behaviour is part of the gender role for males in many societies.

gender socialization the different ways in which girls and boys are socialized, or learn to belong to society

general deterrence the discouragement, through fear of punishment, of the commission of crimes. This type of deterrence targets members of the general population who have never committed crimes
themselves.

genes biological building blocks that determine a person's hair colour, eye colour, height, and other physical characteristics

genitor in pastoralist cultures, the biological father of a child

ghetto in many central cities, an area in which poor people are forced to live to gain access to affordable day care, mental health services, and nutrition programs for children

glass ceiling the invisible barrier that keeps women from rising to the highest levels of management within corporations

global economy an economy in which goods and services, including information, cross national borders with few restrictions

H

hallucinations experiences in which a person sees or hears something that is not really there

heathen according to members of a more politically powerful culture, a person who does not belong to the religion of the more politically powerful culture and is therefore regarded as having no religion. This term was often applied to Aboriginal peoples by early settlers to Canada.

heritable a characteristic that is acquired through the genes

heroism conduct or qualities that show courage and nobility. A mark of heroism may be facing down danger while helping another.

hidden curriculum a set of unwritten goals of education. Conflict theorists consider these goals to include obedience to authority. Conflict theorists believe that the purpose of the education system is to achieve these goals in the lives of students in order to turn them into good workers.

humanities those disciplines that focus on the creative side of the human experience, such as art or literature

hypothesis a proposition or theory that a researcher is trying to prove

I

id the term used by Sigmund Freud for the pleasure-seeking, often self-destructive, part of the unconscious mind

identical twins twins who inherit identical genes

identity crisis a period in a person's life during which the person's self-concept and beliefs are challenged

ignorance lack of information or knowledge

immersion in Atkinson et al.'s stage model, the act of accepting a set of beliefs and incorporating them into one's life

impersonal institutions social institutions such as the government that affect the activities and behaviours of large groups of people

incongruity the result of putting ideas together in an unexpected or illogical way

independent variable a factor that has an effect on a second factor

Indian Act a Canadian government policy of 1876 that made Aboriginal peoples "wards of the state" by placing them on reserves and under the direct control of the federal government

individuality a psychological concept for the condition of being oneself and understanding who that self is in relation to others

individual psychology a system of therapy originated by Alfred Adler that focuses more on people's conscious minds than on their unconscious minds. Adler assumed that people are normally aware of the goals and values that motivate them.

Industrial Revolution the dramatic transformation of society resulting from the bulk of the working population turning from agriculture to industry

inferiority complex the term used by Alfred Adler for normal human feelings of inferiority that can, in extreme circumstances, lead to the inability to function normally

informal group a group in which members' interactions with one another are not determined by rules or a defined power structure

informants members of a group who provide information to social scientists who are studying the group

Information Revolution the dramatic transformation of society resulting from technologies such as the computer, the Internet, and other innovations in communications

informed consent the requirement that subjects must understand and agree to their participation in an experiment or observation before the results can be used

institutionalization the process whereby a person's ability to make decisions and live independently is destroyed because he or she has lived in a strictly controlled environment for too long

integrator a person who manages conflict by seeking to hear a variety of opinions before making a decision

intelligence quotient (IQ) a measurement of a person's general intelligence, obtained through written tests and comparisons of the results of the test with data on average intelligence

intervening variable a factor that causes difficulty in making a link between two other variables

introspection in Atkinson et al.'s stage model, questioning both one's own values and those of others while developing ethnic identity

introvert the term used by Carl Jung to describe an emotionally self-sufficient people who does not encourage a large number of close associations with others and who draws strength or energy from her or his inner life

irony a way of expressing oneself in which one says the opposite of what one really means

I-self one of the two selves that sociologist George Herbert Mead believed we create depending on the social setting we find ourselves in. Mead believed the I-self is our true self and is only revealed to those closest to us.

isolates children raised in almost total isolation within human households

J

job a piece of work done for hire or profit

job satisfaction the extent to which a person's job meets the person's expectations or desires

K

kin selection preferring and showing kindness towards one's relatives or family to help them survive. The result is that the genes of relatives or family, which are similar to one's own genes, have a better chance of spreading.

kinship relationships among members of a social group that are based on members' descent from common ancestors

Kpelle *moot* an informal system of justice in Africa in which the accused, the complainant, a mediator, and the community all attend a meeting to determine the resolution of a conflict

L

labour unions organized associations of workers formed to protect and further their rights and interests and to bargain collectively with employers

latent function the hidden purpose of an institution. For example, one of a school's latent functions is to teach students how to work together in unfamiliar situations.

looking-glass self the idea of self originated by Charles Cooley, which claimed that our view of ourselves is derived from how we think others perceive us

low self-control the characteristic of requiring instant gratification of all desires

M

mainstream the term describing the culture or customs of the majority of a population

manifest function the visible purpose of an institution. For example, one of a school's manifest functions is to help students develop academic skills.

material culture physical objects, such as CDs or prayer books, that are important to a culture

mechanization the introduction of machinery into factories

Me-self one of the two selves that sociologist George Herbert Mead believed we create depending on the social setting we find ourselves in. Mead believed the Me-self is our public self, guided by the rules and expectations of the roles we play.

militant the term describing people who are prepared to use extra-legal means, including violence, to achieve a social goal

modelling theory the psychological theory developed by Albert Bandura that states that humans learn aggression by observing others who behave in an aggressive manner

monogamy a form of marriage in which one woman is married to one man at a time

myth a true or fictional story that recounts supernatural events that are significant to members of a culture

N

nature-nurture debate the debate over whether nature (inherited, biological characteristics) or nurture (learned, environmental forces) has more of an impact on personality development

neo-Marxist the branch of sociology, based on the work of Karl Marx, that studies how humans compete for power and control in society (another name for **conflict school**)

neurosis a type of psychological disorder. People suffering from a neurosis usually experience very high levels of anxiety or tension but are generally able to manage their daily affairs.

new economy the term coined at the end of the twentieth century for the global economy of the twenty-first century

"no-fault" divorce a type of divorce practised in Canada that resulted from changes to The Divorce Act in 1968. In this type of divorce, no grounds are needed other than the separation of a couple for a period of time.

non-governmental organizations (NGOs) international charities or advocacy groups that scrupulously maintain their independence from national governments

non-profit organizations also known as "not for profit organizations," organizations whose purpose is not to make money but to provide the best service possible to its members or customers

normative bureaucracies organizations such as charities or religions that operate to help others or make society a better place

norms the behaviours that society expects from its members

nuclear family a family type that consists of a wife and husband and their biological children

O

obliger a person who manages conflict by playing down the differences between people while looking for common ground

obsessive-compulsive disorder a disorder in which a person has an obsession (recurring, uncontrollable thought or impulse) to be compulsive (engage in meaningless, repetitive behaviour)

Oedipus complex the term used by Sigmund Freud for the rare case of a son's sexual attraction to his mother and hostility toward his father

overload the state that results when a person take on too much work

P

participant observation the anthropological method of study where a researcher lives with a cultural group for an extended period to obtain an insider's understanding of the group

pastoralist the term describing cultures based on animal herding

pater in pastoralist cultures, a female who acts as the legal father of a child

patrilineal the term describing the kinship structure of certain societies. It means that property is bequeathed from the father to the male children of the family.

peer group a social group whose members are similar in age and status and share similar interests

personal institutions social institutions such as the family that affect individuals' lives intimately

personality an individual's relatively unchanging personal qualities and character

phenylethylamine a chemical hormone whose production in the brain can be triggered by eye contact or nad-touching with another person with thom one feels to be "in love." Alone one of around 300 chemicals in chocolate.

phobia an irrational and often debilitating fear

physical anthropology the study of the evolution of humankind, including the comparison of human genetic characteristics with those of apes, gorillas, and chimpanzees

polyandry a form of marriage in which a woman has more than one husband at a time

polygamy a form of marriage in which either a man has more than one wife at a time or a woman has more than one husband at a time

polygyny a form of marriage in which a man has more than one wife at a time

positivism the term originating in Auguste Comte's work for the belief that society can only be understood by rigidly applying the scientific method of analysis

post-industrial economy an economy that no longer relies on heavy industry

prejudice a preconceived opinion or judgment that does not take into account all relevant facts

primary group a group in which members have strong emotional or close personal attachments to each other

primary socialization the process of learning how to function in society at the most basic level

primary sector the sector of the economy dealing with the extraction of natural resources from the environment

primate a member of the mammal group with the most developed brains, such as a human, an ape, a gorilla, or a chimpanzee

production the creation of goods and services

profession a vocation or calling, or a declaration or avowal, often of belief in a religion

professionalizing with regard to conflict, seeing the conflict as a breakdown in teamwork rather than a result of the personal shortcomings of the individual(s) involved

progressive the term describing beliefs or practices that emphasize equality of individuals and freedom of choice in personal decisions

progressive philosophy the belief that the major purpose of schools is to provide students with a wide variety of experiences and to teach a flexible curriculum. It is believed that, as a result, students will better understand themselves and how to fit into society.

projection a defence mechanism by which we see negative traits and feelings in other people that we sense in ourselves but to which we cannot openly admit

proletariat the term used by Karl Marx for the poor and powerless groups in society who survive by selling their labour

psychiatry the study and medical treatment of mental disorders

psychoanalysis the school of psychology founded by Sigmund Freud in which hypnosis and dream analysis is used to study a person's unconscious mind

psychological disorder a disease of the mind that makes it difficult to cope with the

ordinary stresses of daily life

psychology the systematic study of people's thoughts, feelings, and behaviour

psychosis a type of psychological disorder. People suffering from a psychotic disorder often lose touch with the real world and require treatment to be able to live a "normal" life.

R

race a term for a group of people, often with similar physical characteristics, who are assumed to share a common descent or origin. The term is no longer accepted by the American Anthropological Association.

rationalization a defence mechanism by which we invent an excuse to explain a failure, loss, error, or our bad behaviour

re-engineering changing the structure of a business or other organization, usually by introducing improved technology and reducing staff, to improve efficiency

reflexivity the practice by anthropologists of analyzing their own thought processes and belief structures to understand how these affect how they interpret their observations

regression to the mean the idea maintained by psychologists that intelligence, while not inherited, is distributed consistently throughout a population from generation to generation

rehabilitation one of the functions of punishment. This function consists of reforming or improving an offender.

reliable the term describing an experiment or

observation that, if repeated, will produce exactly the same results

repression a defence mechanism by which we push unpleasant urges or thoughts out of our conscious minds and into our subconscious

rescuers people who help others escape harm. During the Holocaust, rescuers helped others escape persecution and death.

residential schools institutions run by the federal government and four Canadian churches. Their aim was to strip Aboriginal children of their own culture and assimilate them into Euro-Canadian culture.

resistance in Atkinson et al.'s stage model, the act of deliberately rejecting a set of beliefs or values

resocialization the process in which society replaces negative aspects of a person's behaviour with new learnings

retribution one of the functions of punishment. This function is born of society's need and/or desire for inflicting suffering on the offender that is comparable to the suffering caused by the offence. The outcome of this function is protection of the moral order.

rightsizing changing the size of a company, most often by downsizing (firing workers) and eliminating positions

romantic love a type of love based on physical attraction, shared values and goals, and compatible personalities. In Robert Sternberg's triangular theory of love, a kind of love having passion and intimacy but not commitment.

S

sanctioned violence violence that is encouraged and unpunished. Such violence occurs in competitive sports games.

sapienization the anthropological term for the process of learning about the components of society—for example, marriage and the family—that make society distinctly human

scapegoat a person or group of people who are unfairly blamed for the sins, shortcomings, or troubles of others

secondary group a group in which the members relate less personally and more formally with each other than do members of primary groups

secondary sector the sector of the economy dealing with the transformation of raw materials into manufactured goods

secondary socialization the process of learning how to function in group situations

selective perception seeing certain things while being blind to others

self an individual's personhood. The self includes an individual's positive and negative qualities as well as the individual's feelings about his or her identity.

self-concept our sense of who we are, based on our ideas about our strengths, weaknesses, values, beliefs, hopes, dreams, achievements, and disappointments

self-determination a psychological term for the ability to identify and achieve goals based on a foundation of knowing and valuing oneself

self-employment working for oneself rather than an employer, often as a freelancer or owner of a business

self-enhancers people who see themselves more positively than others do and who tend to be emotionally well-adjusted

self-government government by the same group of people being governed. Self-government includes developing and implementing laws and policies on health, education, justice, and child welfare. Aboriginal peoples have consistently insisted on being self-governed, and Canadian law is increasingly recognizing self-government as their right.

sexual orientation a category for identifying whether a person is attracted to members of the same sex, members of the opposite sex, or both

sibling rivalry any unresolved tension or negative feelings between two siblings

slapstick humour humour that involves physical stunts such as walking into doors

social anthropology the study and analysis of the social organization of living peoples

social dynamics the term originated by Auguste

Comte for the study of the forces that result in change within a society, such as war, revolution, economic growth. and catastrophe.

social integration the socialization of individuals into mainstream culture. Functionalists consider social integration to be one of the purposes of education.

social sciences those disciplines that use research and analysis to study human behaviour, such as anthropology, psychology, and sociology

social statics the term originated by Auguste Comte for the study of the forces that give a society stability, such as customs, institutions, and laws

socialization the life-long process through which humans learn the skills and attitudes they need to function in society

sociology the scientific study of the development, structure, and functioning of human society

special status a status that may be accorded to people that results in their being treated differently from other people

specific deterrence the discouragement, through fear of punishment, of the commission of crimes. This type of deterrence targets individuals who already have committed crimes and already have been punished for them. Specific deterrence functions to deter them from committing further offences.

stage models theories claiming that individuals proceed through life in stages. At each stage, the individual must successfully resolve a set of conflicts before being able to move on to the next stage.

statistics numbers that are collected and analyzed by social scientists and others

status set a sociological term for the many roles we play simultaneously in our lives

stereotypes preconceived, standardized, and oversimplified generalizations that consider all members of particular groups to share certain characteristics

stereotyping assuming that all members of a particular group share certain characteristics without considering the actual characteristics of individual group members

Stockholm Syndrome the tendency of victims of crimes such as hostage-taking, under certain conditions, to identify with the perpetrators and to resist those who try to rescue them

stratified divided into layers. The layers may be based on various factors, including educational achievement, income level, and social importance.

subsistence economy an economy that produces only enough goods to sustain workers for a short time

superego the term used by Sigmund Freud for the part of the unconscious mind that acts as a conscience, serving as a referee between the id and the ego

surplus an amount left over when requirements have been met

symbolic interactionist school the branch of sociology that focuses on the beliefs and actions of individuals and the meanings that individuals give to their beliefs and actions

synergistic articulation in Atkinson et al.'s stage model, resolving all previous conflicts and developing an ethnic identity with which one is at peace

systemic racism racism that is embedded into social institutions in contrast to racism that is directed from one individual to another

T

Taliban the governing group that came to power in Afghanistan in 1994 and introduced strict Islamic laws

telecommuting working from home, communicating by modem, telephone, fax, or other electronic means

tertiary sector the sector of the economy dealing with the provision of services

The Human Genome Project an international project, launched in 1989, aimed at identifying the location and function of all human genes

tiu lien "loss of face" in Asian cultures

total institutions institutions such as prisons that are designed to give individuals new, positive socialization experiences to replace the negative results of their prior socialization. Sociologist Erving Goffman originated this term and identified key features of such institutions, such as isolating people from the rest of society.

traditional philosophy the belief that schools should teach students what society considers to be the correct answers to questions, downplaying the individual search for the truth

transferable skills specific aptitudes that can be applied in a wide variety of jobs or careers

U

unconditioned response the term used by Ivan Pavlov for a response that is natural, such as shivering when you are cold

unconditioned stimulus the term used by Ivan Pavlov for a stimulus—for example, hot food on a cold day—that causes a natural response in a subject—for example, warming up the subject—without the subject's having to learn the response

unconscious mind the term used by Sigmund Freud for the part of our minds of which we are unaware, but which Freud believed is responsible for most of our behaviour

unemployment rate the percentage of people in the labour force who are without work but are looking and available for work

universals characteristics that can be observed in every human culture and society, such as ethics, gestures, and superstitions

utilitarian bureaucracies commercial bureaucracies that operate to make a profit for their owners

V

vague notes notes that, because they provide only a sketchy description of an incident, are unusable at a later date for drawing conclusions

virtual community a group of computer users who communicate regularly in cyberspace

vocation a strong feeling of fitness for a particular career or occupation, or a divine call to the religious life, or a form of employment that requires dedication

W

wage labour work for which wages are paid

wheat boom the period of prosperity and expanded economic activity brought about by the completion of the transcontinental railway in 1885, opening up the Canadian West to wheat farmers

Y2K bug a flaw in computer hardware that many people feared would have caused the world's computers to crash on 1 January 2000. These fears did not come to pass.

Acknowledgements of Sources

Note: Statistics Canada information is used with the permission of the Minister of Industry, as Minister responsible for Statistics Canada. Information on the availability of the wide range of data from Statistics Canada can be obtained from Statistics Canada's Regional Offices, its World Wide Web site at http://www.statcan.ca, and its toll-free access number 1-800-263-1136.

4 Adaptation of 'Workplace stress hurts, bosses learning' by Eric Beauchesne, Southam News, from *Calgary Herald*, 10 September 1999. Reprinted by permission of Southam News. **8** Reprinted from George E. Pataki, 'Death Penalty Is a Deterrent', *USA Today* magazine, March 1997, by permission of the Society for the Advancement of Education, © 1997.
8 Excerpts from 'What Prosecutors Won't Tell You' by Robert M. Morgenthau from *The New York Times*, 7 February 1995. Copyright © 1995 by the New York Times Co. Reprinted by permission. **17** Excerpts from 'What a Difference a Gene Makes' by Clay Shirky reprinted from FEED Magazine (www.feedmag.com). Copyright © 2000. **44** Excerpts from 'Racial intelligence at issue' by Steve Buist from *The Hamilton Spectator*, 15 April 2000. Reprinted courtesy of The Hamilton Spectator. **74** Excerpts from 'Designer babies: Another hard choice for parents: Their babies' genes' by Daniel Q. Haney, Associated Press, 21 March 2000. Reprinted with permission of The Associated Press. **87** Excerpts from 'My Genes Made Me Do It' by Stanton Peele and Richard DeGrandpre from *Psychology Today*, July/August 1995. Reprinted with permission from *Psychology Today Magazine*, Copyright © 1987 Sussex Publishers, Inc. **89-90** Evelyne Michaels, quote from 'High Anxiety' from *Chatelaine*, January 1994. Courtesy of Chatelaine magazine © Rogers Publishing Ltd. Reprinted by permission. **96-97** Excerpts from 'The Queen of Cunning' by Rosie DiManno from *The Toronto Star*, 4 November 1999. Reprinted with permission - The Toronto Star Syndicate. **97-99** Excerpts from 'Dorothy Homolka: Mother Supports Daughter's Campaign' by Kerry Gillespie and Michelle Shepard from *The Toronto Star*, 4 November 1999. Reprinted with permission - The Toronto Star Syndicate. **101** Excerpts from *Today's Parent*, 1 June 1998. **108-109** Excerpts from 'Men have to work at humoring women' by Dave Barry from *The Kitchener-Waterloo Record*, 18 March 2000. **113-114** 'Dismantling the Wall, Brick by Brick' by Kerry Gillespie from *The Toronto Star*, 21 February 1999. Reprinted with permission - The Toronto Star Syndicate. **117** 'Starving for Acceptance' by Robert Shelley from *The Globe and Mail*, 17 July 2000. *To come from Ann??* **135** Adaptation of 'Concrete Validity' from Internet Source Validation Project by Doug Furey et al reprinted by permission. **141, 142** Quotes from *The Guru's Gift* by Cynthia Mahmood and Stacy Brady (Mountain View, CA: Mayfield Publishing, 2000). **152** Excerpt from 'Russia's Harvest of Have-Nots' by Vanora Bennett from *The Los Angeles Times*, 22 September 1998. Copyright 1998, Los Angeles Times. Reprinted by permission. **160-161** Excerpt from 'The Kpelle Moot' by James L. Gibbs from *Africa*, 33(1), 1963. *To come from Ann??* **164-165** Excerpts from 'Fear Imprisons Debate on Jail Issue' by Carol Goar from *The Toronto Star*, 28 November 1998. Reprinted with permission - The Toronto Star Syndicate. **166** Figure, 'Age of Offenders Admitted to Federal Custody, Canada, 1996-97' from Statistics Canada, *Adult Corrections Survey*, Catalogue 85F0018XIE (Ottawa: Canadian Centre for Justice Statistics, Statistics Canada, 1997). **173** Excerpt from 'Never Met? Say 'Hello' and 'I Do" by Valerie Gibson from *The Toronto Sun*, 11 February 1999. Reprinted by permission of the author. **185** Figure, 'Monogamy Polyandry' from *Natural History*, 96(3). **186** Excerpt from 'African Polygyny: Family Values and Contemporary Changes' by Philip L. Kilbride in *Applying Cultural Anthropology*, 4th Edition, by Aaron Podolefsky and Peter J. Brown (Mountain View, CA: Mayfield, 1999). Reprinted by permission of Philip L. Kilbride, author of *Plural Marriage for Our Times: A Reinvested Option?*, Professor of Anthropology, Bryn Mawr College, USA. **187-188** Waiel Faleh, 'Mass Weddings Help Couples Navigate Sanctions Against Iraq' reprinted with permission of The Associated Press. **189** Excerpts from 'Wed Through the Web' by Jennifer Isaac, *The Calgary Sun*, 24 March 2000. Reprinted by permission of the author. **196** Excerpts from 'A Lesson in Finding Work' by Robin Harvey from *The Toronto Star*, 20 June 2000. Reprinted with permission - The Toronto Star Syndicate. **201** Cartoon by Dwane Powell © Tribune Media Services, Inc. All Rights Reserved. Reprinted with permission. **202-203** Excerpts from 'A Media Colossus' by Katherine Macklem from *Maclean's*, 25 September 2000. Reprinted by permission. **206** from *The Quality of Work: A People-Centred Agenda* by Graham s. Lowe (Toronto: Oxford University Press Canada, 2000). Copyright © Graham S. Lowe 2000. Reprinted by permission. **210** from *The Quality of Work: A People-Centred Agenda* by Graham S. Lowe (Toronto: Oxford University Press Canada, 2000). Copyright © Graham S. Lowe 2000. Reprinted by permission. **213-214** Excerpts from 'Telecommuting Finding Its Place' by Susan G. Strother from *The Orlando Sentinel*, 8 August 2000. Reprinted by permission of The Orlando Sentinel. **217** Figure, 'More and More Canadians Create Their Own Jobs' from Statistics Canada, *Labour Force Historical Review*, Catalogue 71F0004XCB (Ottawa: Statistics Canada, 1998). **220** Figure, 'Winners and losers' from 'The Wealth Gap' by Mary Janigan from *Maclean's*, 28 August 2000. Reprinted by permission. **222** Figure, 'Working 50 hour weeks' from Statistics Canada, *Labour Force Historical Review*, Catalogue 71F0004XCB (Ottawa: Statistics Canada, 1998). **223** Figure, 'Unemployment Rates: Youth, Students, Non-Students, and Adults' from Statistics Canada, *Canadian Labour Force Historical Review*, Catalogue 71F0004XCB (Ottawa: Statistics Canada, 1997). **224-225** Quiz, 'Did Your Parents Discipline You Fairly?' from *Because I Said So: Recognize the Influence of Childhood Dynamics on Office Politics and Take Charge of Your Career* by Amy Stark, (New York: Pharos Books, 1992). **226** Quiz, 'Do You Create Sibling-Rivalry Situations at Work?' from *Because I Said So: Recognize the Influence of Childhood Dynamics on Office Politics and Take Charge of Your Career* by Amy Stark, (New York: Pharos Books, 1992). **233** 'School Code Step Forward' from *The London Free Press*, 27 April 2000. Reproduced with permission from The London Free Press. Further reproduction prohibited without written permission from The London Free Press. **246** Figure, 'Scholarship Sampler' from 'Shopping for Scholarships' by John Schofield from *Maclean's*, 20 November 2000. Reprinted by permission. **247** Excerpts from *The Schools of Ontario, 1876-1976*, by Robert M. Stamp (Toronto: University of Toronto Press, 1982). Reprinted by permission of University of Toronto Press Inc. **248** Excerpts from *The Schools of Ontario, 1876-1976*, by Robert M. Stamp (Toronto: University of Toronto Press, 1982). Reprinted by permission of University of Toronto Press Inc. **254** Excerpt from Plains Indians Cultural Survival School's Web site, http://www.cbe.ab.ca reprinted by permission of Plains Indians Cultural Survival School. **255** Excerpts from Leo Ussak Elementary School's Web site, http://www.arctic.ca/LUS, reprinted by permission. **256** Adaptation of 'Self-esteem Fleeting, Fragile for Canadian Kids' by Chris Morris, *The Canadian Press*, 28 October 1999. Reprinted by permission. **256** Adaptation of 'Are the Schools Failing Boys' by Sean Fine from *The Globe and Mail*, 5 September 2000. Reprinted with permission from The Globe and Mail. **262-263** Excerpts from 'Online School Registration Guide' reprinted from Alberta Distance Learning Centre's Web site, http://www.adlc.ab.ca by permission of Alberta Distance Learning Centre. **266** Source: Freedman, Joe. 1997. *Charter Schools in Atlantic Canada* (Atlantic Institute for Market Studies, March 1997), http://www.aims.ca/Publications/charterschool/charterpg1.html#top. Reprinted by permission of Atlantic Institute for Market Studies, a public policy think tank based in Halifax, NS. **266** Adaptation of 'Charter Schools Take Us Backward, Not Forward' by Heather-Jane Robertson from *Education Monitor* (Ottawa: The Canadian Centre for Policy Alternatives), Summer 1997. Reprinted by permission. **269-272** Excerpts from 'Canadians Say No to Advertising in Schools', Canadian Teachers' Federation's poll conducted by Environics Research Group. Reprinted by permission of Canadian Teachers' Federation. **280** Excerpts from 'France adopts

tough anti-sect law' by Jon Henley from *The Guardian*, 22 June 2000. Copyright © Jon Henley. Reprinted by permission of Guardian Newspapers. **300** Used with permission from Women's Legal Education and Action Fund - LEAF. Excerpted from "About LEAF" from http://www.leaf.ca. **300** Excerpts from http://www.realwomenca.com reprinted by permission. **302** Excerpts from 1999 Nobel Peace Prize acceptance speech by Dr James Orbinski, President, Médicins Sans Frontières, 1998-2000, on 10 December 1999, Oslo, Norway. Reprinted by permission. **304** Adaptation of 'Child Labour: What Can Be Done: Seven Steps to Sweatfree Status' (2001) from http://www.freethechildren.com. Reprinted by permission. **305-306** Excerpt from 'Who's In Charge of the Global Economy?' by Maude Barlow, Chairperson of the Council of Canadians, Canada's longest public advocacy organization, http://www.canadians.org. Reprinted by permission. **308** Reprinted by permission of the Ontario Coalition Against Poverty. **323** Abridged from 'Welcome to the gender wars' by Ann Dowsett Johnston from *Maclean's*, 27 September 1999. Reprinted by permission. **325** Figure, 'Estimates of some costs of violence against women in British Columbia, 1996' from *Paying for Violence: Some of the costs of Violence Against Women in B.C.* by Richard Kerr and Janice McLean (Victoria: Province of British Columbia, May 1996). **327** Adapted from 'Murder, He Wrote: A Newfoundland Anthropologist Has Become an Expert on Serial Killers' by John DeMont from *Maclean's*, 31 November 1994. Reprinted by permission. **341** Excerpt from 'Do Korean Men Still Beat Their Wives? Definitely' by Nicholas D. Kristof from *The New York Times*, 5 December 1996. **341** Excerpt from 'Women Under Virtual House Arrest' by Kenneth J. Cooper from (*The Washington Post*, 7 October 1996. **341** Excerpt from 'Justice in Peru: Rape Victim Is Pressed to Marry Attacker' by Calvin Sims from *The New York Times*, 12 March 1997. **343** Abridged from 'Can a Man of 25 Claim Age Bias?' by John Cloud, *Time*, 16 August 1999. © 1999 Time Inc. Reprinted by permission. **347** Excerpt from 'Abuse of Trust' by Jane O'Hara from *Maclean's*, 26 June 2000. Reprinted by permission. **349-350** Excerpts from *Canada and the World Backgrounder*, 1 May 1997. **358-359** Adaptation of 'Survival of the Kindest' by Frans B.M. De Waal from *The Chronicle of Higher Education*, 7 August 1998. **362** Adaptation of 'He Saves Lives' by Stan Grossfeld, *The Boston Globe*, 19 June 2000. Reprinted courtesy of The Boston Globe.

Photo Credits

t=top; b=bottom; c=centre; l=left; r=right

Bettman=Bettmann/CORBIS/MAGMA PHOTO
CP=CP Picture Archive
Everett=Everett Collection, New York, NY
Glenbow=Glenbow Archives, Calgary, Canada
Granger=The Granger Collection, New York, NY
NAC=National Archives of Canada

1 Jean-Marc Bouju/Wide World Inc./CP; 6 Andy Sacks/Stone; 9 CP; 11 Tom Hanson/CP; 13 Everett; 20 (t) © Bettmann, (b) Kean Collection/Archive Photos; 21 (t) © Bettmann, (c) North Wind Picture Archives, (b) Granger; 22 Granger; 26 (t) Granger, (b) © Bettmann; 27 (t) and (b) © Bettmann; 28 © Bettmann; 33 (t) and (br) © Bettmann; 34 © Hulton Deutsch Collection/CORBIS/MAGMA PHOTO; 35 Wide World Inc./CP; 36 (t) and (c) © Bettmann, (b) B.I. DeVore/Anthro-Photo; 37 (t) Jean-Marc Bouju/Wide World Inc./CP, (br) Courtesy of Dr. Birutė Galdikas/Orangutan Foundation International; 38 Robert Campbell/NGS Image Collection; 46 PhotoDisc; 48 © Bettmann; 51 Napoleon Chagnon/Anthro-Photo; 57 Reunited identical twins, Daphne Goodship and Barbara Herbert, the "giggle twins." Photo credit: Dr. Nancy L. Segal, California State University, Fullerton and author of "Entwined Lives: Twins and What They Tell Us About Human Behaviour"; 59 John Lamb/Stone; 64 Greg Baker/Wide World Inc./CP; 71 Tony Joyce/VALAN PHOTOS; 76 Patti Henderson; 79 Skjold Photographs; 81 Eastcott/Yva Momatiuk/VALAN PHOTOS; 86 Skjold Photographs; 89 C. Mohr/First Light; 91 Courtesy of North West Airlines; 92 Everett; 94 Vancouver Sun/CP; 96 Frank Gunn/CP; 98 Paul Chiasson/CP; 101 Tony Joyce/VALAN PHOTOS; 102 Mark and Ellen Sereda; 104 Images/First Light; 107 J. Feingersh/First Light; 111 "Don't blame me, work with me," article by Erma Collins, artwork by John Overmyer, Toronto Star, April 19, 1994, p. A21.; 113 The Toronto Star/Andrew Stawicki; 119 Ivy Images; 121 Dick Hemingway; 125 V. Wilkinson/VALAN PHOTOS; 127 Patti Henderson; 128 Everett; 130 Doug Crawford/CP; 133 Mark and Ellen Sereda; 139 Skjold Photographs; 141 Chuck Stoody/CP; 144 Santiago Lyon/Wide World Inc./CP; 149 John Kenney/CP; 154 Patti Henderson; 159 Joe Bryksa/CP; 162 Kevin Simpson/Wide World Inc./CP; 170 National High Magnetic Field Lab/Florida State University; 174 © Annie Griffiths Belt/CORBIS/MAGMA PHOTO; 179 © Kelly-Mooney Photography/CORBIS/MAGMA PHOTO; 180 John Kenney/CP; 183 Irv DeVore/Anthro-Photo; 186 Lincoln University; 188 Reuters/Faleh Kheiber/Archive Photos; 191 BC Archives/I-46770; 193 Eastcott/Momatiuk/VALAN PHOTOS; 199 (l) Glenbow Archives/NA-1367-10, (r) "Power loom weaving" 1834, after Thomas Allom, Private Collection/Bridgeman Art Library; 203 Phil Snell/Maclean's; 204 The New Zealand Herald; 208 Lee/Anthro Photo File; 217 Adrian Wyld/CP; 219 PhotoDisc; 225 Barros & Barros/The Image Bank; 226 PhotoDisc; 227 Patti Henderson; 228 Walter Hodges/Stone; 237 Juan Silva Productions/The Image Bank; 239 Paul Chiasson/CP; 240 (l) and (r) Reuters/HO/Archive Photos; 243 PhotoDisc; 244 A. Skelley/First Light; 245 Patti Henderson; 248 Saskatchewan Archives Board/R-A14067; 249 Courtesy of Mr. William Thompson; 250 NAC/PA-111241; 253 Marc Gallant/CP; 254 Calgary Herald; 257 John Lehmann/CP; 259 Ivy Images; 263 Dick Hemingway; 264 Rebecca Lavallee; 265 Western Report; 267 Photo: Peter Thompson, Courtesy of Laurie Pedwell; 277 The Toronto Star/B. Spremo, C.M.; 283 Hugh V. Green/VALAN PHOTOS; 285 Bruce Ayres/Stone; 287 Dick Hemingway; 289 Eastcott/Momatiuk/VALAN PHOTOS; 291 Ryan Remiorz/CP; 294 Glenbow /NA-1399-1; 296 Nick Procaylo/CP; 299 CP; 301 Peter Parsons/CP; 303 Courtesy of Canada World Youth; 305 Courtesy of Craig Kielburger and Kids Can Free the Children, www.freethechildren.com, www.leaderstoday.com; 307 © Nik Wheeler/CORBIS/MAGMA PHOTO; 308 The Toronto Star/B. Spremo, C.M.; 312 Copyright © 1965 by Stanley Milgram. From the film "Obedience," distributed by The Pennsylvania State University, Audio Visual Services; 313 Gary Moore/CP; 314 Hulton Getty/Archive Photos; 318 Everett; 319 Patti Henderson; 325 Patti Henderson; 327 Keith Gosse/CP; 329 Tony Mihok/Ivy Images; 330 © David & Peter Turnley/CORBIS/MAGMA PHOTO; 332 CTV Sportsnet/CP; 335 Dick Hemingway; 338 Rudi Blaha/World Wide Inc./CP; 342 © Jonathan Carlson, 2001; 345 Neg. No 11604/Courtesy Department of Library Services, American Museum of Natural History; 348 Jacques Boissinot/CP; 349 Keith Anderson/CP; 352 Sean Murphy/Stone; 357 (l) and (r) Dick Hemingway; 358 Chris Bakers/Stone; 360 Zigy Kaluzny/Stone; 362 Christopher Navin

Index

N

O

P

Y

Z